THE M & E HANDBOOK SERIES

Company Law

M. C. Oliver

M.A.

Barrister
Head of the Department of Law
City of London Polytechnic

EIGHTH EDITION

MACDONALD AND EVANS

Macdonald & Evans Ltd.
Estover, Plymouth PL6 7PZ

First published 1966
Second Edition 1967
Reprinted 1968
Reprinted 1969
Reprinted 1970
Third Edition 1971
Reprinted (with amendments) 1972
Fourth Edition 1973
Reprinted 1974
Reprinted 1975
Fifth Edition 1976
Sixth Edition 1977
Seventh Edition 1979
Reprinted 1980
Eighth Edition 1981

Richard Clay (The Chaucer Press) Ltd,
Bungay, Suffolk

Preface

The idea of writing a small introductory handbook I owe in the first place to Mr M. B. Wintoki, B.Sc. (Econ.), who, as he left the college at the end of his course, told me with relief that he could at last understand the textbook. It occurred to me then that if a student of his marked ability and industry found the textbooks difficult because he had no previous legal training, there must be many more people for whom a very simple book might be useful.

This HANDBOOK is intended to meet this need. I have tried to be as simple as possible, in the hope that readers will pursue the subject in more advanced books. Thus I have unswervingly adopted the "realist" or "organic" theory of the corporate person, without mentioning other theories, because I think this is the easiest approach for the beginner. I have devoted more space to matters which cause difficulty than to matters of importance, for this is a teacher's function, and I have attempted to meet the examination needs of solicitors, company secretaries, accountants and students of business management. Progress tests have been set at the end of each chapter, and specimen examination questions will be found in the Appendix. The progress tests are the ones which I normally use in class, so that they are the result of experiment. For the use of the specimen examination questions I am greatly indebted to the Institute of Chartered Secretaries and Administrators, the Institute of Chartered Accountants and the Association of Certified Accountants, all of whom kindly allowed me to use questions from their past papers.

The only advice that I can give as to method of study is that which I once heard given by that distinguished and much-loved teacher of law, Dr J. W. C. Turner, LL.D., of Trinity Hall, Cambridge, to a student who was engaged during a lecture on the laborious completion of a cross-word puzzle. "Can you think of a four-letter word beginning with W and ending with K?" he asked.

Students should read each chapter three times. The first time, the chapter should just be carefully read. The second time, it should be learnt, paragraph by paragraph, with constant reference to the relevant statutory provision or clause of Table A. It is essential for each student to have his own copy of each of the four Companies Acts so that he can make notes in the margins and cross-reference the sections. The third time, the chapter should be read straight through once again. Then the student should see if it has a shape in his mind, if he can make a synopsis of it, and if he can do the progress test on it. If so, he knows it.

It cannot be too often stated that Company Law is not difficult. It merely requires *Work*. Precision is essential and gossip useless, so that students who are privately convinced that they are going to be gifted personnel managers or administrative cyclones with a nest of telephones in pastel colours must shed their Walter Mitty. They will find some satisfaction when they discover that hardly anyone has much knowledge of Company Law. It may not be nice, but it *is* rare.

I should like to express my thanks to Mrs M. Foard of the South West London College, who patiently typed the manuscript for me in spite of the already heavy demands on her time. I also wish to thank my colleague Mr William T. Major, M.A., Barrister, for his determined assistance with the manuscript at the time when I most needed help. I owe more than I can say to all those whom I have ever taught. And I must acknowledge finally that the completion of this little book resulted largely from the loyal misapprehension of my family that I can write a book as easily as I can bake a cake. Without them and the encouragement of Mr J. E. C. Trechman, A.C.I.S., I should never have had the temerity to write it, and I hope that it compensates them a little for my domestic shortcomings.

Soon after this book was first published the Companies Act 1967 added many important provisions to the law relating to companies. These were included in the second edition. The Companies Acts 1976 and 1980 have made further important changes so that, as stated above, students will require a copy of each of these three Acts as well as of the Companies Act 1948 before commencing study.

Despite the fundamental nature of the provisions of the Companies Act 1980, in this, the eighth, edition the structure of the book still remains largely unchanged. I have, however, removed from Chapter XXVII the two sections on the oppression of minorities and added a new chapter—Chapter XXXI—on shareholder protection in the expectation of rapid development in this area. I hope that I shall not prove to have been over-optimistic. I have also continued to modify the text (often as a result of student comment) and included, as usual, the recent judicial decisions of importance. It is, however, not an over-statement to say that the Companies Act 1980, which according to Lord Lloyd of Kilgerran "passed like a snowball racing downhill, picking up new and complex clauses", requires an entirely new approach to a number of basic aspects of the subject. This is the case even though, for the sake of simplicity, I have omitted all reference to the transitional provisions.

Finally, students should be aware that although many sections of the Companies Acts 1948 and 1967 refer to the Board of Trade this institution, after a prolonged identity crisis, finally emerged as the Department of Trade and is so described in the text.

September, 1980   M. C. OLIVER

Contents

Table of Cases

Table of Statutes

CHAPTER I

The Basic Principles of Company Law

1. The nature of the subject. Company Law consists partly of the ordinary rules of common law and equity, and partly of statute law. The basic principles are very few, and the main difficulty encountered in learning the subject is the memorising of details. If, however, the principles are thoroughly understood, the details are easier to learn, and in the chapters which follow an attempt has been made to arrange the material so that a student can memorise it with as little effort as possible.

The subject is a modern one. The Companies Act of 1862 put Company Law on its present footing, and major Acts were passed in 1908, 1929 and 1948. Amending Acts of 1967, 1976 and 1980 have now been added to this massive legislation and further Acts are expected in due course for, as Viscount Trenchard observed during the debate in the House of Lords on the 1980 Act: "This subject of company law and Companies Bills is an endless one".

The student is concerned as a rule only with the 1948, 1967, 1976 and 1980 Acts and should not attempt to study the subject without a copy of each. These four Acts are here collectively termed "the Companies Acts 1948–80" although in fact that expression carries, under s. 90(2) Companies Act 1980, a somewhat wider meaning. All references in this book, however, are to sections of the 1948 Act unless it is expressly stated or clear from the context that a later Act applies.

2. Fundamental concepts. There are two fundamental legal concepts to be grasped in Company Law:

    (*a*) The concept of *legal personality*.

    (*b*) The theory of *limited liability*.

Both are explained below.

As well as fully understanding these, the student will find the detail much easier to learn if he once appreciates the following fact: nearly all the statutory rules are intended for one of two purposes, namely (*a*) the *protection of creditors* (e.g. the rules preventing reduction of capital without proper safeguards) or (b) the *protection of investors* (e.g. the rules concerning the prospectus and the accounts).

3. The starting-point. Every subject should have a starting-point which a beginner with no previous knowledge can understand. Here it is suggested that the easiest way of beginning to study Company Law is to imagine that you yourself are about to "go into business", i.e. that you have a little money saved or lent to you and are about to start a small business.

The first legal question which arises is: in which legal form shall the business operate? In order to decide this question it is necessary to examine the legal forms of a business and understand the differences between them. There are three:

(a) You may be a *sole trader*.
(b) You may form a *partnership* with one or more other persons.
(c) You may form a *limited company* by registration under the Companies Act.

Each of these must now be considered in turn.

4. A sole trader. A sole trader is so called because *he alone* bears the responsibility for running the business, and *he alone* takes the profits.

He may of course be helped by his wife and family, or he may employ other people to work for him, but this does not alter the fact that the management is entirely in his hands. A man in this position has not formed any kind of "association" in law and is not in any way regulated by special rules of law.

5. A partnership. In a partnership the members "associate", i.e. they form collectively an association in which they all participate, as a rule, in management and in sharing the profits.

(a) *Number of partners.* Obviously there must be at least two members in a partnership, but there may be more. There is, however, in most cases a maximum number. Section 434 Companies Act 1948 states that this maximum is twenty, but ss. 120 and 121 Companies Act 1967 exempt from this limit both partnerships and limited partnerships (*see* **6**) of solicitors, accountants and stockbrokers—a relaxation which has not been greeted with universal enthusiasm among the professions specified. If a partnership exceeds the maximum number, the members must *incorpor-*

ate themselves. This process of *incorporation* will be described in detail below (*see* IV).

The special provisions relating to the number of members in a banking partnership have all been repealed by the Banking Act 1979.

(*b*) *Liability of partners.* In a partnership the legal position of the members is not very different from that of a sole trader. If the firm gets into financial difficulties, all the partners may find that their creditors are seeking to make them bankrupt, and since all the partners are liable for the debts of the firm, they are not protected against the possibility of total bankruptcy. At the same time, just because they are liable for the firm's debts, they may find that tradesmen are willing to give them credit on the grounds, for example, that one of the partners is known to be a very wealthy man.

(*c*) *Legal position of partners.* The members of a partnership may sue and be sued collectively by using the name of the firm, but this is a matter of legal procedure only, and does not alter the fact that the action is being brought by or against the *partners*. All the partners are *agents* for each other, i.e. each one can bind the others when he makes contracts on behalf of the firm. It follows that each partner is a *principal*. They are therefore all in a *fiduciary relation* with each other, i.e. they must not only tell each other the truth in conducting the business, but they must disclose the whole truth. For instance, no partner may make a secret profit. The word "fiduciary" comes from the Latin *fides*, meaning trust or confidence.

(*d*) *Rights of partners.* Usually the rights of the partners are regulated by a contract drawn up between them and put in writing, called the "articles" of partnership or the "partnership deed". The partners may make what arrangements they like in this contract, but when they have not made any provision at all the position is regulated by the Partnership Act 1890. A partnership need not be created formally, however, and may arise through an oral agreement or even by conduct.

6. A limited partnership. There is a special type of partnership which is very rare but should be mentioned. It is called a *limited partnership* and is regulated by the Limited Partnerships Act 1907. Here it is possible for all the partners except one to be "limited partners". A limited partner puts into the firm a certain amount of money, e.g. £500, and then he is not responsible for the debts of the firm above that figure. This means that he can lose his £500, but cannot be made bankrupt or made to pay more than this sum. The £500 is the "limit" of his liability. He cannot, however, take part in the management of the firm.

There must always be at least one partner whose liability for the firm's debts is not limited in this way, and he is called a general partner. He manages the business, bears the risk, but normally gets the bulk of the profits. Limited partnerships are very rare because in the same year in which they were introduced the Companies Act 1907 made it possible to form a *private company*, which is a much more convenient way of running a small business. The ordinary type of partnership described in **5** above, however, is very common and will be referred to later when a comparison will be drawn between it and the limited company (*see* IV, **11**).

7. The meaning of the word "company". Partnerships often describe themselves as "Smith, Brown and Co.", but this is misleading because they are not companies in the strict sense of the word. The difficulty is caused by the fact that the word "company" has a variable meaning and can be used in many ways. The meaning depends on the context. When a partnership describes itself in this way the partners are simply indicating that there are other persons in their association besides Smith and Brown. They are *not* indicating that their business is a company registered under the Companies Act.

8. A limited company formed by registration under the Companies Act. If you choose this form for your business you are *incorporating* it, i.e. you are forming a corporation. You are also going to acquire *limited liability*. The actual process of incorporation by registration forms the subject-matter of the first part of this book and there is much detail to be learnt about it, but before this process is described it is essential to clarify the two legal concepts which have already been mentioned as being the basis of Company Law, i.e. legal personality and limited liability (*see* **9–12** below). For in a limited company both these concepts can be seen operating together.

9. The concept of legal personality. A *human* person is a man, woman or child and usually recognisable as such, but a *legal* person is not quite the same thing. In the first place, a legal person is not always human. In the second place, in some societies (though not in ours today) a human person is not necessarily a legal person.

A legal person can be described as any person, human or otherwise, who has rights and duties at law, i.e. who can seek the aid of the court and against whom the aid of the court can be sought by others. It is clear that in a modern civilised community all human persons fall into this category, but slaves, when slavery was lawful, did not: they were regarded as property, not persons, and they could be owned and dealt with as property. Today it is almost universally true that no-one may own another person. Generally speaking, a husband does not own his wife, nor a father his child. In a modern state all human persons, whatever their sex or age, can enforce their rights in the court and can be made liable for breach of their legal duties by the court.

A human person is, therefore, a legal person all his life, i.e. from birth to death. But it is important to remember that for some purposes he has pre-natal rights and the courts protect him even before he is born, while for other purposes his rights remain enforceable after death for specified periods. Students learn more about this when they study Criminal Law and the Law of Tort, but it is outside the proper scope of this book.

Though all human persons are legal persons, not all legal persons are human. The non-human legal persons are called *corporations*, a word derived from the Latin "*corpus*" (body). A corporation is a legal person created by a process other than natural birth. It is therefore sometimes called an *artificial* legal person, but it should not be called "fictitious" because it really exists. For instance, if a man has a carnation in his button-hole it may be a real one or an artificial one, but it can hardly be said to be fictitious if it is there.

10. Types of corporation. There are many types of corporation and they can be classified in various ways, e.g.:

(*a*) *Sole* (where one human being constitutes the corporation and has a dual personality, one corporate and the other human or natural. The Crown is an example of this type of corporation).

(*b*) *Aggregate* (where the corporation consists of two or more persons).

Another classification is into:

(*a*) *Lay* (e.g. Woolworth's or the Institute of Chartered Secretaries and Administrators).

(b) *Ecclesiastical* (e.g. the Archbishop of Canterbury).

A third classification is into:

(a) *Trading* (e.g. Woolworth's).
(b) *Non-trading* (e.g. the Institute of Chartered Secretaries and Administrators).

Thus the particular type of corporation which we are about to study is a lay trading corporation aggregate.

For our purposes, however, by far the most useful classification is based on the method of formation. Corporations may exist as a result of:

(a) *Common law*, e.g. the Crown or a bishop.
(b) *Prescription*, i.e. the corporation has existed so long that the law presumes that it had a charter which was lost.
(c) *Royal charter*.
(d) *Statute*.
(e) *Registration under the Companies Act*.

The corporation we are studying is formed in this last way.

NOTE: Students are often confused by being told that a corporation can be statutory, i.e. formed by statute, and that this is a different method of formation from registration under the Act. They feel that both these types of corporation are "statutory". The difference, however, is that a statutory corporation is directly created by a particular Act of Parliament which is passed for that specific purpose. The Companies Act, on the other hand, does not itself create any corporations at all. It merely lays down a *process* by which any two or more persons who so desire can themselves create a corporation by complying with the rules for registration which the Act prescribes.

11. The nature of the corporate person. The corporate legal person is very different from the natural or human legal person. It has neither body, mind nor soul. In the *Case of Sutton's Hospital* (1612), it was said that it "is invisible, immortal, and rests only in intendment and consideration of the law". Corporations "cannot commit treason, nor be outlawed, nor excommunicate, for they have no souls". A corporation is not subject to "death of the natural body".

It is not surprising, therefore, that a variety of legal problems, of which space does not permit treatment here, have arisen as to its criminal and tortious liability. There were at one time procedural difficulties in prosecuting it, and there were bound to be practical difficulties in punishing it. These have been largely overcome. If in 1682 the Recorder of London demanded: "Must they hang up its common seal?", the law today makes a valiant effort to do the equivalent of just that. Thus s. 68(5) Companies Act 1967, defiantly proclaims: "An insurance company which contravenes a restriction ... shall be guilty of an offence and liable on conviction on indictment to imprisonment for a term not exceeding two years". One can only marvel at the advances of science.

Less progress, however, seems to have been made on the spiritual plane. In *Rolloswin Investments, Ltd.* v. *Chromolit Portugal, etc.* (1970), Mocatta J. declared: "A limited company is incapable of public worship or repairing to a church or exercising itself in the duties of piety and true religion, either publicly or privately, on any day of the week". More recently, in *Re Armvent, Ltd.* (1975), Templeman J. said: "The company has no soul and no feelings", and he was accordingly "not horrified" at the prospect of winding it up.

All corporations, then, however they came into existence, have *perpetual succession*, i.e. they were not born and so cannot die. They have been created by a process of law and can only be destroyed by a process of law and until so destroyed will continue to exist. They will exist even if all their human members are dead, for every corporation is a *separate* legal person from those legal persons who compose it.

In the latter part of this book the methods of destruction or dissolution are dealt with.

12. Limited liability. Students sometimes confuse the idea of limited liability with the principle outlined above concerning the independent legal personality of a corporation. It is true that in a large number of corporations the members have limited liability, but this is not necessarily so. Later we shall see that the Act itself provides for the creation of an unlimited company—i.e. a company where the members have unlimited liability.

The meaning of liability must be understood: it means the *extent to which a person can be made to account at law*. He is either fully liable, i.e. he can be made to pay the full amount of the debts owed, or he is liable only to a limited extent, i.e. he can be made to pay towards those debts only up to a certain limit, but not beyond it. In our company we shall see that the member's liability for the debts of the company is normally limited to the amount unpaid on his shares. Thus, if he buys 100 £1 shares "at par", i.e. at £1 per share, and pays up 50p on each share, he has paid up £50 and can be made to pay another £50, but he cannot be made to pay more than £100 in all. This is so even if the debts of the company amount to many thousands of pounds.

Notice that it is only the *members'* liability for the *company's* debts which is limited. The company itself, the artificial legal person, is always fully liable and so has unlimited liability. It follows that so long as there are assets available to pay the debts, it must pay them. It will be seen later that these debts must be paid in a strict order laid down by the law and certain classes of creditor receive preferential treatment.

Of course a company, like a human person, may not have enough assets to pay its debts. It will then be dissolved by liquidation, while a human person in such a case would be made bankrupt. This condition of insolvency is in no way related to limited liability. Insolvency is a simple matter of *fact*: a person cannot pay his debts because he has not enough money. Liability is a matter of *law*: a person is liable to pay his debts to a limited or unlimited extent regardless of whether he has enough money. Thus, *ability* to pay one's debts must never be confused with *liability* to pay them.

PROGRESS TEST 1

1. What type of association is a legal person with the liability of its members unlimited? (**12**)

2. What type of association is not a legal person, though the liability of its members is limited? (**6**)

3. In a company limited by shares, is the liability of the *company* for its debts limited or unlimited? (**12**)

4. Which of the following are legal persons:

(*a*) a dog? (**9**)

(*b*) Bloggins, Grindinghalt & Co., Solicitors? (**7**)

(*c*) an infant? (**9**)

(*d*) a soldier? (**9**)

5. What is the maximum number of persons who may lawfully form a partnership?

Are there any cases where this maximum does not apply? (**5**)

6. If a larger number of persons than this maximum wish to form a business association, what should they do? (**5**)

CHAPTER II

The Memorandum of Association

1. Who may form a registered company? Section 1(1), as amended by s. 2(1) and s. 88(1) and (2) Companies Act 1980, tells us who may form a company under the Companies Act and by what process. It states that any two or more persons may form a company and that these persons must be associated for a lawful purpose. No company may have an illegal object. These same two persons must subscribe their names to, i.e. sign, a document called a *memorandum of association*. They must also comply with the requirements of the Companies Acts 1948–1980 in respect of registration.

If they fulfil these conditions they can form an incorporated company or association, i.e. a corporation registered under the Act with or without limited liability. This means that the members' liability for the company's debts may be limited or unlimited (*see* **3**).

2. Classification of companies. The Companies Act 1980 introduced a classification of companies entirely different from that which formerly existed. It gives, for the first time, a statutory definition of a public company and defines a private company as any company which does not fall within it. While the number of public companies in England and Wales (approximately 15,000) is small compared with that of private companies (approximately 650,000), it includes many large companies well-known to the ordinary person.

Section 1(1) Companies Act 1980 defines a public company as a company which is *either*:

(*a*) limited by shares; *or*

(*b*) limited by guarantee with a share capital (*see* **36**);

    provided that:

    (*i*) its memorandum states that it is to be a public company; and

    (*ii*) the statutory provisions governing the registration of a public company have been complied with.

A public company, accordingly, is now always a limited company. It follows that an unlimited company is necessarily a private company.

It should also be noted that s. 1(2) Companies Act 1980 prohibits a company limited by guarantee from having a share capital unless it did so before the Act came into force. This type of company is therefore of diminishing importance and will cease to exist in time.

3. Limited and unlimited companies. Section 1(2) enlarges on the subject of liability. A company may be:

(a) *limited by shares* (i.e. the liability of the members is limited by the memorandum to the amount unpaid on their shares); *or*

(b) *limited by guarantee* (i.e. the liability of the members is limited by the memorandum to the amount which the members have undertaken or guaranteed to contribute to the assets of the company on winding up); *or*

(c) *unlimited* (i.e. there is no limit to the liability of the members. Here, although the association is a corporation and not a partnership, the extent of the members' liability is the same as that of partners. Unlike partners, however, they are not directly liable to the creditors, but to the company).

4. The contents of the memorandum. The contents of the memorandum are prescribed in the main by s. 2 Companies Act 1948, as amended by the Companies Act 1980, and s. 1(1) Companies Act 1980, although other Acts give further relevant details. The document must contain:

(a) The name of the company (*see* **7–12**).

If the company is a public company, s. 2(2) Companies Act 1980 requires its name to end with the words "public limited company".

If the company is a private company, the last word of its name must be "limited": s. 2(1) Companies Act 1948.

(b) A statement that the company is to be a public company, where appropriate (*see* **2** *and* **13**).

(c) The domicile of the company, i.e. whether the registered office is to be in England, Scotland or, under s. 30 Companies Act 1976, in Wales (*see* **13–14**).

(d) The objects of the company (*see* **23–34**).

(e) The limitation of the liability of the members, if the company is limited by shares or guarantee (*see* **35–40**).

(*f*) The amount of share capital, divided into shares of a fixed amount (*see* **41**).

These six clauses are usually referred to as the *compulsory clauses* and each of them is considered separately later in this chapter. Other clauses, however, are often included.

Where the memorandum states that the registered office is to be in Wales, s. 30(3) Companies Act 1976 permits it to state a private company's name with "cyfyngedig" as the last word, instead of "limited". Similarly, under s. 2(2) Companies Act 1980, the name of a Welsh public company may end with the words "cwmni cyfyngedig cyhoeddus", instead of "public limited company".

Furthermore, none of these expressions is required to be given in full. Section 78 Companies Act 1980 permits abbreviations to be used in all cases, as follows:

For "limited", "ltd."
For "public limited company", "p.l.c."
For "cyfyngedig", "cyf."
For "cwmni cyfyngedig cyhoeddus", "c.c.c."

5. The form of the memorandum. The Finance Act 1970, has abolished the first requirement of s. 3 that the memorandum should be stamped as a deed, but the second requirement of the section remains. The memorandum must be signed by each subscriber in the presence of at least one witness. Anyone may be a witness so long as he is old enough to understand what he is doing.

Section 2(4) requires each subscriber to take at least one share and to write against his name the number of shares he takes.

In Part I of the 1st Schedule to the Companies Act 1980 a model form of memorandum of a public company limited by shares can be found, while Table B of the 1st Schedule to the Companies Act 1948, formerly applicable to all companies limited by shares, gives a form of memorandum now restricted to private companies: s. 2(4) Companies Act 1980. In both forms, after the compulsory clauses, appears what is known as the *association clause* by which the subscribers bind themselves together to form a company, but no other mention of this clause is made in the Acts.

6. Alteration of the memorandum. Section 9(5) European Communities Act 1972, states that where a company alters its memorandum (other than under s. 5 Companies Act 1948, which already contains this requirement: *see* **33**), it must send to the registrar of companies a printed copy of the memorandum as altered. Section 9(3)(*b*) requires the registrar to publish in the *Gazette* the receipt by him of any document relating to an alteration of the memorandum.

If the company fails to notify him of such an alteration and cannot show that it was known at the time to the person concerned, then it cannot rely on the alteration against that person: s. 9(4)(*b*).

The registrar of companies is the Department of Trade official on whom the Companies Acts place wide administrative duties and responsibilities regarding the formation, operation and liquidation of companies. Where a company is required by statute to send to him a printed copy of any document, he will accept a document produced by any clear and durable process, e.g. lithography or electrostatic photocopying.

Section 4 Companies Act 1948 deals with the legal rules relating to alteration of the memorandum. Slightly amended by the Companies Act 1980, it is an important section governing the *whole document* and states that a company may not alter the clauses in its memorandum except in the cases, in the mode and to the extent for which the Acts expressly provide.

The result of this section is that each clause of the memorandum must be separately studied, for the rules regarding alteration of the clauses are not all the same.

7. The choice of a name for the company. In dealing with the name we must consider the provisions of s. 2, s. 17, s. 18, s. 19, s. 108 and s. 439 Companies Act 1948, s. 46 Companies Act 1967, s. 30 and s. 42 Companies Act 1976, s. 2, s. 76, s. 77, s. 78 and s. 80 Companies Act 1980 and s. 58 Companies Act 1947. There is also some important case-law on this topic.

Regarding the choice of a name, s. 17 states simply that the name chosen must not be undesirable in the opinion of the Department of Trade. The Act gives no further guidance on this point, but the Department publishes a pamphlet or Practice Note giving details of what it considers undesirable.

Broadly speaking, a name will be undesirable and therefore rejected if it is either:

(*a*) too *similar* to the name of another company; *or*

(*b*) *misleading*, e.g. suggesting that the company is connected with a government department, a member of the Royal family, a district or a country, or that it is an association of a particular type, when this is not the case.

If, despite these rules, a company is registered by a name so similar to that of another company that the public are likely to be deceived, the court will grant an injunction restraining it from using that name.

> Thus in *Ewing* v. *Buttercup Margarine Co. Ltd.* (1917), the plaintiff, who carried on business under the name of the *Buttercup Dairy Co.*, obtained an injunction against the defendant on the grounds that the public might think that the two businesses were connected, the word "buttercup" being an unnecessary and "fancy" one.

An injunction will not be granted, however, to prevent the use of a purely descriptive word with a definite meaning and in common use. If the names of two companies contain such a word, a very trifling distinction between their names will suffice to make them acceptable.

> Thus in *Aerators, Ltd.* v. *Tollitt* (1902), the plaintiff was not granted an injunction restraining the defendant from using the name of *Automatic Aerators Patents, Ltd.*

8. Publication of the company's name. Once the Department of Trade has accepted the company's name as "not undesirable", the company must comply with s. 108 and the later Acts regarding its publication.

(*a*) *Publication of name.* Section 108(1) makes it compulsory to have the name painted or affixed on the *business premises*, engraved on the *seal*, and mentioned on all *business documents and negotiable instruments*.

We have already seen in **4** that the word "limited" or "cyfyngedig" must appear in the name of a limited company so as to indicate the true legal position of the members regarding the company's debts. Where the name of a public company contains the words "cwmni cyfyngedig cyhoeddus", s. 77 Companies Act 1980 requires the fact that it is a public limited company to be stated in English also on all business documents and in a notice on the business premises.

Conversely, however, under s. 439 as amended by s. 42 Companies Act 1976, any person who carries on business under a name of which "limited" or "cyfyngedig" is the last word, without being incorporated with limited liability, commits an offence. Section 76(1) Companies Act 1980 contains a similar provision, stating that any person who is not a public company and who carries on business under a name which includes the words "public limited company", or their equivalent in Welsh, commits an offence.

Finally, s. 76(2) Companies Act 1980 makes it an offence for a public company to use a name which may reasonably be expected to give the impression that it is a private company in circumstances where the fact that it is a public company is likely to be material.

(b) *Fines for non-compliance.* The rest of s. 108, as amended by the Companies Act 1980, imposes fines on the company and the officers in default for non-compliance with the section. The fines, which have all been altered by s. 80 and the 2nd Schedule to the Companies Act 1980, need not be learned in detail, but the exact meaning of "officer in default" and of "officer" is important.

Section 440(2) states that the expression "officer in default" means an officer who *knowingly and wilfully* authorises or permits the default, while s. 455, the definition section alphabetically arranged, defines "officer" as including *director, manager or secretary*.

(c) *Personal liability.* Section 108(4) has an important provision. It not only imposes a fine on the officer in default for using the seal or signing a business document or negotiable instrument without the company's name on it, but it states that he will be personally liable to the holder of such a negotiable instrument for the amount thereof unless it is duly paid by the company. This could be a serious matter for an officer of a company, as a negotiable instrument may be for any amount and could involve him in personal liability which far exceeds the amount of the fine. The omission of any part of the name is sufficient to render him personally liable in this way.

Thus in *Hendon* v. *Adelman* (1973), where an ampersand was omitted, and in *Penrose* v. *Martyr* (1858) and *British Airways Board* v. *Parish* (1979), where the word "limited" was not on the instrument, the officers were in every case held personally liable. In *Stacey & Co. Ltd.* v. *Wallis* (1912), however, it was held not only that the abbreviation "Ltd." was permissible—a rule now enshrined in s. 78 Companies Act 1980 (*see* 4)—but also that it did not matter whereabouts on the instrument the company's name appeared, so long as it was correctly stated.

Further, if the error in the name is caused by the holder of the instrument, he will not be able to enforce the resulting liability against the officer who signed it: *Durham Fancy Goods* v. *Jackson* (*Michael*) (1968).

9. Power to dispense with the word "limited". There are certain circumstances where, even in a limited company, the last word of the name need not be "limited". Section 19(1) states that where an association is to be formed for promoting commerce, art, science, religion, charity or any other useful object, its profits used to promote its objects, and the payment of dividends prohibited, it may apply to the Department of Trade for a licence to register *with limited liability*, but *without "limited" as part of its name*.

Section 19(5) gives the Department power to revoke the licence, and s. 19(6) gives it power to vary the licence by making it conditional if the company should alter its objects.

Finally, s. 19(4) relieves a company to which a licence has been granted from the obligation not only of using the word "limited" as part of its name, but also of publishing its name (*see* **8** above) and of sending lists of members to the registrar of companies.

These provisions, however, were deprived of some of their effect by s. 9(7)(*c*) European Communities Act 1972, which requires such a company to have the fact that it is limited mentioned in all business letters and order forms, even though it may continue to dispense with "limited" as part of its name. Furthermore, the Companies Act 1980 now restricts the application of s. 19 to *private* companies so that a public company can no longer take advantage of it: s. 88(1) and para. 5 of the 3rd Schedule.

10. Company resolutions. Section 18 concerns alteration of the name and must be carefully studied. But first the student should be familiar with the meaning of a company resolution and the types of resolution which exist.

A company is managed by the board of directors to whom the members have delegated management. The directors are appointed and can be removed by the members. But to appoint directors, or to remove them, or to do any act which must be done by the members themselves at a meeting, requires a vote from the members who have voting rights.

A question on which a vote is about to be taken is called a *motion*, but this is a word which is used only once in the Acts and seldom in textbooks on Company Law. Once the motion has been put to the members and they have voted in favour of it, it becomes a company *resolution*.

The Acts repeatedly refer to resolutions, of which there are three different types:

(*a*) An *ordinary* resolution. This is a resolution passed by a simple majority. The Act does not state the period of notice required, but it must always be at least 14 days, as this is the minimum period of notice required for an extraordinary general meeting.

(*b*) An *extraordinary* resolution. This is a resolution passed by a majority of 75%, under s. 141(1). The period of notice required is again unspecified, so that it must be at least 14 days as in (*a*) above.

(*c*) A *special* resolution. This is also a resolution passed by a majority of 75%, but the period of notice required under s. 141(2) is 21 days.

In all cases the majority is of those members present and voting, i.e. absentees and abstentions are not counted. A shareholder can therefore be said, to some extent at least, to have the company which he deserves.

11. Alteration of name and certificate. We can now return to s. 18 which tells us how we can alter the company's name.

(*a*) Section 18(1) states that the name may be altered by special resolution with the written consent of the Department of Trade. This is a *general permission* to any company to alter its name at any time and as often as it wishes, but of course the new name must also be "not undesirable" in the opinion of the Department.

The 3rd Schedule of the Companies Act 1967 has been repealed by the Companies Act 1976 which states in s. 37(1) that the fees to be paid to the registrar of companies are to be laid down in regulations made by statutory instrument and fixed by the Secretary of State. The fee for registration of a new name in pursuance of a special resolution passed under s. 18(1) is £40: Statutory Instrument No. 1749 of 1980.

(*b*) Section 18(2) applies only where there is a similarity of names. First, it states that where a company has for any reason become registered by a name which is too similar to that of an existing company, it *may* change its name with the sanction of the Department. Here the type of resolution required is not stated, which means that an ordinary resolution will suffice.

Secondly, it states that, in these same circumstances, the

Department can *direct*, i.e. compel, that company to change its name, provided it acts within six months of registration. If the Department gives such a direction, the company must comply within six weeks. This is clearly intended to cover the case of a company which will not of its own accord change a name which is too similar to an already existing one. The Department's power, however, expires after six months from the registration of the company, after which any other company seeking protection for its name must apply to the court.

(*c*) Once the alteration of the name has been made, s. 18(3) directs the registrar of companies to issue an altered certificate of incorporation, while s. 18(4) states that a change of name does not affect the company's legal position, and legal proceedings by or against it may be continued under the new name.

(*d*) Section 46(1) Companies Act 1967 empowers the Department to direct a company to change its name if, in their opinion, its registered name gives *so misleading an indication of the nature of its activities* as to be likely to cause harm to the public. Section 46(2) requires the company to comply with such a direction within six weeks unless, under s. 46(3), it applies to the court within three weeks to set the direction aside. The court may set the direction aside or confirm it, in which case it must specify the period within which the company must comply.

12. Registration of the business name. While many companies trade under their registered names, some companies have a business name which is not the same as their corporate or registered name. In such circumstances, s. 58 Companies Act 1947 requires them to register the business name under the Registration of Business Names Act 1916.

13. The distinction between domicile and residence. In the case of a public company the second clause of the memorandum will be, as explained in **4**, a statement that the company is to be a public company. The alteration of the memorandum with regard to this clause is best considered in Chapter XIX on private companies.

We come now, therefore, to the second or, in the case of a public company, the third compulsory clause of the memorandum. This states the country in which the registered office of the company is situated, thus giving the company's domicile. Section 9(7)(*a*) European Communities Act 1972 requires both the domicile and the registration number of the company to be mentioned in all business letters and order forms. The registration number of a company is given on its certificate of incorporation (*see* IV, **2**).

Domicile must be distinguished from *residence*. The domicile of a company is the place where it was incorporated or registered, and this domicile adheres to the company throughout its existence. A company can have only one domicile, which cannot be changed.

The test of residence, on the other hand, is not registration but the place where the company does its business, i.e. the place of its management and control. This will usually be the place where the board of directors meets. The main importance of residence is with regard to taxation, for which purpose a company may have more than one residence.

14. The importance of the registered office. Although the domicile of the company cannot be changed, the address of the registered office within that domicile can be changed freely at any time to suit the company's convenience. Section 9(7)(*b*) European Communities Act 1972 requires that address to be mentioned in all business letters and order forms.

Section 107 has been repealed by the Companies Act 1976 and replaced by s. 23 of that Act. Section 23(1) makes it compulsory for a company to have a registered office at all times. Its intended situation must, under s. 23(2), be specified in the statement delivered to the registrar prior to incorporation (*see* IV, **1**), while any subsequent changes in its situation must, under s. 23(3), be notified to the registrar within fourteen days.

Section 9(3)(*e*) European Communities Act 1972, as amended by s. 23(6) Companies Act 1976, requires the registrar to publish in the *Gazette* the receipt by him of notice of any change in the situation of a company's registered office. If the company fails to give the required notice and cannot show that the change was known at the time to the person concerned, it cannot rely on the change against that person as regards service of any document on it: s. 9(4)(*d*) European Communities Act 1972.

The importance of the registered office is that it is the address where writs may be served on the company and where communications may be sent. It is also the address at which the following registers and documents must normally be kept:

(*a*) The register of members: s. 110.
(*b*) The register of debenture-holders: s. 86.
(*c*) The register of directors and secretaries: s. 200.

(d) The register of directors' interests in shares and debentures: s. 29 Companies Act 1967.

(e) The register of charges: s. 104.

(f) Copies of instruments creating the charges: s. 103.

(g) Minute books of general meetings: s. 146.

(h) The register of interests in voting share capital: s. 34 Companies Act 1967.

This list must be carefully learnt. The order in which the eight items are memorised is not important, but they have been arranged above as far as possible so that they fall into couples in order to facilitate learning them.

NOTE: All these documents are open to members free, during business hours for at least two hours a day. (e) and (f) are also open to creditors free, while (b) is open to debenture-holders free. (a), (b), (c), (d), (e) and (h) are open to the public on payment of the prescribed fee.

15. The statutory books. Often the student is required to state what are the statutory books. This is a list of the registers and documents which every company is required by law to keep. There are eight items here:

(a) The register of members: s. 110.

(b) The register of directors and secretaries: s. 200.

(c) The register of directors' interests in shares and debentures: s. 29 Companies Act 1967.

(d) Directors' service contracts: s. 26 Companies Act 1967.

(e) The register of charges: s. 104.

(f) The minute books of general and directors' meetings: s. 145.

(g) The register of interests in voting share capital: s. 34 Companies Act 1967.

(h) The accounting records, which are:
   (i) receipts and expenditure;
   (ii) assets and liabilities;
   (iii) statements of stock held and sales and purchases of goods: s. 12 Companies Act 1976.

NOTE: The two lists are very similar. Most of the statutory books must be kept at the registered office since they appear in both lists. But the minute books of directors' meetings and the accounting records may be kept at any convenient place: they do not appear in the first list and therefore there is no obligation to keep them at the registered office. Directors' service contracts must be kept at an appropriate place, defined as the registered office or the principal place of business.

On the other hand, while there is no obligation to keep a register of debenture-holders at all, most companies do so in practice, in which case the register must be kept at the registered office.

Directors' service contracts are open to members free, during business hours for at least two hours a day. The accounting records are open to the officers of the company at all times, though not to members. However, it was held in *Conway* v. *Petronius Clothing Co.* (1978) that the right of a director to inspect the accounting records is not a statutory right but a common law right, and the court accordingly has a discretion as to whether or not to assist him in enforcing it.

16. Types of security. It will be seen that in both the lists the register of charges appears, and some explanation of charges is given below since constant references to them are made throughout the subject.

When a person owes money to another, either because he has borrowed it or for any other reason, the sum owed is a *debt*. This debt can be either *unsecured* or *secured*.

When the debt is unsecured, the creditor has only one remedy: to sue for the amount owed, i.e. a right of action. He is not, therefore, at all safe if the debtor goes bankrupt or disappears. He has no security. Ordinary trade debts are usually unsecured, as is money borrowed from a friend when a person unexpectedly finds that he has not enough money in his pocket for his fare home.

A wise creditor, therefore, will demand security, i.e. a right over the debtor's *property* which is *in addition* to his right of action. A bank overdraft, for instance, is often secured by a deposit of the title deeds of the borrower's house (a mortgage), or of his share certificates (*see* XX, **18**). An unpaid seller of goods who is still in possession of them has a lien on those goods for the price, under the Sale of Goods Act 1979. An unpaid repairer of goods, e.g. a cobbler, has a lien at common law on the goods he has repaired, i.e. he can retain them until he is paid the amount owed to him. A bank may ask a customer who wishes to borrow money whether he can find another person of means to guarantee his overdraft, i.e. someone who is willing to undertake to repay the bank if the borrower does not do so. And a pawn-broker or pledgee has possession of the goods pledged to him. Thus a mortgage, a charge, a lien, a guarantee and a pledge are all *types of security*, i.e. methods by which a creditor's position is made safer.

17. Security given by companies. A company, like any other person, can give its creditors security. Often it mortgages or charges its property to its *debenture-holders*, i.e. the persons who have lent money to it (*see* XXI). These persons will then not only be able to sue the company for the amount of money which they have lent to it, but they will be able also to enforce their security, i.e. claim that the property charged belongs to them. The charges given by a company fall into two categories:

(*a*) *Fixed or specific charges.*

These are charges on definite or specific property of a permanent nature, e.g. land or heavy machinery, and may be either legal or equitable (*see* XIII).

(*b*) *Floating charges.*

These are charges which do not initially attach to the property charged and are thus necessarily equitable. They are useful when the assets to be charged are of the kind turned over in the course of trade, e.g. stock, for the company may continue to deal in the usual way with the property charged without the consent of the creditor. A floating charge will attach to the particular property then in the company's possession if:

(*i*) the company goes into liquidation; *or*

(*ii*) the company ceases to carry on business; *or*

(*iii*) the debenture-holders take steps to enforce their security, e.g. by appointing a receiver (*see* XXI, **13**).

It is then said to become fixed or to crystallise.

NOTE: Section 104 requires *all* charges given by a company to its creditors to be shown in the company's register of charges, which must contain:

(1) a short description of the property charged;

(2) the amount of the charge; and

(3) the names of the persons entitled to the charge.

18. Charges which must be registered with the registrar. Quite apart from the company's own register of the charges which it has created over its property, s. 98 requires the registrar to keep another register of charges for each company. There are nine types of charge which are registrable in this register, and these are listed in s. 95(2). They are here re-arranged for memorisation:

(a) A charge to secure debentures.
(b) A floating charge.
(c) A charge on uncalled share capital.
(d) A charge on calls made but not paid.
(e) A charge on land.
(f) A charge on a ship or, under Statutory Instrument No. 1268 of 1972, on an aircraft.
(g) A charge on book debts.
(h) A charge on goodwill, patents, trade marks or copyrights.
(i) A charge created by an instrument which, if executed by an individual, would require registration as a bill of sale.

NOTE

(1) This list will be most easily memorised if learnt in four couples and one odd item at the end. Most of these charges require some explanation, so that they can be connected with each other.

(2) The first two are placed together because debentures, though they may be secured by a fixed charge, are very often secured by a floating charge and so the one reminds the student of the other. The third couple are placed together because ships and land have certain obvious similarities. The fourth couple are all choses in action (intangible personal property). But students are often puzzled by the second couple and the ninth charge at the end.

(3) The second couple are charges on capital. Let us assume that a company has a share capital of 100 £1 shares issued at par, of which A holds 50 and B holds 50. This means that both A and B can ultimately be compelled to pay £50 each to the company. Usually they will have done this when they applied for the shares, and if so they will then have no further liability towards the company. But sometimes they will have paid only part of this sum, so that their shares are partly paid and therefore partly unpaid.

Let us assume now that they have each paid up 50p per share. We then say that the company has an issued share capital of £100, but a paid-up capital of £50. It therefore has unpaid capital of £50, and at some point, when more money is required, the directors will call up, i.e. demand, this unpaid capital. Until they do so, this unpaid capital is also the un-called capital of the company.

Since the uncalled capital has not been received, or even demanded, by the company, it is still a fund which can be charged in favour of a creditor, in the same way as a book debt. Thus, when it is finally received by the company, the creditor has a right to such part of it as will pay off the debt owed to him. This is the charge on *uncalled share capital*. Furthermore, at some point, as we have seen, the directors call up this money, and even after they have done so it may still be charged by the company before it is actually received. This is the charge on *calls made but not paid*.

(4) The ninth charge is not as complicated as it sounds. When an individual, i.e. a human person, mortgages his goods as security to a creditor, he does so by a document, i.e. an instrument, called a mortgage or conditional bill of sale. When goods are mortgaged in this way, the debtor remains in possession of them, though he no longer owns them. His position is exactly the reverse of a pledgor, who loses possession but retains ownership. This might be very misleading to other persons, since the mortgagor will look much richer than he is, and therefore the Bills of Sale Act 1882 requires such instruments to be registered in a public registry so that they are available for inspection by any interested person.

This Act, however, does not apply to companies, and therefore s. 95(2) has to include in its list of registrable charges a *charge created by an instrument which, if executed by an individual, would be registrable as a bill of sale*, thus making the same provision for mortgages of goods by companies as does the Bills of Sale Act for those created by human persons.

(5) A book debt is a debt arising in the course of a business which would in the ordinary course of such a business be entered in well-kept books, whether it is in fact so entered or not, and includes a *future* book debt: *Independent Automatic Sales, Ltd.* v. *Knowles and Foster* (1962). It does not include, however, a policy issued to a company by the Export Credits Guarantee Department of the Department of Trade guaranteeing payments to cover losses sustained by the company in export transactions: *Paul and Frank* v. *Discount Bank* (*Overseas*) (1966).

(6) In a contract for the sale of land by a company *an unpaid vendor's lien* is not registrable under s. 95(2) because such a lien arises by operation of law, and is not "created" by the company within s. 95(1): *London and Cheshire Insurance Co.* v. *Laplagrene Property Co.* (1971). On the other hand, the

deposit of title deeds to land by a company in order to secure a debt creates an equitable charge on the land which is registrable under s. 95(2), for it arises by presumption of law into the contract made by the parties and therefore, although implied and not express, is "created" by the company within s. 95(1): *Re Wallis and Simmonds (Builders) Ltd.* (1974).

(7) In recent years difficulties have arisen where a supplier of goods has, under the contract, retained an interest in those goods by way of security until he has been paid in full for them. Thus where a seller supplied goods to a company under a contract containing a "reservation of title" clause providing that the title to the goods should not pass until full payment was made, the right to trace the proceeds of sale of the goods if the company re-sold them was held not to be a charge on a book debt within s. 95(2), since those proceeds already belonged in equity to the supplier: *Aluminium Industrie Vaassen BV* v. *Romalpa Aluminium Ltd.* (1976).

On the other hand, in *Re Bond Worth Ltd.* (1979) where the supplier retained merely *equitable* ownership under the contract and the *legal* title to the goods passed to the company, Slade J. held that the reservation of equitable ownership amounted to the creation of a floating charge by the company over its property which was registrable within s. 95(2).

Further, in *Borden (U.K.) Ltd.* v. *Scottish Timber Products* (1979), where there was a reservation of the *legal* title to resin supplied by the seller for use in the manufacture of chipboard, the Court of Appeal held that since the resin had been amalgamated with other ingredients into a new product by an irreversible process, "the resin and the title and the security disappeared without trace" (*per* Templeman L.J.), so that no charge was created. Had the wording of the contract been held to confer a charge on the chipboard, however, it is clear that such a charge would have been registrable as falling within (*i*) in the list given at the beginning of this section.

19. Particulars to be entered in the registrar's register of charges. When any of these nine charges is registered, the particulars which must be given are found in s. 98(1)(*b*), and are:

(*a*) the date of creation of the charge;
(*b*) the amount secured by the charge;
(*c*) short particulars of the property charged; and
(*d*) the persons entitled to the charge.

NOTE: These particulars are the same as those which must be entered in the company's register of charges, except for the addition of the date of creation.

If the charge is one to which the *holders of a series of debentures* are entitled, then the particulars which must be given, according to s. 98(1)(*a*), are those set out in s. 95(8). These are:

(*a*) the total amount secured by the whole series;
(*b*) the dates of the resolution authorising the issue of the series and the deed, if any, creating the security;
(*c*) a general description of the property charged; and
(*d*) the names of the trustees, if any, for the debenture-holders.

The deed containing the charge, if any, or if none, one of the debentures of the series, must also be delivered to the registrar.

Section 98(2) provides that the registrar's certificate of registration of a charge is conclusive evidence that the statutory requirements as to registration have been complied with. It is thus conclusive evidence both of the date of creation of the charge and of the amount for which it was given: *Re C. L. Nye, Ltd.* (1970).

20. The effect of non-registration of a registrable charge. Section 95(1) provides that if any registrable charge is not registered within 21 days from its creation by the company, it is *void* against the liquidator and any creditor of the company. The charge is not made void against the *company*, however, so that the company itself cannot claim that the charge is void for non-registration: *Independent Automatic Sales, Ltd.* v. *Knowles and Foster* (1962).

Moreover, the debt in respect of which it was given remains *valid*, although the creditor has not got the security of the charge and is totally unsecured: *Re C. L. Nye, Ltd.* (1970). This debt becomes immediately payable under the subsection, and he can thus sue for it at once.

Section 96(1) states that it is the duty of the company to register the charge, but if it does not do so, then any person interested (normally the creditor) may do so. There is now no fee payable for registration.

Where a company borrows money in order to purchase land on the condition that once it has acquired the land it will grant the lender a first legal charge on it to secure the loan, and the charge, though duly granted, is void for non-registration under

s. 95(1), the lender is a mere unsecured creditor. He cannot claim that he is entitled by way of subrogation to the unpaid vendor's lien which the vendor of the land would have had if he had not been paid with the lender's money and which would not, of course, have been registrable (*see* **18**, note (6)): *Burston Finance, Ltd.* v. *Speirway, Ltd.* (1974).

21. The memorandum of satisfaction. After a charge has been created and registered, the debt may be paid by the company, or the creditor may release some of the property charged to him, or, in the case of a floating charge, the property may no longer form part of the company's assets.

In such a case the company should notify the registrar, who enters on the register of charges a *memorandum of satisfaction* recording this fact: s. 100.

22. Rectification of the register of charges. If a charge is not registered within the proper time, or if there is an omission or mis-statement in the register or in a memorandum of satisfaction, s. 101 empowers the court to extend the time for registration or rectify the omission or mis-statement. The section does not, however, give the court jurisdiction to delete a whole registration; it can merely rectify an omission by adding what is required, or a mis-statement by correcting it: *Re C. L. Nye, Ltd.* (1970).

The persons who may apply to the court for such an order are the company or any interested person, and the court must be satisfied that the failure to register the charge or the error or omission in doing so was accidental or due to inadvertence or some other sufficient cause, or not prejudicial to the creditors or shareholders, or that on other grounds it is just and equitable to grant relief.

23. The objects clause. The third or, in the case of a public company, the fourth compulsory clause in the memorandum sets out the objects or *vires* of the company. It is of great importance because it determines the *capacity* of the company wherever the *doctrine of ultra vires* applies. We must now see where this doctrine is applicable, what are its effects, what changes in the law were recommended by the Jenkins Committee and what changes were made by the European Communities Act 1972.

(The Jenkins Committee was appointed in 1959 by the President of the Board of Trade to review the provisions and workings of the Companies Act 1948 and to state what alterations to the law it considered desirable.)

24. Application of the doctrine of ultra vires. This doctrine has never applied to chartered corporations, but only to statutory and registered ones. A chartered corporation will of course have objects or *vires*, which will be set out in its charter, but it nevertheless has at law the full capacity of a human person, so that even if it acts outside those objects the transaction will be valid. If however, it persistently violates its charter, there is a procedure by which the charter can be forfeited, called *scire facias*.

Statutory and registered corporations, on the other hand, are in an entirely different position. The statutory corporation has its *vires* set out in the statute, i.e. the Act of Parliament, creating it, while a registered corporation has its *vires* stated in the objects clause. The doctrine of *ultra vires* applies to them both, so that if either of them acts outside the *vires* the transaction is *void*. The *vires* limit their contractual capacity. It is obvious that it is of great importance to know whether any particular transaction is *intra* (within) or *ultra* (outside or beyond) *vires*, for on this depends its validity.

25. Construction of the objects clause. The court will always construe the objects clause reasonably. The clause usually ends, as may be seen from the model forms of memorandum mentioned in **5**, with a general permission to do anything "incidental or conducive" to the stated objects, but this adds nothing to the general rule of law. Moreover, in recent years the courts have construed objects clauses in an increasingly liberal manner. Thus in *Re New Finance and Mortgage Co., Ltd.* (1975), where the material events took place before the entry of the United Kingdom into the European Communities so that it was unnecessary to consider the effect of the European Communities Act 1972, Goulding J. gave a very wide construction to the words "merchants generally", holding that they covered "all purely commercial occupations".

Usually there are several objects set out in the clause. If this is done, the first object is regarded as the *main object* or *substratum* of the company, and if it fails the company may be wound up by the court under s. 222(*f*): *Re German Date Coffee Co.* (1882). To avoid this result the memorandum may provide by what is called an "independent objects" clause at the end that *all* the objects shall be regarded as main or substantive ones, so that the failure of any one of them will not prevent the company from carrying on with the others. This was done successfully in *Cotman* v. *Brougham* (1918), where there were thirty objects and also in *Anglo-Overseas Agencies* v. *Green* (1960). The decision in *Introductions, Ltd.* v. *National Provincial Bank, Ltd.* (1969), however, shows that there are limits to the success of this device. It was there held that, despite an independent objects clause, a power to borrow could not stand by itself, but was necessarily for some purpose. This purpose must be legitimate and *intra vires* for the borrowing to be valid. Moreover, Harman L.J. indicated that this was not the only power about which he would take a similar view (*see* XXI, **2**).

26. The effect of ultra vires transactions. When an act is *ultra vires* and void, it can never be subsequently ratified and validated, even if every shareholder consents to it: *Ashbury Carriage Co., Ltd.* v. *Riche* (1875). All that can be done is for the company to alter its objects clause for the future, and such an alteration will never have a retrospective effect. It is therefore essential to study carefully the legal position both of the company and of the persons who deal with it under an *ultra vires* transaction.

The European Communities Act 1972 has made an important change here and it is necessary to consider the position both before and after that Act.

27. Effect of ultra vires contract on other party before the European Communities Act 1972. Where the contract was *executory*, a person who had agreed to supply goods or perform services for the company under an *ultra vires* contract had no action for breach if the company repudiated the contract before he had performed it.

Where the contract had been *executed by the other party*, i.e. where he had performed his bargain, he did not have any action for the price of goods supplied by him, nor for services rendered by him. *At common law*, however, he was sometimes able to "follow" goods supplied to the company and recover them. He could do this only if he could identify the goods and if they had not been consumed by the company. He based his claim on the fact that the *title* to the goods was still his, since no property can pass under a void contract.

Even where the goods had ceased to be identifiable, he might *in equity* be able to "trace" them under the equitable doctrine of restitution. By means of a tracing order he might obtain an equitable charge on a *mixed mass of assets* out of which, or the proceeds of which, he could satisfy his claim. The property, at least in equity, remained his: *Sinclair* v. *Brougham* (1914).

28. Effect of ultra vires contract on company before European Communities Act 1972. Although an *ultra vires* contract was void, it seems that any property obtained by a company under such a transaction could be protected by it against damage by other persons, even though it should not have acquired the property in the first place. Thus a company which, acting *ultra vires*, built a factory was nevertheless entitled to sue a person who threw stones through the windows.

Furthermore, we must examine the legal position from another point of view. It might not be the *supplier* who wished to enforce the *ultra vires* contract, or who had performed it and demanded payment. It might instead be the *company* who sued the other party for breach of contract. Here it seemed logical to argue that since the contract was void, the company was in no better a position to enforce it than the supplier, and that even if the company had performed its part of the bargain it would not be able to bring a successful action for payment.

Nevertheless, until recently this was not universally accepted as the correct view and textbooks differed on the question, so that it was helpful to have the position clarified by the judgment of Mocatta J. in *Bell Houses* v. *City Wall Properties* (1966), even though his decision was reversed in the Court of Appeal on the construction of the particular objects clause in question. Mocatta J. said:

"A defendant when sued on a contract by a company is entitled to take the point *by way of defence* that the contract was *ultra vires*. The contract is void and in the eyes of the law non-existent. There is no ground for distinguishing between executory and executed contracts."

29. The recommendations of the Jenkins Committee regarding the doctrine of ultra vires. From paragraph **27** it will be seen that the former state of the law concerning the third party was obviously not a satisfactory one, especially since he has no means of telling whether a transaction is *intra vires* or *ultra vires* without actually reading and understanding the objects clause of the memorandum. Moreover, *he was always deemed to have done this whether he had in fact done it or not*, i.e. he was said to have *constructive* knowledge of the contents of the memorandum in all cases where he did not have *actual* knowledge of them.

Thus, in legal theory a supplier to a company was formerly not safe unless he took the trouble to read the objects clause and see whether his particular transaction was within it. In practice, however, the business world is peopled by individuals who seldom concern themselves with such hazards until they are involved in them, and hardship could, and did, result.

The Jenkins Committee therefore made certain recommendations to improve the third party's position. These were as follows:

(*a*) The position of the company should be unchanged. The doctrine of *ultra vires* should be retained because to abolish it would place too much power in the hands of the directors, as the company's agents. Moreover, if the company delegated only restricted powers to the directors, the third party would be concerned with whether the directors were exceeding them, which would result in as many difficulties as arose at the moment.

(*b*) A third party acting *bona fide* should be able to enforce the *ultra vires* contract if he had performed it.

(*c*) The doctrine of *constructive* notice should be abolished. The third party should no longer be deemed to know the contents of the memorandum and articles where he had no actual knowledge of them.

(*d*) The third party should be able to enforce the contract even where he had *actual* notice of the contents of the memorandum and articles, if he honestly and reasonably did not appreciate that they precluded the company, or the directors on its behalf, from entering into the contract.

30. The provisions of the European Communities Act 1972. Section 9(1) European Communities Act 1972 provides that in favour of a person dealing with a company in good faith, any transaction decided on by the directors shall be deemed to be within the company's capacity (i.e. *intra vires*), and the directors' powers to bind the company shall be deemed free of limitations under the memorandum or articles. Such a person need not inquire into the company's capacity or the directors' powers, and is presumed to have acted in good faith unless the contrary is proved.

This provision seems to lack the customary precision of English legislation. It certainly destroys the doctrine of constructive notice (*see* **29**) in these circumstances, and implements recommendations (*a*), (*b*) and (*c*) of the Jenkins Committee as they are set out above. But how much further, if any, does it go? What is the position if the contract is still entirely executory? What is the position if a third party is given, or already has in his possession, a copy of the memorandum but does not trouble to read it? Does that position differ according to whether he *forgets* to read it or whether, believing that ignorance is bliss, he is *afraid* to read it? If he is afraid to read it, he is hardly *bona fide*; yet the company must prove his bad faith—an impossible task. What is the position if he reads it but does not understand it and later finds that the transaction is actually *ultra vires* when he thought it was *intra vires*, or else does not understand the importance of the point at all? Is he protected by his own stupidity? Has recommendation (*d*) above been implemented also? If so, stupidity becomes thoroughly advantageous. Finally, can this cosseted third party take the point *by way of defence* that the contract was *ultra vires*? If so, the law still seems unduly severe towards companies. A man is not necessarily either nice or honest merely because he does not carry on his business in corporate form.

We must await with interest judicial decisions on these matters. It seems, however, unfortunate that the opportunity was not taken to eradicate the doctrine completely from English law. Originally the doctrine was said to have two purposes, namely, to protect both investors and creditors; but at the present day it is hard to see that it achieves either. It was said to prevent the unrestricted use of the shareholders' money for any transaction in which the directors, as the company's agents, cared to engage, with the possible resulting loss to both members and creditors. But today, under modern economic conditions, it can be equally dangerous for a company to have only one type of enterprise, and objects clauses have become increasingly wide so as to enable a company to engage in the maximum range of commercial activities which could be of benefit to it. The doctrine from the point of view of businessmen is no more than an outdated irritant, and because it is deeply rooted in English company law they will doubtless look encouragingly at a legislature which has now taken the first slightly uncertain step in the right direction.

31. Gratuitous payments by companies. One further matter connected with the doctrine of *ultra vires* must be considered: namely, how far a company may make gratuitous payments out of its assets for political, charitable and educational purposes.

The Jenkins Committee declined to comment on *political* donations, taking the view that these were not a matter of Company Law since they raised constitutional issues. As regards *charitable* donations, the Committee pointed out that these had never been challenged in the courts, and that they would continue to be permissible on the grounds that they preserved goodwill. They took the same view of *educational* donations, citing *Evans* v. *Brunner Mond and Co., Ltd.* (1921), where a donation for scientific research by chemical manufacturers was held *intra vires*.

In *Parke* v. *Daily News* (1961), however, a gratuitous payment to the employees of a company who had become redundant on an amalgamation was held *ultra vires*, and the court decided that *ex gratia* payments out of the assets are only *intra vires* and valid if they are:

(*a*) *bona fide*;
(*b*) reasonably incidental to the carrying on of the company's business; and
(*c*) made for the benefit and prosperity of the company.

Thus in *Re W. and M. Roith* (1967), the controlling director of a company, after many years' service without any contract, was given a service agreement providing for payment of a pension to his executors on trust for his wife. He died in office two months later and the pension was paid for several years. Then the company went into liquidation. The executors claimed the capitalised value of the pension, but the liquidator rejected their claim. HELD: The payment of the pension was not reasonably incidental to the carrying on of the company's business, nor undertaken *bona fide* for the benefit and prosperity of the company, and the claim was therefore rightly rejected.

Some doubt was thrown on these rules by the decision in *Charterbridge Corporation, Ltd.* v. *Lloyds Bank, Ltd.* (1969). In that case the court held that where a company is carrying out the purposes expressed in its memorandum, and does an act within the scope of an express power in the memorandum, the *state of mind* of the parties concerned is immaterial on the issue of *ultra vires*. If this is so, then for an act to be *intra vires* the only one of the three conditions mentioned above which needs to be satisfied is (*b*). Motive becomes a relevant factor in determining whether any act is a *bona fide* exercise of the directors' power to do it, but is irrelevant in determining whether or not they have that power.

In any event, s. 74(1) Companies Act 1980 resolves the difficulty to a limited extent by stating that the powers of a company shall be deemed to include power to provide for its past and present employees and those of any of its subsidiaries on the *cessation or transfer* of the whole or any part of its undertaking or that of any subsidiary. Moreover, under s. 74(2), the company may exercise the power even when it is not in its best interests to do so—a novel principle indeed! Section 74(6), however, stipulates that any such provision, if made before the commencement of winding up, may be made out of distributable profits (*see* XVI, **3–5**), while if made after the commencement of winding up, it may be made out of the assets available to shareholders.

Section 74(3) imposes certain conditions on the exercise of the power. It must be sanctioned:

(*a*) in a case not falling under (*b*) or (*c*) below, by an *ordinary resolution*; *or*

(*b*) if so authorised by the memorandum or articles, a *directors' resolution*; *or*

(*c*) if the memorandum or articles require the sanction of a resolution for which a higher majority is necessary, a *resolution of that kind.*

Furthermore, any other requirement of the memorandum or articles must also be observed.

If, before winding up has commenced, the company has decided to make a payment in accordance with these conditions, the fact that it later goes into liquidation will not affect the position. Section 74(4) expressly authorises the liquidator to make the payment in these circumstances, although if the company is being wound up by the court his power to do so, like all the powers mentioned in s. 245 Companies Act 1948 (*see* XXVII, **21**), is subject to the control of the court: s. 245(3).

If winding up has already commenced, s. 74(5) governs the position. It authorises the liquidator, after providing for the costs of winding up and discharging the company's liabilities, to exercise the company's power to make a payment. The conditions stated in s. 74(3) above, however, again apply with the exception of (*b*) which can have no application to a company in liquidation since on winding up the powers of directors cease (*see* XXVII, **9** (*f*)).

It should be noted that if there should be any conflict between the rules governing the power to make a payment to employees under s. 74(4) or s. 74(5) and the normal rules relating to distribution of assets in liquidation (*see* IV, **5**), s. 74(8) makes it clear that the former prevail.

Finally, s. 19(1) Companies Act 1967 as amended by S.I. No. 1055, 1980, requires the directors' report to contain particulars of money given by the company for *political* or *charitable* purposes if, in a financial year, the total sum given exceeds £200 in amount.

In each case the report must state the *amount* of money given. In the case of money given for *political* purposes, it must also state:

(*a*) the name of each person to whom more than £200 has been given and the amount given;

(*b*) if more than £200 has been given by way of donation or subscription to a political party, the identity of the party and the amount given.

32. Alteration of the objects clause. So far, as regards this clause of the memorandum, only the doctrine of *ultra vires* has been considered. It is now important to see how the clause can be altered where this is desired.

Section 5(1) enables the company to alter the objects at any time by *special resolution* in order to:

(*a*) carry on its business more economically or efficiently; *or*
(*b*) attain its main purpose by new or improved means; *or*
(*c*) enlarge or change the local area of operations; *or*
(*d*) carry on some business which may be conveniently combined with its own; *or*
(*e*) restrict or abandon any of its objects; *or*
(*f*) sell or dispose of all or any of its undertaking; *or*
(*g*) amalgamate with another company.

NOTE: The *first four* of the above *increase* the scope of the company's activities, while the *last three* do not. The list should be carefully learnt.

33. Objections to alterations. Once the special resolution is passed, the company must wait for a period of twenty-one days to see whether or not any application to the court is made to cancel the alteration. If the twenty-one days elapse without such an application having been made, s. 5(7)(*a*) requires the company, within a further period of fifteen days, to deliver to the registrar a printed copy of the memorandum as altered.

It may be, however, that during the permitted period of twenty-one days specified in s. 5(3) an application to the court for cancellation of the alteration is made. Section 5(2) states that such an application can be made only by:

(a) the holders of at least 15% of the issued share capital, or any class thereof, or, if the company is not limited by shares, 15% of the members; *or*

(b) the holders of at least 15% of any debentures secured by a floating charge and issued before the 1st December 1947: s. 5(5).

NOTE: One person may hold the requisite 15% and so be able to apply to the court on his own.

If an application to the court for cancellation of the alteration is made, s. 5(1) states that the alteration is then ineffective unless confirmed by the court, but this is the *only time* when the consent of the court is required. Under s. 5(4) the court may make such order as it thinks fit, or may adjourn the proceedings in order that an arrangement may be made for the purchase of the share-holdings or other interests of the dissentient persons. It should be noted, however, that the proviso to s. 5(4) has been amended by s. 88(1) and para. 4 of the 3rd Schedule to the Companies Act 1980. A court order under s. 5 may now provide for the purchase by the company of the shares of any members and for the resulting reduction of capital (*see* XI, **9**). It can also make any alterations to the memorandum or articles which are thereby rendered necessary and prohibit the company from making subsequent alterations to these documents. The company may then make such alterations only with the leave of the court.

As soon as an application is made, s. 5(7)(b) requires the company to notify the registrar. Then when the court order is made, the company must deliver to the registrar within fifteen days an office copy of the order and, if it confirms the alteration, a printed copy of the altered memorandum.

34. Unauthorised alterations. The above provisions of s. 5 clearly state within what limits the objects clause can be altered, and how and by whom an objection to an alteration within these limits can be made. They do not, however, cover the case where an alteration is made which is *outside the permitted limits*. Yet it is obviously possible for a company to pass a special resolution altering its objects quite beyond these limits, and one might think that such an alteration, in view of s. 4, would be totally ineffective.

Nevertheless, s. 5(9) states that the validity of an alteration of the objects clause cannot be questioned on the grounds that it was not authorised by s. 5(1) except within 21 days. Thus presumably any member could object to an unauthorised alteration, provided he did so within 21 days, but after that period has elapsed the alteration cannot be challenged. From the viewpoint of an outsider dealing with the company, such a provision is essential, for if the *vires* of a company could be questioned at any times on the grounds that they were the result of an unauthorised alteration of the objects clause, the outsider could never be sure whether his particular transaction was *intra* or *ultra vires*.

35. The liability clause. The fourth or, in the case of a public company, the fifth compulsory clause of the memorandum states that the liability of the members is limited if in fact this is the case.

In the normal trading company, as we have seen, the members' liability will be limited to the amount, if any, unpaid on their shares. But in a company limited by guarantee, it will be limited to the amount which the members have agreed to contribute to the assets in the event of liquidation. This amount will be the sum specified in the fifth or, in the case of a public company, the sixth clause of the memorandum of such a company.

36. Companies limited by guarantee. Some details concerning companies limited by guarantee may be considered here. Such companies are normally formed for educational or charitable purposes, and may or may not have a share capital. If there is a share capital, then a member has a double liability, for he is liable not only up to the amount unpaid on his *shares*, but also up to the amount of the *guarantee* whatever it may be.

Model forms of memorandum for companies limited by guarantee with a share capital are found in Table D of the 1st Schedule to the Companies Act 1948 and, in the case of a public company, in Part II of the 1st Schedule to the Companies Act 1980, but it should be borne in mind that no more companies of this type can be created (*see* **2**).

If there is no share capital, the member is liable only up to the amount of the guarantee which is, as stated above, not payable until liquidation (*see* Table C in the 1st Schedule). Companies limited by guarantee with no share capital normally obtain their funds through subscriptions or endowments.

37. Alteration of liability. Section 16(1) permitted an *unlimited* company to convert into a *limited* company by the process of re-registration. It did not permit the opposite operation.

Section 45 Companies Act 1967, however, states that the power to register an unlimited company as limited under s. 16 is to cease, and ss. 43 and 44 Companies Act 1967 provide entirely new procedures for altering liability. Since the unlimited company has to some extent replaced the exempt private company as the favourite of the law, these provisions are now of some importance.

A company cannot however use *both* procedures. Thus once a limited company has re-registered as unlimited under s. 43 it cannot re-convert itself into a limited company under s. 44, or vice versa.

38. Re-registration of limited company as unlimited. Section 43(1) Companies Act 1967 states that a *limited* company may be re-registered as *unlimited* by application to the registrar. There is a re-registration fee of £5 under Statutory Instrument No. 1749 of 1980. The application must be framed in the prescribed form, signed by a director or the secretary, and lodged with the registrar together with certain other documents.

Section 43(2) requires the application to set out such alterations in the memorandum and, if articles have been registered, in the articles as are necessary to conform with the requirements of the Companies Act 1948 as regards unlimited companies with share capital or, if the company is not to have a share capital, as are necessary in the circumstances. If articles have not been registered, appropriate printed articles must be annexed and their registration requested.

Section 43(3) requires the application to be accompanied by:

(*a*) the *form of assent* to the company's being registered as unlimited, subscribed by *all the members*;

(*b*) a *statutory declaration* by the directors that the persons subscribing the form of assent constitute the whole membership of the company;

(*c*) a printed copy of the *memorandum* and, if articles have been registered, of the *articles* incorporating the alterations set out in the application.

Section 43(4) requires the registrar to retain the application and other documents, to register the articles if annexed, and to issue to the company an appropriate certificate of incorporation. On the issue of this certificate the status of the company is changed from limited to unlimited, and the alterations in the memorandum and, if articles were previously registered, in the articles take effect as if made by resolution of the company.

Section 43(5) states that the certificate of incorporation is conclusive evidence of compliance with the requirements of the section as to re-registration.

It must now be remembered, however, that owing to the definition of a public company in s. 1(1) Companies Act 1980 (*see* **2**), the procedure laid down in s. 43 is confined to private companies: s. 88(1) and para. 43 of the 3rd Schedule to the Companies Act 1980.

39. Re-registration of unlimited company as limited. Section 44(1) Companies Act 1967 states that an *unlimited* company may be registered as *limited* if a *special resolution* is passed to that effect and an application made to the registrar. There is a re-registration fee of £50 under Statutory Instrument No. 1749 of 1980. The application must be framed in the prescribed form, signed by a director or the secretary, and lodged with the registrar, together with certain other documents, on or after the day on which a copy of the resolution is received by him (*see* XXIII, **39**).

Section 44(2), as amended by the Companies Act 1980, requires the resolution to state whether the company is to be limited by shares or by guarantee and, if limited by shares, what the share capital is to be. It must also provide for such alterations to the memorandum and articles as are necessary to conform with the statutory requirements.

Section 44(3) requires the application to be accompanied by a printed copy of the memorandum and articles as altered.

Section 44(4) requires the registrar to retain the application and other documents, and to issue to the company an appropriate certificate of incorporation. On the issue of this certificate the status of the company is changed from unlimited to limited, and the alterations in the memorandum and articles specified in the resolution take effect.

Section 44(5) is similar to s. 43(5) (*see* **38**).

It must again be stressed that this procedure is now confined to *private* companies: s. 7(4) Companies Act 1980.

40. Other statutory provisions regarding liability. There are a number of other statutory provisions regarding liability, some of which are of importance while others are rarely used. They are as follows:

(*a*) Section 22 states that the liability of a member cannot be increased without his written consent.

(*b*) Section 31, as amended by s. 88(1) and para. 7 of the 3rd Schedule to the Companies Act 1980, states that where a company carries on business for more than six months without having at least two members, any person who, for the whole or any part of the period that it carries on business after those six months:

(*i*) is a member of the company; and

(*ii*) knows that it is carrying on business with only one member,

is liable, jointly and severally with the company, for the payment of the company's debts contracted during that period or the relevant part of it. Such a person thus *loses the protection of limited liability*.

The horrifying effect of this section can be avoided by a member quite easily, since under s. 222 a reduction of members below the statutory minimum is a ground for winding up by the court, and under s. 224 this is one of the occasions on which a member can present a winding up petition and so protect himself.

(*c*) Section 202 states that the memorandum may provide that the *directors* in a limited company shall have *unlimited liability*, but that they must be notified of this before accepting office by the promoters, existing directors or secretary.

If they are not notified, then though their liability will still be unlimited, the person responsible for the failure to notify them is liable for any damage which they may sustain.

(*d*) Section 203 states that a limited company with authority in its articles may by special resolution alter its memorandum so as to make the liability of a director unlimited.

Section 202 and s. 203 are rarely used in practice. Stock Exchange rules now permit stockbroking firms to become limited companies provided the directors give an undertaking that they will be personally liable without limitation to the Stock Exchange in respect of stock exchange transactions. Such an undertaking, however, does not confer unlimited liability on the directors either to the company or to its creditors and thus does not give rise to the position contemplated by these two sections: *Mitton Butler Priest & Co. Ltd.* v. *Ross* (1976).

(*e*) Section 332 deals with *fraudulent trading*. In subsection (1) it states that where, in the course of liquidation, it appears that the company's business has been carried on with intent to defraud creditors or for any fraudulent purpose, the official receiver, the liquidator, a creditor or a contributory may apply to the court, which may declare that any persons knowingly parties to the transactions shall be personally responsible *without any limit on their liability* for all or any of the debts of the company.

To be a "party" within this section, a person must take some *positive steps* in the carrying on of the company's business in a fraudulent manner: *Re Maidstone Buildings Provisions, Ltd.* (1971). However, a creditor who accepts money knowing that it has been procured by carrying on the business with intent to defraud other creditors for the very purpose of paying him is a "party" within the section: *Re Gerald Cooper Chemicals Ltd.* (1978). "A man who warms himself with the fire of fraud cannot complain if he is singed," said Templeman J. of the creditor in question. He further held that even an isolated transaction can be within the section provided that it amounts to a fraud on a creditor perpetrated in the course of carrying on business.

Lastly, in *Re Sarflax Ltd.* (1979) it was held that the expression "carrying on business" in s. 332 had a wider meaning than carrying on trade. It included the collection of assets acquired in the course of business and their distribution in discharge of business liabilities provided there was a "continuous course of active conduct". The court further held that the mere preference of one creditor over another did not amount to an "intention to defraud" within the section.

41. The capital clause. Consideration of this topic will be postponed, since it requires a chapter to itself. Two points, however, should be noted at this stage:

(*a*) The figure given in the capital clause of the memorandum is the *nominal* or *authorised* capital of the company. The Act does not state any *minimum figure* for share capital in the case of a private company. This can, in theory, be of any amount, provided the subscribers to the memorandum take at least one share each. Thus one private company was incorporated with a capital of $\frac{1}{2}d$ divided into two shares of $\frac{1}{4}d$ each. Presumably today the minimum capital for a private company would be 1p.

In the case of a public company, however, s. 3(2) Companies Act 1980 requires the capital clause of the memorandum to state a figure which is *not less than the authorised minimum*. Section 85(1) Companies Act 1980 defines the authorised minimum as £50,000 or such other sum as the Secretary of State may specify by order made by statutory instrument. Presumably the definition is designed to allow the Secretary of State sufficient latitude to take account of inflation.

(b) The shares must have a *fixed value* which can also be of any amount. This fixed value is called the *par* or *nominal* value of the share.

Once the share is allotted, the holder will be able to sell it at its current *market* value, which is a fluctuating figure and may be either above or below the par value according to the prosperity and prospects of the company. When the market value is *above* the par value, the share is said to be standing *at a premium*. When the market value is *below* the par value, the share is said to be standing *at a discount*.

Similarly, when shares are first issued by the company, they may be issued at par or at a premium, although not at a discount.

42. Other clauses in the memorandum. The compulsory clauses of the memorandum have now been separately considered in this chapter, but of course the memorandum may have other clauses containing matters which might equally well have been put in the articles instead.

The alteration of any such non-compulsory clauses is governed by s. 23, which states that they may be altered by special resolution, with the same provision for dissentients to apply to the court to cancel the alteration as was made by s. 5 regarding alterations of the objects clause, except that debenture-holders have no right of application.

There are, however, three cases where s. 23 does not apply:

(a) If the memorandum expressly, or by reference to the articles, lays down a method of alteration of the particular clause, then that method must be used.

(b) If the memorandum prohibits alteration, then the clause can only be altered with the leave of the court under s. 206.

(c) Section 23 does not apply to class rights. The nature of class rights and the method of alteration required will be considered later.

PROGRESS TEST 2

1. What is the minimum number of persons required to form a registered company? (**1**)

2. Give the definition of a public company found in s. 1 Companies Act 1980. (**2**)

3. Section 1 Companies Act 1948 states that three types of company may be formed by registration under the Act. What are they? **(3)**

4. What are the compulsory clauses in the memorandum of association? **(4)**

5. Where does one find:

(*a*) a model memorandum for a public company limited by shares?

(*b*) a model memorandum for a private company limited by shares? **(5)**

6. What is the association clause? **(5)**

7. Give the provisions of s. 4 Companies Act 1948. **(6)**

8. Give the *statutory* provisions on the choice of a name. **(7)**

9. Where can guidance on the choice of a name be obtained? **(7)**

10. Once the name has been chosen and accepted, where must it appear? **(8)**

11. Give the provisions of the Companies Act 1980 governing the publication of its name by a public company. **(2, 8)**

12. Define an officer of a company. **(8)**

13. If the secretary of a company signs a cheque on its behalf without putting the word "limited" anywhere on the document, what is the possible effect? **(8)**

14. What companies may dispense with the use of the word "limited" as part of their name, even though they are limited companies? **(9)**

15. Give the majorities and periods of notice required in order validly to pass:

(*a*) an ordinary resolution;
(*b*) an extraordinary resolution;
(*c*) a special resolution. **(10)**

16. How are voting majorities calculated? **(10)**

17. How may a company change its name? **(11)**

18. Can a company be compelled to change its name? **(11)**

19. What is a company's domicile, and can it be changed? **(13)**

20. Can the address of the registered office within the domicile be changed? **(14)**

21. What documents must normally be kept at the registered office? **(14)**

22. What are the statutory books? **(15)**

23. What particulars must be entered in the *company's* register of charges? **(17)**

24. What charges must be registered with the registrar? **(18)**

25. What particulars must be entered in the *registrar's* register of charges? **(19)**

26. What particulars must be entered in the registrar's register of charges where the charge is one to which the holders of a series of debentures are entitled? **(19)**

27. What is the legal effect of failure to register a registrable charge? **(20)**

28. Who is entitled to register a registrable charge? **(20)**

29. What is a memorandum of satisfaction? **(21)**

30. If a registrable charge is not registered within the prescribed period, is there any remedy? **(22)**

31. Outline the nature and advantages of a floating charge. **(17)**

32. Explain what is meant by "crystallisation" of a floating charge. **(17)**

33. What remedy had a supplier of goods to a company under an *ultra vires* contract before the European Communities Act 1972 if:

(*a*) the company refused to take delivery of the goods;

(*b*) the company took delivery and the goods were on the premises;

(*c*) the company took delivery and the goods were then consumed? **(27)**

34. What remedy before the European Communities Act 1972 had a company which had made an *ultra vires* contract with an outsider who refused to perform it? **(28)**

35. What were the recommendations of the Jenkins Committee regarding the doctrine of *ultra vires*? **(29)**

36. Discuss the provisions of the European Communities Act 1972 with regard to the doctrine of *ultra vires*. **(30)**

37. How far is it lawful to make gratuitous payments out of a company's assets? **(31)**

38. By what method and within what limits may the objects clause of a company's memorandum be altered? **(32)**

39. Who may apply to the court to cancel an alteration of the objects clause? **(33)**

40. What are the powers of the court on such an application? **(33)**

41. How far can a limited company convert itself into an unlimited company? And vice versa? Describe the procedures available. (37, 38, 39)

42. Can the liability of a member be *increased*? (40)

43. What constitutes *fraudulent trading* by a company and what is its possible result? (40)

44. The number of members in a company became reduced to one on 28th April 1980. The company incurred trade debts on 29th April 1980, 20th September 1980, 27th October 1980 and 28th October 1980. How far is the remaining member liable for these debts? (40)

45. How can the non-compulsory clauses of the memorandum, if any, be altered? (42)

46. What is the *authorised minimum* of share capital required to be stated in the capital clause of the memorandum of a public company? (41)

CHAPTER III

The Articles of Association

1. The nature of the articles of association. The articles of a company are the regulations for its internal management, corresponding to the partnership deed in a partnership. The management of every company is governed by articles, though not every company need *register* articles with the registrar, as will be seen later.

2. The contents of the 1st Schedule to the Act. Section 11 applies both to the memorandum and the articles, and states:

(*a*) The memorandum of a company limited by shares must be in accordance with Table B (II, **4** and **5**).

In the case of a public company, however, Part I of the 1st Schedule to the Companies Act 1980 has superseded Table B: s. 2(4) Companies Act 1980.

(*b*) The memorandum and articles of a company limited by guarantee and not having a share capital must be in accordance with Table C (II, **36**).

(*c*) The memorandum and articles of a company limited by guarantee and having a share capital must be in accordance with Table D (II, **36**).

In the case of a public company, again, Part II of the 1st Schedule to the Companies Act 1980 has superseded Table D: s. 2(4) Companies Act 1980.

(*d*) The memorandum and articles of an unlimited company with a share capital must be in accordance with Table E.

The section does not mention Table A, nor does it refer to the articles of a company limited by shares which do not, therefore, have to be in any specified form.

NOTE: The 1st Schedule to the Act should now be examined carefully. It contains the five Tables A–E, and the student should know the *nature of each Table* as stated in s. 11. He need not learn the *contents,* apart from Table B which was studied extensively in Chapter I, and Table A, to which constant reference will be made throughout the book.

3. The nature of Table A. It should be observed that Table A is divided into two parts. Part II has been repealed by the Companies Act 1980: s. 88(1) and para. 36 of the 3rd Schedule. Part I is now a model form of articles for both public and private companies limited by shares. Many of the clauses in it must eventually be learnt, but at this stage it is best simply to glance at the headings in order to see the type of material normally found in the articles of companies limited by shares.

4. The obligation to register articles. Section 6 states that a company limited by shares *may* register articles, i.e. may do so if it wishes, while a company limited by guarantee or an unlimited company *must* (shall) do so.

Section 11 has already indicated the form which the articles of companies limited by guarantee and unlimited companies must take.

Section 6 also states that the articles are signed by the subscribers to the memorandum, i.e. the same persons sign both documents.

5. The application of Table A. It is clear from s. 6 that a company limited by shares need not register articles, though other types of company are required to do so. The section does not, however, tell us what happens if a company limited by shares fails to register articles.

Section 8 deals with this situation. Section 8(1) merely gives a general permission for the articles of any company to adopt the Table A provisions, but s. 8(2) is of great importance. It deals exclusively with companies limited by shares, and states that Table A applies to such companies *automatically, unless excluded or modified.*

It is essential to grasp the fact of the automatic application of Table A. The result of s. 8(2) is that if a company limited by shares does not register any articles, Table A automatically applies. Moreover, even if it *does* register articles of its own, Table A will still apply automatically unless it has been excluded or modified.

The company can easily exclude Table A by express words to that effect in its articles. Modification can be either *express*, as where the company's articles state that some clauses of Table A will apply with certain alterations, or *implied*, as where the company's articles are inconsistent with Table A, in which case they will prevail.

Students often find s. 8(2) a little difficult to understand. Its meaning, as explained above, is quite simple, and it should be read slowly several times until it becomes clear. The words "those regulations" in the fifth line refer, of course, to Table A.

. Companies formed prior to 1948. A question which arises in connection with Table A is whether a company is always governed by the Table A of the 1948 Act or, if it was formed prior to 1948, of the particular Companies Act under which it was registered. Each Act has a Table A of its own, and each differs to some extent from the others, so this can be an important point.

The rule here is that a company is always governed by the Table A of the Act *under which it was registered* with *one exception*: under s. 134(*a*) the *method of service of notice of meeting* is regulated in every case by the Table A of the 1948 Act, no matter when the company was formed, unless the company's own articles stipulate some other method.

. Statutory requirements regarding articles. The Finance Act 1970, has abolished the requirement in s. 9(*c*) that the articles should be stamped as if they were contained in a deed, but the other requirements of s. 9 remain.

Articles must therefore be:

(*a*) printed (*see* II, **6**);
(*b*) in numbered paragraphs;
(*c*) signed by the subscribers to the memorandum in the presence of at least one witness.

. The duties of the subscribers to the memorandum. The duties of the subscribers must at some stage be noted, and since we have already come across three of them, they can now conveniently be listed in full:

(*a*) They must sign the memorandum.   (II, **5**)
(*b*) They must sign the articles.
(*c*) They must take at least one share each.   (II, **5**)
(*d*) They normally appoint the first directors.   (XXII, **4**)

. Alteration of the articles. Section 10 states that a company may alter its articles by special resolution. This may be done at any general meeting and as often as required. There are, however, certain important rules regarding alteration:

(*a*) Under s. 10, the alteration must be subject to the provisions of the memorandum, and if the two documents conflict, the memorandum will prevail.

(*b*) The alteration must be lawful. It must not conflict with the provisions of the Act, nor with the general law.

(*c*) If, in response to an application by the prescribed minority for the cancellation of an alteration of the company's objects clause, the court has made an order under s. 5 prohibiting any alteration to the articles, the company may not alter them without the leave of the court (*see* II, **33**).

(*d*) If, in response to an application by the prescribed minority for the cancellation of a resolution by a public company to be re registered as a private company, the court has made an order under s. 11 Companies Act 1980 prohibiting any alteration to the articles, the company may not alter them without the leave of the court (*see* XIX, **5**).

(*e*) If, in response to a petition on the ground that the company's affairs are being conducted in a manner unfairly prejudicial to the interests of some part of the members, the court has made an order under s. 75 Companies Act 1980 prohibiting any alteration to the articles, the company may not alter them without the leave of the court (*see* XXXI, **5**).

(*f*) Under s. 22, the alteration may not increase the liability of any member without his written consent (*see* II, **40**).

(*g*) If the alteration concerns class rights, s. 72 protects dissentients, i.e. persons who disagree. (Section 72 and class rights are discussed in XV, **15**.)

(*h*) The alteration must be *bona fide* for the benefit of the company as a whole. Provided this condition is satisfied, individual hardship is irrelevant: *Allen* v. *Gold Reefs of West Africa* (1900); *Shuttleworth* v. *Cox Bros. & Co., Ltd.* (1927); *Sidebottom* v. *Kershaw, Leese & Co., Ltd.* (1920).

(*i*) If the alteration involves a breach of contract, it will still be valid, but the injured party will have all the normal remedies against the company for the breach.

NOTE: The first seven of these rules have a restrictive effect on the company's statutory power to alter its articles freely by special resolution under s. 10, while the last two rather emphasise its power to alter its articles as it wishes.

Section 9(5) European Communities Act 1972 provides that where a company alters its articles it must send a printed copy of them as altered to the registrar. Section 9(3)(*b*) requires him to publish in the *Gazette* the receipt by him of any document relating to an alteration of the articles. If the company fails to notify him of such an alteration and cannot show that it was known at the time to the person concerned, then it cannot rely on the alteration against that person: s. 9(4)(*b*).

10. The legal effect of the articles. Section 20(1) states that the memorandum and articles bind the company and the members as though signed and sealed by each member, and as though they contained covenants (i.e. promises under seal) by each member to observe their provisions.

Section 20(2) states that money payable by the member to the company under the memorandum or articles is a *specialty debt*, i.e. the period of limitation is twelve years and not the normal six. It appears, however, that this is not the case as regards debts owed by the company to the members, e.g. declared dividends (*see* XVI, **9**).

The effect of the articles is therefore as follows:

(*a*) The company is bound to the members *in their capacity of members*.

(*b*) The members *in their capacity of members* are bound to the company.

(*c*) The members are contractually bound *to each other*.

(*d*) The company is *not bound to any person*, except to members in their capacity of members.

Results (*a*) and (*b*) are obvious from the wording of s. 20; results (*c*) and (*d*) are dealt with in **11** and **12** below.

11. The members are bound to each other. This result of s. 20 is not quite so obvious. In *Clarke* v. *Dunraven* (1897) it was held that the members of a yacht club were bound *to each other* by the rules of the club, so that one member could sue another *directly* to enforce the rules. But a yacht club is not a corporation, and therefore not a legal person, so that a club member in joining the club is contracting directly with all the other members. A company, however, is a legal person and a member in becoming a shareholder is contractually bound in respect of his shares to the *company*.

Perhaps this should be regarded as one of the occasions mentioned in discussing *Salomon* v. *Salomon & Co., Ltd.* (1897), (*see* IV, **6**), when the "veil of incorporation" is lifted, i.e. the member is contractually bound to the company, but the company consists of the members behind the veil of the corporate person, and therefore in this sense each member can be said to be *directly bound* to the others. The law, however, has not so far established this, and until recently it was clear that the *direct enforcement* of the members' rights *inter se* was not permitted. If we try to put this in the form of a diagram, it will look like this:

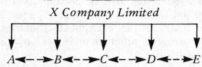

X Company Limited

A ←--→ B ←--→ C ←--→ D ←--→ E

Each member is contractually bound to the company, and the company to him, *in respect of his shares*. Each member is bound to the other members, but he may not be able to sue another member directly—the action must be brought by the company itself or, if it is in liquidation, by the liquidator.

12. The articles are not a contract between the company and any person in a capacity other than that of member. This rule is seen clearly in the leading case of *Eley* v. *Positive Life Assurance Co., Ltd.* (1876), from which it follows that a person cannot rely on the articles as a contract of employment or supply since they only bind the company to members in respect of their membership rights, and not contractual rights of other kinds. This is so whether he is a member or not.

In *Eley* v. *Positive Life Assurance Co., Ltd.* (1876), the articles provided that E should be the company's solicitor *for life*. He was employed by the company and took shares in it, but later the company dismissed him from his employment with it. He sued for breach of contract. HELD: His action failed, for the articles on which he relied were not a contract between the company and any other person, except in respect of their *membership* rights.

Where, however, a person performs services for the company at its request without any contract, he may sue in *quasi-contract* for a reasonable sum (*quantum meruit*) for the work done. A clause in the articles then may be *evidence* of what the parties thought reasonable, and though unable of itself to create contractual rights of this type, may be of evidential value in a quasi-contractual claim such as was made in *Craven-Ellis* v. *Canons, Ltd.* (1936).

In *Craven-Ellis* v. *Canons, Ltd.* (1936), C was appointed the company's managing director by a contract in writing and under the company's seal, by a resolution of the board of directors. The articles imposed a share qualification on the directors, none of whom ever obtained it. C sued for his salary under the contract and, alternatively, for reasonable remuneration (*quantum meruit*) for work done, in quasi-contract. HELD: His claim on the *contract* failed, for under the articles his appointment could not be valid owing to his failure to take up his qualification shares. His claim in *quasi-contract*, however, succeeded, for he had performed services for the company at its request.

13. Difficulty in application of rules regarding legal effect of articles. In recent years the decision in *Rayfield* v. *Hands* (1958), has given rise to difficulty in connection with rules (*c*) and (*d*) in the last paragraphs.

In *Rayfield* v. *Hands* (1958), Clause 11 of the articles of a private company provided: "Every member who intends to transfer shares *shall* inform the directors, who *will* take the said shares equally between them at a fair value". The plaintiff, a member, informed the defendants, the directors, of his wish to transfer his shares. The directors denied liability to take and pay for them. HELD: (*a*) "Will" indicated an *obligation* to take the shares. (*b*) The article created a *contractual relationship* between the *plaintiff as a member* and the *defendants as members*.

It is submitted that (*a*) above is correct in that it probably gives effect to the intention behind the clause, although one may well wonder why, if obligation was intended, the word "shall" was not used again. But (*b*) is more difficult to understand. The defendants in the case were in fact members, but the clause imposed the obligation to buy the shares on the *directors*. If one of them had not been a member, would he too have been bound? Can an article which refers to a person as a director, or employee, or coal-supplier, bind him *as a member* if he also happens to be one? And how far does such an article give a *direct right of action* between one member and another? Is the position now similar to that in *Clarke* v. *Dunraven* (*see* **11**)?

It can at least be said that it should be carefully considered how far this decision has affected rules (*c*) and (*d*). Moreover, it does not stand entirely alone. Much the same reasoning appears to have been adopted by Plowman J. in *Re Richmond Gate Property Co.* (1974), a case which concerned a managing director's claim for remuneration, and where in his judgment Plowman J. said: "The effect of Article 9, coupled with Article 108 of Table A, *coupled with the fact that the applicant was a member of the company,* in my judgement is that a *contract exists between himself and the company*".

Perhaps it will soon be correct to say that where a person is a member of a company, the articles constitute a contract between the company and himself in any capacity in which they refer to him. If so, the decision in *Eley* v. *Positive Life Assurance Co., Ltd.* may no longer be the law.

PROGRESS TEST 3

1. What is Table A? To which companies and when does it apply?　(**3 and 5**)

2. If a company limited by shares was formed in 1945 and did not register articles, is it governed by the Table A of the Companies Act 1929, or the Companies Act 1948?　(**6**)

3. What are the statutory requirements regarding the articles?　(**7**)

4. What are the duties of the subscribers to the memorandum?　(**8**)

5. By what method may a company alter its articles? What rules govern alteration?　(**9**)

6. What is the legal effect of the articles?　(**10, 11, 12, 13**)

CHAPTER IV

Registration

1. Documents to be delivered to the registrar on registration. We have now dealt with the memorandum and articles of association and it remains to consider the next step after preparation of these documents.

Section 12 states that the memorandum and articles, if any, must be delivered to the registrar, who retains and registers them. But this is not enough, and the complete list of documents which must be delivered to him is as follows:

(*a*) The memorandum: s. 12.

(*b*) The articles, if any: s. 12.

(*c*) A statement signed by the subscribers of the memorandum:

(*i*) containing the names and particulars of the directors and secretary and a consent signed by each of them to act in the relevant capacity; and

(*ii*) specifying the intended situation of the company's registered office: s. 21 and s. 23 Companies Act 1976.

(*d*) A statement of capital: s. 47(3) Finance Act 1973.

(*e*) A statutory declaration of compliance signed by a solicitor engaged in the formation of the company, or a person named as director or secretary in the statement delivered under s. 21 Companies Act 1976: s. 3(5) Companies Act 1980.

2. The certificate of incorporation. Once the required documents have been delivered the registrar, under s. 3(1) Companies Act 1980, must satisfy himself that all the requirements of the Companies Acts in respect of registration have been complied with. He then, in accordance with s. 13(1), issues a certificate of incorporation (the company's "birth" certificate).

Section 13(2), as amended by the Companies Act 1980, provides that on the issue of the certificate the company becomes a body corporate by the name contained in the memorandum. This occurs, according to the subsection, from the *date on the certificate*, even if that is *not* in fact the date when it was issued: *Jubilee Cotton Mills* v. *Lewis* (1924). If the company's memorandum states that it is to be a public company, the certificate of incorporation must also contain a statement to that effect: s. 3(3) Companies Act 1980.

Section 15 was repealed by the Companies Act 1980 and replaced by s. 3(4) and (5) of that Act. Section 3(4) states that the certificate, once issued, is conclusive evidence that the company has been duly registered and, if it contains a statement to that effect, that the company is a public company. Section 9(3)(a) European Communities Act 1972 requires the registrar to publish notice of its issue in the *Gazette*.

The company is now formed, i.e. it is now a "registered" corporation.

3. Summary of the statutory provisions studied so far. It is at this stage helpful to look at the first twenty sections of the Act and to see that some comprehension of them should now have been achieved:

Sections 1–4 deal with formation and the memorandum.

Section 5 deals with the objects clause of the memorandum.

Sections 6 and 8–11 deal with the articles.

Sections 12 and 13 deal with incorporation.

Section 16 dealt with liability and re-registration, but is no longer effective. Sections 43–44 Companies Act 1967 now deal with alterations of liability.

Sections 17–19 deal with the name.

Section 20 deals with the effect of the memorandum and articles.

Apart from s. 15 which has been repealed and replaced, as stated in 2 above, by s. 3(4) and (5) Companies Act 1980, the only sections not mentioned are s. 7, which relates to companies limited by guarantee and unlimited companies and is therefore outside the scope of this book, and s. 14, which relates to the holding of land by registered companies, but has now been repealed by the Charities Act 1960. All registered companies have now unrestricted power to hold land in the same way as a private person.

4. The expenses of formation. These are as follows:

(*a*) A registration fee of £50 under Statutory Instrument No. 1749 of 1980.

(*b*) Stamp duty of £1 per cent on the actual value of assets of any kind contributed by the members less any liabilities assumed or discharged by the company as consideration for them: s. 47(5) and 19th Schedule, Finance Act 1973.

In addition, the cost of professional services and preparing the requisite documents must be defrayed.

5. The order of distribution of a company's assets in liquidation. Now that we have formed a registered company and have created an artificial legal person, we must consider the implications. This is best done by studying two famous cases: *Salomon* v. *Salomon & Co., Ltd.* (1897), and *Foss* v. *Harbottle* (1843). The first of these cases, however, can only be thoroughly understood if a student already knows the order of distribution of a company's assets when it goes into liquidation. This is therefore given below and should be carefully studied and thoroughly learnt.

Note that on liquidation the usual important distinction between capital and revenue ceases and these merge to become, collectively, the company's *assets* which the liquidator must assemble and distribute in the following order:

(*a*) Secured creditors with *fixed* charges usually take payment out of their security. If their security is inadequate, they rank as unsecured creditors for the balance of their debts.

(*b*) The costs of liquidation (including the liquidator's remuneration).

(*c*) Preferential creditors. (Section 319 lists them, and will be studied later, *see* XXX.)

(*d*) Secured creditors with *floating* charges.

(*e*) Unsecured creditors.

(*f*) Debts due to members *as members*, e.g. dividends declared but not yet paid, and interest on calls paid in advance: s. 212(1)(*g*).

(*g*) Repayment of capital to members *pari passu* (i.e. proportionately in relation to their shareholdings) unless the articles or terms of issue provide otherwise. (Often they give priority to the preference shareholders, but this is a modification by contract of the basic rule.)

(*h*) Surplus assets divisible among the members *pari passu*, unless the articles or terms of issue provide otherwise.

From this order it is apparent that the law protects the creditors of the company at the expense of the members. Even a debt due to a member in his capacity of member is deferred below the claims of the unsecured creditors by s. 212(1)(*g*).

Moreover, the normal rule by which secured creditors rank before unsecured ones is reversed by s. 319(5), which provides that preferential debts (which are unsecured) rank *before* secured creditors with floating charges. Floating charges are often over the whole of the company's assets generally, so if s. 319(5) did not make this provision there would be a much greater risk to the preferential creditors who include, of course, the Revenue.

A secured creditor part of whose debt is preferential and who realises his security for less than the amount owing to him may appropriate the proceeds of sale to that part of his debt which is non-preferential, thus leaving his preferential claim outstanding: *Re William Hall (Contractors)* (1967).

Debenture-holders, being simply creditors, fall into (*a*), (*d*) or (*e*) according to whether they have a fixed charge, a floating charge, or are "naked", i.e. unsecured and have no charge at all.

Finally, under s. 302 the assets of a company must be applied to its liabilities *pari passu*, subject to the claims of its preferential creditors. Thus unsecured creditors all rank equally and if the assets are insufficient to discharge their debts in full, they will each receive a proportionate amount. Even a *judgment* creditor has no priority although he has brought a successful action for his debt. If, therefore, a contract is made which would result in a distribution of the company's property in a manner contrary to s. 302, the court will refuse to give effect to it, even though it was made for good business reasons and without any thought for the effect of insolvency on the arrangement agreed under it: *British Eagle International Airlines* v. *Compagnie Nationale Air France* (1975).

NOTE: Students often ask whether a floating charge which has *crystallised* (II, **17**) and so become fixed is promoted, as it were, from (*d*) to (*a*) on crystallisation. This is not the case. One of the events which causes crystallisation is liquidation, and if the holders of floating charges which had crystallised were in the same position as the holders of fixed charges, there would be no need to put the holders of floating charges into a separate category as shown above.

6. Salomon v. Salomon & Company, Ltd. The facts of this leading case were as follows:

Salomon ran a boot business which he decided to incorporate. He formed a registered company by the process of registration as described above, and then sold his business to the company at an over-valuation. This was a common feature of a company promotion, and provided the profit made by the promoter was disclosed it was, as will be seen later in VI, **1**, quite permissible even in the case of a public company, until the Companies Act 1980 was passed. The only members of the company were Salomon, his wife, and his children, who by luck or judgment were just sufficient in number to form a registered company. (The minimum number of subscribers required to form a public company was seven until the Companies Act 1980 reduced it to two, and it was not possible to form a private company with the smaller minimum number of members until 1907.) Since all the members knew of the entire arrangement, the over-valuation was quite in order.

Salomon's wife and children each held one share in this company, and the remainder were held by Salomon himself. In payment for the business these shares were allotted to Salomon fully paid up, but part of the purchase-price was left outstanding as a debt due to Salomon from the company. He was careful to see that it was secured by a floating charge over the company's assets.

When at length the company went into liquidation, these assets were insufficent to pay all the debts. The unsecured trade creditors claimed that they were entitled to such assets as existed, on the grounds that the whole transaction was a sham, and that the secured debentures originally issued to Salomon were therefore invalid. They regarded the company as in essence the same person as Salomon himself, since he controlled it.

The House of Lords either had to agree that this was so, thereby rejecting the whole principle of incorporation and the theory of the corporate legal personality, or to hold that once a corporation has been formed, it is an entirely different legal person from the members who compose and control it. They chose the latter course, and accordingly the company was treated as a different legal person from Salomon. It followed that since the debentures originally issued to him were secured by a floating charge, the holder had priority over the unsecured trade creditors, who in consequence received nothing.

This famous case, establishing beyond all doubt the existence of the "veil of incorporation", i.e. the legal personality of the corporation through which the identity of the members cannot be perceived, is not without its exceptions. There are several instances where the veil is "lifted" and the identity of the members can be seen, not through a glass darkly, but face to face, but these exceptions are best left until the end of the subject.

7. The rule in Foss v. Harbottle. This case is usually considered in textbooks in connection with meetings. Strictly speaking, however, it relates, like Salomon's case, to the theory of the corporate personality, and can well be studied at this point. The facts were as follows:

> The minority shareholders brought an action against the directors to compel them to make good losses incurred by the company due to their fraud. HELD: The action failed, for the proper plaintiff for wrongs done to the company is the company itself, and the company can act only through its majority shareholders.

This decision is the logical result of the principle that a company is a separate legal person from the members who compose it. Once it is admitted that the company is a legal person, it follows that if a wrong is done to it, the company is the proper person to bring an action. This is a simple rule of *procedure* which applies to all wrongs: only the injured party may sue. If, for instance, A intentionally pushes B down the stairs because he does not like him, and B breaks his leg in consequence, it is no use if C, who has seen the whole incident, brings an action against A. C has not been hurt: he is not the injured party; he is the wrong plaintiff. The right plaintiff is B, or, sometimes, persons who are injured by having been deprived of B's services. But if a person has not been injured, he cannot sue.

Of course, as applied to companies, the rule appears a little more complicated. After all, the directors who have been fraudulent have injured the *company*. The company is composed of *members*. Losses to the company affect *all the members*, not simply the majority or the minority or any particular member. Why, then, should an individual member not sue, since he has been injured?

The answer is that injury is not enough. The plaintiff must show that the injury has been caused by a *breach of duty* to him. In the course of existence a person suffers many injuries for which no action can be brought, for no duty to him has been broken; and individual shareholders, or even the minority shareholders as a body, who try to show that the directors owe a duty to *them personally* in their management of the company's assets will assuredly fail. The directors owe no duty to the individual members, but only to *the company as a whole*. A company is a person, and if it suffers injury through breach of a duty owed to it, then the only possible plaintiff is the company itself acting, as it must always act, through its majority.

NOTE: *Foss* v. *Harbottle* concerned a wrong done to the company by the *directors*, but it is immaterial by whom it was done. In *Leon* v. *York-O-Matic* (1966), it was stated that for wrongs done by a *liquidator*, such as selling the company's assets at an undervalue, the proper plaintiff would have been the *company*, and not a creditor or a director.

8. Advantages of rule in Foss v. Harbottle. There are two main advantages to the rule in *Foss* v. *Harbottle*, of a purely practical nature:

(*a*) Clearly, if every individual member were permitted to sue anyone who had injured the company through a breach of duty, there could be as many actions as there are shareholders. Legal proceedings would never cease, and there would be enormous wastage of time and money.

(*b*) If an individual member could sue a person who had caused loss to the company, and the company then ratified that person's act at a general meeting, the legal proceedings would be quite useless, for a court will naturally hold that the will of the majority prevails.

9. Apparent exceptions to the rule in Foss v. Harbottle. There are a number of occasions on which *an individual member may bring an action*, and these are as follows:

(*a*) Where the act done is *ultra vires* the company or *illegal*.

(*b*) Where the act can only validly be done by a special or extraordinary resolution, but in fact has been done by a simple majority.

(*c*) Where the majority are committing a fraud on the minority.

In *Prudential Assurance Co. Ltd.* v. *Newman Industries Ltd.* (*No. 2*) (1980) Vinelott J. held that dicta in *Foss* v. *Harbottle* indicated that an action might be brought not only where the wrongdoers were a majority with voting control, but also where they "were able ... by manipulation of their position in the company to ensure that the action is not brought by the company", i.e. where they had merely *de facto control* and the interests of justice would be defeated if an action were not allowed.

He further stated that the "fraud" lies in the controllers' "use of their voting power, not in the character of the act or transaction giving rise to the cause of action"—a useful and penetrating distinction.

(*d*) Where a minority shareholder has no other remedy and

the directors are using their powers, either fraudulently or negligently, in a manner which benefits themselves at the expense of the company: *Daniels* v. *Daniels* (1978).

(*e*) Where the *personal* rights of the *individual member* have been infringed: *Edwards* v. *Halliwell* (1950).

(*f*) Where a company meeting cannot be called in time to be of practical effect: *Hodgson* v. *National and Local Government Officers Association* (1972).

These six occasions are often said to be exceptions to the rule in *Foss* v. *Harbottle*—exceptions which, to quote again the incisive Lord Lloyd of Kilgerran, "have taken the matter into the realms of near incomprehensibility". If, however, they are considered carefully it appears that five of them are unconnected with it and based not so much on legal logic as on common sense. In the first four the wrongful act is done not so much *to* the company as *by* it. If the majority act *ultra vires* or illegally, or alter the objects clause by ordinary resolution, or oppress the minority, it is the *company* who is doing these things. One cannot say that the majority constitutes the company for one purpose and not for another. And if the company is doing these things, who is to stop it except the minority? Thus the law permits the minority to sue and, since the decision of the Court of Appeal in *Wallersteiner* v. *Moir* (1975), to be indemnified by the company against all costs reasonably incurred in the proceedings.

The fifth occasion is of an entirely different nature. Here the wrong has been done to the individual member *as such*. His dividend has been withheld, or his vote disallowed. The company's duty to him has been broken, and he is injured thereby. Naturally in such a case he is not merely the proper plaintiff, but the only possible one, for he has contractual rights against the company, and injury has been caused to him by their breach. Thus here we have not so much an exception to *Foss* v. *Harbottle* as an example of the very principle which *Foss* v. *Harbottle* enunciates.

Only in the sixth occasion, therefore, do we have a genuine and entirely proper exception.

10. The form of the action. On all the occasions mentioned above in **9** with the exception of (*e*), where the individual member is bringing his own action, the minority shareholders are bringing *the company's* action, since it is the company which has been injured. Because their right of action is *derived* from the company, the proceedings are known as a *derivative action* and the damages payable, if any, will be paid to the *company*.

It may well be, however, that in addition to the company's cause of action each of a number of shareholders has a separate claim in tort for injury caused to him. Because the injury to each of them will have been caused by the same illegal conduct, it is sufficient if one of them brings a *representative* action on behalf of himself and all other members who have been similarly injured. This avoids the necessity of repeatedly proving the illegal conduct before the court.

In a representative action the successful plaintiff will normally obtain only *declaratory* relief, i.e. the court will hold that the illegal conduct has been satisfactorily proved. The plaintiff can then go on to claim damages on the basis of the declaration and the other injured members can do likewise.

In *Prudential Assurance Co. Ltd.* v. *Newman Industries Ltd.* (*No. 2*) (1980) Vinelott J. held that the two claims are not mutually exclusive. Thus a derivative claim can be joined with a representative claim in the same proceedings. In a previous hearing, however, the judge had held that in order to succeed in a representative action three conditions must be satisfied:

(*a*) A court order for relief must not confer a right of action on a member who would not otherwise have been able to assert it in separate proceedings, or bar a defence otherwise available to the defendant in such proceedings.

(*b*) There must be an "interest" shared by all the members of the injured class—a common ingredient in the cause of action of each of them.

(*c*) The court must be satisfied that it is for the benefit of the injured class that the plaintiff be allowed to sue in a representative capacity.

11. Differences between a company limited by shares and a partnership. It is sometimes convenient at this stage to set out the differences between a company limited by shares and a partnership. The process of incorporation has been completed and its implications discussed, so that comparisons can now be drawn. There are a large number of differences, but the most important are as follows:

(*a*) A limited company is an *artificial legal person*.

A partnership is not. It is an association of two or more legal persons, in the same way as a company, but the *association itself* has no legal personality and outsiders deal directly with the members.

(*b*) In a limited company the *liability* of the members is *limited* to the amount unpaid on their shares.

In a partnership, the *liability* of the partners is *unlimited* except in the case of a limited partnership, and even then there must be at least one general partner with unlimited liability.

(*c*) A limited company must be *formed by the process of regis-tration* described above.

A partnership may be formed quite *informally*, e.g. orally, or even by conduct, though it is wise to have a written agreement or articles, often called the deed of partnership.

(*d*) In a *public* limited company the *shares* are usually *freely* transferable.

In a partnership no partner may transfer his share without the *consent* of the others.

(*e*) In a limited company the members are *not ipso facto agents* of the company.

In a partnership each partner is an *agent* of the others, and each therefore is also a principal. A partnership is thus a collec-tion of principals and agents.

(*f*) In a limited company the *death or bankruptcy* of a member (or even of all the members) has *no effect* on the existence of the company.

In a partnership death or bankruptcy of a partner causes *dis-solution* unless the articles provide otherwise.

(*g*) A limited company is subject to many *special rules of law*, both statutory and otherwise, e.g. it cannot normally buy its own shares.

In a partnership the partners are *free* to make any arrangement they like which would be lawful between private persons.

PROGRESS TEST 4

1. What documents must be delivered to the registrar on regis-tration of a company? (**1**)

2. From what date is a registered company incorporated? (**2**)

3. What is the legal effect of the certificate of incorpora-tion? (**2**)

4. Give the order of distribution of a company's assets in liquidation. (**5**)

5. Give an account of the decision in *Salomon* v. *Salomon & Co., Ltd.* (**6**)

6. Outline the Rule in *Foss* v. *Harbottle*, explaining its practical advantages and its so-called exceptions. (**7–9**)

7. What are the main differences between a company limited by shares and a partnership? (**10**)

CHAPTER V

Commencement of Business and Contracts

1. Commencement of business. A *private* company can commence business on incorporation. Once it has received its certificate of incorporation, nothing further is required.

A company registered as a *public* company on its *original incorporation*, however, must obtain a *second* certificate, often called a *trading certificate*, before it can commence business or exercise its borrowing powers. In order to obtain its trading certificate, the company must comply with s. 4 Companies Act 1980. (Section 109 Companies Act 1948, which formerly dealt with the matter, has been repealed.)

2. Procedure for obtaining trading certificate. In order to obtain its trading certificate the company must apply to the registrar. Section 4(2) and (3) require the application to be made in the prescribed form and accompanied by a statutory declaration signed by a director or the secretary of the company.

The statutory declaration must state:

(*a*) that the nominal value of the company's allotted share capital is not less than the authorised minimum (*see* II, **41**);

(*b*) the amount paid up on the company's allotted share capital;

(*c*) the amount of the company's preliminary expenses and the persons who paid them; and

(*d*) any amount paid or benefit given to any promoter and his consideration for it.

Section 4(4) states that any shares allotted under a share scheme for employees must be disregarded for the purposes of (*a*) above unless they are paid up at least as to one quarter of their nominal value and the whole of any premium.

Finally, s. 9(3) European Communities Act 1972, as amended by para. 45 of the 3rd Schedule to the Companies Act 1980, requires the registrar to publish in the *Gazette* the receipt by him of such a declaration.

3. Issue of trading certificate. If the registrar is satisfied as to (*a*) above and has received the statutory declaration, s. 4(2) requires him to issue a trading certificate.

Section 4(6) provides that this certificate is conclusive evidence that the company is entitled to do business and exercise its borrowing powers.

If the company is not issued with a trading certificate within a year from incorporation, it may be wound up by the court under s. 222(*b*) Companies Act 1948, as amended by para. 27 of the 3rd Schedule to the Companies Act 1980 (*see* XXVII, 1).

4. Contracts. In studying the contracts of a company, it is important first to grasp the situations which may arise.

In the case of a *private* company, there are only two:

(*a*) Contracts made on behalf of the company before incorporation.

(*b*) Contracts made after incorporation.

Owing to s. 4 Companies Act 1980, however, in the case of a *public* company, there are three:

(*a*) Contracts made on behalf of the company before incorporation.

(*b*) Contracts made after incorporation but before obtaining the trading certificate.

(*c*) Contracts made after obtaining the trading certificate.

These situations must be dealt with separately.

5. Pre-incorporation contracts. The rules here are the same both for public and private companies. Clearly no legal person, natural or artificial, can contract before he or it exists. Therefore a contract made by a promoter on behalf of the company before incorporation never binds the company, because the company is not yet formed. It has no legal existence. Even if the parties act on the contract, it will not bind the company: *Re Northumberland Avenue Hotel Co.* (1886).

Problems formerly arose, however, with regard to the promoter. It must be remembered that he was not automatically bound simply because the company was not yet in existence. He was bound only if he had shown an intention to be bound, and this intention was deduced from his conduct and the surrounding circumstances. Similarly, he could not enforce the contract unless he had shown such an intention, since the right to enforce a contract normally accompanies liability to perform it.

Although the principle was clear enough, the question of whether the promoter had shown an intention to be bound often rested on what the Jenkins Committee described as "subtle differences in the terminology employed". Thus in *Kelner* v. *Baxter* (1866), the directors were held personally liable on a pre-incorporation contract where they had signed it "A, B and C, on behalf of the X Company". But in *Newborne* v. *Sensolid, Ltd.* (1954), Newborne was held unable to enforce the contract (and therefore presumably not bound by it) because he had signed it "Leopold Newborne and Co., Ltd.", even though underneath he had added his own name, "Leopold Newborne".

The Jenkins Committee criticised the state of the law, and recommended that the next Companies Act should provide that a company might unilaterally adopt after incorporation contracts made on its behalf by the promoter prior to incorporation, and that unless and until the company did so the promoter should be both bound and entitled to sue.

The Companies Act 1967 contained no provision on this matter, but s. 9(2) European Communities Act 1972 now provides that, unless otherwise agreed, a pre-incorporation contract shall have effect as a contract entered into by *the person purporting to act as agent for the company*, who is personally liable on it.

6. Contracts made after incorporation but before issue of trading certificate. This situation can arise, as we have seen, only in the case of a *public* company.

Section 4(8) Companies Act 1980 states that failure to obtain its trading certificate will not affect the validity of any transaction entered into by a company.

If, however, a company contravenes the section by entering into a transaction before its trading certificate has been issued, and then fails to comply with its resulting obligations within twenty-one days from being called upon to do so, the directors become jointly and severally liable to indemnify the other party to the transaction in respect of any loss which he has suffered through such failure.

7. Contracts made after issue of the trading certificate in the case of a public company and after incorporation in the case of a private company. These are, of course, valid provided they are *intra vires*, but it must always be remembered that the doctrine of *ultra vires* restricts the contractual capacity of companies, and that the *vires* will always depend on the objects clause of the memorandum.

There are, however, some statutory provisions relating to form and other matters which must be studied.

8. Form of contracts made by companies. Section 32(1) states in effect that the contracts of a company may be made in the same form as those of a private person.

At common law the contracts of a corporation were required to be by deed, but today statute has rendered this rule practically obsolete. The result of s. 32 is that a registered company never needs to contract by deed unless a deed would also be required in the case of a private individual, e.g. for a lease exceeding three years.

Thus today the company's common seal is required by law only in the case of the following documents:

  (a) Contracts which would be required to be by deed if entered into by a private person.
  (b) Deeds.
  (c) Share certificates: s. 81.
  (d) Share warrants: s. 83.

Section 33, of less importance, states that a bill of exchange or promissory note will be in order if made, accepted or endorsed in the name of the company by any person acting under its authority.

Section 36 states that a document requiring authentication by a company may be signed by a director, secretary or other authorised officer and need not be under its seal.

9. The official seal. Section 35(1) states that a company whose objects comprise the transaction of business in foreign countries may, if authorised by its articles, have for use in any place outside the United Kingdom an official seal. This is a facsimile (copy) of the common seal, with the addition on its face of the name of the place where it is to be used.

PROGRESS TEST 5

1. With what statutory requirements must a public company comply in order to commence business or exercise its borrowing powers? **(2)**

2. Discuss the legal effect of pre-incorporation contracts. **(5)**

3. What is the legal effect of a contract made by a public company after incorporation but before obtaining its trading certificate? **(6)**

4. In what form may registered companies contract? **(8)**

5. On which documents is the company's seal required? **(8)**

6. What is the official seal of a company? **(9)**

CHAPTER VI

Promoters and Subscribers
to the Memorandum

1. The legal position of a promoter. There is no general statutory definition of a promoter, though he is indirectly described in s. 38(1) as a person "engaged or interested in the formation of the company", and s. 43(5) gives a definition for the purpose of that section only, stating:

> "the expression 'promoter' means a promoter who was a party to the preparation of the prospectus, but does not include any person by reason of his acting in a professional capacity for persons engaged in procuring the formation of the company."

Here again the promoter is referred to as a person "engaged in the formation of the company", and though this definition is expressed to be for the purpose of the section only, it is clear that in the normal way persons assisting the promoters by "acting in a professional capacity" do not thereby become promoters themselves. Thus the solicitor or counsel who drafts the articles, or the accountant who values the assets of a business to be purchased, are merely giving professional assistance to the promoters. They will be paid for their services, but they will not be implicated further. Perhaps the true test of whether a person is a promoter is whether he has a *desire* that the company shall be formed, and is prepared to take some steps, which may or may not involve other persons, to implement it.

While the accurate description of a promoter may be difficult, his legal position is quite clear. He is said to be in a *fiduciary* position towards the company, analogous to the relation of an agent with his principal, and, like an agent, he may not make a secret profit. The fiduciary relation requires *full disclosure* of the relevant facts, including any profit made. Students of the law of contract will recall many examples of this relation.

NOTE: It is important to understand that it is not the profit made by the promoter which the law forbids, but the non-disclosure of it. Provided full disclosure is made, as was done in *Salomon* v. *Salomon & Co., Ltd.*, the profit is permissible. It must be disclosed to an independent board of directors, if there is one, but if, as is often the case in a private company, the promoter is himself the only director, it must be disclosed to the shareholders. Frequently they will be the promoter's own family, and he will in practice be free to make what arrangements he likes, since their fortunes rise and fall with his.

2. Remedies of the company against a promoter. As regards public companies, s. 24 Companies Act 1980 introduced strict rules on the valuation of non-cash consideration for an allotment of shares (*see* IX, **18–20**). These statutory rules greatly diminish the importance of the remedies evolved by the courts against a promoter for non-disclosure of profit in a public company. In private companies, however, these remedies remain the only sanction and continue to be of significance. In theory, the remedies apply with respect to all companies, public or private.

If any profit made is not disclosed, the company has a remedy against the promoter which varies according to the circumstances. These can be divided into two possible situations:

(*a*) *Where the promoter was not in a fiduciary position when he acquired the property which he is selling to the company, but only when he sold it to the company.*

Here the promoter, as in Salomon's case, has had the property for a considerable period of time. He can hardly be said to be in a fiduciary position towards the company if he bought a business ten years before its formation, and though the moment at which his fiduciary relation arises may be difficult to determine, it can at least be said that it does not arise until he contemplates, i.e. considers the possibility of, forming a company to take over his business.

The remedy for non-disclosure in such a case is that the company may rescind the contract with the promoter, which of course means that it restores the property to him and recovers its money.

(*b*) *Where the promoter was in a fiduciary position both when he acquired the property, and when he sold it to the company.*

Here the promoter bought the property with a view to selling it to the company, and the company will then have a choice of remedy. It may either:

 (*i*) rescind the contract as in (*a*) above; *or*
 (*ii*) retain the property, paying no more for it than the promoter, thereby depriving him of his profit; *or*
 (*iii*) where the above remedies would be inappropriate, such as when the property has been altered so as to render rescission impossible, and the promoter has already received his inflated price, the company may sue the promoter for misfeasance (breach of the duty to disclose). The measure of damages will be the difference between the market value of the property and the contract price.

3. Remuneration of promoters. It is clear that a promoter, if he makes proper disclosure, may expect to be rewarded for his efforts. In practice he is recompensed in one of the following ways:

 (*a*) He may sell his own property to the company for *cash* at an over-valuation of which proper disclosure has been made; *or*

 (*b*) He may sell his own property to the company for *fully paid shares*, again having fully disclosed any over-valuation; *or*

 (*c*) He may be given an *option* to take up further shares in the company *at par* (i.e. at their *nominal* value) after their true value has risen and is reflected in their market price; *or*

 (*d*) The articles may provide for a fixed sum to be paid to him. Such a provision has no contractual effect and he cannot sue to enforce it (III, **10**), but if it is acted on—and the promoter can in practice probably make sure that it is—the company cannot recover its money.

It must again be borne in mind that in a public company s. 24 Companies Act 1980 will normally operate to prevent any over-valuation.

4. Suspension of promoters. Section 188 empowers the court, *inter alia*, to suspend a promoter from taking part in the management of a company for a limited period.

This section must be carefully studied, for it is not easy to learn. It deals, as the margin says, with the court's power to restrain fraudulent persons from managing companies.

Section 188(1) states that where:

 (*a*) a person is convicted of a promotion or management offence; *or*

(*b*) in liquidation it appears that a person:
    (*i*) has been guilty of fraudulent trading (s. 332); *or*
    (*ii*) has been guilty while an officer of any fraud or breach
       of duty,

then the court may order that he shall not be a director or take part in the management of a company for a period not exceeding five years without the leave of the court.

5. Valuation of non-cash assets acquired from subscriber. The subscribers to the memorandum are not normally the promoters of the company. Nevertheless, s.26 Companies Act 1980 introduced rules to ensure that where, in a public company, a subscriber sells non-cash assets to the company, those assets are valued by an independent person in exactly the same way as is prescribed by s. 24 in relation to payment for shares (*see* IX, **18–20** and XII, **1**).

Section 26(1) prohibits a public company from entering into an agreement with a subscriber for the transfer by him, within two years from the date of issue of its trading certificate, of a non-cash asset to the company for a consideration equal to *one tenth or more of the nominal value of its issued share capital* unless four conditions are satisfied.

These are:

(*a*) the consideration to be received by the company and any consideration other than cash to be given by it must have been *valued*;

(*b*) a *report* on the consideration so received and given must have been made to the company during the six months immediately preceding the agreement;

(*c*) the terms of the agreement must have been approved by an *ordinary resolution* of the company; and

(*d*) not later than the giving of notice of the meeting at which the resolution is proposed, copies of the resolution and the report must have been *circulated to the members* and, if the subscriber in question is not then a member, to him: s. 26 (3).

Section 27(2) requires a copy of the resolution, together with the report, to be delivered to the registrar within fifteen days of the passing of the resolution, while s. 9(3) European Communities Act 1972, as amended by para. 45 of the 3rd Schedule to the Companies Act 1980, requires the registrar to publish in the Gazette the receipt by him of the report.

6. Report on non-cash assets acquired from subscriber. Section 26(5) Companies Act 1980 provides that s. 24(4) and (6) apply to the valuation and report, requiring the valuation to be made by an independent person qualified to be an auditor (the "expert"), or some other qualified person chosen by him (*see* IX, **18** and **19**).

Further, s. 27(1) entitles the person making the valuation or report to require from the company's officers any necessary information and explanation.

Under s. 26(6) the report must:

(*a*) state the consideration to be received by the company, describing the asset in question, specifying the amount to be received in cash, and the consideration to be given by the company, specifying the amount to be given in cash;

(*b*) state the method and date of valuation;

(*c*) contain a note as to the matters mentioned in s. 24(7) (*a*)–(*c*) (*see* IX, **19**); and

(*d*) contain a note that on the basis of the valuation the value of the consideration to be received by the company is not less than the value of the consideration to be given by it.

7. Effect of contravention of s. 26. Section 26(7) provides that where a public company enters into any agreement with a subscriber to its memorandum which contravenes s. 26(1) and *either*:

(*a*) the subscriber has not received a report; *or*

(*b*) there has been some other contravention of s. 26 or of s. 24(4) or (6) which he knew or ought to have known amounted to a contravention,

the company is entitled to recover from him any consideration which it gave under the agreement or a sum equivalent in value, and the agreement itself is *void*.

PROGRESS TEST 6

1. What do you understand by the term "promoter"?   (**1**)

2. What remedies has a company against a promoter who fails to disclose his profit?   (**2**)

3. In what ways may a promoter be remunerated for his services?   (**3**)

4. Give an account of the statutory provisions which prevent fraudulent persons from managing companies.   (**4**)

5. What rules were introduced by the Companies Act 1980

concerning the valuation of non-cash assets acquired from subscribers to the memorandum in public companies? **(5)**

6. What are the contents of the report on non-cash assets acquired from a subscriber to the memorandum? **(6)**

7. What effect does contravention of the rules on the valuation and report have on the agreement between the company and the subscriber? **(7)**

CHAPTER VII

The Prospectus

1. The raising of capital. A company raises its share capital in the first instance by issuing shares to optimistic persons who hope to benefit by investing their money in a rapidly developing enterprise. It repeats this process as many times as is required in the course of its existence, so that the first issue of shares may well be followed by other later issues as the company's business expands and new capital is needed.

When the issue of shares is on a small scale to a few relatives or friends, the Act does not protect these persons from the results of their enthusiasm. But where capital is raised from persons who have no direct knowledge of the undertaking, e.g. the public generally, there are a large number of statutory provisions aimed at their protection. These provisions must be carefully studied. It is also important to know when they are applicable.

Broadly speaking, there are *three methods* by which a company may raise capital from the public:

(*a*) *By issuing a prospectus.*

Here the prospectus is normally published in a newspaper and the investor reads it and applies for shares on the strength of it. Attached to the prospectus will be an application form which the investor will fill in, stating the number of shares which he wishes to buy, and will then send with his cheque to the company.

Prospectus

Company - - - - - - ➤ Public

(*b*) *By an offer for sale.*

Here the company sells all the shares to an *issuing house*, i.e. a company or firm whose business is finance, and which may be involved in many types of financial enterprise, including the handling of new issues.

The issuing house sells the shares to the public at a higher price than it paid for them by publishing a document called an offer for sale with an application form attached. This document is deemed to be a prospectus in law.

This method is more common than (*a*) above, as it relieves the company from the administrative work of a new issue, and at the same time ensures that the whole issue is sold, i.e. the issue here is *underwritten firm* (see VIII, **4**).

Offer for sale

Company – – – –➤ Issuing House – – – – – – – – –➤ Public

deemed a prospectus

(*c*) *By placing.*

Here a broker finds persons—normally his clients—who wish to buy the shares. He is a mere agent, and his function is simply to produce buyers for the shares, i.e. to "place" them.

Company – – – – – – – –➤ Public

(introduced by broker as agent)

The statutory provisions on the prospectus are of great importance. In the case of (*a*) above they naturally apply, while in the case of (*b*) they apply, with modifications, because under s. 45 an offer for sale is deemed to be a prospectus. But in the case of (*c*) they apply only if the shares can be said to be offered to the public, and this, as will now be seen, is sometimes a question of great difficulty.

The three methods must now be considered in turn.

2. Definition of the prospectus. Section 455 gives the statutory definition of the prospectus which should be carefully learnt. It states that "prospectus means any prospectus, notice, circular, advertisement, or other invitation offering to the public for subscription or purchase any shares or debentures of a company".

NOTE

(1) *The word "offering" is misleading.* The prospectus is not an offer in the contractual sense, but an invitation to treat, like a teapot in a shop window marked 75p. The investor who applies for shares makes the true offer, and the company either accepts or rejects it, as will be seen later.

(2) *The word "public" raises difficulty.* It is impossible to say exactly how many persons constitute "the public", and s.55, which deals with interpretation, is not altogether helpful. Section 55(1) states that "public" includes any section of the public, however selected. This means that if a document invit-

ing persons to buy shares is issued, for example, to all doctors, or to all Roman Catholic students, or to all Japanese persons resident in the United Kingdom, or to all the clients of a particular stockbroker, or to all the shareholders in a particular company, it is still issued to "the public" within the meaning of the Act and therefore in this respect complies with the statutory definition of a prospectus: *Re South of England Natural Gas and Petroleum Co., Ltd.* (1911). This apparently would still be the case even if in fact there were only one person in the particular section of the public selected.

(3) *Non-renounceable letters of allotment.* Section 55(2), however, limits the effect of s. 55(1) by stating that the invitation is *not* made to the public if only those persons to whom it is made are likely to be the ultimate shareholders, e.g. if the letter of allotment sent by the company to the applicant is non-renounceable. (This means that the applicant must then become the registered holder of the shares. He cannot "renounce" the letter of allotment in favour of some other person who will then become the registered holder, in effect selling the shares for which he has applied before becoming a member.)

(4) *Domestic invitations.* Section 55(2) also states that the invitation is *not* made to the public if it is the domestic concern of those making and receiving it. What the expression "domestic concern" means is doubtful, but in *Sherwell* v. *Combined Incandescent Mantles Syndicate* (1907), where the invitation was issued to a few friends of the directors, it was held that it had not been issued to the public. Perhaps this expression would cover such circumstances, but the section is still not easy to apply. Are not friends a "section of the public"?

For private companies, however, the position has been slightly clarified by para. 11 of the 3rd Schedule to the Companies Act 1980 which adds two further subsections to s. 55. Section 55(3) and (4) provide that an offer of shares or debentures of a *private* company shall be regarded as a "domestic concern" if it is *either*:

(a) an offer made to an existing shareholder of the company or a member of his family, or an existing employee of the company or a member of his family, or an existing debenture-holder; *or*

(b) an offer to subscribe for shares or debentures to be held under a share scheme for employees.

In view of s. 15 Companies Act 1980 (*see* XIX, 1) these rules are now of considerable importance.

(5) *The meaning of "subscription or purchase"*. A more recent case of some importance is *Governments Stock Investment Co., Ltd.* v. *Christopher* (1956). Here it was held that the word "subscription" in the definition means taking the shares *for cash*, while the word "purchase" can only apply to *issued* shares. Hence an offer of new shares to the shareholders of certain companies in exchange for their shares in these companies was not an offer for subscription or purchase within the definition. Moreover, the letters of allotment here were non-renounceable, and therefore, according to s. 55(2), the invitation was not to the public, so that the document by which it was made could not be a prospectus within the definition.

Once the difficulties arising out of the definition have been considered, and it is realised that the first question which arises with regard to any document inviting persons to buy shares is *whether or not it is a prospectus within that definition*, the sections of the Act which apply to the document *if it is a prospectus* can be studied. They range from ss. 37–46, and the simplest method of learning their contents is to look at them in that order, as far as possible.

3. Dating and contents of the prospectus. Section 37 requires a prospectus to be dated.

Section 38(1) requires a prospectus to contain the matters and reports specified in the 4th Schedule to the Act. Here the nature of these matters and reports must be considered. The 4th Schedule specifies *eighteen matters and three reports*, which should be learnt, but it will be seen at once that learning these in the order in which they appear in the Schedule is not easy. The eighteen matters have therefore been re-arranged, grouped and considerably shortened below purely in order to facilitate learning them. In fact they can be arranged in any way that the student finds best.

They are as follows:

(*a*) Directors (names, addresses and descriptions).
(*b*) Directors' qualification shares and remuneration (amount need not be stated).
(*c*) Directors' interest in the promotion.
(*d*) Auditors.
(*e*) Preliminary expenses.
(*f*) Promoters' remuneration.
(*g*) Particulars of options on shares or debentures.

(*h*) Underwriting commission and brokerage.

(*i*) The minimum subscription.

(*j*) The time of the opening of the subscription lists.

(*k*) Amount payable on application and allotment.

(*l*) Voting and class rights.

(*m*) Deferred shares.

(*n*) Particulars of shares and debentures issued otherwise than for cash.

(*o*) Particulars of material contracts.

(*p*) Vendors of property to the company.

(*q*) Amount paid for property, stating amount paid for goodwill.

(*r*) Length of time the business has been carried on, if less than three years.

This list, though it is hoped a little easier to learn than the 4th Schedule, is sufficient for the student to memorise. The first group of four items concerns the directors and auditors. The second group of four items relates to the expenses of formation. The third group of five items consists of practical matters in which an investor would be interested ((*i*) and (*j*) will be explained in detail later). The last group of five items concerns the property and business of the company.

To these eighteen matters must be added the three reports required by the 4th Schedule. These have been shortened, but not re-arranged:

(*a*) An *auditors' report* showing:

(*i*) Profits or losses in each of the last five years.

(*ii*) Rate of dividend during the last five years.

(*iii*) Assets and liabilities at the date of the last accounts.

(*iv*) Similar details of subsidiary companies, if any.

(*b*) Where the proceeds of the issue are to be used *to buy a business*, a *report by named accountants* on its profits or losses for the last five years, and its assets and liabilities at the date of the last accounts.

(*c*) Where the proceeds of the issue are to be used *to buy shares in a subsidiary*, a similar report as in (*b*) above.

Finally, s. 16 Companies Act 1980 may require, in certain circumstances, one further item to be included in the prospectus (*see* IX, **24**).

4. The minimum subscription. Of the matters and reports in the 4th Schedule, one—the minimum subscription—is of particular importance. It is ninth in the list given above, but in fact is in para. four of the 4th Schedule, and consists of four items which must be carefully learnt.

The minimum subscription is the amount which, in the opinion of the directors, must be raised by the issue in order to provide for the following matters:

- (a) The price of any property to be paid for out of the proceeds of the issue.
- (b) Preliminary expenses and underwriting commission.
- (c) Repayment of money borrowed by the company for (a) and (b).
- (d) Working capital.

It will be remembered that under s. 4(2) Companies Act 1980 one of the requirements which must be satisfied before a public company can obtain its trading certificate is that the nominal value of its allotted share capital must reach the authorised minimum (*see* V, **2**), while s. 22(1) Companies Act 1980 prohibits a public company from allotting any shares at all unless they are paid up at least as to one quarter of their nominal value and the whole of any premium.

It is clear from s. 20(1) Companies Act 1980, however, that the Act contemplates a payment for shares in something *other than money*, e.g. property (*see* XII, **1**), and that the capital requirements for commencement of business can be satisfied without the company necessarily having that capital in the form of *cash*.

In the case of a public company which issues a prospectus the requirement that there must be a *minimum subscription* for the shares ensures that the company will have sufficient money to cover the four items mentioned above, for under s. 47(2) the minimum subscription is reckoned *only in cash* (*see* IX, **22**).

5. Waiver of the requirements of s. 38. Once the 4th Schedule and the definition of the minimum subscription have been learnt, the rest of s. 38 may be studied.

Section 38(2) states that compliance with the section cannot be waived by the applicant. Even if he should be willing or persuaded to waive it, the waiver would be void. The statutory safeguards are regarded as of such importance that a shareholder cannot dispense with them even if he is prepared to do so.

6. Exceptional cases where 4th Schedule prospectus is not required. Section 38(3) states that no application form can be issued for shares or debentures unless it is accompanied by a prospectus complying with the section. There are, however, five exceptions to this, where a 4th Schedule prospectus is not required even though a document of some kind will in practice normally be sent out.

These five exceptions are:

(*a*) Underwriting agreements: s. 38(3).

(*b*) Shares or debentures which are not offered to the public: s. 38(3).

(*c*) Issues to existing members or debenture-holders, whether the letters of allotment are renounceable or not: s. 38(5).

(*d*) Issues of shares or debentures uniform with those previously issued and listed on a prescribed stock exchange: s. 38(5) as amended by the Companies Act 1976.

(*e*) Where a certificate of exemption is granted: s. 39.

The five exceptions are of the greatest importance. It should be noted that in the case of the first two the public are not involved, and therefore not protected. In the case of the last three the shareholder will have enough information about the company to protect himself, either because he is already a member and therefore receives the accounts, or because the shares are dealt in on the stock exchange and their true value is reflected in their market price, or, in the fifth case, because a large number of particulars about it will have to be published under s. 39 even though a full 4th Schedule prospectus is not required. Section 39 will be discussed in more detail later.

7. The distinction between civil and criminal liability. We come now to the effect of contravention of s. 38. It is not normally necessary to learn the innumerable penalties imposed on the officers of a company by the Act, and they are, to say the least of it, discouraging. But in the case of the prospectus the civil and criminal liability which may attach to officers and experts should be studied. The liability imposed by each section is, therefore, dealt with separately, but it must be remembered that the penalties have been altered by s. 80 and the 2nd Schedule to the Companies Act 1980.

Sometimes, however, students do not grasp the distinction between civil and criminal liability, and without embarking on a jurisprudential discussion which might possibly be beyond the scope of the reader and is certainly beyond that of the writer, it can be said briefly that the hallmark of *criminal* liability is *punishment*, i.e. a fine or a term of imprisonment. *Civil* liability, on the other hand, involves a *remedy* to the injured party, e.g. damages or an injunction.

The same conduct can, of course, give rise to both types of liability. Thus it is possible to sue a burglar, if only his identity and whereabouts can be discovered, and recover damages from him if he has any assets out of which to pay them. He will also receive a term of imprisonment as punishment for his crime if he is prosecuted for it.

8. The effect of contravention of s. 38. Under s. 38(3), as amended by s. 80 and the 2nd Schedule to the Companies Act 1980, there is a fine of an unspecified amount on conviction on *indictment*, while on *summary conviction* there is a fine not exceeding the statutory maximum. This is, of course, the criminal liability. The expression "statutory maximum" is defined in s. 87(1) Companies Act 1980 as meaning the prescribed sum within s. 28 Criminal Law Act 1977 (i.e. £1,000 or such other sum as is fixed under s. 61 of that Act to take account of inflation).

Section 38(4) gives any director or other person responsible for the prospectus three defences against this liability:

(a) As regards an omission from the prospectus, that he was not cognisant (i.e. ignorant) of it; *or*

(b) That the contravention arose from an honest mistake of fact; *or*

(c) That the contravention was immaterial or ought reasonably to be excused.

It should be noted that, as with all the defences against liability imposed by the sections on the prospectus, the burden of proof is on the *director*, i.e. he is automatically liable for the contravention unless he can show that one of the three defences applies to him, and this may be very difficult.

The section does not impose any civil liability for contravention, i.e. it does not give the injured party any remedy against the directors. But in *Re South of England Natural Gas and Petroleum Co., Ltd.* (1911), it was held that damages are recoverable for omissions from the prospectus. It is doubtful whether the three defences given above apply also to this civil liability, but probably they do, since s. 38(4) specifically states that they apply to *any* liability, and not merely to that imposed by the section.

9. The certificate of exemption. We can now move on to s. 39. This concerns the certificate of exemption, and the fifth exception to the rule that a full 4th Schedule prospectus is always required. It states that if a company is applying to a stock exchange for its shares to be listed, it may also ask for a certificate of exemption. This is a certificate from the stock exchange that, having regard to the size and other circumstances of the issue, and to the persons to whom it is to be made, compliance with the 4th Schedule would be *unduly burdensome*.

If the certificate is granted, and an advertisement for the shares is published which complies with the regulations of the stock exchange, then that advertisement is *deemed to be a 4th Schedule prospectus,* and the requirements of the Act are satisfied.

10. The expert's consent. Section 40 deals with the expert. It gives an important definition of him in s. 40(3), where it states that "expert" includes engineer, valuer, accountant, and any other person whose profession gives authority to his statement.

Section 40(1) states that a prospectus including a statement by an expert must not be issued unless two conditions are satisfied:

(*a*) He must have given and not, before delivery of a copy of the prospectus for registration, withdrawn his written consent to the issue with his statement included, and

(*b*) A statement that he has so given and not withdrawn his consent must appear in the prospectus.

11. Registration of the prospectus. Section 41 concerns the registration of a copy of the prospectus with the registrar, referred to in (*a*) of the last paragraph. Section 41(1) states that a prospectus may not be issued unless a copy of it, signed by every person named therein as a director or proposed director, or by his agent authorised in writing, has been delivered to the registrar for registration. The copy must have attached to it:

(*a*) Any *expert's consent*: s. 40.

(*b*) *Copies of contracts* required to be stated in the prospectus or, if not in writing, particulars of them.

(*c*) When the persons making the reports have made adjustments to them, a signed statement by them stating *the adjustments* and the reasons for them.

Section 41(2) requires the prospectus to state expressly that a copy has been duly delivered, and to specify the documents required to be attached. Section 41(3) prohibits the registrar from registering the prospectus unless it is dated (s. 37), the copy duly signed, and the specified documents attached.

12. Civil liability for mis-statements in the prospectus. Section 42 has been repealed by the Companies Act 1980, so that now follow two important sections on liability: s. 43 dealing with civil liability for mis-statements in the prospectus, and s. 44 dealing with criminal liability for mis-statements. Unlike s. 38, which imposes liability for *omissions,* i.e. leaving out items which the 4th Schedule requires to be disclosed, these two sections impose liability for *mis-statements*, i.e. inserting untrue statements. Here we have sins of commission as opposed to omission, and s. 43, on civil liability, deals with them at length.

Section 43(1) states who is liable, for what, and to whom. The *persons liable* under the section are:

    (*a*) The directors at the time of issue.
    (*b*) Persons named in the prospectus as present or future directors.
    (*c*) The promoters.
    (*d*) Persons who have authorised the issue.

Experts are not liable under (*d*) above except in respect of their own untrue statements.

The liability is for untrue statements. *Fraud is irrelevant*: the liability arises whether the untrue statement is made "knowingly", or "without belief in its truth" (*Derry* v. *Peek* (1889)), or whether it is made innocently by an honest man. Its mere untruth is enough. This, like the remedy given by the Misrepresentation Act 1967, is thus a valuable enlargement of the protection given by the rules of common law and equity which will be considered later.

Once the untruth of the statement has been proved, compensation for the injury sustained is recoverable, i.e. damages. And the persons who can recover it are those who have subscribed for shares or debentures on the faith of the prospectus. The use of the word "subscribed" here confines the use of this remedy to those who take their shares by allotment directly from the company.

It should be noted that the section gives no remedy against the *company*. The proceedings must be taken against persons falling within one of the four categories given above. Section 2 Misrepresentation Act 1967, however, provides that where a person has entered into a contract after a misrepresentation has been made to him by another party, and as a result has suffered loss, the party making the misrepresentation will be liable to damages even if it was not made fraudulently, unless he proves that he believed on reasonable grounds that his statement was true. Presumably, therefore, the *company* is liable under this Act to compensate the allottee, so that he has now a choice of defendant as he has in the case of fraud (*see* **18**).

13. The defences to liability under s. 43 available to persons other than experts. The rest of the section concerns the defences available to those against whom proceedings have been taken for untrue statements included in the prospectus. They are not easy to learn, and there are altogether nine of them—six for persons other than experts and three for experts. They have been shortened and set out as simply as possible for learning purposes below.

The six defences available to *persons other than experts* are found in s. 43(2), which states that a person shall not be liable if he proves:

(*i*) that he withdrew his consent to acting as director before the prospectus was issued, and it was issued without his authority or consent; *or*

(*ii*) that the prospectus was issued without his knowledge or consent, and on becoming aware of its issue he gave reasonable public notice of that fact; *or*

(*iii*) that after the issue of the prospectus and before allotment he became aware of the untrue statement, withdrew his consent to it, and gave reasonable public notice of the withdrawal and his reasons; *or*

(*iv*) that as regards an untrue statement not purporting to be made on the authority of an expert or public official document, he believed on reasonable grounds that the statement was true; *or*

(*v*) that as regards an untrue statement purporting to be made by an expert it fairly represented the statement, and he believed on reasonable grounds that the expert was competent, and that the expert had complied with s. 40; *or*

(*vi*) that as regards an untrue statement purporting to be a statement from a public official document, it was a correct and fair representation.

NOTE: When a student is trying to commit these defences to memory, it sometimes helps him if he can remember that the first three apply to *different moments of time*, while the last three relate to *the part of the prospectus* in which the untrue statement is found. He can then make an even shorter list to assist him when revising, which might look like this:

(1) Before issue of prospectus.
(2) Issue of prospectus without his knowledge.
(3) Aware of untruth only after issue of prospectus.
(4) Belief in truth of statements other than (5) and (6).
(5) Relied on expert's statement.
(6) Relied on statement from public official document.

Note also that the burden of proof is again on the defendant to show that one of these six defences applies to him. If he cannot show this, he will be liable.

14. Defences available to experts. The three defences available to experts only are found in s. 43(3), which states that an expert shall not be liable if he proves:

(*a*) That having given his consent under s. 40 he withdrew it in writing before delivery of a copy of the prospectus for registration; *or*

(*b*) That after delivery of a copy of the prospectus for registration and before allotment, he became aware of the untrue statement, withdrew his consent in writing, and gave reasonable public notice of the withdrawal and his reasons; *or*

(*c*) That he was competent to make the statement, and believed on reasonable grounds that it was true.

Here again the first two defences apply to *different moments of time,* i.e. before and after the registration of a copy of the prospectus which we have seen is required by s. 41. Unfortunately the moments of time do not correspond with those in the first three defences available to persons other than experts given above, and though a belief on reasonable grounds that the statement was true is a defence in both cases, as regards experts it must be accompanied by a proof of competence. These lists therefore require very careful learning.

15. Criminal liability for mis-statements in the prospectus. In contrast to this formidable section, s. 44 is short and simple.

Section 44(1), as amended by s. 80 and the 2nd Schedule to the Companies Act 1980, states that where a prospectus contains an untrue statement, any person authorising its issue is liable:

(*a*) on conviction on indictment (i.e. before a jury) to a term of imprisonment not exceeding two years or a fine, or both;

(*b*) on summary conviction (i.e. before magistrates without a jury) to a term of imprisonment not exceeding six months or a fine not exceeding the statutory maximum, or both (*see* **8**).

Again, the accused is criminally liable unless he can prove that one of the two defences available to him under the section applies. These are:

(*a*) that the statement was immaterial; *or*
(*b*) that he believed on reasonable grounds that it was true.

Section 44(2) specifically excludes experts from the ambit of the section.

16. Rules of interpretation. Finally (for s. 45 will be postponed till later), there is s. 46 giving two rules of interpretation. It provides:

(*a*) That a statement shall be deemed untrue if it is misleading.
This means that a perfectly true statement, as in *R*. v. *Kylsant* (1932), where it was stated that the company had been paying dividends, is deemed untrue for the purposes of the Act if it is misleading, i.e. gives a false impression. Some people, especially the very young and the very old, are experts at this type of truthful lie, and the Act is merely recognising human nature as being what, unfortunately, it often is.

(*b*) That a statement shall be deemed included in a prospectus if it is contained in the prospectus itself or in any report or memorandum issued with it.
This merely extends the scope of the sections to documents which in substance are part of the prospectus, even though they may not be presented as such.

17. Non-statutory remedies for mis-statements in the prospectus. We have now considered all the sections on the prospectus, but there are two other remedies for mis-statements in it which are available to an injured party under the general law. These are

(*a*) damages for fraud; *or*
(*b*) rescission of the contract (*see* **18** and **19** below).

18. Damages for the tort of deceit or fraud. This remedy exists at *common law* for the plaintiff who can prove that he suffered damage by acting on a deceitful statement addressed to him. Thus, as a rule, only allottees taking their shares directly from the company may sue for deceit, though exceptionally a transferee may be able to prove that he was intended to be affected by the statement.

Deceit was defined in *Derry* v. *Peek* (1889), as "a false statement made *knowingly*, *without belief in its truth*, or *recklessly*, careless whether it be true or false". Thus in law something less immoral than a deliberate lie amounts to deceit: the defendant may merely have been reckless, i.e. he did not care whether the statement was true or not. But not caring involves considering the possibility that the statement might be false, and making it just the same, regardless of the consequences to the plaintiff. Thus the defendant is equally liable whether he made the false statement *knowing* that it was untrue, or *thinking that it might be*, for in both cases the possibility of deception was in his mind.

It is clear from this that to succeed in a claim for fraud, the plaintiff has to prove a certain state of mind in the defendant. This may well be "as much a fact as the state of his digestion", but it is even harder to prove. Consequently s. 43 and s. 2 Misrepresentation Act 1967 provide a much more reliable remedy: it will be remembered that to recover damages under those sections fraud need not be proved, and the mere untruth of the statement is enough. It is then up to the defendant to show, if he can, that he reasonably believed that the statement was true, and so escape liability.

The action for damages for fraud may be brought either against the company or the directors. If, however, the plaintiff sues the *company*, he must rescind his contract to take the shares. He may not sue the company for fraud in the prospectus and at the same time remain a member. There seems to be no good reason for this rule: a member may sue the company for other types of wrong done to him without having to abandon his membership, and this exception does not seem to be based on any general rule of law.

If he sues the *directors*, he need not rescind, though he may of course do so if he wishes.

19. Rescission. This remedy exists in *equity* for the plaintiff who can prove a mis-statement, either innocent or fraudulent.

The rules here are the ordinary rules of misrepresentation familiar to students of contract, so that the plaintiff must prove a mis-statement of fact which had an effect on his mind and induced him to buy the shares. He may then rescind and return the shares, receiving his money back with interest at 4%. But it is important to remember that this is an equitable remedy which is basically discretionary and may be lost in certain circumstances. Thus the plaintiff will not be allowed to rescind if:

(a) he displays laches, i.e. delays in taking proceedings. Delay defeats equity.

(b) he does some act showing a clear manifestation of ownership, e.g. attends meetings or tries to sell the shares.

(c) the company goes into liquidation. Here the rights of creditors are involved, and the law always favours creditors at the expense of members.

20. The offer for sale. So far this chapter has dealt only with the first of the three methods of raising capital from the public, i.e. the prospectus method. The second method, the offer for sale, must now be considered. Section 45 gives details about the offer for sale which must be carefully studied, for it is an important section.

Section 45(1) states that where a company allots shares or debentures to an issuing house with a view to their being offered for sale by the issuing house to the public, the document by which the offer for sale is made is deemed a prospectus, and all the rules as to contents and liability apply.

This vital subsection brings into operation all the rules, statutory and otherwise, which we have just studied with regard to the prospectus, so that no evasion of the safeguards to the public is possible by selling the shares through the medium of an issuing house. Moreover, the subsection not only makes the company just as liable for the offer for sale as if it had issued it itself, but expressly states that this is without prejudice to the liability of the persons by whom the offer was made, so that the issuing house will also be liable.

It is clear from s. 45(1) that the offer for sale will have to comply with the 4th Schedule. But that is not enough. Section 45(3) provides that it must also state *two further matters:*

(a) The consideration received by the company for the shares or debentures, i.e. the price paid for them by the issuing house.

(b) A place and time at which the contract between the company and the issuing house can be inspected.

Section 45(4) states that where the offer for sale is made by a company, it must be signed by two directors or their agents authorised in writing, and where it is made by a firm (i.e. a partnership), it must be signed by not less than half of the partners or their agents authorised in writing.

NOTE: Section 45 will not apply at all, however, unless the company allotting the shares to the issuing house does so *with a view to* the shares being offered for sale to the public. This means that the company must *intend* that the public shall ultimately be able to buy the shares from the issuing house. The proof of intention is always a matter of great difficulty, and the company might deny this intention altogether and so escape the provisions of the section.

To help combat this danger, s. 45(2) states that it is evidence of this intention if:

(1) the offer for sale is made within six months of the allotment to the issuing house; *or*

(2) at the date of the offer for sale the company has not yet been paid the whole consideration for the shares.

This is not, of course, the only evidence permissible. Other evidence of intention can be given. Moreover, it is only *prima facie* evidence, i.e. it stands only unless the contrary is proved.

21. Placing. With regard to the third method of raising capital from the public, there are no further statutory provisions to be considered. As was stated at the beginning of the chapter, the necessity for a 4th Schedule prospectus in a placing depends on whether the shares can be said to be offered to the public, and in the case of doubt it is always better to be on the safe side and produce one.

PROGRESS TEST 7

1. Give the statutory definition of a prospectus, explaining what is meant by the words "offering", "public" and "subscription or purchase". (**2**)

2. What are the contents of a prospectus complying with the 4th Schedule? (**3**)

3. Define the minimum subscription. (**4**)

4. In what cases is a prospectus complying with the 4th Schedule *not* required? (**6**)

5. Discuss the liability which can arise as a result of omissions from the prospectus of matters required by the 4th Schedule. (**8**)

6. What is a certificate of exemption? By whom is it granted and what is its effect? **(9)**

7. Give the statutory definition of an expert. **(10)**

8. What conditions must be satisfied before a prospectus containing a statement by an expert may be issued? **(10)**

9. What are the statutory requirements regarding registration of the prospectus? **(11)**

10. Discuss the statutory liability, civil and criminal, which arises as a result of an untrue statement in the prospectus. **(12–15)**

11. Discuss the non-statutory remedies available to a person who has suffered damage by reason of an untrue statement in the prospectus. **(17–19)**

12. What is an offer for sale? **(1, 20)**

13. What are the statutory requirements as to (*a*) the contents and (*b*) the signature of an offer for sale? **(20)**

14. What liability arises under the Act for omissions from and mis-statements in the offer for sale? **(20)**

CHAPTER VIII

Underwriting Commission and Brokerage

1. The meaning and purpose of underwriting. For all companies the raising of capital is a matter of practical importance, since without capital a newly formed company can neither start nor purchase a business. For public companies it is also a legal necessity for, as was seen in V, **2** and **3**, no trading certificate will be granted unless the company's allotted share capital reaches the authorised minimum. The success of any issue to the public, however, depends on many factors and will always be doubtful to some extent, and therefore to ensure that the shares will be taken up even if the issue is a failure as far as the public are concerned, a company normally arranges for it to be underwritten.

This involves entering into an agreement with an *underwriter*, i.e. a financial house which undertakes to buy as many of the shares as are not taken up by the public. If the issue is a large one several underwriting agreements may be made with different underwriters, since one alone may not be prepared to bear the risk. Alternatively, the principal underwriters may pass on the risk by entering into a *sub-underwriting agreement*, i.e. arranging for one or more other underwriters to underwrite them, while they underwrite the whole of the company's issue. If the issue is being handled by an issuing house by means of an offer for sale, the issuing house will make the same sort of arrangement.

2. Underwriting commission. The underwriters make their profit by charging a commission on the number of shares underwritten. This commission is still payable even if the issue is a complete success so that all the shares are bought by the public and the underwriters are not compelled to take up any of them. Where the underwriters have entered into a sub-underwriting agreement, the underwriting commission is passed on to the sub-underwriter and is known as *sub-underwriting commission,* while the principal underwriters retain some part of it, called *overriding commission*, for their services. Thus overriding commission is the difference between underwriting and sub-underwriting commission.

3. Statutory control of underwriting commission. A company which has been in existence for some years and is making, for instance, its third issue of shares to raise capital for expansion may have revenue reserves out of which it can pay the underwriting commission, or funds in its share premium account which, under s. 56, may lawfully be used for this purpose although a capital reserve. But a new company making its first issue will have no reserves of any kind. Any commission paid, therefore, will have to be provided out of the capital obtained from the issue, and this clearly reduces the amount of capital which the company will ultimately derive from that issue. Since the preservation of capital is one of the most important aims of the Act, s. 53 permits the payment of underwriting commission only on certain conditions.

4. Power of company to pay underwriting commission. Section 53(1), as amended by the Companies Act 1980, states that it is lawful to pay underwriting commission if:

(*a*) it is authorised by the articles, and

(*b*) it does not exceed 10% of the price at which the shares are issued, or the rate specified in the articles, whichever is the less, and

(*c*) it is disclosed in the prospectus or, where the shares are not offered to the public, in a statement in the prescribed form delivered to the registrar, and

(*d*) the number of shares which have been underwritten firm is similarly disclosed.

Table A, Article 6, authorises the maximum rate of 10%.

It will be noted that the section does not mention the word "underwriter" and that it is very loosely phrased so that it might appear to cover the payment of a commission to anyone who undertakes to buy shares in a company. This was not, of course, what it was intended to do, but misuse of the section has sometimes occurred.

It will also be seen that the section uses the words: "subscribe absolutely or conditionally". To subscribe *conditionally* is to enter into the kind of agreement described above in **1**, i.e. to undertake to buy as many shares as are not taken up by the public. The underwriter here is agreeing to take up the shares only on a condition, namely, that the public do not do so. To subscribe *absolutely* is to agree to take up the shares, i.e. underwrite them *firm*, and then re-sell them at a higher price to the public. Thus an issuing house making an offer for sale, as described in VII, **1**, is in effect underwriting firm. Either way the company can be sure that the entire issue will be taken up, and that the risk of its failure lies with the underwriters.

NOTE

(1) Section 53(2) states that a company may not pay underwriting commission out of *capital* "save as aforesaid", i.e. unless it complies with the conditions laid down in s. 53(1). It does not, however, refer to the payment of commission out of *revenue*, i.e. profits, and this therefore seems to be unrestricted by the section.

(2) Section 53(2) refers not only to *commission*, but also to *discount* or *allowance*. This is because it is possible to pay a commission by allowing a discount: thus it makes no difference whether £1 shares are issued at £1 and the underwriters then receive 5p for each share underwritten, or whether they are issued to the underwriters at 95p. Either way the company is left with 95p for each £1 share issued. Thus s. 53 is the only *statutory* exception to the rule that shares may not be issued at a discount.

(3) Section 53 refers only to shares and does not mention debentures, since they are not capital and can therefore be issued at a discount freely.

5. Brokerage. Brokerage is the sum paid to a person by the company for *placing* shares. Section 53 does not restrict it in any way, and s. 53(3) expressly states that the section in no way affects the payment of "lawful brokerage".

Lawful brokerage is reasonable brokerage, but it must be paid to a person carrying on the business of broker, and not to a private person: *Andreae* v. *Zinc Mines of Great Britain* (1918). Moreover, there must be authority in the articles (Table A, Article 6, gives it), and the brokerage must be disclosed in the prospectus.

PROGRESS TEST 8

1. Describe what is meant by underwriting commission, subunderwriting commission, and overriding commission. (**1, 2**)

2. Under what circumstances is it lawful for a company to pay underwriting commission out of capital? (**4**)

3. What rules govern the payment of brokerage? (**5**)

CHAPTER IX

Allotment

1. The meaning of allotment. Although allotment is only one of several methods by which a person can become a member of a company, it is one of considerable importance and complexity owing to the large number of statutory provisions which apply to it. When this method of acquiring membership is employed, shares are taken to be allotted when a person acquires the unconditional right to be included in the company's register of members in respect of them: s. 87(2) Companies Act 1980.

In this chapter the rules governing allotment are considered. It will be seen that its basic feature is that the investor acquires the shares from the *company* and not from a previous holder.

2. The contract to take shares. It will have been seen from VII that a prospectus issued by a company or an offer for sale made by an issuing house is not an offer in the contractual sense, but merely an invitation to treat. It is the applicant for the shares who makes the offer, and it is the company which accepts or rejects it. The transaction is governed by the normal rules of contract and no special form is required. In practice, the applicant makes his application in writing on the application form issued with the prospectus, but in theory it could be oral.

NOTE: Where the contract is made by post, as it usually is, the ordinary rules of contract again apply to the position. These rules are fully dealt with in textbooks on the law of contract, and they are outside the scope of this book.

There are, however, three points of importance where special rules apply regarding:

(*a*) the persons to whom the shares are offered;
(*b*) variation of the offer to buy shares; and
(*c*) revocation of the offer to buy shares.

These will now be discussed in turn.

3. The person to whom the shares are offered. Section 17 Companies Act 1980 introduced *pre-emption rights* for existing shareholders who now normally have a statutory right to be offered shares in proportion to their present holdings whenever a new issue is made (*see* **10–13**).

Formerly, such rights were given only by the company's articles or, in the case of listed companies, by the rules of the Stock Exchange.

4. Variation of the offer to buy shares. The law of contract requires the acceptance of an offer to be entire. If the acceptance introduces a new term, or varies the offer to the slightest degree, it will amount in law to a counter-offer and itself require acceptance by the original offeror.

This rule could obviously lead to difficulty where the issue of shares is *over-subscribed*, i.e. where the public have applied for more shares than the company is issuing. This is a common occurrence, and the company usually deals with it by "scaling down" the numbers of shares applied for, or by holding a ballot, or some other method intended to be a fair solution. The law of contract would allow the company either to accept an applicant's offer, or to reject it, but it would not allow any variation of the offer by allotting the applicant a lesser number of shares than the number for which he applied.

In consequence the application form is worded: 'I agree to accept —— shares, or such lesser number as may be allotted to me", and the company is then able to accept the offer by allotting the applicant any number of shares not in excess of the number for which he applied. This may, of course, involve sending the applicant a cheque back for the difference between the value of the shares applied for and those ultimately allotted.

5. Revocation of the offer to buy shares. The normal contractual rule is that an offer may be revoked at any time before acceptance. A person could therefore apply for shares, and then revoke his application before acceptance if he thought that the issue was going to be a failure, were it not for s. 50(5).

Section 50(5) states that an application may not be revoked until after the expiration of the third day after the time of the opening of the subscription lists.

Section 50(1) defines the time of the opening of the subscription lists as the beginning of the third day after that on which the prospectus is first issued.

Section 50(6) states that in computing the days Saturdays, Sundays and bank holidays must be disregarded, so that the practical effect of these provisions is that if the prospectus is issued on Friday 1st, the lists will open on Wednesday 6th and an application may not be revoked before Tuesday 12th, by which time the company will probably have allotted the shares for which application was made.

NOTE: The purpose of these rules is to prevent "stagging", i.e. applications for shares by persons who have no intention of holding them permanently, but hope that the new issue will be over-subscribed. If they are allotted any shares they can then sell them as soon as dealings start at a higher price than the price of issue. Such persons would naturally try to withdraw their applications at once if they thought that the issue were a failure, for they frequently apply for shares without having the funds to pay for them, relying on the popularity of the new issue to enable them to sell the shares immediately and make a profit.

6. Conditional applications. An application for shares, like any other offer, may be conditional, i.e. subject to a *condition precedent*. Then if the condition is not fulfilled, no contract for the shares can result.

Thus in *Simpson's Case* (1869), the applicant for the shares made his offer conditional on his being given a building contract by the company. He was allotted the shares, but was never given the building contract, so that the condition on which he had made his application was never fulfilled. HELD: He was not bound to pay up the amount unpaid on the shares.

This is exactly the result to be expected, of course, from the ordinary law of contract.

7. Applications subject to a condition subsequent. With regard to a *condition subsequent*, however, the ordinary law of contract does *not* apply to applications for shares. In most types of contract the parties may agree that their contractual relationship shall be terminated on the happening of an event: this is one form of discharge by agreement. Such arrangements are often made when a contract is to endure for a considerable period of time, and either or both of the parties fear a change in circumstances which might render it no longer beneficial to them. But in shareholding, as in marriage, it would hardly be in the public interest if the parties to the agreement decided that on the happening of a certain event their contract should be terminated, for the company's creditors could never be certain how many of the present members might suddenly become entitled to have their capital returned to them.

The law, of course, permits an allotment to be set aside for fraud or error, just as it permits a marriage to be destroyed by certain events or conduct, but it will not allow the parties themselves to agree to discharge their contract on the happening of an event which they, but not the law, find sufficient to make termination of their relationship desirable. Their contractual freedom is restricted: they may make, but not break, their agreement.

It follows, therefore, that an applicant who is allotted shares in the company may not set the allotment aside merely because he and the company have agreed that it should become invalid on the happening of an event. Once the applicant becomes a member, he is liable to pay for the shares. Similarly, where he has applied for shares and at the same time made a *collateral agreement* with the company, i.e. another contract *side by side* with his contract to take the shares, he cannot set the allotment aside merely because the company has broken the collateral agreement.

Thus in *Elkington's Case* (1876), the applicants for the shares relied on an agreement which they had made with the company that they should pay 30s. per share in *cash*, and the balance should be set off against goods with which they were to supply the company. The company never ordered the goods. HELD: The applicants were liable to pay the balance due on the shares in cash, since the arrangement concerning the goods merely amounted to a collateral agreement, and not to a condition precedent.

A collateral agreement of this type will of course, if a valid contract in itself, give rise to all the normal remedies for breach if either party should break it. But it in no way affects the validity of the allotment.

Here is yet another example of the law's preference of creditors to members.

8. The statutory provisions on allotment. The statutory provisions on allotment in the Companies Act 1948 range from s. 47–52, immediately following those on the prospectus. Section 48, however, was repealed by the Companies Act 1980 which itself contains no less than nine sections—s. 14, s. 16, s. 17, s. 18, s. 22, s. 23, s. 24, s. 25 and s. 28—on the same topic.

Each of these fourteen sections will now be considered in turn. It is essential to notice in each case to which companies the particular section applies and it will be seen that the provisions in the Companies Act 1980 are of much greater significance than those in the 1948 Act. For this reason they have, with one exception, been considered first.

9. Authority of company required for allotment. Section 14 Companies Act 1980 is the most comprehensive of the fourteen sections on allotment, applying to *all companies, public and private*. It provides in s. 14(1) that the directors may not allot "*relevant securities*" of the company unless they are *authorised* to do so by either:

(*a*) a general meeting; *or*
(*b*) the articles.

Section 14(10) defines "relevant securities" as shares in the company *excluding those*:

(*a*) shown in the memorandum as having been taken by the subscribers thereto; *or*
(*b*) allotted under a share scheme for employees.

The expression includes, however, a *right to subscribe for,* or *convert any security into*, shares in the company other than those comprised in (*b*) above. Thus it would include a convertible debenture (*see* XXI, **5**).

Under s. 14(2) the company's authority to the directors may be general or particular, conditional or unconditional, but in all cases s. 14(3) requires it to state:

(*a*) the maximum amount of relevant securities which may be allotted under it; and
(*b*) the date on which it will expire.

The date of expiration may not be more than five years from whichever of the following dates applies:

(*a*) where on the company's original incorporation the authority was contained in the articles, the *date of incorporation*;
(*b*) where this is not the case, the *date of the resolution* giving the authority.

Whether given by the articles or by a resolution, the authority may always be revoked or varied by the company in general meeting.

Section 14(4) permits the authority to be renewed by a resolution of the general meeting as many times as is desired, but never for a period exceeding five years. The resolution must always state the amount of relevant securities to be allotted, or which still remains to be allotted, as well as the date on which the renewed authority will expire.

Section 14(6) permits any resolution mentioned in the section, regardless of whether it gives, varies, revokes or renews the authority, to be an *ordinary* resolution, even if it alters the articles of the company (*see* III, **9**). It must, however, be filed with the registrar (*see* XXIII, **39**) who, under s. 9(3) European Communities Act 1972 as amended by para. 45 of the 3rd Schedule to the Companies Act 1980, is required, in the case of a *public* company, to publish his receipt of it in the *Gazette*.

Although it can be seen that the rules imposed by the section are stringent, the validity of an allotment is not affected if they are broken: s. 14(8).

10. Pre-emption rights. Section 17 Companies Act 1980 for the first time gives existing shareholders a statutory right of pre-emption on a new issue of shares. In s. 17(1) it prohibits any company, public or private, from allotting *equity securities* to any person unless it has first offered to each holder of *relevant shares* or *relevant employee shares,* on terms at least as favourable, a proportion of them equal in nominal value to that already held by him of the total relevant shares or relevant employee shares already issued.

Further, it is not enough for the company merely to make such an offer: the prohibition on allotment endures until either the period for the acceptance of the offer has expired (*see* **11** *below*) or the company has, in every case, been notified of its acceptance or refusal.

This important subsection introduces three technical expressions given in italics above, the definitions of which are found in s. 17(11). It will be seen that the most crucial of the three is that of *relevant shares.*

(*a*) *Relevant shares* means shares in the company *excluding*:
  (*i*) shares having a limit on their right to participate in distributions of both dividend and capital (*see* XI, **15** for a comparison with the term *equity share capital*); and
  (*ii*) shares held under a share scheme for employees.

(*b*) *Relevant employee shares* means shares which would be relevant shares within (*a*) above if they were not held under a share scheme for employees.

(*c*) *Equity security* means a relevant share in the company *excluding those*:

(*i*) shown in the memorandum as having been taken by the subscribers thereto; *or*

(*ii*) issued as bonus shares.

It includes, however, a *right to subscribe for,* or *convert any security into,* relevant shares (*see* **9**).

It often happens that the company's memorandum or articles contain a clause giving a pre-emption right to holders of a *particular class* of shares in the event of any further issue of shares of that class. Section 17(3) covers this situation and states that where such a clause exists, the provisions of s. 17(1) apply *only to the balance of the securities which remains unallotted.* Thus such shareholders have "double" pre-emption rights—the first as holders of a particular class of shares, and the second as members of the company.

11. Procedure for making pre-emption offer. Whether made under s. 17(1) or under a clause in the memorandum or articles, s. 17(6) requires the company's offer of the new shares to be served on each person entitled to receive it in the usual manner of the serving of notices under Table A, Articles 131–133 (*see* **XXIII, 19**). If this is impossible because he is the holder of a share warrant (*see* **XX, 16**), or not entitled to receive notices of general meetings, it may be published in the *Gazette.*

Section 17(7) requires the offer to state a period of at least twenty-one days during which it may be accepted. It cannot be revoked before the end of that period.

12. Contravention of rules governing pre-emption rights. Where there is any contravention of s. 17 or of a class pre-emption clause in a company's memorandum or articles, s. 17(10) provides that the company, and every officer who knowingly authorised or permitted the contravention, shall be jointly and severally liable to compensate any person entitled to receive an offer for any damage suffered or expenses incurred due to the contravention.

Such a person must, however, commence proceedings within two years.

13. Exclusion, withdrawal or modification of pre-emption rights. In the case of a *private* company s. 17(9) permits the above rules to be entirely excluded by the company's memorandum or articles. Even in the case of a *public* company, however, s. 18 Companies

Act 1980 permits the company to dispense with or modify the
statutory pre-emption rights given by s. 17 if it so desires.

Where the directors have been given a *general* authority to exercise the company's power of allotment under s. 14 (*see* **9**), s.
18(1) permits the articles or a special resolution of the company
to empower them to allot equity securities either entirely free
from any pre-emption rights, or with those rights modified in
whatever manner they decide.

Under s. 18(2), of much narrower application, the company
may by special resolution withdraw or modify the pre-emption
rights as regards any specified allotment. In this case it is immaterial whether the directors' authority to allot the equity securities in question is general or particular.

Whenever the directors' authority to allot is revoked or expires, their power under s. 18(1) or the special resolution under
s. 18(2) to dispense with or modify the pre-emption rights
terminates with it. In consequence, on the renewal of their
authority a special resolution will be required to renew that
power or special resolution if the company desires to do so: s.
18(3).

A special resolution passed under s. 18(1), (2) or (3) must,
like all special resolutions, be filed with the registrar under s.
143 Companies Act 1948. In the case of a *public* company the
registrar is then required, under s. 9(3) European Communities Act 1972 as amended by para. 45 of the 3rd Schedule to the
Companies Act 1980, to publish his receipt of it in the *Gazette*.

14. Further rules regarding specified allotments. Further rules
apply where the special resolution to withdraw or modify the pre-
emption rights relates to a particular specified allotment and
therefore falls under s. 18(2).

Section 18(5) provides that no such special resolution, or
special resolution for its renewal, can be proposed unless:

  (*a*) it is recommended by the directors; and
  (*b*) a written statement by the directors has been circulated
       with the notice of the relevant meeting giving:
    (*i*) their reasons for recommending it;
    (*ii*) the amount to be paid to the company in respect of the
          allotment; and
    (*iii*) the directors' justification of that amount.

Section 18(6) gives penalties for false or misleading matter in
the statement.

15. Minimum amount to be paid before allotment. The three sections considered above all apply to both public and private companies. The next ten sections to be considered apply to *public companies only*.

Section 22(1) Companies Act 1980 states that a public company may not allot a share unless it is paid up at least as to *one quarter of its nominal value and the whole of any premium on it*.

If the company makes an allotment which contravenes this rule, s. 22(2) requires the shares in question to be treated *as if the minimum amount had been received,* but renders the allottee liable to pay that amount, less the value of any consideration applied in payment for the allotment, with interest at the appropriate rate. *Bonus shares* are not affected by this subsection unless the allottee knew or ought to have known of the contravention: s. 22(3).

None of the above provisions applies to shares allotted under a *share scheme for employees*: s. 22(4).

Finally, in s. 22(5) the section extends the liability of the allottee under s. 22(2) to *subsequent holders* by making applicable by reference the provisions of s. 20(4). Accordingly, where a person becomes liable through a contravention of the section to pay an amount in respect of the shares, any subsequent holder also becomes liable, jointly and severally with him, unless *either*:

(*a*) he is a purchaser for value without actual notice of the contravention at the time of the purchase; *or*

(*b*) he derived title to the shares from a person who acquired them after the contravention and was not himself so liable.

There is thus a chain of liability which can be broken only by an innocent purchaser (the *bona fide purchaser for value*).

16. Allotment for non-cash consideration. The Companies Act 1980, in s. 23, s. 24 and s. 25, introduced special rules to apply in public companies where the consideration to be furnished by the allottee for the allotment is not in cash but in some other form. It has been mentioned earlier (*see* VII, **4**) that it is entirely proper for an allottee to furnish consideration for the allotment in a form other than money, but the detailed rules on this topic will be found in Chapter XII.

Section 23(1) Companies Act 1980 prohibits any public company from allotting shares as fully or partly paid up otherwise than in cash if the consideration consists of or includes an undertaking which is to be or may be performed *more than five years after the date of the allotment*.

Where the company makes an allotment which contravenes subsection (1) the allottee, under s. 23(2), becomes liable to pay to the company an amount equal to the nominal value of the shares, together with any premium—i.e. he becomes liable to pay for his shares in *cash*, with interest at the appropriate rate.

The same rule applies, under s. 23(5), where the terms of the contract for allotment, without any fault on the part of the company, have not been complied with by the allottee within the prescribed period.

In both these cases—i.e. whenever the allottee becomes liable to pay for his shares in cash—any subsequent holder also becomes liable, jointly and severally with the allottee, to pay for the shares in cash unless *either*:

(*a*) he is a purchaser for value without actual notice of the contravention at the time of the purchase; *or*

(*b*) he derived title to the shares from a person who acquired them after the contravention and was not himself so liable: s. 23(6), applying s. 20(4).

This last provision is similar to that applied by s. 22(5) (*see* **15**) and once again liability in a subsequent holder does not arise if the chain is broken.

17. Exemption from liability under s. 23. Section 28(1) Companies Act 1980 provides that where a person is liable to a company under s. 23 regarding payment for his shares, he may apply to the court for relief from that liability.

The court may then exempt him from liability if it appears just and equitable to do so: s. 28(2).

18. Valuation of non-cash consideration. Section 24 Companies Act 1980 gives detailed rules for the valuation of non-cash consideration in public companies. In s. 24(1) it prohibits any public company from allotting shares as fully or partly paid up otherwise than in cash unless:

(*a*) the consideration has been valued in accordance with the section;

(*b*) a report on its value has been made to the company by a person appointed by the company during the six months immediately preceding the allotment; and

(*c*) a copy of the report has been sent to the proposed allottee.

Section 24(4) requires the valuation and report to be made by an *independent person*, i.e. a person qualified to act as the company's auditor. Such a person is termed an "expert" in the margin to the Act—a less cumbersome expression which is in general use and will therefore be adopted in the paragraphs which follow.

If the expert thinks it reasonable to do so, he may arrange for the valuation to be made by some other person provided such person appears to him to have the requisite knowledge and experience and would not be disqualified under s. 161(2) and (3) Companies Act 1948 from acting as auditor to the company (*see* XVII, **13**). Such other person must then make a report to the expert which will enable him to make his own report as required by s. 24(1)(b).

Whoever carries out the valuation or makes the report under s. 24 is entitled, under s. 25(1), to require any information and explanation which he thinks necessary from the company's officers. Any person who responds by knowingly or recklessly making a statement to him which is misleading, false or deceptive in a material particular is guilty of an offence under s. 25(3) for which s. 25(5) prescribes penalties.

Lastly, s. 25(2) requires the company receiving the report to deliver a copy of it to the registrar for registration at the same time that it files its return of allotments for the shares in question (*see* **27**). The registrar must then, under s. 9(3) European Communities Act 1972 as amended by para. 45 of the 3rd Schedule to the Companies Act 1980, publish his receipt of it in the *Gazette*.

19. Contents of expert's report. Section 24(5) requires the expert's report to state:

(*a*) the nominal value of the shares to be wholly or partly paid for by the consideration in question;

(*b*) the amount of any premium payable on them;

(*c*) the description of the consideration and the method and date of valuation:

(*d*) the extent to which the nominal value of the shares and any premium are to be treated as paid up:

(*i*) by the consideration;

(*ii*) in cash.

Where a valuation is made by some person other than the expert the latter's report, under s. 24(6), must also state:

(*e*) the fact that the valuation was made by some other person;

(*f*) that other person's name and relevant knowledge and experience; and

(*g*) the description of the consideration valued by him and the method and date of valuation.

Finally, s. 24(7) requires the expert's report either to contain or be accompanied by a *note* by him:

(*a*) that it appeared reasonable to him to arrange for the valuation to be made by another person if in fact it was so made;

(*b*) that the method of valuation was reasonable;

(*c*) that it appears to him that there has been no material change in the value of the consideration in question since the valuation; and

(*d*) that on the basis of the valuation the value of the consideration, together with any cash to be paid for the shares, is not less than the amount treated as paid up on the shares allotted.

20. Effect of contravention of s. 24. Section 24(8) and (9) provide that where a public company allots shares in contravention of s. 24(1) and *either*:

(*a*) the allottee has not received a report; *or*

(*b*) there has been some other contravention of s. 24 which the allottee knew or ought to have known amounted to a contravention;

the allottee becomes liable to pay to the company an amount equal to the nominal value of the shares together with any premium, or such proportion of that amount as is treated as paid up by the consideration, with interest at the appropriate rate.

Section 24(10) applies the now familiar provision contained in s. 20(4) and previously encountered in s. 22(5) and s. 23(6) (*see* **15** and **16**) to the effect that whenever the allottee becomes liable through a contravention of the section to pay an amount under it in respect of the shares, any subsequent holder also becomes liable, jointly and severally with the allottee, to pay the amount in question unless *either*:

(*a*) he is a purchaser for value without actual notice of the contravention at the time of the purchase; *or*

(*b*) he derived title to the shares from a person who acquired them after the contravention and was not himself so liable.

Thus once again a subsequent holder or purchaser is not liable if a previous holder or purchaser was not liable. Further, s. 28 again applies to any person liable under s. 24 (*see* **17**).

21. Cases where valuation of non-cash consideration is not required. Section 24(2) Companies Act 1980 gives two cases where no valuation is required even though a public company is allotting shares for non-cash consideration. These are:

(*a*) where the company is making an offer to shareholders in another company to acquire their shares as consideration for an allotment to them of shares in itself (popularly known as "*a take-over bid*"); or

(*b*) where the company is making an allotment of its shares in connection with a *merger* between itself and another company.

Both these operations are considered in detail in Chapter XXXII.

22. The minimum subscription. Once the important rules introduced by the Companies Act 1980 have been considered, the five sections still in force in the Companies Act 1948 must be examined.

The first of these is s. 47 which now deals only with the minimum subscription since s. 47(3) was repealed by the Companies Act 1980. It should be noted at the start that s. 47(5) states that an applicant for shares may not waive the requirements of this section: thus he may not dispense with them even if he is willing to do so.

Two further points are of importance. First, s. 47(6) states that the section applies only to the *first* allotment of shares to the public by a company, so that s. 47(1) must be read with this in mind. Secondly, since a private company is prohibited by s. 15 Companies Act 1980 from offering its shares or debentures to the public, it is clear that the section applies only to public companies.

Section 47(1) thus places an important restriction on the *first*—but only the first—allotment of shares to the public by a public company. It states that a company may not allot any shares offered to the public for subscription until the minimum subscription (*see* VII, **4**) has been subscribed, and the sum payable on application for it has been paid to and received by the company.

Section 47(2) states that the minimum subscription must be reckoned in *cash* (*see* VII, **4**), i.e. an applicant who is paying for his shares with property (a perfectly proper arrangement as has already been explained in **16**) is not contributing towards the minimum subscription, which must be in the form of *money*. Section 47(1) states, however, that if a cheque is received in good faith and the directors have no reason for suspecting that it will not be met, then the amount of the cheque is to be deemed paid and received.

Section 47(4) states that if the minimum subscription has not been subscribed within forty days from the issue of the prospectus, all money received from applicants must be repaid to them at once. If it is not repaid within forty-eight days from the issue of the prospectus, the directors become jointly and severally liable to repay it with interest at 5% from the end of the forty-eighth day, unless they can prove that the default in repayment was not due to their misconduct or negligence.

NOTE: From the wording of s. 47(1) it might be thought that an allotment made in contravention of the section is void. In fact, it is clear from s. 49 that it is not void, but only *voidable*, and that the allottee may therefore retain his shares if he wishes, even though the minimum subscription has not been subscribed.

It should also be noted that s. 47(4) applies only where such an irregular allotment has *not* been made. Once it has been made, the position is governed by s. 49.

23. Effect of an allotment which is irregular under s. 47. Section 49, as amended by the Companies Act 1980, deals with the effect of any allotment which is irregular under s. 47.

Section 49(1) states that such an allotment is *voidable* by the applicant within one month after the date of the allotment, even if the company is in liquidation.

Section 49(2) makes a director who knowingly contravenes s. 47 liable to compensate the company and the allottee for the resulting loss or damage, but stipulates that the action to recover this compensation must be brought within *two years*—an unusual period of limitation now found again in s. 17 Companies Act 1980 (*see* **12**).

24. Disclosure in prospectus where issue not fully subscribed. It is convenient here to return briefly to the Companies Act 1980 in order to consider the provisions of s. 16, for it will be seen that these are linked to the two sections just discussed.

Section 16(1) and (3) Companies Act 1980 prohibit any allotment of shares in a public company, whether *for cash or otherwise*, unless *either*:

(*a*) the shares are fully subscribed; *or*

(*b*) the prospectus states that, even if the shares are not fully subscribed, those subscribed for will be allotted in any event.

Section 47(4) and (5) and s. 49 Companies Act 1948 again apply in a corresponding way: s. 16(2) (*see* **22** and **23**).

25. Time of allotment. Section 50 Companies Act 1948 deals with the time of allotment. Some of its provisions, namely those dealing with the revocation of the application for shares, were discussed in **5**, so here we need to consider only s. 50(1) and (3).

Section 50(1) states that no allotment may be made of shares or debentures in pursuance of a prospectus until the time of the opening of the subscription lists.

Section 50(3) states that if the section is contravened, the validity of the allotment is not affected, though the company and every officer in default will be fined. This means, then, that even if contravention of the section occurs, the allotment remains *valid*.

26. Application to stock exchange for listing of shares. Section 51 concerns permission for shares or debentures to be listed. Section 51(1), as amended by the Companies Act 1976, provides that where a prospectus states that application has been or will be made for the shares or debentures to be listed on any stock exchange, then the allotment is *void*:

(*a*) if the permission has not been applied for before the time of the opening of the subscription lists; *or*

(*b*) if the permission has been refused within three weeks from the closing of the subscription lists.

It will be seen that the effect of this subsection is to make the obtaining of permission for the shares or debentures to be listed a *condition precedent* to the allotment once the prospectus has stated that it has been or will be applied for.

NOTE: The reason for this is that it is a tremendous advantage to the investor if his shares are listed on a stock exchange, since it greatly increases their marketability and therefore their value. If, therefore, the prospectus has stated that the company has applied for permission for the shares or debentures to be listed, the investor who relies on that prospectus is entitled to regard the obtaining of a stock exchange listing as a fundamental term of his contract.

Section 51(3) states that all money received from applicants must be kept in a separate bank account as long as there is a possibility of it having to be repaid.

Section 51(2) states that where the allotment is void under

s. 51(1), the company must repay the application money at once to the applicants, and if it is not repaid within eight days the directors are jointly and severally liable to repay it with interest at 5% from the end of the eighth day, unless they can prove that the default in repayment was not due to their misconduct or negligence. (Note the similarity of this provision to that in s. 47(4) discussed in **22**.)

Section 51(4) contains the now familiar provision that the section cannot be waived.

27. The return of allotments. The last of the sections on allotment is s. 52, dealing withe the return of allotments. This important document must be delivered to the registrar within one month of the allotment whenever any limited company, public or private, allots shares. Capital duty of £1 per cent on the actual value of assets contributed must be paid at the same time. In the case of a public company s. 9(3) European Communities Act 1972, as amended by para. 45 of the 3rd Schedule to the Companies Act 1980, then requires the registrar to publish his receipt of the return in the *Gazette*.

Section 52(1) states that the company must deliver:

(*a*) a return of allotments, stating:

    (*i*) the number of nominal amount of the shares allotted,

    (*ii*) the names, addresses and descriptions of the allottees,

    (*iii*) the amount paid and payable on each share, *and*

(*b*) where shares are allotted fully or partly paid up *otherwise than in cash*:

    (*i*) a written contract constituting the title of the allottee to the shares,

    (*ii*) the contract of sale or for services or other consideration for which the allotment was made, and

    (*iii*) a return stating the number and nominal amount of the shares so allotted, the extent to which they are paid up, and the consideration for which they were allotted.

Section 52(2) states that where there is no written contract available the company must deliver particulars of it, stamped with the same stamp duty as would have been payable if the contract had been in writing.

Section 52(1) must be studied and learnt very carefully. It is not difficult to understand, but it is not easy to learn. It will help if it is seen that *in every case* the company will have to deliver the return under (*a*) above, but will only have to deliver the contracts and return under (*b*) where the shares have been paid for *otherwise than in cash,* i.e. with property, goods or services.

Where the company makes a *capitalisation issue* (XVI, **12**) and issues bonus shares paid up out of undistributed profits or reserves, it is nevertheless necessary to make not only a return of allotments (*a*), but also to file a contract between the company and the members constituting the title of the allottees (*b*). This is because bonus shares, though not paid for with property, goods or services, are not paid for in "cash" within the meaning of the section, for this expression is confined to cases where the member provides the company with further capital. For the same reason, issues of bonus shares are not subject to capital duty.

NOTE: The Jenkins Committee, however, recommended that the filing of a contract in such a case should no longer be required.

If the company fails to comply with s. 52, there is a fine on every officer in default, but the *validity of the allotments is not affected.* Thus whether or not they are irregular in any other way, the fact that no return of allotments is made will not render them void.

28. Summary of statutory provisions on allotment. The statutory provisions on allotment are so numerous that it is sometimes helpful to have a summary for easy reference, such as that given below.

No reference to the penalties mentioned in the summary has been made in the text since students are not normally required to learn them. They have been inserted into the summary only in order to give a complete picture of contravention of the various sections.

PUBLIC AND PRIVATE COMPANIES

SECTION		EFFECT OF CONTRAVENTION
s. 14 Companies Act 1980	Company's authority required for allotment	Penalty on directors: s. 14(7) Allotment remains VALID: s. 14(8)
s. 17 Companies Act 1980	Pre-emption rights	Company and officers liable to pay compensation: s. 17(10)
s. 52 Companies Act 1948	Return of allotments	Penalty on officers in default: s. 52(3) Allotment remains VALID

PUBLIC COMPANIES ONLY

SECTION		EFFECT OF CONTRAVENTION
s. 22 Companies Act 1980	25% of nominal value to be paid before allotment	Penalty on company and officers in default: s. 30(1) Allottee liable to pay amount due. Liability extended to all subsequent holders except purchasers for value without notice: s. 22(2)(5) (applying s. 20(4))
s. 23 Companies Act 1980	Non-cash consideration to be transferred within 5 years of allotment	Same as for s. 22: s. 30(1) and s. 23(2)(5)(6) (applying s. 20(4)) + Relief from liability: s. 28
s. 24 Companies Act 1980	Non-cash consideration to be valued by expert	Same as for s. 23: s. 30(1) and s. 24(8)(9)(10) (applying s. 20(4)) + Relief from liability: s. 28
s. 47 Companies Act 1948	Minimum subscription to be subscribed before FIRST allotment	Directors liable to pay compensation: s. 49(2) Allotment VOIDABLE: s. 49(1)
s. 16 Companies Act 1980	Disclosure in prospectus before allotment where issue not fully subscribed	Same as for s. 47 Companies Act 1948: s. 16(2)
s. 50 Companies Act 1948	No allotment before time of opening of subscription lists	Penalty on company and officers in default: s. 50(3) Allotment remains VALID: s. 50(3)
s. 51 Companies Act 1948	Stock exchange listing	Penalty on company and officers in default: s. 51(3) Allotment VOID: s. 51(1)

PROGRESS TEST 9

1. When are shares regarded as being allotted? **(1)**

2. How does a company deal with the legal difficulty which arises where an issue of shares is over-subscribed? **(4)**

3. Give an account of the statutory provision which prevents an applicant for shares from revoking his offer for a prescribed period. **(5)**

4. Define the time of the opening of the subscription lists. **(5)**

5. What is the legal effect of a conditional application? **(6)**

6. What is the legal effect of an application subject to a condition subsequent or accompanied by a collateral agreement? **(7)**

7. What is the minimum amount payable for shares before allotment? **(15)**

8. How may directors be authorised to make an allotment of shares? For how long may the authority last? **(9)**

9. Give the rules relating to pre-emption rights. **(10–14)**

10. What special rules apply where allotment is made for non-cash consideration consisting of an undertaking to be performed in the future? **(16)**

11. Outline the rules governing the valuation of non-cash consideration. **(18–21)**

12. What are the statutory rules on allotment regarding the minimum subscription? **(22)**

13. What is the legal effect of an allotment which is irregular because the minimum subscription has not been subscribed? **(23)**

14. What special rules apply where an issue of shares in a public company is not fully subscribed?

What is the effect of contravention of those rules? **(24)**

15. What are the statutory provisions regulating the time of an allotment of shares?

What is the legal effect of an allotment which is made in breach of these provisions? **(25)**

16. What is the effect on an allotment where the prospectus states that application for permission for the shares or debentures to be listed has been or will be made, and that permission is not granted? **(26)**

17. What rules govern the delivery and contents of the return of allotments? **(27)**

CHAPTER X

Membership

1. Methods of becoming a member. A person may become a member in the following ways:

(*a*) *Allotment.* Here the member takes the shares *directly from the company.* The statutory provisions on allotment have been fully discussed in IX.

(*b*) *Transfer.* Here the member acquires the shares *from an existing member* by sale, gift or some other transaction.

(*c*) *Transmission.* This is an involuntary transfer occurring on the *death* or *bankruptcy* of a member. Later it will be seen that the ownership in the shares then *automatically*, i.e. by operation of law, passes from the dead or bankrupt member to his personal representatives or trustee in bankruptcy, as the case may be, who may then be registered in respect of them. (The student who wrote that transfer was by act of parties, while transmission was by act of God, was somewhat overstating the divine responsibility.)

(*d*) *Subscribing the memorandum.* The subscribers must take their shares directly from the company, and not by transfer from another member.

Section 26(1) states that the subscribers to the memorandum shall be deemed to have agreed to become members, and must be entered in the register of members.

(*e*) *Estoppel.* If a person's name is improperly placed on the register of members, and he knows and assents to it, he will then be *estopped from denying* that he is a member.

Estoppel is simply a *rule of evidence* which prevents a person from denying the legal implications of his conduct. Thus a man may behave as though he is a partner in a firm, and be "held out" by the other partners as being one of their number: neither he nor they will then be allowed to deny that he is a partner, for they will be estopped from doing so. The same rule applies to a person who behaves as though he is a member of a company by allowing his name to be placed on the register.

NOTE: Section 26(2) states that every other person who agrees to become a member and whose name is entered on the register of members shall be a member. This clearly covers allotment, transfer, transmission and estoppel.

2. The conditions of membership. It will be seen from the above that there are two conditions to membership:

(*a*) the *agreement* to become a member, either by subscribing the memorandum, or by allotment or transfer, or after transmission has occurred, or as a result of estoppel; *and*

(*b*) the *entry on the register of members* of the shareholder's name.

Thus as a general rule all members are shareholders, and all shareholders are members, so that the two words are synonymous. Later on, however, it will be seen that there is an exception to this, namely, where share warrants have been issued. Also, in the case of death or bankruptcy, there will be a period of time when the person on the register no longer owns the shares, because he is either dead or bankrupt and transmission has occurred.

3. Joint holders. Where two or more persons own shares jointly, the *jus accrescendi* or right of survivorship applies. This means that on the death of any joint holder, the survivor or survivors simply *continue to own* the shares, which do not pass to the personal representatives of the deceased for distribution under the will or intestacy.

Joint holders may be entered on the company's register of members in any order which they desire, and the articles usually provide that the vote of the senior must be accepted to the exclusion of the votes of the others. Seniority is determined by the order in which the names stand in the register. Table A, Article 63, contains a provision to this effect.

Joint holders may require the company to split their holding equally among them. This will give them each a smaller holding but an equal number of votes. A similar result is obtained if their holding is split and their names in respect of each holding are placed in a different order. They will then all continue to own all the shares, but each will have the same voting rights as the others.

4. Methods of ceasing to be a member. There are a large number of ways in which a person may cease to be a member of a company, many of which will be discussed in detail in later chapters:

(*a*) *Transfer*. Here the transferor ceases to be a member when the transferee is placed on the register.

(*b*) *Forfeiture*. The articles may provide that a member's shares may be forfeited for non-payment of calls.

(*c*) *Surrender*. This is a short-cut to forfeiture, in order to avoid the formalities.

(*d*) *Sale by the company under its lien.*

(*e*) *Transmission to personal representatives on death of member*. In the next chapter we shall see that the dead member only ceases to be a member of the company when some other person is registered in his place.

(*f*) *Transmission to trustee in bankruptcy of member*. Here again the bankrupt member only ceases to be a member when some other person is registered in his place.

(*g*) *Disclaimer by trustee in bankruptcy of member*.

(*h*) *Liquidation*. On liquidation the company will be dissolved and members will have their capital returned to them as far as possible. Since the existence of the company comes to an end, membership also ceases.

(*i*) *Issue of share warrants*. Under s. 112 a member is struck off the register on the issue of a share warrant, but it should be noted that s. 112(5) provides that the bearer of a share warrant may be deemed to be a member to the extent to which the articles provide.

(*j*) *Redemption of redeemable preference shares under s. 58.*

(*k*) *Repudiation by infant.*

(*l*) *Rescission for misrepresentation in the prospectus.*

(*m*) *Court order*, e.g. s. 5 Companies Act 1948; s. 11 and s. 75 Companies Act 1980.

(*n*) *Section 209*. Where a "take-over bid" is made, the shares of the dissenting minority may under certain conditions be bought by the transferee company.

(*o*) *Section 287*. Where a liquidator is empowered to sell the company's property in return for shares in another company, those members who dissent from the arrangement can compel the liquidator either to abandon it or to buy their shares.

PROGRESS TEST 10

1. In what ways may a person become a member of a company? **(1)**

2. What is the legal position of joint holders of shares? **(3)**

3. In what ways may a person cease to be a member of a company? **(4)**

CHAPTER XI

Legally Abnormal Persons

1. Introduction. A *legally normal* person is any natural legal person of full age who is sane, sober and solvent.

Some legal persons are abnormal from their beginning, such as corporations which, as we have seen, are artificial legal persons. Others, whether by a disorder of their mind, body or finances, become abnormal in the course of their lives. Moreover, all normal persons are born: they are therefore infants, or minors, and legally abnormal for the first eighteen years. They also die, creating a legal situation to which special rules apply.

This chapter is concerned with the rules which apply to legally abnormal persons as shareholders, and deals therefore with infants, lunatics, personal representatives, trustees in bankruptcy and corporations. Drunkenness, though studied in the law of contract, does not affect shareholding unless of so persistent a nature that it leads to incapacity of mind, when the rules regarding lunacy will apply.

2. Infants. An infant may hold shares in a company, provided the company is willing to place his name on the register. Often the articles prohibit the transfer of shares to an infant, but even if they do not the company cannot be compelled to register him as a member.

(*a*) *A transfer to an infant is voidable.* If, therefore, the company has unknowingly registered an infant, it can still apply to the court to have the transfer set aside and the transferor put back on the register, but it must act promptly. If it acquiesces in the transfer, or delays too long before applying to have the register rectified, the infant shareholder will have to be recognised.

(*b*) *An infant shareholder may likewise repudiate his contract* either before attaining majority or within a reasonable time afterwards, and on doing so can avoid all future liability on partly paid shares. He cannot, however, recover money already paid on the shares unless there has been a total failure of consideration. If the shares have a market value, however small, the infant has received some consideration and therefore cannot recover his money: *Steinberg* v. *Scala, Ltd.* (1923).

(*c*) *An infant may subscribe the memorandum*, but can afterwards repudiate liability in the normal way.

(*d*) *A transfer of shares by an infant* is usually said to require an order from the court, though there is conflict of opinion on the point.

3. Lunatics. A person of unsound mind may be a shareholder, but his voting rights will be exercised by his committee, receiver or other person appointed by the court to deal with his affairs. Table A, Article 64, specifically authorises this.

Such person may also be given authority to transfer the shares and to deal generally with the lunatic's property.

4. Personal representatives. The expression "personal representatives" covers both *executors*, who are appointed by the testator in his will, and *administrators*, who are appointed by the court when the testator fails to appoint an executor, or when the deceased has made no will.

It is essential to understand first that when a person dies, all his property vests at the moment of death in his personal representatives. This is known as *transmission*, or *transfer by operation of law*, or *involuntary assignment*, according to the context, but it can be expressed most simply by saying that because a deceased person cannot own anything, the ownership of all his property passes at the moment of death to those who legally represent him. These persons, under the Administration of Estates Act 1925, are his personal representatives.

This raises no difficulties where the deceased has appointed an executor, but if he has not, there will be a period of time which must obviously elapse before the court makes the necessary appointment of an administrator. Nevertheless, the ownership of the property vests in the administrator, once he is appointed, *from the moment of death*, and his title *relates back* to the date when the deceased died.

Personal representatives, therefore, have in all cases the *legal* ownership of the deceased's property. But they are *trustees*: they hold the property *on trust* for those entitled to it under the will or the rules of intestacy. The position which arises where a person is a trustee of shares will be fully discussed later, but meanwhile these basic principles should be kept in mind.

5. Provisions of the Act and Table A regarding personal representatives. These are two sections in the Act concerning personal representatives.

Section 82 states simply that the production to a company of any document which is by law sufficient evidence of probate of the will, or letters of administration of the estate, or confirmation as executor of a deceased person, must be accepted by the company as sufficient evidence of the grant, regardless of anything in the articles.

NOTE: This section does not make the personal representatives members of the company. The deceased is still on the register. But it impliedly recognises that the *ownership* in the shares has passed from the deceased to the personal representatives. Note here how membership is divorced from ownership, an exceptional position.

Section 76 proceeds further to implement this principle. It states that a transfer of the shares of the deceased made by a personal representative who is not a member of the company is as valid as if he were a member. Not only does he own the shares, but he may deal with them without his name being entered on the register of members.

Table A, Article 134, states that notice of meetings must be sent to the personal representative. But Article 32, while it gives him the right to dividends and other benefits attached to the shares, states that he shall not have any rights relating to meetings until his name is on the register of members. Thus while he receives the notice of a meeting, he will not be able to vote at it unless he has become registered as a member.

6. Registration of personal representatives as members. Unless the articles provide otherwise, personal representatives are entitled to be registered as members of the company if they wish, and may make their desire known to the directors by a *letter of request*. They may, however, prefer not to be registered, and this may be inconvenient for the company as there is then no-one who can vote in respect of the deceased's shares. Article 32 provides for this situation, allowing the directors to require the personal representatives either to become registered as members or to transfer the shares. If they do not comply within 90 days, then the directors may withhold all dividends and other moneys payable in respect of the shares until they do. While this is not exactly compulsion, it is certainly persuasion.

If the shares are partly paid, personal representatives who are on the register of members are personally liable for calls, but they will have a right of indemnity against the deceased's estate for the amount paid. If they have not become registered as members, then the calls will be made on the estate and payable out of it. Section 215 provides that if the personal representatives default in paying the calls, the company itself may take administration proceedings in order to obtain the money due to it.

7. Trustees in bankruptcy. When a member of a company becomes bankrupt, the legal position is very similar to that arising on death. The debtor's name will be on the register of members, but he will no longer own the shares, for when he was adjudicated bankrupt the ownership passed by operation of law to his trustee in bankruptcy. Moreover, the title of the trustee in bankruptcy again *relates back* to a previous moment of time, namely the *commencement of the bankruptcy*. This is not the date of the adjudication order, but the first act of bankruptcy committed by the debtor within three months before the presentation of the bankruptcy petition.

NOTE

(1) *The trustee in bankruptcy*, though not on the register of members, becomes *entitled as owner of the shares* to deal with them, to control the debtor's vote, and to be registered as a member if he wishes. Article 134 provides that notice of meetings is to be sent to him, and Article 32 applies to him in the same way as to personal representatives.

(2) *If the shares are partly paid*, the company may prove in the bankruptcy both for calls in arrears and liability for future calls, but the trustee in bankruptcy may *disclaim* the shares within twelve months if they are onerous. If he disclaims, the company may prove for the damage resulting to it from the disclaimer, which will of course be the loss of the amount unpaid on the shares. The company may mitigate this damage by re-issuing the shares, as in the case of a forfeiture.

8. Corporations. A company may own shares in *another company*, and s. 139 then authorises it to appoint a person to act as its representative at meetings.

A company may not, however, normally own shares *in itself*. This was formerly known as the rule in *Trevor* v. *Whitworth* (1887), where the articles authorised the company to buy its own shares, but were held illegal on the grounds that this would amount to a reduction of capital.

The rule is now given statutory form by s. 35(1) Companies Act 1980 which, with two exceptions given below, prohibits any limited company from acquiring its own shares, whether by purchase, subscription or otherwise. In subsection (3) the Act imposes penalties on the company and every officer in default for contravention of the section and provides that any illegal acquisition of shares is *void*.

The two exceptions to the rule are found in s. 35(2) which expressly permits:

(*a*) a company limited by shares to acquire any of its own *fully paid* shares *otherwise than for valuable consideration* (i.e. by way of gift); and

(*b*) any company to acquire its own shares in a *reduction of capital duly made*.

Neither exception is new. A more limited version of the first, (*a*), was formerly found in two well-known cases—*Kirby* v. *Wilkins* (1929) and *Re Castiglione's Will Trusts* (1958). It is helpful to have it in a broader statutory form. The second, (*b*), does no more than state the obvious, having regard to the very wide provisions of s. 66 Companies Act 1948 on reduction of capital (*see* XV, **22**).

It is clear, of course, that if a company has issued 100 £1 shares at par, and then uses £25 of that share capital to buy 25 shares from an existing member, it will still have an issued capital of 100 shares, but will only have £75 in cash. The capital of the company is reduced by the amount which it has used to buy its own shares.

If, however, a company has been in existence for some time, and has accumulated revenue reserves, and then uses those reserves to buy its own shares from an existing member, this is not a reduction of *capital* in the strict sense of the word. Nevertheless, it would still be unlawful, both at common law and under s. 35, for it has reduced the amount of the company's *assets*, and on liquidation there would be less available to meet the claims of creditors. Thus the rule seems to be based not so much on an illegal reduction of capital, as on an illegal use of the company's assets generally, by returning money to a shareholder and so potentially depriving creditors of that amount.

9. Cases falling outside s. 35. Section 35(4) Companies Act 1980 gives six cases which do not amount to acquisition of its own shares by a company within s. 35(1), despite the fact that in four cases out of the six the company purchases its own shares.

These six cases are:

(*a*) Where the company, under its articles, redeems redeemable preference shares (*see* XV, **10**).

Here, due to the provisions of s. 58 Companies Act 1948, no reduction of capital occurs.

(*b*) Where the court makes an order for the purchase of shares in the company by the company under s. 5 Companies Act 1948 (*see* II, **33**).

(*c*) Where the court makes an order for the purchase of shares in the company by the company under s. 11 Companies Act 1980 (*see* XIX, **5**).

(*d*) Where the court makes an order for the purchase of shares in the company by the company under s. 75 Companies Act 1980 (*see* XXXI, **5**).

In these last three cases the court will also by order provide for the resulting reduction of the company's capital.

(*e*) Where, under the company's articles, forfeiture of shares occurs (*see* XX, **22**).

(*f*) Where the company accepts a surrender of shares in lieu of forfeiture (*see* XX, **24**).

10. Statutory extension of s. 35. Section 54 Companies Act 1948, which formerly was regarded as an extension of the common law rule in *Trevor* v. *Whitworth*, can now be seen as an extension of s. 35 Companies Act 1980. It broadens the rule in s. 35 in order to prevent attempted evasions of it.

Thus, if a company is approached by Smith and asked if it will *lend* him money in order to enable him to buy shares in that company, and it does so, then the company will have parted with some of its assets in return for a *debt* due to it from Smith. Probably Smith will repay it in due course, with interest, and the company may benefit from the arrangement. But possibly he will not. He might be adjudicated bankrupt, or he might disappear. Then the loan will not be repaid and the company will have lost that amount of money.

Again, if Smith approaches the company saying that he wishes to buy shares in it, but has no cash available, and has therefore asked his bank manager for a loan which will be forthcoming provided the company acts as his *guarantor*, the same situation will result. Possibly Smith will repay the loan to the bank, and the company will never be liable on its guarantee, but possibly he will not, and the company may then have to pay to the bank the amount of the loan. There is a potential liability to the company here, a potential reduction of its assets.

Even if the company obliges Smith by providing *security* to his bank, e.g. by charging its assets in favour of the bank as security for the loan made to Smith, there is the same possibility that Smith will not repay the bank, which will then enforce its security. The company's assets will therefore be diminished by the value of that security.

Section 54(1) makes all these transactions illegal. It states that it is unlawful for a company to give, directly or indirectly, and whether by means of a loan, guarantee or security, any financial assistance towards the purchase of shares in itself or, if it is a subsidiary company, in its holding company. (The expressions "subsidiary" company and "holding" company are explained below.)

Moreover, the prohibition against financial assistance is not confined to that given to a purchaser, but extends to financial assistance *to whomsoever it is given* for the purpose of or in connection with a purchase of the company's shares: *Armour Hick Northern Ltd.* v. *Armour Trust Ltd.* (1980).

Furthermore, there will be a breach of s. 54 whenever the sole purpose, or one of the several purposes, of a transaction is to assist a person to buy shares in the company. It is irrelevant that the transaction was in the commercial interests of the company or that the price paid for anything bought by the company was a fair one. The determining factor in each case is the *intention*, where the company is buying something, that the proceeds of the transaction should be used for the purchase of shares in the company: *Belmont Finance Corporation* v. *Williams Furniture Ltd.* (1980).

Despite these strict rules the proviso to s. 54(1), as amended by para. 10 of the 3rd Schedule to the Companies Act 1980, gives *three exceptions* where a company is permitted to give financial assistance to persons who wish to buy shares in it:

(*a*) Where the company is a *money-lending company*, and the loan is in the *ordinary course of its business*.

In *Steen* v. *Law* (1963) it was held that this exception can apply only where the money lent is at the free disposition of the borrower so that he can do what he likes with it, and that it can never cover a loan made for the direct purpose of financing a purchase of the company's shares.

(*b*) Where the company provides money under an *employee share scheme* for the purchase of subscription of *fully paid shares* in the company or its holding company by *trustees of the scheme*.

(*c*) Where the company lends money to *employees other than directors* to enable them to buy *fully paid shares* in the company or its holding company.

These exceptions are of great importance and should be studied carefully. They have been qualified, however, in the case of *public* companies by para. 10 of the 3rd Schedule to the Companies Act 1980 which has added two new subsections to s. 54.

Section 54(1A) accordingly provides that a public company may give financial assistance under the proviso only if its *net assets* are not reduced by doing so or, to the extent that they are reduced, if the financial assistance is provided out of *distributable profits* (*see* XVI, **5**).

Section 54(1B) states that "net assets" means the aggregate assets less the aggregate liabilities.

NOTE: If a company should contravene s. 54 and provide, for instance, unlawful security, it might be expected that the transaction would be void for illegality. At the present time, however, the law on this point is uncertain. Section 54(2), as amended by s. 80 and the 2nd Schedule to the Companies Act 1980, imposes greatly increased penalties on the company and officers in default for contravention of the section, but the effect of the "unlawful" transaction remains doubtful.

In *Victor Battery Co. Ltd.* v. *Curry's Ltd.* (1946) *security* given in breach of the section was held to be valid, while in *Selangor United Rubber Estates Ltd.* v. *Cradock* (1968) a *loan* contravening the section was held void. In *Heald* v. *O'Connor* (1971) Fisher J. reviewed these decisions and held that a debenture giving a charge on the company's assets in breach of the section was void. It is regrettable that the Companies Act 1980 did not expressly deal with the matter.

The effect on the directors of the company is nevertheless quite clear. In *Wallersteiner* v. *Moir* (1974) Lord Denning M.R., with his customary lucidity, said:

"Every director who is a party to a breach of s. 54 is guilty of a misfeasance and breach of trust; and is liable to recoup to the company any loss occasioned to it by the default."

11. Acquisition of shares in company by company's nominee. The prohibition given in s. 35 Companies Act 1980 is fortified by s. 36. Under s. 36(1) and (6)(*a*) where a limited company has a beneficial (i.e. equitable) interest in:

(*a*) shares which are issued, not to the company itself, but to its nominee; *or*

(*b*) partly paid shares which are acquired by the company's nominee from a third person,

the shares in question must be treated as held by the nominee on his own account and the company must be regarded as having no beneficial interest in them.

If he is called on to pay an amount in respect of them, s. 36(2) provides that he must comply within twenty-one days. If he fails to do so, then:

(*a*) if the shares were issued to him as a subscriber to the memorandum, the *other subscribers*; *or*

(*b*) if not, the *directors* of the company at the time when he acquired them,

are jointly and severally liable with him to pay the amount in question.

12. Special rules applicable only to public companies. Section 37 Companies Act 1980 imposes stringent additional rules applying to *public companies only*. In subsection (1) the Act gives four cases where these rules apply, the first of which will be considered in **XX, 25** since it relates to forfeiture or surrender of shares. The remaining three relate, respectively, to circumstances envisaged in s. 35 and s. 36 Companies Act 1980 and s. 54 Companies Act 1948 and are as follows:

(*a*) where shares in the company are acquired by the company and the company has a beneficial interest in them; (s. 35)

(*b*) where the company's nominee acquires shares in the company from a third person *without* financial assistance from the company and the company has a beneficial interest in them; (s. 36)

(*c*) where *any person* acquires shares in the company *with* financial assistance from the company and the company has a beneficial interest in them. (s. 54)

In each of these three cases s. 37(2) and (11) provide that the shares in question, or the company's interest in them, must, within three years from their acquisition in the case of (*a*) and (*b*) and within one year in the case of (*c*), be either *disposed of* or *cancelled* by the company. If they are cancelled the company's share capital must be diminished accordingly and if in consequence it falls below the authorised minimum, the company must apply for re-registration as a private company.

Thus in each of these cases the company's shareholding or interest will be purely temporary and the holder of the shares in question is meanwhile debarred by s. 37(3) from exercising any voting rights in respect of them.

Finally, the Companies Act 1980 places strict limits in s. 38 on the cases where a *public* company may acquire an equitable interest in its own shares by way of *security*, e.g. a lien. This topic is discussed in XX, **21**.

13. Cross-holdings. A cross-holding arises where two companies own shares in each other. We have already seen that it is lawful for a company to own shares in *another company* (**8**). It is also lawful for two companies to own shares *in each other*, though when this position is carefully considered it will be seen that if the share capital of *both* companies is regarded *as a whole*, then *that capital is always reduced by the amount of the cross-holdings*.

Thus if Mr and Mrs Smith form Company A with a share capital of 100 £1 shares, taking 40 shares each, and then Company B with a share capital of 100 £1 shares, again taking 40 shares each, and if Company A then buys the remaining 20 shares in Company B, while Company B buys the remaining 20 shares in Company A, the combined issued share capital will be 200 £1 shares, though the actual cash in both companies together will be £160.

Nevertheless, there is nothing unlawful about this situation, with one important exception: cross-holdings are lawful *provided the companies involved do not constitute a group*.

It is therefore essential to know what a group is, and how it arises.

14. The nature of a group. A group exists wherever two or more companies are in the relationship of *holding* and *subsidiary* to each other. The Act gives an important definition of a subsidiary company in s. 154.

Section 154(1) states that a company is a subsidiary of another where that other:

(*a*) is a member of it and controls the composition of the board of directors; *or*

(*b*) holds more than half its equity share capital.

This definition must be studied with the utmost care. Often students do not understand its implications.

NOTE

(1) *Observe that* (*a*) *and* (*b*) *are alternatives. Either* situation will result in a group. In order to satisfy the requirements of (*a*), the holding company *need own only one share*: the section states that it must be a member, and the ownership of a single share is enough to constitute membership. But membership alone does not suffice: the holding company must also control the composition of the board of directors. This means that, in the normal way, it has *voting control*, for the directors are appointed and removed by the company, and the company acts by a majority of votes. Usually in order to have voting control it is necessary to hold the majority of the voting shares, but sometimes *weighted voting* exists so that very few shares carry the majority of the votes, and the owner of those few shares has control without having a large shareholding.

For instance, in *Investment Trust Corporation* v. *Singapore Traction Co.* (1935), where there were 400,000 shares, a particular single share could outvote the other 399,999.

(2) *In order to satisfy the requirements of* (*b*), on the other hand, the holding company need only hold more than half of the equity share capital, and *votes are irrelevant*. The shares held may carry votes, or they may not: it is immaterial. It is common for companies to issue non-voting shares to maintain control in present hands, so that sometimes part of the equity share capital may consist of such shares. But the group relationship here depends simply on whether or not *more than half* of the equity share capital is owned by another company and not, as in (*a*), on voting control. (The Jenkins Committee felt that the definition of a subsidiary company should be based solely on control, and therefore recommended that (*b*) should be repealed. This would certainly simplify the position.)

15. Meaning of equity share capital. This is defined in s. 154(5) in language calculated to depress the most enthusiastic student. The meaning of the subsection can be more simply expressed by saying that equity share capital consists of those shares on which there is *no legal limit* either as to the *amount of dividend* payable, or as to the *participation in surplus assets* on liquidation.

Thus preference shares, which carry the right to a fixed dividend and are often precluded by the articles from participation in surplus assets on winding up, are not normally equity share capital. Participating preference shares, however (where there is no ultimate limit on the dividend payable since they participate along with the ordinary shares once a certain level has been reached), will be part of the equity share capital even if there is a limit to participation in surplus assets on liquidation.

Ordinary shares are normally equity share capital unless there are deferred shares, which carry the residue of profits after a certain level has been reached on the dividend to the ordinary shareholders. The test is always the *absence of a limit to participation* either with regard to dividends or to surplus assets. If there is a limit on *both*, the shares are not part of the equity share capital.

16. Subsidiaries of subsidiaries. Section 154(1) further states that *the subsidiary of a subsidiary is also the subsidiary of the holding company*. In other words, where Company A holds Company B (e.g. by owning more than half its equity share capital), and Company B holds Company C (by owning more than half its equity share capital), then Company C is not only the subsidiary of Company B, but also of Company A. The result is that Company A has two subsidiaries, and Company C two holding companies, while the group relationship between them is *indirect*. It arises *only because* Company B is the subsidiary of Company A and the holding company of Company C.

17. Size of groups. From these statutory provisions it will be seen that a group can be quite small, e.g. two companies, one of which is the holding company of the other, or very large, e.g. one holding company with twenty subsidiaries, which in turn have subsidiaries of their own. The chain can be very long: in theory it is infinite. Where there are several subsidiaries, the term *co-subsidiary* is sometimes used to describe their relationship with one another. Often companies in a group are said to be similar to a family, and the holding company is referred to as the "parent" company, but non-technical descriptions must be viewed with caution for it is the legal technicalities which are important here. No grand-parent has ever yet become the parent of its grandchild, despite strenuous efforts.

18. Unlawful cross-holdings. It will now be clear that in all cases where two companies are in a *direct* group relationship the holding company is a member of the subsidiary. If the relationship arises under (*a*) (*see* **14**), then the holding company must own at least one share; if it arises under (*b*), then it must own more than half the equity share capital. If, therefore, the subsidiary company owns shares in the holding company, this will be a *cross-holding*, and it may here be affected by s. 27. In fact, s. 27 is intended to cover *all* group relationships, even where they are *indirect* as described in **16** so that there is no cross-holding.

Section 27(1) states that a subsidiary company cannot be a member of its holding company, and any allotment or transfer of shares in the holding company to its subsidiary is void.

This dogmatic provision can lead to a difficult position. The section was a new one in 1948, and therefore it was obvious that when the Act came into force there would be many groups in which the subsidiary owned shares in the holding company. This suddenly became unlawful. Consequently s. 27(3) carefully provided for these circumstances, stating that where a subsidiary company owned shares in the holding company *at the commencement of the Act*, it could continue to hold them, but could not vote at meetings.

There was, however, another set of circumstances for which the section made no provision. If Company A holds 40% of the equity share capital of Company B, and Company B holds 40% of the equity share capital of Company A, then this is a lawful cross-holding because neither company is the holding company of the other (unless by any chance there is voting control) so that there is no group relationship. But if Company A acquires more than another 10% of the equity share capital of Company B, it will become the holding company and Company B will become the subsidiary.

Section 27(1) does not help us here. It states that a subsidiary company *cannot be* a member of its holding company, *but it is*. It states that an allotment or a transfer of shares *to the subsidiary* is void. But when Company B acquired its 40% holding in Company A, *it was not a subsidiary*; it did not become one until Company A acquired its additional holding raising the fraction of the equity share capital owned to more than 50%.

NOTE: The Jenkins Committee have recommended here (though for different reasons) that a future Companies Act should contain a provision similar to s. 27(3) to cover these special circumstances. This would mean that in such a case the subsidiary could continue to own the shares in the holding company, but could not vote at meetings.

19. The exceptions to s. 27(1). Finally, there are two statutory exceptions to s. 27(1). Section 27(2) expressly permits a subsidiary company to own shares in the holding company where it does so in the capacity of:

(*a*) personal representative (e.g. if the subsidiary is a banking company acting as executor to a deceased owner of shares in its holding company); *or*

(*b*) trustee, provided the equitable interest in the shares is owned by persons outside the group (e.g. if the subsidiary is a banking company appointed the trustee of a family settlement created by a settlor owning shares in the holding company).

There is one case, however, where the equitable interest may be owned by a company within the group, namely, when it arises by way of security for a loan made by a money-lending company in the ordinary course of business (e.g. where the trustee wishes to raise a temporary loan, and mortgages the shares as security to a banking company within the group).

20. Disclosure in accounts of holding and subsidiary companies. Section 3 Companies Act 1967 requires a holding company to disclose in its accounts with respect to each subsidiary:

(*a*) its name;

(*b*) if it is incorporated in Great Britain but in a different country from that in which the holding company is registered, the country in which it is registered, and if incorporated outside Great Britain, the country in which it is incorporated; and

(*c*) the class or classes of shares and the proportion of nominal value of the issued shares of each class held.

Conversely, s. 5 Companies Act 1967 requires a subsidiary company to disclose in its accounts the name of the company regarded by the directors as being its ultimate holding company and, if known to them, the country in which it is incorporated.

21. Associated companies. The expression "associated companies" is a commercial one with no precise technical legal significance. It is normally used to indicate a shareholding of 10–50% by one company in another, so that the two companies are not usually in the group relationship described in **14** above. Such a holding is often acquired for business reasons and may well lead to the formation of a group at a later date by the companies concerned.

The only recognition given by the Companies Acts to this type of relationship between companies is in regard to accounts. Section 4 Companies Act 1967 requires any company which holds:

(a) more than *one-tenth in nominal value* of the issued shares of any class of equity share capital, or

(b) shares of an amount exceeding *one-tenth of the assets*

of another company which is *not its subsidiary* to disclose in its accounts with respect to that company the same information as is required with respect to subsidiary companies (*see* **20** above).

PROGRESS TEST 11

1. What is the legal position of an infant shareholder? (**2**)

2. Can an infant subscribe the memorandum? (**2**)

3. Give an account of the statutory provisions concerning the position of personal representatives of a deceased member. (**5**)

4. Give an account of the clauses of Table A concerning the position of personal representatives of a deceased member. (**5, 6**)

5. What is the legal position of a trustee in bankruptcy regarding the shares of a bankrupt member of a company? (**7**)

6. May a company own shares in another company? (**8**)

7. How far may a company lawfully acquire its own shares? (**8, 9**)

8. What special rules applicable to nominee holdings are found in the Companies Act 1980? (**11, 12**)

9. Give an account of the statutory provisions which restrain a company from providing financial assistance to any person for the purchase of shares in itself. Are there any exceptions? (**10**)

10. What special rules apply in public companies where the company has a beneficial interest in its own shares? (**12**)

11. Explain what is meant by a cross-holding. How far are cross-holdings lawful? (**13**)

12. Define a subsidiary company. (**14**)

13. Define equity share capital. (**15**)

14. In what cases is it lawful for a subsidiary company to own shares in its holding company? (**18, 19**)

CHAPTER XII

Payment for Shares

1. Methods of payment for shares. It is essential to understand at the outset that shares must always be paid for. The company cannot give them to the allottee, for the law always seeks to ensure that the company's actual capital is at least equal to the nominal value of its issued capital.

The basic rule at common law was that as long as the company receives some consideration for the shares, it is immaterial whether they are issued for money, i.e. *cash*, or for property, goods or services, i.e. *consideration other than cash*.

This rule was given statutory form in s. 20(1) Companies Act 1980 which provides that shares allotted by a company may be paid up in *money or money's worth* (including goodwill and know-how). There are, however, three limitations on it which are applicable only to *public* companies:

(*a*) Section 20(2) Companies Act 1980 prohibits a public company from accepting payment for its shares, whether on account of the nominal value or of premium, by means of an *undertaking to do work or perform services* for the company.

The result of this prohibition is that shares in a public company must necessarily be paid up either in *cash* or in *non-cash assets*.

Section 87(3) Companies Act 1980 states that a share shall be taken to have been paid up in *cash* if the consideration is:

(*i*) cash received by the company; *or*
(*ii*) a cheque received by the company in good faith which the directors have no reason for suspecting will not be paid; *or*
(*iii*) the release of a liability of the company for a liquidated sum; *or*
(*iv*) an undertaking to pay cash to the company at a future date.

Section 87(1) states that "non-cash asset" means *any property or interest in property other than cash*.

Where a company contravenes s. 20(2) by accepting an undertaking for work or services in payment for its shares, the holder of those shares becomes liable to pay the amount of their nominal value, together with any premium, to the company, with interest at the appropriate rate.

Moreover, s. 20(4) expressly contains the provision applied by reference in s. 22(5), s. 23(6) and s. 24(10) (*see* IX, **15–20**) that where a person becomes liable through a contravention of the section to pay an amount in respect of the shares, any subsequent holder also becomes liable, jointly and severally with him, to pay that amount unless *either*:

> (*i*) he is a purchaser for value without actual notice of the contravention at the time of the purchase; *or*
>
> (*ii*) he derived title to the shares from a person who acquired them after the contravention and was not himself so liable.

Section 28 again applies to any person liable under s. 20 (*see* IX, **17**).

(*b*) Section 29 Companies Act 1980 requires shares issued by a public company to a subscriber to the memorandum in pursuance of his undertaking in it, together with any premium, to be paid up in *cash*.

(*c*) Section 47(2) Companies Act 1948, already considered in IX, **22**, requires the minimum subscription to be reckoned in *cash* in order that a public company may be able satisfactorily to finance its initial requirements.

2. The meaning of payment otherwise than in cash. If the allottee is simply buying the shares from the company and paying for them either on application (which is usual) or partly on application and partly when called upon later, no problems arise. The shares are either fully paid or partly paid according to their condition, and the only other relevant matters, namely premiums and discounts, are dealt with in this chapter.

If, however, he is providing the company with property, goods or services, there are two possible situations which should never be confused:

(*a*) *Where there is no express agreement to pay for the shares otherwise than in cash.*

It sometimes happens that a shareholder provides the company with property, goods or services for which he is owed a sum of money, and that at the same time he has taken shares in the company for which he owes a sum of money.

There are *two separate transactions* here, one under which the company is receiving some benefit for which it has agreed to pay, and another under which the allottee is receiving shares for which he must pay, and concerning which no agreement to pay otherwise than in cash has been made. There are therefore *two debts*, one from the company to the allottee, and another from the allottee to the company.

Clearly, if the two debts are for exactly the same amount of money, it would be unnecessarily complicated for the company to pay the sum owed only to receive it back again. Even if the two debts are not for exactly the same amount, it is still easier for the party who owes the bigger debt to pay the balance due after deducting the amount he is owed than for each party to pay the full amount. Consequently, provided the two debts are presently payable, the law permits them to be set off against each other. But since this arrangement is only a substitute for two cash payments, the shares issued to the allottee are still paid for in *cash*.

Thus in *Spargo's Case* (1873), S bought shares from the company at the same time as he sold a mine to the company. The two debts were due on the two transactions at the same time, and one was set off against the other as described above. HELD: The shares were paid for in cash.

(*b*) *Where there is an express agreement to pay for shares otherwise than in cash.*

If in the first place the company agrees to allot shares to a person in return for property, goods or services, the shares are then said to be issued *otherwise than for cash*. There is *only one agreement* here, under which the shares are to be paid for with property, goods or services, and it will have to be registered under s. 52 (*see* IX, **27**).

Moreover, the limitations in respect of public companies mentioned in **1** must be borne in mind.

3. Inadequate consideration in private companies. It is no longer possible for consideration to be inadequate in a public company owing to the rules introduced by the Companies Act 1980. Shares in a public company must be paid for either in cash or non-cash assets under s. 20, and non-cash assets must be valued by an independent person under s. 24. Neither of these safeguards, however, applies to a private company which may therefore lawfully accept work or services, or non-cash assets without a valuation, in payment for its shares.

In any such arrangement there is always the possibility that the property, goods or services received by the company will be over-valued, so that they will not in fact be equal to the nominal value of the shares issued in exchange. The consideration is real, but inadequate. One might expect this to be unlawful, for it has the effect of an issue of shares at a discount, but this is not the case. The law here preserves the normal contractual rule that each man is free to make a bad bargain. Consideration must be real, but need not be adequate, and as a rule the court will not inquire into the true value of the consideration received by the company in return for the shares issued.

There are, however, three cases where it will do so:

(a) Where there is *fraud*.

(b) Where it appears *on the face of the agreement* that the consideration is, or may be, inadequate.

(c) Where the consideration is in fact entirely *illusory*, i.e. unreal.

A good example of (b) occurred in *Hong Kong and China Gas Co.* v. *Glen* (1914), where the company agreed to allot *one-fifth of all future increases of capital* fully paid in return for the consideration it had received from the allottee. HELD: The agreement could not be allowed to stand, since in time the number of fully paid shares issued to the allottee might obviously become wholly disproportionate to the consideration provided by him.

4. Issue of shares at a discount. So far we have seen two cases where shares may lawfully be issued at a discount, namely, under s. 53 by way of underwriting commission and, in a private company, where they are issued in exchange for over-valued consideration as described above.

Section 21 Companies Act 1980 repeals s. 57 Companies Act 1948 and in s. 21(1) prohibits allotment at a discount in all other cases. Where shares are allotted in contravention of s. 21(1) they are treated as paid up to their nominal value less the amount of the discount, but the allottee remains liable to pay that amount to the company with interest at the appropriate rate: s. 21(2).

As usual, where the allottee is liable through a contravention of the section to pay an amount under it in respect of the shares, any subsequent holder also becomes liable, jointly and severally with him, to pay that amount unless *either*:

(a) he is a purchaser for value without actual notice of the contravention at the time of the purchase; *or* (*b*) he derived title to the shares from a person who acquired them after the contravention and was not himself so liable: s. 21(3) applying s. 20(4).

Lastly, it should be noted that s. 21, like s. 53 Companies Act 1948, applies only to shares and not to debentures which, as was pointed out in VIII, **4**, are not part of the share capital and may therefore be issued at a discount whenever required.

5. Issue of shares at a premium. In contrast to an issue at a discount, an issue of shares at a premium, i.e. at a price *above* the par or nominal value, may be made whenever desired. In practice it is usual to issue shares at a premium.

The only statutory requirement here concerns the premium, i.e. the amount in excess of the par value. This must be transferred, under s. 56(1), to the *share premium account*, whether the company is issuing the shares for cash, or otherwise than for cash, i.e. for property, goods or services which are worth more than the nominal amount of the shares issued in exchange: *Shearer* v. *Bercain* (1980).

6. The nature and uses of the share premium account. Section 56(1) makes it quite clear that the share premium account is to be regarded as *share capital* as far as reduction of capital is concerned, even though it is not, of course, divided up into shares. Section 56(2), however, allows it to be used for *four specific purposes*:

(*a*) To pay up bonus shares to be issued fully paid to members.

(*b*) To write off the preliminary expenses.

(*c*) To write off commissions or discounts, or the expenses of any issue of shares or debentures.

(*d*) To provide the premium payable on the redemption of redeemable preference shares or debentures.

The share premium account is often called a *statutory capital reserve*, since it is regarded as part of the company's capital and its use is strictly controlled by the Act. It must be disclosed in the balance sheet. The provisions of s. 56 are very important, and they will be discussed again later in XV.

PROGRESS TEST 12

1. Explain what is meant by payment for shares otherwise than in cash. **(2)**

2. What limitations exist on the allotment of shares for a consideration other than cash? **(1)**

3. In what cases may shares lawfully be issued at a discount? **(4)**

4. What is the legal effect of an unlawful issue of shares at a discount? **(4)**

5. What are the statutory requirements regarding the issue of shares at a premium? **(5)**

6. Outline the nature and uses of the share premium account. **(5, 6)**

CHAPTER XIII

The Register of Members

1. The sections to be studied. In II, **15** the register of members was listed as one of the statutory books, and in II, **14** as one of the registers and documents which the company must keep at its registered office. It must now be considered in detail.

The sections of the Act which are concerned with it range from ss. 110–118, but the student should commit to memory only the main points. These are given below, where it will be seen that s. 114 has been entirely omitted, while s. 112 has been postponed to a later chapter in which share warrants are discussed. The sections have not been dealt with in their statutory order, since s. 117 is of major importance and requires more lengthy explanation.

The provisions of ss. 119 and 120 on the dominion register are also given in this chapter.

2. The contents of the register of members. Section 110(1) requires every company to keep a register of members, and to enter in it:

(*a*) the names and addresses of members, the shares held by each member, with distinguishing numbers, if any, and the amount paid up;

(*b*) the date of entry in the register;

(*c*) the date of cessation of membership.

Stock is entered instead of shares where appropriate.

Section 118 states that the register is *prima facie* evidence of the matters inserted in it.

3. The place where the register of members must be kept. Section 110(2) requires the register of members to be kept at the registered office unless it is made up elsewhere, when it may be kept there, or by some other person, when it may be kept at his office. It may never be kept outside the domicile.

Section 110(3) states that notice must be given to the registrar of where the register is kept, and of any changes, unless it has always been kept at the registered office.

4. The index of members. Section 111(1) requires every company with more than fifty members to keep an index, unless the register is already in the form of an index. It must alter the index within fourteen days of altering the register.

Section 111(2) states that the index must indicate how the account of each member may be readily found in the register of members.

Section 111(3) requires the index to be kept at the same place as the register of members.

5. Inspection of the register of members and index. Section 113(1) states that, except when closed under the provisions of s. 115, the register of members and the index must be open to inspection by members free, and by other persons on payment of a fee, for at least two hours a day during business hours. The fee, under Statutory Instrument No. 1749 of 1980, is £1.

Section 113(2), authorises any person to require a copy of the register, or of any part of it, on payment of a fee of 30p per page: Statutory Instrument No. 1749 of 1980. The copy must be supplied within ten days.

Section 113(4) states that if inspection is refused, or a copy not sent within the ten days, the court may order that inspection be allowed or that the copy should be sent.

Section 115, however, permits the company, on giving notice in a local newspaper, to close the register for not more than thirty days in each year.

6. Rectification of the register. Section 116(1) states that if:

(a) the name of a person is entered in or omitted from the register of members without sufficient cause; *or*

(b) default or delay occurs in entering a cessation of membership;

the aggrieved person, or any member, or the company may apply to the court for rectification.

Section 116(2) states that the court may either refuse the application, or may order rectification and payment by the company of damages for losses sustained by an aggrieved party.

Section 116(3) empowers the court also to decide questions of title (i.e. ownership of the shares) and any other necessary questions.

Section 116(4) requires the court to order that notice of any rectification shall be given to the registrar.

NOTE: This useful section deserves careful study, as much for its practical as for its academic importance. Note especially the three possible applicants, and the width of the powers given to the court. Often rectification proceedings provide the only remedy available to a person who thinks that he ought to be registered as a member, but who is rejected by the company.

7. Notice of trusts. Section 117 is a short section in simple language but with far-reaching consequences. It states merely that *no notice of any trust shall be entered on the register,* but many students find the concept of the trust difficult to understand and so do not entirely follow the meaning and purpose of the section.

An attempt, therefore, has been made to give a brief explanation of the trust before embarking on the effect of the section.

8. Legal ownership. In the normal way a person accepts the idea of *ownership* without question or analysis. If a student leaves a pen-knife behind after a class, and the lecturer asks to whom it belongs, he will reply: "Mine." He seldom troubles to think of what he means because this one word, if true, gives him the right to pick it up and take it with him.

If, however, he is asked to think about it, he will readily agree that because he owns the knife he can carry it around with him, or keep it in his desk, or use it for its intended purpose of sharpening pencils, or its unintended purposes such as opening tins and bottles or slicing cucumber. He can sell it, or lend it to a friend, or hire it out to a friend at tenpence per week, or pledge it to a pawnbroker. He can throw it in the dustbin or lose it without incurring liability to anyone. In fact, the only things which he may *not* do with it are *acts unlawful in themselves*, such as stabbing the lecturer or cutting the pages out of a library book.

Provided he is acting lawfully, then, the ownership of the knife gives him the right to do a very large number of things with it, and has therefore been described as "a bundle of rights". Intangible property, like shares, can be treated in the same way within the limits of its non-physical existence. Thus the owner of shares whose name, as we have seen, normally appears on the register of members, can deal with his shares in any lawful way, and can give them to a friend, sell them, mortgage them or dispose of them by will.

When we talk of ownership in this way, we are referring to a right, or a bundle of rights, recognised and protected by the *common law*. Common law ownership is often called *legal* ownership, to distinguish it from *equitable* ownership which arises under a *trust*.

A brief account of equitable ownership is given below.

9. The origin of equitable ownership.

(*a*) The royal courts of common law had superseded the local and feudal courts and were giving general protection to litigants by the end of the thirteenth century. Their growth since the Conquest in 1066 had by this time led to jurisdiction in all types of case. It was only because the common law had severe disadvantages that the Chancellor, in his court of "equity" or *natural justice*, started to protect a petitioner who could claim merely a *moral* or *equitable* right to property, and his jurisdiction in this field did not become comprehensive until at least a century later. The first independent decree of the Chancellor in the Court of Chancery was given in 1474. Thus common law or legal ownership is historically earlier, and the idea of equitable ownership emerged afterwards to meet difficulties and defects.

(*b*) We cannot here consider all the disadvantages of the common law ownership of land, the most important type of property in mediaeval times. It is enough to know, for explanatory purposes, that a man could not devise his land by will at common law, and that all conveyances of land were required to be effected in public so that the ownership should never be in doubt. This latter rule was aimed mainly at preventing the evasion of the feudal incidents, i.e. the dues and other burdens which fell on the common law owner of land, whoever he might be. It is hardly surprising that the mediaeval landowner set out to improve his position in much the same way as the modern citizen wrestles with the Inland Revenue.

(*c*) Though the earliest examples of trusts of land appeared in the thirteenth century, it was not until the fourteenth century that it became a common practice for an owner of land to transfer it to a number of friends *on trust for himself*. By this device he had, *at common law*, no interest in the land at all, yet continued to enjoy it. As far as the common law courts were concerned, his friends owned it, and that was the end of the matter. They owned it as joint tenants, so that if any one of them died, the others merely continued as owners by the right of survivorship or *jus accrescendi*. As long as there were at least two of them, this avoided the worst of the feudal burdens, since these arose on the death of the landowner. If the original owner died, no dues became payable since at common law he was no longer connected with the land in any way. Moreover, he could dispose of the land by will by directing his friends to hold it on trust after his death for anyone he wished to name.

(*d*) Of course, at first a landowner who adopted this method of evading the disadvantages of common law ownership was taking the risk of his friends proving dishonest and taking advantage of their impregnable position at common law by depriving him of enjoyment. He had no remedy against them in that event, for at common law they were the owners and he was not. But from about the beginning of the fifteenth century the Chancellor, in the early court of equity, started to intervene to protect him.

(*e*) The Chancellor did this not by opposing the common law, but by ordering the defaulting friends to act equitably, and threatening them with imprisonment if they refused. In other words, he gave the petitioner a *remedy*, and where a court gives a remedy, the citizen has a *right*. The right here was merely in the Court of Chancery, but it was none the less effective against dishonest persons, and because it was recognised by the Chancellor in his equitable jurisdiction, it is called an *equitable right*, or, more usually, an *equitable interest*.

10. The enforceability of equitable interests. In the course of time the Chancellor protected the equitable interest of the petitioner not only against his defaulting friends, but against *any person to whom they should transfer the land* in breach of trust, with *one exception*: the petitioner *was never allowed to enforce his equitable interest against a person who took the land for valuable consideration and without notice of the equitable interest*.

From this development we can now see that there are *two essential rules* to remember:

(*a*) A legal or common law interest in property cannot be defeated by anyone.

At common law, with the exception of a sale in market overt, only the owner can deprive himself of ownership.

(*b*) An equitable interest in property can always be defeated by a *bona fide* purchaser for value of the legal interest in that property, though it cannot be defeated by anyone else.

Later these rules will be studied in relation to shares.

11. The nature of a trust. It will be seen from the above explanation that wherever there is an equitable interest in property, there is what is often called *duality of ownership*. By this expression we mean that one person is regarded as the owner of the property *at common law* (i.e. he is the *legal* owner), while another is regarded as the owner in *equity*.

Wherever this duality of ownership exists, there is a *trust*. The *legal* owner is the *trustee*, while the equitable owner is called the *beneficiary* or *cestui que trust*. There are many types of transaction which produce this duality of ownership, for the trust has developed enormously since mediaeval times, and is often said to be the most important feature of our law. An account of the occasions on which a trust arises is, however, outside the scope of this book and should be sought in manuals dealing with equity.

12. The purpose of s. 117. Let us now return to s. 117 which, as we have seen, states that *no notice of a trust shall be entered on the register of members*. It must be understood that the section does *not* say that there cannot be a trust of shares. It merely says that if there is a trust, it must not be entered on the register. We already know that the correct entry in the register is the name of the member, i.e. the person who *owns* the shares. This, of course, is the person who is the *legal* or *common law* owner, the *trustee* in the case of a trust. It is the *equitable* owner who must be kept off the register, whom the company must not recognise. Note that this is a purely *administrative* section. Its whole object is to simplify administration from the company's viewpoint.

There are in fact *two main reasons* for the section. First, it is possible for *several equitable interests* to arise in a single piece of property. Thus there can be several equitable interests in one holding of shares, while the legal ownership is in the member whose name is on the register. It is therefore possible for a dispute to arise among the owners of the equitable interests as to which of them has priority, i.e. the better claim to the shares.

If their names were to appear on the register, the company might be involved in this dispute, and therefore to prevent the company from being implicated in lengthy argument as to which owner of an equitable interest in the shares has priority, the section simply forbids the company from taking any notice of equitable interests at all. It is concerned solely with the *legal* owner, and if he happens to be a trustee and decides to commit a flagrant breach of trust, the company is not to blame unless it has actual knowledge not only of the trust, but also of the breach—a very unlikely circumstance.

NOTE: An extreme example of the protection afforded to the company can be seen in *Simpson* v. *Molsons' Bank* (1895), where the company registered a transfer of shares by executors (who are trustees) in breach of the terms of the will of the deceased. The Act incorporating the company provided that it should not be bound to see to the execution of any trust to which its shares were subject. The company had a copy of the will in its possession and its president was one of the defaulting executors and the testator's brother. The company and the executors employed the same law agent. It was held that though the company knew that the shares in question were held by the executors in that capacity, it had no knowledge of their breach of trust, and the knowledge of the executor and law agent could not be imputed to the company so as to affect it with liability.

Without a statutory provision of this kind a company might never dare to register a transfer of shares at all, for fear that it might be party to a breach of trust. Later it will be seen that equivalent provisions exist with regard both to the register of directors' interests (XXII, **17**), and to the register of interests in voting share capital (XX, **13**), and that while equitable interests must be shown on both these registers, the company is protected from involvement.

Secondly, it is a rule of equity that anyone who meddles with trust property becomes himself a trustee. If the company, therefore, were able to recognise trusts it might become concerned with trust property and so become a trustee, with all the attendant duties and liabilities. This is hardly the proper function of a trading company, and so the section prevents this result from occurring by entirely precluding the company from recognising trusts.

13. Priority of equitable interests. Although s. 117 simplifies the position of the company, it is still sometimes necessary to know how the priority of equitable interests is regulated if there should be several in a single shareholding.

There are *two basic rules* for this:

(*a*) If none of the owners of the equitable interests has succeeded in getting his name put on the company's register of members, then the person whose equitable interest is the earliest has priority.

This rule is often much more neatly expressed by the equitable

maxim: *Where the equities are equal, the first in time prevails.* By
"equal" here is meant that the *moral* or *equitable* claims of the
persons concerned are all equally good. Priority must obviously
be regulated by something, so it is based on time.

Thus in *Peat* v. *Clayton* (1906), C assigned his property, including some shares, to P who never obtained the share certificates and never became the registered holder, so that he had
merely an equitable interest in them. C subsequently sold the
shares to a purchaser who, under the contract of sale, also
obtained an equitable interest in the shares. Before either party
became registered, P started proceedings claiming that he had
the prior equity and therefore the right to have the shares registered in his name. HELD: He was entitled to registration. (He
had in fact notified the company of his equitable interest, but
the notice was of course quite ineffective because of the section, and his priority depended simply on the rule given
above.)

(b) If any one of the owners of the equitable interests succeeds
in getting his name put on the register of members, so that he
becomes the *legal* owner of the shares, the equitable interests of
other persons, even though created earlier, will be destroyed provided he acted *bona fide*.

This rule is expressed by the equitable maxim: *Where the
equities are equal, the law prevails.* By "law" here is meant the
common law, and we have already seen (**10**) that an equitable
interest has a single but important weakness: it can be destroyed
by what Maitland describes as that "extremely rare and extremely lucky person"—the *bona fide* purchaser for value of the
legal interest in the property.

The good faith of the person who succeeds in getting registered
is an essential factor.

Thus in *Coleman* v. *London County and Westminster Bank*
(1916), a debenture-holder transferred some debentures to a
trustee on trust for his own sons, but the transfer was never
registered so that the legal interest remained in the original
holder. One of the sons sold his equitable interest to a purchaser. Many years later the registered holder deposited the
debentures with the bank as security, thus giving the bank an
equitable interest in them. When the bank discovered that a
purchaser of an equitable interest in the debentures already
existed, it applied for registration and succeeded in becoming

registered as the legal owner. HELD: It could not obtain priority over the earlier equitable interest in this way, for it was not acting *bona fide*. It *knew* that the earlier interest existed.

These rules are easy to apply provided they are carefully learnt. It cannot be sufficiently stressed that the priority of equitable interests in shares or debentures is regulated by time, but that all equitable interests can be destroyed by a *bona fide* purchaser for value of the legal interest in the property.

14. The stop notice. The student may at this stage feel that the owner of an equitable interest is in a very difficult position. He may not tell the company that he has such an interest, because if he does the company is simply not concerned with the information. Section 117 says so. Consequently he must remain in a precarious state: he has an interest in shares of which the registered holder is the legal owner. How can he protect himself against the holder's dishonesty? If he discovers that the holder is defrauding him, he can of course start legal proceedings. But how can he find out *in time*, i.e. before a *bona fide* purchaser for value has become the registered holder and so defeated his equitable interest entirely?

The answer is that there is a simple process by which he can compel the company to inform him of a pending transfer of the shares. This is to serve on the company a *stop notice* (formerly known as a notice in lieu of distringas), under Order 50, Rules of the Supreme Court, 1965.

The effect of this notice is that the company becomes bound to inform the person serving it of any request to transfer the shares. Thus the owner of the equitable interest will be told of any impending threat to his position. He can then, if he likes, apply to the court within eight days for an injunction restraining the company from transferring the shares. If he does not do so, the company may register the transfer in the normal way.

NOTE: The company is not concerned with the equitable interest; its sole duty is to inform the owner of an impending transfer of the shares. It is entirely up to him to protect his equitable interest by application to the court, and if he does not wish to do this the company is under no obligation to protect it for him.

15. Legal position where company acquires equitable interest. One final problem can arise where *the company itself* acquires an equitable interest in the shares of a member, e.g. under its lien. It will be seen later that where the articles of a company give it a lien on the shares of a member for money due in respect of them, the lien is an equitable interest.

If in such a case there were already earlier equitable interests in the shares, and if a dispute broke out between their owners and the company so that all claimed to be entitled to the legal ownership of the shares, it might be thought that s. 117 gives the company an unfair advantage in that it prevents the company from having notice of the equitable interests of other persons.

This is not so. The rule applying here is that *the company's equitable interest ranks after any prior equitable interest of which it knows*, and *it cannot rely on s. 117 to say that it does not know*. It must always be borne in mind that the purpose of s. 117 is administrative convenience, and not to place the company in a better legal position than the holders of other equitable interests.

Thus in *Bradford Banking Co.* v. *Briggs* (1886), the articles gave the company a lien on the shares for the debts of a member. A member deposited his share certificate with the bank as security, thus giving the bank an equitable interest. The bank notified the company— a notice which in the normal way would be completely ineffective because of s. 117. The member then became indebted to the company, so that a second equitable interest in his shares was created under the company's lien. The question of the priority of the interests arose. HELD: The bank had priority, since s. 117 never operates to deprive the company of notice of an equitable interest *when the company itself is involved*. It gives no undeserved priority.

16. The dominion register. Section 119(1) states that a company with a share capital whose objects comprise the transaction of business in any part of Her Majesty's dominions outside Great Britain may keep there a branch register of members resident there, called a dominion register.

Section 119(2) requires the company to give notice to the registrar of the office where the dominion register is kept, and of any changes in that office, and of the discontinuance of the register, within fourteen days.

Section 120(1) states that the dominion register is deemed part of the company's principal register, and s. 120(2) requires it to be kept in the same manner as the principal register.

Section 120(3) requires the company to:

(*a*) send to its registered office a copy of every entry in its dominion register as soon as possible; and

(*b*) keep a duplicate of the dominion register at the place where its principal register is kept.

PROGRESS TEST 13

1. What are the contents of the register of members? (**2**)

2. What are the statutory requirements as to the index of members? (**4**)

3. What rights of inspection of the register and index of members are given by the Act? Can the register of members ever be closed? (**5**)

4. Who may apply for rectification of the register of members, and under what circumstances? (**6**)

5. What are the powers of the court when application is made for rectification of the register? (**6**)

6. What are the provisions of s. 117? What is their purpose? (**12**)

7. What are the rules for determining the priority of equitable interests in shares? (**13**)

8. What is a stop notice? (**14**)

9. What is the legal position where a company acquires an equitable interest in its own shares? (**15**)

10. Give an account of the statutory provisions concerning the dominion register. (**16**)

CHAPTER XIV

The Annual Return, the Accounts and other Statutory Duties of Disclosure

THE ANNUAL RETURN

1. The duty to make the annual return. Section 124(1) states that every company with a share capital must, at least once in every calendar year, make a return to the registrar in accordance with the 6th Schedule.

It need not, however, do so in the year of its incorporation, nor in the following year if s. 131 does not require it to hold an annual general meeting in that year.

Section 131(1) states that although a company must hold an annual general meeting every calendar year, and that not more than fifteen months may elapse between such meetings, it need not hold one in the year of its incorporation nor the following year provided the first annual general meeting is held within eighteen months of incorporation.

Thus a company incorporated in September, 1979, need not hold an annual general meeting or make an annual return in either 1979 or 1980, since it can hold its first annual general meeting early in 1981 without infringing the regulations.

2. The contents of the annual return. The 6th Schedule states that the contents of the annual return are:

(*a*) The address of the registered office.

(*b*) The address where the registers of members and debenture-holders are kept, if they are kept elsewhere.

(*c*) A summary distinguishing between shares issued for cash and shares issued as paid up otherwise than in cash, stating:

(*i*) The amount of share capital and the number of shares.

(*ii*) The number of shares taken up to the date of the return.

(*iii*) The amount called up, received and unpaid.

(*iv*) Commission and discount in respect of shares or debentures.

(*v*) Forfeitures.

(*vi*) Details of share warrants.

(*d*) Total amount of indebtedness in respect of registrable charges.

(*e*) A list containing:

   (*i*) The names and addresses of those who are members on the fourteenth day after the annual general meeting, and of those who have ceased to be members since the date of the last return.

   (*ii*) The number of shares held by each member, stating the shares transferred since the date of the last return.

   (*iii*) An index of names where necessary.

(*f*) Particulars of the directors and secretary.

This very important list of contents has been shortened and slightly re-arranged to facilitate learning, but it has been reduced to its minimum and every student should make sure that he is thoroughly familiar with it.

Section 124(1) also states that if the company has converted its shares into stock, the return should give the same particulars with regard to the stock as are required for shares. Moreover, it only requires a complete list of members and their holdings every third year. In the intervening years only changes need be given.

All statements in the return are admissible as evidence of the truth of their contents: *R.* v. *Halpin* (1975).

3. The time for completion of the annual return. Section 126(1) states that the annual return must be completed within 42 days after the annual general meeting, and the company must at once send a copy signed by a director and the secretary to the registrar.

There is a registration fee of £20: Statutory Instrument No. 1749 of 1980.

THE ACCOUNTS

4. The accounting reference period. Section 2(1) Companies Act 1976 permits any company to give notice to the registrar within six months from incorporation specifying a date on which, in each calendar year, the accounting reference period of the company is to end.

If the company gives such a notice, then the specified date becomes, under s. 2(2), the company's *accounting reference date*. If no such notice is given, the accounting reference date is 31st March.

Section 3(1) Companies Act 1976 permits a company to alter

its *current and all subsequent* accounting reference periods by giving notice to the registrar at any time in the course of a period specifying a new accounting reference date. Section 3(2) permits a holding or subsidiary company (*see* XI, **14–16**) to alter its *previous and all subsequent* reference periods by giving notice to the registrar at any time after the end of a period specifying a new accounting reference date which *coincides* with the accounting reference date of its subsidiary or holding company, as the case may be.

5. The delivery of accounts to the registrar. Section 127 has been repealed and replaced by s. 1(7) Companies Act 1976 which requires the directors, in respect of each accounting reference period of the company, to deliver to the registrar a copy of *every document required to be comprised in the accounts*.

The documents required to be comprised in the accounts are, under s. 1(5) and s. 8(1) Companies Act 1976:

(*a*) the profit and loss account;
(*b*) the balance sheet;
(*c*) the auditors' report;
(*d*) the directors' report; and
(*e*) where a company has subsidiaries, group accounts.

Section 1(8) Companies Act 1976 exempts from this duty the directors of an *unlimited company*, provided that during that accounting reference period:

(*a*) the company was not, to its knowledge, the subsidiary of a limited company;
(*b*) there were not, to its knowledge, held or exercisable by *two or more* limited companies shares or powers which, if held or exercisable by *one* of them, would have made it the subsidiary of that company;
(*c*) it was not the holding company of a limited company;
(*d*) it was not carrying on business as the promoter of a trading stamp scheme.

Section 9(3)(*d*) European Communities Act 1972, as amended by s. 1(10) Companies Act 1976, requires the registrar to publish in the *Gazette* the receipt by him of any documents delivered by a company under s. 1(7) Companies Act 1976.

6. The laying of accounts before the general meeting. Section 148 has been repealed and replaced by s. 1(6) Companies Act 1976 which requires the directors, in respect of each accounting reference period of the company, to lay before the company in general meeting a copy of *every document required to be comprised in the accounts* (*see* **5**).

7. Period allowed for laying and delivering accounts. Section 6(2) Companies Act 1976 provides that the period allowed for laying and delivering accounts (*see* **5** and **6**) shall be:

(a) in the case of a private company, ten months after the end of the accounting reference period;

(b) in the case of a public company, seven months after the end of the accounting reference period.

8. Signature of balance sheet. Section 155(1), as amended by the Companies Act 1976, requires every balance sheet of a company, and every copy of it laid before the company in general meeting or delivered to the registrar under s. 1 Companies Act 1976, to be signed by two directors on behalf of the board or, in the case of a sole director, by that director.

9. Profit and loss account and auditors' and directors' reports. Section 156(1), as amended by the Companies Act 1976, requires the company's profit and loss account and any group accounts of a holding company to be annexed to the balance sheet.

The auditors' report, under s. 156(1), and the directors' report, under s. 157(1), must be attached to the balance sheet.

OTHER STATUTORY DUTIES OF DISCLOSURE

10. Disclosure under the Industry Act 1975. Section 28 Industry Act 1975 authorises the Secretary of State or the Minister of Agriculture, Fisheries and Food to require certain information from companies wholly or mainly engaged in the *manufacturing industry*.

The information required must be necessary in the Minister's opinion:

(a) to form or further national economic policies; *or*

(b) for consultation between Government, employers or workers on the outlook for the industry.

Furthermore, the Minister must consider that:

(a) the company makes a significant contribution to a sector of the industry which is important to the economy, and

(b) it is desirable that the company should provide the

Government and the representatives of the trade unions concerned with the information.

Section 34 imposes a fine not exceeding £400 for:

(a) refusal or failure without reasonable cause to comply with the requirements of the Act; *or*
(b) knowingly or recklessly making a false statement in doing so.

Where the offence is committed by a company with the consent or connivance of an officer of that company, or is due to his neglect, the officer as well as the company is liable to the fine.

Section 30 states that the Minister may require information regarding *the following matters only*:

(a) employees;
(b) capital expenditure;
(c) fixed capital assets and their disposal and acquisition;
(d) productive capacity and capital utilisation;
(e) output and productivity;
(f) sales and exports of products;
(g) sales of industrial or intellectual property;
(h) expenditure on research and development.

Section 30(5) expressly excludes the Minister's right to information about the details of any research or development programme.

11. Disclosure under the Employment Protection Act 1975. Section 17 Employment Protection Act 1975 imposes a duty on an *employer* (whether a company or not) to disclose to the representatives of the trade unions concerned all information about the undertaking in his possession:

(a) without which the trade union representatives would be impeded in carrying on collective bargaining with the employer; and
(b) which it would be in accordance with good industrial relations practice to disclose for the purposes of collective bargaining.

Section 100 of the same Act requires any employer proposing to dismiss as redundant:

(a) 100 or more employees at one establishment within 90 days or less; *or*
(b) 10 or more employees at one establishment within 30 days or less,

to notify the Secretary of State and the representatives of any trade union concerned.

The Secretary of State may then require the employer to give him further information.

Section 105(1) imposes a fine not exceeding £400 for failure to give notice to the Secretary of State in compliance with s. 100. Section 117(1) states that where an offence is committed by a company with the consent or connivance of an officer of that company, or is due to his neglect, the officer as well as the company is liable to the fine.

PROGRESS TEST 14

1. What are the statutory provisions regarding the duty to make the annual return?   (1)

2. What are the contents of the annual return?   (2)

3. Within what period must the annual return be completed, and who is required to sign the copy sent to the registrar?   (3)

4. What documents are required to be comprised in the accounts and what duties are imposed by the Companies Acts on the directors in respect of them?   (5–8)

CHAPTER XV

Capital

1. The meaning of capital. The word "capital" is as variable in meaning as the word "company". It means different things to different people, and in particular a lawyer will think of it in a different way from an accountant, and both of them will be perplexed by the economist. Since many students learn Company Law at the same time as Accounting and Economics, it is no wonder that they sometimes find definition impossible.

Most ordinary people—and lawyers, as far as Accounting is concerned, are ordinary people—think of capital as *something the company has got*. It has got the money which it has raised by the issue of shares. It uses this money to buy the things which it needs, such as business premises and stock-in-trade, and these things are then called the *fixed* capital and the *circulating* capital respectively. Always the concept of capital is a *positive* one, based on the notion that what the company has obtained by issuing shares to members it must preserve at all costs.

There is nothing wrong with this idea and the lawyer survives happily until he looks at a company's balance sheet. Here he finds on the left-hand side clearly headed "Liabilities" not only the share capital of the company, but also the debentures or "loan capital" and, what is even worse, the trade creditors.

Slowly the truth begins to dawn upon him that the accountant thinks of capital in a *negative* way as *something the company owes*. The share capital is owed to the members, the loan capital is owed to the debenture-holders, and the trade debts are owed to the trade creditors. Almost certainly he will then wish that he knew some accounting principles, but when he asks an accountant for assistance he will probably be told that the idea of capital as a debt of the company flows directly from the law. Did not *Salomon* v. *Salomon & Co.* show that a company is a separate legal person from the members? Why, then, should the money contributed by the members to the company not be regarded as a debt due back to them? What could be more logical? The lawyer will be compelled to agree, but his viewpoint will have been disturbed. The accountant sounds as though he knows what he is talking about, and the lawyer has suddenly seen the picture from a new angle.

NOTE: The only advice which can safely be given to students on this point is to tread warily and always try to find out in what sense the book or the lecturer is using the word "capital". Unless the term is defined at the beginning, any subsequent discussion will be both useless and dangerous.

In this chapter it is used in the sense adopted by most legal textbooks and means *share capital*, i.e. the money raised by the issue of shares. Money raised by the issue of *debentures* is simply money which the company has *borrowed* at a fixed rate of interest and *is not capital in this sense*, though the confusing expression "loan capital" is often used in books on business management and economics to mean money raised in this way.

2. The use of the word. There are many expressions involving the use of the word "capital". The *issued capital* of the company, for instance, means as a rule the share capital which has been allotted to members, although "issue" is also a variable word and is not always used in this sense. The *paid-up capital* means that amount of the issued capital which has been paid up by members, so that if the shares are not fully paid this will leave the *unpaid capital* which is the amount still unpaid on the issued capital and which can be called up at any time that it is required. The issued capital can of course never exceed the *nominal* or *authorised* capital, i.e. the figure given in the capital clause of the memorandum of association, and if it is desired to issue more shares than the number authorised by this clause, then the nominal capital must be increased to cover the required amount. In this chapter the method of doing this and of making other alterations to capital will be discussed.

Section 9(7) European Communities Act 1972 provides that if there is a reference to the company's share capital on its business stationery or order forms, that reference must be to the *paid-up* share capital.

3. Reserve capital. Lastly, there is the *reserve capital*. This must never be confused with a *capital reserve*, which is entirely different. *Reserve capital can only be created under s. 60*, and if one turns to s. 60 the expression is clearly explained. Note that the margin of the Act refers to the reserve *liability*, while the section itself states how this reserve capital or liability is created. It provides that a company may determine by special resolution that its uncalled capital (i.e. the amount of the issued capital which is still unpaid and which has not yet been called up by the directors) may not be called up except on liquidation.

Once the company has created reserve capital in this way, it cannot charge it as it can the uncalled capital. (It will be remembered that a charge on uncalled capital is one of the nine types of registrable charge mentioned in s. 95(2): II, **18**.) The reserve capital is not under the directors' control, and once the special resolution creating it has been passed, it cannot be revoked except under a scheme of arrangement with the consent of the court, for to do so would be a threat to the position of creditors who are relying on the existence of this fund of money. Reserve capital can, however, like all share capital, be reduced under s. 66 with the consent of the court.

Since it is possible to charge the uncalled capital, a difficult situation can arise if the company converts into reserve capital uncalled capital which has already been charged. In this case it would be injurious to the secured creditor with a charge on the uncalled capital if his charge could be destroyed by the simple expedient of converting the uncalled capital into reserve capital. The position here, therefore, is probably that the charge remains outstanding, although any further charges on what is now reserve capital are not permissible.

4. The meaning of capital reserve. As stated above, it is very important that the *reserve capital* should not be confused with a *capital reserve*, and the meaning of the latter will now be considered.

The only assistance provided by the Act on this point is in para. 27 of the 8th Schedule. This Schedule has now been extensively amended by s. 9 Companies Act 1967 in accordance with the 1st Schedule of that Act. The entire Schedule is set out in its amended form in the 2nd Schedule of that Act, and para. 27 gives us the meaning attached by the Schedule to the words *provision* and *reserve*. It states that:

(*a*) *Provision* means, *inter alia*, an amount retained to provide for any *known liability of which the amount cannot be determined with substantial accuracy*.

(*b*) *Reserve* does not include an amount retained to provide for any *known liability* or any sum set aside to be used *to prevent undue fluctuations in charges for taxation*.

It no longer distinguishes between capital and revenue reserves, presumably because this distinction, apart from the two *statutory* capital reserves mentioned in **5** (*see* XII, **6** and XV, **10**), is not a matter of law at all, but a matter of expedience. Paragraph 27 of the 8th Schedule of the Companies Act 1948 drew a distinction between *an amount regarded as free for distribution* (a revenue reserve) and *an amount not regarded as free for distribution* (a capital reserve), so that the nature of a reserve was determined by whether it was regarded as distributable. This is doubtless still the case, but practice here will follow policy, so that legal definition is out of place.

These matters often puzzle the student, especially if he has never studied accounting, but perhaps they become clearer if one tries to take a very simple view of a company's position. If the company owes a *precise sum of money* to a creditor, this is a *liability*. It knows that it has a debt, and it knows the exact amount of that debt. If it sets aside a sum of money to meet a debt which it knows that it owes, though it *does not yet know the exact amount*, this is called a *provision*. If it sets aside a sum of money merely out of prudence, and not because it has a known debt in mind, then this is a *reserve*. If this reserve is regarded as *free for distribution* to the members, it is a *revenue reserve*, and if not, it is a *capital reserve*.

5. Types of capital reserve. It is clear that a revenue reserve is profit retained in the business, but which is distributable to the members when desired. It is also clear that a *capital* reserve is a fund which is not regarded as distributable in this way. But in fact there are two types of capital reserve:

(*a*) Those the use of which is strictly controlled by the Act, which impliedly makes them non-distributable by stating the only purposes for which they may be used.

These are:

(*i*) the *share premium account* (s. 56); and

(*ii*) the *capital redemption reserve fund* (s. 58).

They are often termed the *statutory* capital reserves, since the Act controls both their creation and their use.

(*b*) Those the use of which is not controlled by the Act, and which are therefore often termed the *non-statutory* capital reserves. Their only characteristic is that they are *not regarded as free for distribution* to the members, but since they are not controlled by the Act in any way, they can in theory become regarded as free for distribution if desired and transferred to revenue reserve. This might be imprudent, but it would not be unlawful.

Non-statutory capital reserves can arise in several ways, e.g. where a fund is set aside out of profits to replace assets which are wearing out, such as heavy machinery. A well-managed company is one in which the directors plan for the future, and it would be imprudent not to provide for such demands on the company's resources.

NOTE: In the next chapter we shall see that, provided the rules on dividends are observed, there is no *legal* bar to distribution of such funds to the members, though in most cases good management requires their retention in the company's hands. Accountants as a body tend to regard all capital reserves as non-distributable, and view the legal position with gloomy mistrust, but this is due to the belief held by all the members of that profession—or at least by all those known to the author—that caution is the greatest of all virtues. They doubtless greet the strict rules on dividends introduced by the Companies Act 1980 with sanguine expectations of more to come.

6. Reserve fund. Students may be required to distinguish capital reserves from reserve capital, or asked for examples of capital reserves, or for the meaning of the capital redemption reserve fund, which will be explained later in this chapter. But the simple expression "reserve fund" is normally used to mean a sum of money which the company has invested in a readily realisable asset so that it can be made available quickly when needed. It has no technical legal significance.

7. Types of share capital. The shares in any company may be all exactly alike, i.e. they may all carry the same rights to attend and vote at company meetings and to dividends. But often they are of different types with varying rights; in this case the company is said to have different *classes* of shares, and the rights attached to the different classes are called *class rights*. The class rights normally relate to voting, dividends or the return of capital in liquidation, and they will be set out either in the memorandum or articles of association of the company or in the terms of issue of the shares concerned.

Section 33(1) Companies Act 1980 provides that any company allotting shares with rights which are *not* stated in the memorandum, the articles, or a resolution required to be filed with the registrar under s. 143 Companies Act 1948 (*see* XXIII, **39**), and which are not uniform with shares previously allotted, must deliver to the registrar, within one month from the allotment, a statement containing particulars of those rights.

Similarly, under s. 33(3) and (4), where rights attached to shares are varied (*see* **14**), or a class of shares is given a name or other designation, *otherwise* than by an amendment of the memorandum or articles or a resolution required to be filed with the registrar under s. 143, a statement containing particulars of the variation, name or designation must be delivered to the registrar within one month.

These provisions ensure that in all cases, including that where the rights attached to shares are contained in or varied by an *ordinary* resolution, full details of the company's share capital reach the registrar who is then required, under s. 9(3) European Communities Act 1972 as amended by para. 45 of the 3rd Schedule to the Companies Act 1980, to publish his receipt of the statement in the *Gazette*.

There are the following types of share in existence:

    (*a*) Preference shares.
    (*b*) Redeemable preference shares.
    (*c*) Ordinary shares.
    (*d*) Deferred shares.

8. Preference shares. The characteristic of the preference share is that it has a *preferred fixed dividend*, i.e. that the dividend payable on it is fixed at a certain figure, e.g. 7%, and that this dividend must be paid *before* the ordinary shareholders receive anything.

It follows that preference shares are a safe, though far from stimulating, investment, and that when economic conditions are unstable they will be more in demand than when there is a period of prosperous growth or of inflation. On the other hand, nothing is more distressing than to own preference shares in a well-managed company which is making large profits. While the bulk of these profits will be distributed to the ordinary shareholders, whose shares will consequently rise on the market, the preference shareholder will continue to receive his modest fixed percentage. There are thus far more fluctuations in the market value of ordinary shares than of preference shares, providing more excitement to compensate for the greater risk.

Preference shares can be either:

(*a*) *Cumulative*, i.e. if the company is unable to pay a dividend in any particular year, it must *accumulate* the arrears of dividend on the preference shares from year to year until they are all paid, before the ordinary shareholders can receive any of the profits; *or*

(*b*) *Non-cumulative*, i.e. if the company is unable to pay a dividend in any particular year, the preference shareholder will never receive any dividend for that year.

NOTE: They are always *presumed to be cumulative* unless expressly described as non-cumulative.

Preference shares sometimes carry voting rights, but often carry different ones from those of the ordinary shares, or none at all.

Sometimes a company issues *participating* preference shares. These are preference shares which receive their fixed dividend, e.g. 6%, in the normal way, but which then *participate further* in the distributed profits along with the ordinary shares after a certain fixed percentage has been paid on them as well. Note that a participating preference share will be part of the equity share capital unless it participates in profits only up to a further fixed percentage and there is also some restriction on its right to participate in surplus assets in a liquidation.

9. The rights attached to preference shares in a liquidation. In IV, **5** the order of distribution of assets in a liquidation was given. There it was seen that preference shares do not, contrary to popular belief, carry any priority to return of capital in a liquidation unless the memorandum or articles or the terms of issue confer it on them. Such a provision is, however, a common one and where it is made the preference shares *will not have any right to participate in the distribution of the surplus assets*. The right to receive the capital back in priority to the ordinary shareholders is said to be *exhaustive*, i.e. it implies that there is no right to receive anything more, and therefore if in such a case it is desired that the preference shares should also participate in the surplus assets, this right must be *expressly* given to them: *Scottish Insurance Corporation* v. *Wilsons and Clyde Coal Co.* (1949).

Difficulty sometimes arises over the payment of *arrears of dividend* on cumulative preference shares in a liquidation. Clearly, any dividend which has been declared must be paid, for it is a debt. But arrears of dividend, i.e. dividends which have *not* been declared, are not payable in a liquidation *unless the articles so provide*, for they do not constitute a debt. Moreover, the articles must provide for the payment of *arrears*. If they merely provide for payment of *arrears due*, the arrears of dividend will again not be payable unless they have been declared, for the word "due" indicates that the sum is owing and therefore is a debt.

10. Redeemable preference shares. In the normal way shares are not redeemable except in a reduction of capital effected with the consent of the court under s. 66, for if the company could give the members their money back at any time it wished, the creditors could not rely on the company having any money at all. For the same reason it is unlawful for any company to try to *convert* any of its share capital into redeemable preference shares and then to redeem it.

It is, however, lawful to *issue* preference shares which are from the very beginning redeemable, either at a fixed date or after a certain period of time, provided the company complies with the conditions laid down in s. 58(1), as amended by the Companies Act 1980. These conditions are as follows:

(*a*) There must be authority in the articles to make the issue.

(*b*) The shares may be redeemed only out of distributable profits (*see* XVI, **3–5**) or the proceeds of a fresh issue of shares made for the purpose.

(*c*) The shares may be redeemed only if they are fully paid.

(*d*) If there is a premium payable on redemption, it must have been provided out of distributable profits or out of the share premium account before the shares are redeemed.

(*e*) Where the shares are redeemed out of profits, a sum equal to the nominal amount of the shares redeemed is to be transferred out of profits to the *capital redemption reserve fund*. This fund, as we have already seen, is a *statutory capital reserve*, and s. 58(1) expressly states that it is to be treated as *share capital* for reduction purposes, though s. 58(5) allows it to be used for paying up *bonus shares*.

Note how these provisions maintain the capital of the company. If the redeemable preference shares are redeemed out of the proceeds of a fresh issue of shares (which do not have to be redeemable preference shares themselves), then the capital is automatically replaced and no capital redemption reserve fund is required. But if they are redeemed out of distributable profits, then no shares are issued to replace those redeemed, and a capital reserve must be formed in order to keep the total capital of the company constant. This capital reserve may be used for paying up bonus shares, but this merely converts it into share capital as opposed to a capital fund which is not divided into shares. The non-distributable funds are preserved throughout, for the total capital of the company does not alter (*see* XI, **9**).

Section 58(4) states that where a company makes a fresh issue of shares up to the nominal amount of the shares redeemed, this is not to be regarded as an increase of capital for stamp duty purposes, provided the redemption takes place within a month after the making of the fresh issue.

Section 62 provides that notice of the redemption must be given to the registrar within one month. The registrar must then, under s. 9(3) European Communities Act 1972 as amended by para. 45 of the 3rd Schedule to the Companies Act 1980, publish his receipt of the notice in the *Gazette*.

11. Ordinary shares. Ordinary shares normally carry the residue of distributed profits after the preference shares, if any, have received their fixed dividend. If the preference shareholders have priority as to return of capital in liquidation, the ordinary shares will then be entitled to all the surplus assets unless there are also deferred shares. Thus as a rule the ordinary shares are the *equity share capital* of the company.

(*a*) *Voting rights.* While preference shares often carry no voting rights, ordinary shares usually give the holder the right to vote; but this is not invariably the case. In some companies both voting and non-voting ordinary shares are issued, and this practice has been much criticised on several grounds. In principle, it is often thought to be wrong to divorce ownership from control so that those who may have invested the largest amount of money in the company may have no voice whatsoever in its management. Moreover, investors may not realise that their shares give them no voting rights until after they have bought them.

(*b*) *Control.* It is, however, always possible to keep control in the hands of a minority by the device of *weighted voting rights*, without issuing any non-voting shares, and it is sometimes desirable to be able to raise more capital without losing control. For these and other reasons the Jenkins Committee recommended no change in the law with regard to the legality of issuing non-voting shares, though it is thought advisable to give the fullest publicity to the fact that such shares carry no votes, and to give notice of all general meetings and a copy of the chairman's statement to the holders.

12. Deferred shares. Deferred shares are also known as *founders' shares* or *management shares*, since they are often held by the promoters of the company. They are not at all common nowadays.

They usually give the holders the right to the residue of distributed profits after a certain fixed dividend has been paid on the ordinary shares. It follows that in such a case the deferred shares, not the ordinary shares, will constitute the equity share capital of the company.

13. No par value shares. So far all the types of share which we have considered have had a *par* or *nominal value*. This is because, as was explained in II, **41**, shares with no par value cannot be issued in this country, though they exist in certain other countries, notably in the United States.

The rule that shares must have a par value is frequently criticised on two main grounds:

(*a*) The present form of balance sheet is linked to the figure of the nominal capital. This figure is almost certain to become entirely unrealistic in the course of time, for as the company's business expands and becomes more profitable, the market value of the shares will rise, bearing little or no relation to the original par value.

(*b*) Dividends are often declared in the form of a percentage of the nominal value. Thus a dividend of 25% on shares with a par value of £1 but a market value of £5 gives the investor a yield of 5% on his money, and although this is in fact a reasonable figure, it may not appear so to those who do not understand it. Consequently the Jenkins Committee adopted the view expressed by an earlier committee and recommended that shares of no par value should be permitted. The recommendation extends for the first time to *preference* shares which, according to the Committee, would have the following advantages if issued with no par value:

(*a*) They would be less misleading to the investor. If a preference share is described as a 9% preference share, but its market value falls below the price of issue owing to a rise in the market rate of interest, then the yield to the investor who buys at this stage will be more than 9%.

(b) They would enable the company to issue blocks of preference shares which would all rank *pari passu* although issued at different times when there are different market rates of interest, because the price of issue could be varied to suit the demands of the moment. This would increase the marketability of the shares, and be simpler from the company's viewpoint.

It is, however, increasingly unlikely that these recommendations will be implemented, for the company law systems of the other EEC Member States all require shares to have a par value.

14. Variation of rights. We have already seen in **7** that sometimes all the shares in a company are exactly alike, and sometimes they are divided up into different classes. We also saw that the rights attached to the shares are normally to be found in the memorandum, articles or terms of issue. These rights are described as "class rights" only where there are different classes of shares in existence, in which case s. 33 ensures that the registrar receives particulars of them if they are not contained in a document already in his possession (*see* **7**). It is now necessary to consider how these rights can be altered and for this purpose to study each of the two possible situations separately.

Where all the shares in a company are *exactly alike*, the rights—which will not, of course, be class rights—may be specified either in the articles or in the memorandum. If specified in the articles, they may be altered in the same way as any other clause in the articles, i.e. by special resolution. If specified in the memorandum, however, the clause will be covered by s. 23 Companies Act 1948.

This section, as we saw in II, **42**, covers with certain exceptions all the clauses in the memorandum other than the compulsory ones, and states that anything in the memorandum which could lawfully have been inserted in the articles instead can be altered by special resolution with the same provision for dissentients as is given by s. 5 for alterations of the objects clause.

Section 23, however, does not apply if the memorandum itself *stipulates a method* of altering the particular clause, in which case that method must be used. Nor does it apply if the memorandum *prohibits* alteration of the clause, in which case application must be made to the court under s. 206.

15. Variation of class rights. It must first be understood that s. 23 has no application here, for it expressly states in s. 23(2) that it does not apply to a variation of class rights (*see* II, **42**).

Such a variation is now governed by s. 32 Companies Act 1980 which lays down detailed rules not markedly simpler than those which formerly existed. In an attempt to make these rules somewhat easier to learn, an initial distinction has been drawn between those which apply where no provision for variation is contained in either the memorandum or the articles, and those which apply where such a provision exists.

(*a*) *Where there is no provision for variation in either the memorandum or the articles.*

(*i*) Where the class rights are *specified in the memorandum*, any variation requires the consent of *all the members* of the company: s. 32(5).

(*ii*) Where the class rights are *specified elsewhere* (i.e. in the articles or terms of issue), any variation requires *either* the written consent of the *holders of three-quarters of the issued shares of that class*; *or* the sanction of an *extraordinary resolution* passed at a class meeting: s. 32(2).

In addition, any other existing requirements for variation must also be observed, while s. 72 Companies Act 1948, considered below, operates here to protect dissentients: s. 32(8).

(*b*) *Where there is provision for variation in either the memorandum or the articles.*

(*i*) Regardless of whether the class rights are specified in the memorandum or elsewhere, where the variation is connected with *either* the giving, variation, revocation or renewal of *the company's authority to the directors to allot shares* under s. 14 Companies Act 1980, or a *reduction of capital* under s. 66 Companies Act 1948, the rules for variation are *exactly the same as in* (*a*)(*ii*) *above*: s. 32(3).

(*ii*) Where the class rights are *specified in the memorandum* and the articles contain a provision for variation which was included at the time of the company's incorporation, a variation may be made only in accordance with that provision (unless it falls under (*i*) above): s. 32(4).

(*iii*) Where the class rights are *specified elsewhere* and the articles contain a provision for variation, whenever it was first included, a variation may be made only in accordance with that provision (unless it falls under (*i*) above): s. 32(4).

In *all three* of these cases s. 72 operates to protect dissentients. Thus the only time when s. 72 does *not* operate is in (*a*) (*i*) where no dissentients exist.

16. Protection of dissentients on variation of class rights. It will be clear from the wording of s. 72(1) Companies Act 1948 that wherever there are class rights attached to shares in a company and *either the memorandum or the articles prescribe a method of variation* of those rights, the section operates to protect dissentients.

It also operates, under s. 32(8) Companies Act 1980, in one case where a method of variation is *not* so prescribed—namely, where the class rights are specified elsewhere than in the memorandum (*see* **15**,(*a*)(*ii*)).

Section 72(1) and (2) allow the holders of fifteen per cent of the shares of the class in question, who did not consent to the variation, to apply to the court within twenty-one days to have it cancelled. The court may then, under s. 72(3), either cancel or confirm it.

Note that the required percentage of shareholdings by the applicants and the period for making the application are the same as under s. 5 regarding alterations of the objects clause and s. 23 regarding alterations of the non-compulsory clauses in the memorandum (i.e. 15% and 21 days).

17. Further provisions on variation of class rights. Three further points are of importance when considering this topic:

(*a*) Section 32(7) states that any *alteration* of a provision in the articles prescribing a method of variation of class rights, or the *insertion* of such a provision into the articles, is itself to be treated as a variation of those rights.

This brings into operation all the safeguards described above.

(*b*) Section 32(6) states that class meetings connected with a variation of class rights are governed by the normal rules relating to general meetings found in the 1948 Act, but lays down two special rules:

   (*i*) The *quorum* at such a meeting, except an adjourned meeting, is at least two persons holding, or representing by proxy, one-third of the issued shares of the class in question.

   (*ii*) Any holder of shares of the class in question present in person or by proxy may *demand a poll*.

(*c*) Table A, Article 4, states that class rights may be varied with the written consent of the holders of three-quarters of the issued shares of that class, or the sanction of an extraordinary resolution passed at a class meeting.

Note that this article corresponds exactly with the requirements of s. 32(2): (*see* **15**(*a*)(*ii*)).

18. The meaning of variation. It is clear that if there are several classes of shares in a company, and the rights of one class are altered without the rights of the other class or classes being changed in any way, it is possible to change the *control* of the company. The voting rights attached to particular shares can be made quite ineffective by the giving of increased voting rights to another class, or by the issue of further shares of the same class.

In this context, however, the word "variation" has a much more restricted meaning. It only covers *direct alterations*, i.e. if the rights attached to a particular class of shares are altered then that is a variation of rights, but the fact that the effect of the alteration is to remove control from another class of shareholders is immaterial, for this would merely be a *consequential* alteration. Of course the practical effect is to alter their rights, but this is not the meaning given by the law to the word "variation".

Table A, Article 5 expressly states that the issue of further shares of the same class ranking *pari passu* with those already issued is *not* a variation of the rights of the shares of that class, though it is quite possible that the shareholders holding the earlier shares are deprived of any effective control in the company by the dilution of their voting rights.

Section 32(9) Companies Act 1980 provides, however, that in that section and in any provision for variation of class rights contained in a company's memorandum or articles the word "variation" includes *abrogation*. Section 72(6) Companies Act 1948 contains a similar provision.

NOTE: A minority which can show that its interests are being *unfairly prejudiced* has, as will be seen later, a remedy under s. 75 Companies Act 1980. Furthermore, in *Clemens* v. *Clemens Bros. Ltd.* (1976), resolutions to increase the capital and issue the new shares in such a way as to deprive the plaintiff of her "negative control" (i.e. diluting her voting power from 45% to 24·6575%) were set aside as having been passed by an inequitable use of the defendant's voting rights.

19. Alteration of capital. In II we considered the method of alteration of all the compulsory clauses in the memorandum except the capital clause. It must now be seen in what way this can be altered to suit the company's requirements.

Section 61(1) states that a company may alter the capital clause of the memorandum, i.e. its nominal capital, in the following ways:

(*a*) It may increase the nominal capital by creating new shares.

(*b*) It may consolidate its existing shares into larger shares, e.g. by consolidating five 5p shares into one 25p share.

(*c*) It may subdivide its existing shares into smaller shares, but it must keep the proportion paid and unpaid on each share the same. (Shares are sometimes subdivided to make them more marketable, for investors tend to prefer a large number of "cheap" shares to a few "expensive" ones, ignoring the fact that the yield on their investment will be the same whatever the nominal value of the shares.)

(*d*) It may convert fully paid up shares into stock, or vice versa.

(*e*) It may cancel shares which have not been taken up, and diminish the amount of the nominal capital by the number cancelled. (This is *not* a reduction of capital, for these shares have never been allotted to anyone. Section 61(3) makes this quite clear.)

In order to alter its capital clause in any of these ways, the company requires authority in its articles, but if the articles give no power to this effect it can be inserted. Since this involves altering the articles, a special resolution is required, and the same resolution may also be used to make the alteration of capital.

If, however, the articles already contain power to alter the capital an ordinary resolution will suffice to make the alteration, since s. 61 does not require a special one. The articles can, of course, prescribe a special resolution for this purpose, but Table A does not do so.

Section 63 states that notice of any increase in the capital must be given to the registrar within fifteen days.

Section 62 states that notice of all alterations other than increases, including the redemption of redeemable preference shares under s. 58, must be given to the registrar within one month.

20. Stock. We have just seen that s. 61 allows the company to convert its fully paid up shares into stock, and it is therefore important to understand the nature of stock and any advantages which it may have.

Section 455, in defining a share, states that "share includes stock". The *relationship* of a shareholder to the company is in no way altered if his shares are converted into stock and he becomes a stockholder. Table A, Article 43, repeats this provision, and Article 42 gives the stockholder the same rights as to dividends and voting as were carried by the shares before conversion into stock took place. Section 134(*e*) covers the case where the articles make *no provision* for the voting rights attached to the stock, stating that the member shall then have one vote for each £10 worth of stock.

The provisions of s. 61, however, must be carefully observed. It only authorises the conversion of shares into stock if the shares are fully paid. Moreover, it expressly states that shares may be *converted* into stock, and from this it follows that a *direct issue* of stock is not lawful. An issue of *partly paid* stock or of *bonus* stock is therefore *ultra vires* and void, and in theory the same result should ensue from a direct issue of *fully paid* stock. In *Re Home and Foreign Investment Co.* (1912), however, it was held that a direct issue of *fully paid* stock could be validated by *lapse of time*.

Once shares are converted into stock, the stockholder owns £100 worth of stock where formerly he held 100 £1 shares. Thus though his *relationship* with the company remains the same, his *interest* in it is described in a different manner. It is no longer divided up into shares with a nominal value. This raises the question of its divisibility and brings us to consideration of its *advantages*:

(*a*) In legal theory *stock is divisible into any amount required.* Thus it is possible to transfer £4·32 worth of stock, while it is never possible to transfer a fraction of a share.

In practice, however, this advantage seldom exists, since the articles usually prescribe the minimum amount of stock transferable. Table A, Article 41, for instance, empowers the directors to fix this minimum at any figure that they wish, so long as it does not exceed the nominal value of the shares from which the stock arose.

(*b*) *Since stock is not divided up into units, it cannot be numbered.* Shares, on the other hand, must have a number and this causes a certain amount of administrative work. But this advantage of stock is offset to a certain extent by s. 74, which, while requiring shares to be numbered, makes an exception for fully paid shares ranking *pari passu* for all purposes.

21. Serious loss of capital by public company. Section 34(1) Companies Act 1980 applies whenever the net assets of a public company fall to *half or less* of its called-up share capital.

In such a case it requires the directors, not later than twenty-eight days from the day on which that fact first becomes known to a director, to convene an extraordinary general meeting for a date not less than fifty-six days from that day.

The purpose of the meeting is to consider whether any, and if so what, measures should be taken to deal with the situation. It is likely that this will lead, in many cases, to a reduction of capital, the procedure for which is described below.

22. Reduction of capital. A reduction of capial is, of course, an *alteration* of capital, but is an alteration of such importance and of such potential danger to creditors that it is strictly controlled by the Act in s. 66, the requirements of which are far more stringent than those of s. 61 for other types of alteration.

Section 66(1) states that with authority in its articles and the sanction of the court a company may by special resolution reduce its share capital in any way and make the necessary alteration to its memorandum. In particular, it may:

(*a*) extinguish or reduce the liability on unpaid share capital; *or*

(*b*) cancel paid up capital which has been lost or is unrepresented by available assets; *or*

(*c*) pay off any paid up share capital which is in excess of the wants of the company.

NOTE

(1) *The section naturally applies to stock as well as shares*, except that there can be no liability on stock to be extinguished or reduced since, as we have seen, it must always be fully paid. Reserve capital too, it will be remembered, can be reduced under this section, although (*b*) and (*c*) would be inapplicable to it since they can only apply to paid-up capital.

(2) *If the articles do not give the necessary authority*, it is not possible here, as it was under s. 61, to insert the authority and alter the capital in a single resolution. Here a special resolution must first be passed to alter the articles, and then a second

special resolution to reduce the capital, though both can be passed at the same meeting.

(3) *When capital is to be returned to the shareholders*, as under (*c*), it is not simply handed back to them in proportion to their holdings. Their *class rights* will be considered, the court treating the reduction *as though it were a liquidation*. If, therefore, a certain class of shareholders would have priority to return of capital in liquidation, that class will also be the first to have the share capital returned to them in a reduction, and this is so even if they would prefer to remain members of the company: *Prudential Assurance Co. v. Chatterley-Whitfield Collieries* (1949).

23. Creditors' right to object to a reduction. Section 67(2) gives the creditors of the company a right to object to the reduction in any case where their interests are threatened, i.e. where the liability on unpaid share capital is extinguished or reduced, or where paid-up capital is returned to the shareholders. They can object in other cases if the court so directs.

The court settles the list of creditors entitled to object, as far as possible without requiring applications from creditors, and publishes notices fixing a day within which creditors not on the list must claim to be entered on it, or lose their right of objection.

Where a creditor on the list does not consent to the reduction, the court may dispense with his consent if the company secures payment of his debt by appropriating to it, where it admits the debt, the full amount, and where it does not admit it, the amount fixed by the court.

Where a company owns leasehold properties, a list of landlords as creditors is not required if a sum sufficient to pay the rent is set aside or guaranteed. Ten years' rent will suffice for the court to dispense with the list, provided the leases are not onerous: *Re Lucania Temperance Billiards Halls* (*London*) (1966).

24. Confirmation and registration of reduction. Section 68(1) states that if the court is satisfied either that the creditors entitled to object have consented to the reduction, or that their debts have been paid or secured, it may confirm the reduction. Under s. 68(2) it may also direct that the words "and reduced" be added to the company's name for a specified period, and that the company must publish the reasons for the reduction.

Section 69(1) states that when the court order confirming the reduction is produced to the registrar, and a copy of it together with a minute giving the details of the company's share capital are delivered to him, he must register the order and the minute.

The minute specifies:

(a) the amount of the share capital;
(b) the number of shares into which it is divided;
(c) the amount of each share;
(d) the amount paid up on each share.

Section 69(2) states that the reduction takes effect on registration, and s. 69(4), as amended by the Companies Act 1976, requires the registrar to give a certificate of the registration of the order and minute, and that this certificate is conclusive evidence both that the requirements of the Act have been complied with, and that the share capital is now as set out in the minute. The registered minute, under s. 69(5), is deemed to be substituted for the corresponding part of the memorandum.

Section 12 Companies Act 1980 contains special rules to apply where the court order confirming the reduction of the capital of a *public* company brings the nominal value of the company's allotted share capital *below the authorised minimum*. Section 12(1) then prohibits the registrar from registering the order under s. 69(1) unless the court directs otherwise or the company is first *re-registered as a private company*.

Under s. 12(2) the court, in these circumstances, may authorise the company to be re-registered as a private company under s. 10 Companies Act 1980 (*see* XIX, 4) without its having passed the special resolution normally required for that operation. In these circumstances the court must then specify in its order the alterations to be made to the company's memorandum and articles connected with its re-registration.

PROGRESS TEST 15

1. What do you understand by:

(a) the authorised capital?
(b) the issued capital?
(c) the unpaid capital?
(d) the reserve capital? **(2, 3)**

2. What is the difference between:

(a) a provision and a reserve?
(b) a capital reserve and a revenue reserve? **(4)**

3. What are the statutory capital reserves? Discuss their purpose. **(5, 10; XII, 6)**

4. What is a class right? **(7)**

5. What is a preference share? Explain what is meant by the terms:

(*a*) cumulative and non-cumulative;

(*b*) participating and non-participating. **(8)**

6. How far are arrears of dividend on preference shares payable in the event of liquidation? **(9)**

7. Under what conditions may redeemable preference shares be issued? **(10)**

8. What are:

(*a*) founders' shares? **(12)**

(*b*) management shares? **(12)**

(*c*) no par value shares? **(13)**

9. What are the advantages of issuing no par value shares? **(13)**

10. How may class rights be altered? **(15, 16, 17)**

11. How may a company alter its share capital? **(19, 22)**

12. What is stock? Discuss its advantages. **(20)**

13. How may a company reduce its share capital? **(22)**

14. In what cases may a company's creditors object to a reduction of capital? **(23)**

15. What special rules apply where a public company incurs a serious loss of capital? **(21, 24)**

CHAPTER XVI

Dividends

1. The nature of a dividend. A company pays *dividends* to its members, *interest* to its debenture-holders, It is important to distinguish between these two types of payment.

A dividend is a *proportion of the distributed profits* of the company. It may be a *fixed* annual percentage, as in the case of preference shares, or it may be *variable* according to the prosperity of the company, as in the case of ordinary shares, but since it is payable only out of the distributed profits, it follows that if no profits are made, or if none are distributed, no dividend will be declared.

The shareholder cannot insist on the company declaring a dividend, for this is a matter which is at the discretion of the directors. It is the directors who control the management and financial policy of the company, and it is they who recommend the amount of dividend to be paid. If, therefore, the members do not approve of the directors' policy, their proper remedy is to make appropriate changes to the board.

The articles normally contain provisions on payment of dividends but the only statutory provision is contained in s. 59(*c*). This states that a company, with authority in its articles, may pay dividends in proportion to the amount paid up on the shares where a larger amount is paid up on some shares than on others. Table A, Article 118, gives this authority.

2. The nature of interest. The payment of interest is in no way dependent on the existence of profits. Interest is a *debt*. It is payable whether profits are available or not, and may therefore lawfully be paid either out of capital or out of revenue.

In accounting, debenture-holders' interest and the dividends of preference shareholders are often collectively referred to as *prior charges*. This term simply indicates that both these types of payment must be made before the ordinary shareholders receive anything. It is a mistake to think that they are in any way similar in law; even though the debenture-holder is a creditor of the company to the extent of the sum which he has lent and the interest on it, while the shareholder, as we have seen in the last chapter, is regarded in accounting as a creditor to the extent of the capital which he has invested, the *funds out of which they may be paid are different*. The debenture-holder may lawfully be paid his interest out of *any of the company's funds*, including capital. The shareholder, whether he holds preference or ordinary shares, may lawfully be paid dividends *only if profits are available*. Furthermore, while interest on a loan will accrue at the agreed rate per annum and will automatically become a debt, a dividend is not a debt until it is declared, and there is no obligation to declare it.

Thus there are two fundamental distinctions between interest and dividends:

(*a*) *They are payable out of different funds*, interest being payable out of any of the company's moneys, while dividends are payable only out of profits.

(*b*) *Interest is a debt, while a dividend is not a debt until it is declared*. Even then, under s. 212(1)(*g*), in a liquidation it is not payable until *after* the company's debenture-holders and trade creditors have been paid, for it is a debt payable to a member in his capacity of member (*see* IV, **5**).

3. Meaning of distribution, profits and losses. There was formerly little difference between funds which were legally distributable and the concept of "profits". All "profits" were normally distributable so long as the articles did not contain restrictive provisions and the fixed assets as a whole were maintaining their value. Thus the mere description of funds as "profits" indicated that the company had almost complete freedom to use them as it desired.

These lenient rules for distribution were often criticised as a potential danger to creditors for they went far beyond the limits of prudence. It was, for instance, permissible to make a distribution on the strength of an unrealised accretion to a fixed asset: *Dimbula Valley Tea Co. Ltd.* v. *Laurie* (1961). The Companies Act 1980, however, while leaving the concept of "profits" unchanged, introduced stringent rules regarding dividends which considerably restrict the funds out of which they may lawfully be paid. In other words, not all "profits" are now legally distributable.

Before considering these rules it is essential to grasp the meaning given by the Act to the words "distribution", "profits" and "losses".

Section 45(2) states that "distribution" means every description of distribution of a company's assets to its members, whether in cash or otherwise, *except* those made by way of:

(*a*) an issue of fully or partly paid bonus shares;

(*b*) the redemption of preference shares out of the proceeds of a fresh issue of shares made for the purpose and the payment of any premium on redemption out of the company's share premium account;

(*c*) the reduction of share capital by extinguishing or reducing the liability of members in respect of unpaid share capital or by paying off paid up share capital; and

(*d*) a distribution of assets to members on winding up.

Section 45(4) explains that the word "profits" in the Act refers to *both revenue and capital profits*, while the word "losses" refers to *both revenue and capital losses*.

4. Restriction on distribution of assets by public companies. The Companies Act 1980 not only laid down more stringent rules regarding dividends in general but also introduced an additional restriction on distributions of assets applicable only to public companies. In s. 40(1) it permits a public company to make a distribution only:

(*a*) if the amount of its net assets at the time is not less than *the aggregate of its called-up share capital and its undistributable reserves*; and

(*b*) if, and to the extent that, the distribution does not reduce the amount of the net assets to less than that aggregate.

The undistributable reserves, for the purpose of this section, are listed in s. 40(2) as:

(*a*) the share premium account;

(*b*) the capital redemption reserve fund;

(*c*) the amount by which the company's accumulated *unrealised* profits exceed its accumulated *unrealised* losses; and

(*d*) any other reserve which the company is prohibited from distributing by any other enactment or by its memorandum or articles.

An example of (*d*) is found in s. 37(10) Companies Act 1980 which provides that where a public company or its nominee acquires shares or an interest in shares in the company, and those shares or that interest appear in the balance sheet as an asset, then an amount equal to their value must be transferred out of distributable profits to a *reserve fund* which is not available for distribution.

5. Profits available for distribution. With the provisions of s. 45 and s. 40 in mind, the general rules for the payment of dividends can be considered. (The special rules applying to investment companies and contained in s. 41 Companies Act 1980 have been omitted here.)

The basic rule is found in s. 39 Companies Act 1980 which in s. 39(1) prohibits any company, public or private, from making a distribution except out of *profits available for the purpose*. In s. 39(2) these are stated to be a company's *accumulated realised profits less its accumulated realised losses*.

This strict rule is fortified by s. 39(3) which prohibits a company from applying *unrealised* profits in paying up debentures or amounts unpaid on issued shares. It also destroys, with a single statutory blow, all the former leniency of English rules on dividends.

6. Revaluation of fixed assets and provisions. Section 39(5) appears to throw a bone to the corporate dog by providing that if an unrealised profit is made on the revaluation of a fixed asset, and the sum allowed for depreciation after revaluation exceeds the sum which would have been allowed had no such profit been made, an amount equal to the amount of the extra depreciation is to be treated as *realised profit*. Without such a rule directors might be discouraged from effecting revaluations of the company's assets, since depreciation is normally charged against distributable profits.

Revaluation clearly raises difficulties where the cost of an asset is unknown. Accordingly s. 39(6) thoughtfully provides that where there is no record of the original cost, or one cannot be obtained without unreasonable expense or delay, the cost of an asset must be taken to be the value ascribed to it in the earliest available record made after the company acquired it.

Finally, s. 39(4) states that a *provision (see* XV, **4**) must be treated as a *realised loss*, except where it is in respect of a diminution in value of a fixed asset appearing on a revaluation of all the fixed assets of the company.

7. Legality of distribution. Section 43(1) Companies Act 1980 provides that the question whether a company may make a distribution without contravening s. 39 or s. 40, as well as the amount of the distribution, must be determined by reference to the *relevant accounts*, i.e. normally the last annual accounts. The distribution will be unlawful unless the requirements of s. 43 concerning those accounts are complied with.

Section 43(3) gives these requirements:

(*a*) the accounts must have been properly prepared;

(*b*) the auditors must have made a report in respect of them under s. 14 Companies Act 1967;

(*c*) if, because of something referred to in it, their report is *not unqualified*, they must have stated in writing whether, in their opinion, that thing is *material* for the purpose of determining whether the distribution is unlawful; and

(*d*) a copy of any such statement must have been laid before the company in general meeting or delivered to the registrar.

Section 43(8) defines an "unqualified report" as a report without qualification to the effect that in the opinion of the person making it the accounts have been properly prepared.

8. The articles. Section 45(5) Companies Act 1980 makes it clear that all the above rules apply without prejudice to any further restrictions on distributions which may appear in the company's memorandum or articles. Thus the articles may stipulate that dividends may be paid only out of "trading profits" or "the profits of the business", in which case realised profits on fixed assets (capital profits) could not be used for this purpose. They may be even more restrictive, stating that dividends may be paid only out of "the profits of the business for the year", in which case revenue reserves could not be used.

It is accordingly important always to look carefully at a company's articles on this point, although Table A, Article 116, as amended by the Companies Act 1980, merely states that no dividend may be paid except in accordance with the Act.

9. The declaration of dividends. Under the articles of most companies, it is the company which *declares* the dividend, but the directors who recommend its *amount*. The articles usually provide that the dividend shall not exceed the amount recommended by the directors and Table A, Article 114, does this, so that while the shareholders can reduce the amount of the dividend, they cannot increase it.

Unless the company takes advantage of s. 59(*c*) and inserts a clause similar to Table A, Article 118, in its articles, dividends are declared either as a percentage based on the nominal value of the shares, or, less frequently, as a specific sum per share. The amount paid up on the shares is irrelevant.

NOTE

(1) *Debt*. Once declared by the company, the dividend becomes a debt due to the members. It has recently been held that it is not a specialty debt and the period of limitation is thus the normal one of six years: *Re Compania de Electricidad de la Provincia de Buenos Aires* (1978). Unclaimed dividends, however, may give rise to practical problems. It was held in *Jones* v. *Bellgrove Properties, Ltd.* (1949), that a statement of a debt in the balance sheet of a company signed by the company's officers constituted a written acknowledgment of that debt and prevented it from becoming statute-barred under the Limitation Act 1939. The point was further clarified in *Re Gee & Co. (Woolwich) Ltd.* (1974), where it was held that a balance sheet duly signed by the directors was an effective acknowledgment of the state of indebtedness as at the date of the balance sheet, so that the cause of action was deemed to have accrued at that date. However, in *Re Compania de Electricidad de la Provincia de Buenos Aires* (1978) mentioned above, Slade J. further held that a written acknowledgment is not effectively made to a creditor within the Limitation Act unless it actually reaches him.

(2) *Interim dividends*. Sometimes the articles authorise the directors to pay *interim* dividends to the members, i.e. dividends which are paid in between two annual general meetings, usually six months after the final dividend. Table A, Article 115, gives the directors this power. Some companies apply the main part of their distributable profits towards the final dividend, so that the interim dividend is comparatively small. Others aim at making half-yearly dividend payments of approximately the same size.

Where a *public* company proposes to pay an interim dividend which would be unlawful if paid on the basis of the last annual accounts, *interim accounts* will be necessary to show that it is justified: s. 43(2)(*b*) Companies Act 1980. These too must be properly prepared and a copy of them delivered to the registrar of companies, but they do not have to be audited: s. 43(5).

(3) *Debts due to the company and method of payment of divi-*

dends. Table A, Article 119, empowers the directors to deduct from the dividend payable to a member any money owed by the member to the company in respect of his shares. Article 122 states that dividends shall not bear interest. Article 121 states that dividends may be paid by cheque or warrant sent through the post to the registered address of the holder, or to such person as the holder may direct. Many shareholders require the company to send their dividends to their bank, which then informs them of the amount.

(4) *Payment in cash.* Since a shareholder has a right to receive his dividend in *cash* unless there is a provision in the articles authorising payment in some other way, Table A, Article 120, empowers the company to direct payment of a dividend by the distribution to members of specific assets or paid up shares or debentures of any other company.

10. Consequences of unlawful distribution. We have already seen that dividends may be paid only out of profits available for distribution. If, however, other funds of the company are wrongly used for dividend purposes, s. 44(1) Companies Act 1980 makes all shareholders who, when they received the improper dividend, knew or had reasonable ground for believing that it was paid out of undistributable funds liable to repay it to the company.

Presumably where the shareholders are entirely innocent of the illegality, the directors will be liable to replace the funds improperly used, as was the case before there was any statutory provision on the matter.

11. The creation of reserves. As was stated earlier, the directors cannot be compelled to recommend a dividend. They may think it prudent to put all the profits for that year to reserve, and articles usually give them power to do this. Table A, Article 117, states that the directors, before recommending any dividend, may set aside out of profits such sums as they think proper as a reserve.

12. Capitalisation issues. Section 45(3) Companies Act 1980 states that the expression "capitalisation" in relation to the profits of a company means:

(*a*) applying profits in wholly or partly paying up unissued shares to be allotted to members as fully or partly paid *bonus shares*; *or*

(*b*) transferring profits to the capital redemption reserve fund.

The first of these operations, described in (*a*) above, is normally and correctly termed a *capitalisation issue*. It is often called a *bonus issue* which is equally correct, but wrongly gives the impression that the shares are "free" when in fact they have been paid for out of funds which could instead have been distributed to shareholders by way of dividend. Another term for the same operation is *scrip issue*—an expression commonly used by brokers.

In the case of a capitalisation issue the new shares are allotted to members in proportion to their existing holdings fully, or occasionally partly, paid up. The members thus receive shares on which all or some of the money payable has been already paid out of profits retained by the company and on which there is no, or only a partial, further liability. Since this issue of shares is an addition to capital, the shareholder will not pay income tax on it.

NOTE

(1) *Effect of bonus issue.* Such an issue increases the company's capital, and often entails increasing the nominal capital under s. 61. A company may wish to bring its issued capital more into line with the true worth of its undertaking, and the bonus issue frequently achieves this. On the other hand, the increase in the issued capital causes an immediate fall in the market value of the shares of the company, since the cake is now divided up into a larger number of slices each of which must necessarily be smaller than before. The fall in the market price gives investors a good opportunity to buy the company's shares at a low price, for often it is accentuated by shareholders selling their bonus shares as soon as they receive them.

(2) *Authority in articles and funds available for a bonus issue.* In order to make a bonus issue, a company must have authority in its articles. Table A, Article 128, gives it, allowing a company to use for this purpose any amount standing to the credit of any of its reserve accounts or its profit and loss account which is *available for distribution*. Such funds may also be used under this article to pay up any partly paid shares *already held* by members, which would not, of course, result in any increase in the issued share capital although the shares so treated would have a bonus element.

In addition, Article 128 permits a company to apply its share premium account and its capital redemption reserve fund to pay up unissued shares to be allotted to members as fully paid bonus shares. In either of these cases there is no true capitalisation issue, for these funds are already, in law, capital and not profits (*see* XV, **5**).

Finally, para. 36 of the 3rd Schedule to the Companies Act 1980 added a new article—Article 128A—to Table A, made necessary by the increased severity of the rules on dividends. Article 128A authorises a company to use any amount standing to the credit of any of its reserve accounts or its profit and loss account which is *not available for distribution* to pay up unissued shares to be allotted to members as fully paid bonus shares, e.g. an unrealised profit on a fixed asset.

3. Rights issues. A capitalisation issue must not be confused with a rights issue. Here the company wishes to raise more share capital, and having effected any necessary increase in its nominal capital proceeds to issue new shares. These it first offers to its existing members, on favourable terms, in proportion to their existing holdings. The members may then subscribe for the shares and so increase their holdings, or sell their "rights" on the market. If a large number of "rights" are sold, this again may be a good opportunity for an investor to buy shares in the company while they are easily available and the price temporarily depressed.

In reality there is no bonus element in a rights issue, but the members of the company are often pleased to subscribe for more shares at a figure below the market price, and this advantage is often loosely referred to as the bonus element. Payment for the new shares, however, is made entirely by shareholders subscribing fresh capital and not, as in the case of a bonus issue, by the company applying its profits or reserves for that purpose.

It should be noted that where the statutory pre-emption rights apply, an issue of shares will necessarily be a rights issue (*see* IX, **10**).

PROGRESS TEST 16

1. Distinguish between dividends and interest. (**1, 2**)
2. Explain what is meant by the words "distribution", "profits" and "losses" in the Companies Act 1980. (**3**)
3. What special restrictions exist regarding the distribution of assets by public companies? (**4**)
4. What do you understand by "profits available for distribution"? (**5, 6**)

5. How are dividends (*a*) declared, and (*b*) paid? **(9)**

6. What are the consequences of the payment of dividends ou of undistributable funds? **(10)**

7. What do you understand by (*a*) a capitalisation issue, an (*b*) a rights issue? **(12, 13)**

8. On what basis is the legality of a proposed dividend de termined? Are there any special rules for interim dividends? (" 9)

CHAPTER XVII

Auditors

1. Appointment of the first auditors. Section 159 has been repealed and replaced by s. 14 Companies Act 1976.

Section 14(3) states that the *first* auditors may be appointed by the *directors* at any time before the first general meeting at which the documents comprised in the accounts are laid before the company. The auditors so appointed hold office until the end of that meeting.

Section 14(4) states that if the directors do not exercise their power of appointment, the company in general meeting may appoint the first auditors.

2. Appointment of auditors to fill casual vacancies. Section 14(5) Companies Act 1976 provides that the *directors*, or the *company in general meeting*, may appoint auditors to fill casual vacancies, but that the surviving auditors may continue to act during any vacancy.

3. Subsequent appointment of auditors. Section 14(1) Companies Act 1976 requires every company to appoint one or more auditors at each general meeting at which the documents comprised in the accounts are laid before the company. Such auditors hold office from the end of that meeting until the end of the next general meeting at which the documents comprised in the accounts are laid before the company.

4. Power of Secretary of State to appoint an auditor. Section 14(2) Companies Act 1976 states that if no auditors are appointed or reappointed at a general meeting at which the documents comprised in the accounts are laid before the company, the Secretary of State may appoint a person to fill the vacancy. The company must give the Secretary of State notice within one week of the fact that his power has become exercisable.

5. Remuneration of auditors. Section 14(8) Companies Act 1976 states that if the directors appoint an auditor, they may fix his remuneration, and if the Secretary of State makes an appointment, he may fix the remuneration. Apart from this, however, the company must fix it, or else determine the way in which it will be fixed. "Remuneration" here includes sums paid by the company for the auditors' expenses.

Paragraph 13 of the 8th Schedule, as amended by the Companies Act 1967, requires the amount of the auditors' remuneration to be shown as a separate heading in the profit and loss account.

6. Removal of auditors. Section 14(6) Companies Act 1976 states that a company may by ordinary resolution remove an auditor before the expiration of his term of office and despite any agreement between it and him.

Notice of the fact that such a resolution has been passed must be given to the registrar within fourteen days.

7. Resolutions relating to appointment and removal of auditors. Section 160 has been repealed and replaced by s. 15 Companies Act 1976.

Section 15(1) states that *special notice (see* XXIII, **22**) must be given of a resolution at a general meeting:

(*a*) to appoint as auditor a person other than a retiring auditor;

(*b*) to fill a casual vacancy in the office of auditor;

(*c*) to reappoint as auditor a retiring auditor who was appointed by the directors to fill a casual vacancy;

(*d*) to remove an auditor before the expiration of his term of office.

8. The auditor's right to make written representations. Section 15(2) Companies Act 1976 states that when the company receives this notice, it must at once send a copy of it:

(*a*) to the person proposed to be appointed or removed, as the case may be;

(*b*) to the retiring auditor where it is proposed to appoint another person as auditor;

(*c*) to the auditor who resigned where a casual vacancy was caused by his resignation.

Section 15(3) and (5) state that where notice is given of a resolution to appoint as auditor a person *other than the retiring auditor*, or to *remove* an auditor before the expiration of his term of office, and the retiring auditor or the auditor proposed to be

emoved makes *written representations* to the company and asks
hat these should be notified to the members, the company must,
unless it receives them too late:

(*a*) state the fact that they were made in any notice of the
esolution to the members; and

(*b*) send a copy of them to every member to whom notice of
he meeting is sent.

If a copy is not sent out in this way because the representations
vere received too late or because of the company's default, then
he auditor may demand that his statement shall be read out at
he meeting: s. 15(4).

It may perhaps occur that an auditor reacts sharply to the
opy of the special notice of the resolution to appoint someone in
tis place or to remove him, and makes a statement in his own
lefence which is highly defamatory of some other person. Section
5(5) provides for this situation, stating that copies of the repre-
entations need not be sent out, nor need the representations be
ead out, if the company or any aggrieved person applies to the
ourt and the court thinks that the auditor is abusing his rights *to
ecure needless publicity for defamatory matter*. Moreover, the
ourt may order that the company's costs on such an application
hall be paid by the auditor.

NOTE: These provisions in s. 15 Companies Act 1976 concerning the written representations are *exactly the same as those in
s. 184* relating to directors. Once learnt, they apply to both
directors and auditors alike.

. Rights of removed auditor in respect of meetings. Section 15(6)
Companies Act 1976 entitles an auditor who has been removed:

(*a*) to attend the general meeting at which his term of office
vould have expired;

(*b*) to attend any general meeting at which it is intended to fill
he vacancy caused by his removal;

(*c*) to receive all notices and communications relating to such
neetings which a member is entitled to receive;

(*d*) to speak at such meetings on any part of the business
vhich concerns him as former auditor.

0. Resignation of auditors. Section 16(1) Companies Act 1976
rovides that an auditor may resign by giving written notice to
he company at the registered office. Section 16(2), however,
tates that this notice is not effective unless it contains *either*:

(a) a statement that there are no circumstances connected with his resignation which he considers should be brought to the notice of the company's members or creditors; *or*

(b) a statement of such circumstances.

Once an effective notice has been given, s. 16(3) requires the company to send a copy of it:

(a) to the registrar; and

(b) if it contained a statement of the connected circumstances, to every member and debenture-holder of the company.

Under s. 16(4) and (5) the company or any aggrieved person may, within 14 days of the company's receipt of a notice containing a statement of the connected circumstances, apply to the court which, if it thinks that the auditor is using the notice *to secure needless publicity for defamatory matter*, may order that copies need not be sent out. Moreover, it may also order that the company's costs on such an application shall be paid by the auditor.

Finally, s. 16(6) requires the company, within 14 days of the court's decision, to send to every member and debenture-holder

(a) a statement of the effect of the court order, if any;

(b) if none, a copy of the notice containing the statement of the connected circumstances.

11. Resigning auditor's rights. Section 17(1) and (2) Companies Act 1976 confer two rights on the resigning auditor where his notice of resignation contains a statement of the connected circumstances (*see* **10**):

(a) He may deposit with the notice a signed requisition calling on the directors of the company to convene an extraordinary general meeting to receive and consider his explanation of those circumstances.

(b) If he requests the company to circulate to the members before the general meeting at which his term of office expires, or at which it is proposed to fill the vacancy caused by his resignation, or which is convened on his requisition, a written statement of the connected circumstances, the company must, unless it receives it too late:

(i) state the fact that it was made in any notice of the meeting given to the members, and

(ii) send a copy of it to every member to whom notice of the meeting is sent.

Section 17(3), once again, states that if a copy is not sent out in this way because the statement was received too late or because of the company's default, the auditor may demand that his statement be read out at the meeting.

As before, s. 17(4) provides that copies of the statement need not be sent out, nor need the statement be read out, if the company or any aggrieved person applies to the court and the court thinks that the auditor is abusing his rights to *secure needless publicity for defamatory matter*. Moreover, the court may also order that the company's costs on such an application shall be paid by the auditor.

Finally, s. 17(5) entitles a resigning auditor to attend any meeting mentioned in (*b*) above, and to receive all notices and communications relating to such a meeting which a member is entitled to receive. He may also speak at such a meeting on any part of the business which concerns him as former auditor.

12. Qualifications of auditors. Section 161(1), as amended by s. 13 Companies Act 1976, states that an auditor must be *either*:

(*a*) a member of a body of accountants established in the United Kingdom and recognised by the Department of Trade (i.e. the Institute of Chartered Accountants or the Association of Certified Accountants); *or*

(*b*) authorised by the Department as having similar qualifications obtained elsewhere.

Section 13(3) Companies Act 1976 spitefully enables the Secretary of State to refuse an authorisation under (*b*) above to a person who has qualifications obtained outside the United Kingdom if the country in which they were obtained does not confer corresponding privileges on persons qualified in the United Kingdom.

The proviso in s. 161(1) relating to an exempt private company was repealed by the Companies Act 1967.

13. Disqualifications of auditors. Under s. 161(2) and (3) even a qualified accountant cannot act as auditor to a company if he is:

(*a*) an officer or servant of the company; *or*

(*b*) a partner or employee of an officer or servant of the company; *or*

(*c*) an officer or servant, or partner or employee of an officer or servant, of any company within the same group (i.e. if he is disqualified under (*a*) or (*b*) for *any* company within a group, he is disqualified for *all* companies within that group).

Section 161(2) also states that a body corporate cannot act as auditor. It does not prohibit a shareholder in the company from acting as its auditor, but the rules of his professional association are likely to do so.

The proviso to s. 161(2) has been repealed by the Companies Act 1967.

Finally, s. 13(5) Companies Act 1976 prohibits any person from acting as the auditor of a company if he knows that he is disqualified for appointment. If he knowingly becomes disqualified during his term of office he must at once vacate his office and give written notice to the company of his reason for doing so.

14. Auditors' report and rights as to books and meetings. Section 14 Companies Act 1967 repeals s. 162 and the 9th Schedule of the Companies Act 1948 and deals with the same matters with certain additions. It has been slightly amended by the Companies Act 1976.

Section 14(1) states that the auditors must make a report to the members on the accounts examined by them.

Section 14(2) states that this report must be read before the company in general meeting, and be open to inspection by any member.

Section 14(3) requires the report to state whether in the auditors' opinion the company's balance sheet, profit and loss account and group accounts, if any, have been properly prepared and a true and fair view given:

(*a*) in the case of the balance sheet, of the state of the company's affairs as at the end of its financial year;

(*b*) in the case of the profit and loss account, of the company's profit or loss for its financial year;

(*c*) in the case of group accounts, of the state of affairs and profit or loss of the company and its subsidiaries.

Section 14(4) requires the auditors, in preparing their report, to carry out such investigations as will enable them to form an opinion as to the following matters:

(*a*) whether proper accounting records have been kept by the company, and adequate returns have been received from branches not visited by them;

(*b*) whether the balance sheet and profit and loss account agree with the accounting records and returns.

If they think that this is not the case, they must state that fact in their report.

Section 14(5) states that the auditors have a right of access to books, accounts and vouchers of the company. This presumably includes the minutes of board meetings. They may require from the officers of the company any information and explanation which they think necessary and if they fail to obtain it they must, under s. 14(6), state that fact in their report.

Finally, s. 14(7) states that the auditors may attend any general meeting and must receive all notices of general meetings, and may speak at any general meeting on any part of the business which concerns them as auditors.

5. Auditors' powers relating to subsidiaries. Section 18(1) Companies Act 1976 provides that where a company has a subsidiary (*see* XI, **14–17**) incorporated in Great Britain, that subsidiary and its auditors must give the auditors of the holding company such information and explanation as they may reasonably require for the purposes of their duties.

Where a company has a subsidiary incorporated elsewhere, it is the duty of the holding company, if required by its auditors, to take all reasonable steps to obtain such information and explanation from the subsidiary.

6. False statements to auditors. Section 19 Companies Act 1976 makes it a criminal offence for any officer of a company knowingly or recklessly to make, either orally or in writing, to the company's auditors any statement conveying any information or explanation which the auditors require or to which they are entitled and which is misleading, false or deceptive in a material particular.

7. Legal position of auditors. An auditor is not an officer of the company within s. 455, which defines an officer as including a director, manager or secretary. He is, however, an officer for the purposes of certain sections. e.g. s. 328 and s. 330 which impose criminal liability on officers of companies in liquidation, and s. 333, dealing with misfeasance by officers of companies in liquidation.

He is, on the other hand, a servant of the company, and for certain purposes he is also an agent, e.g. s. 167, dealing with an investigation of the company's affairs by the Department of Trade. He is not, however, an agent of the company for the

purposes of acknowledging a debt on its behalf within the Limitation Act, when he signs his report on the balance sheet.

18. Auditors' liability for negligence. An auditor is naturally
liable to the *company* for loss occasioned by breach of his duty of
care, i.e. negligence, for he is in a contractual relationship with it.

Thus in *Re Thomas Gerrard and Son* (1967), a director of a
company falsified the company's accounts by fraudulent entries, *inter alia*, regarding stock. The auditors were suspicious
and asked him for an explanation, but made no further investigation. As a result their estimate of the company's profits
was wrong and the company declared dividends which it
would not otherwise have done, paying tax which would not
otherwise have been payable. The company went into liquidation and the liquidator took misfeasance proceedings against
the auditors under s. 333 (*see* **XXX, 12**). HELD: The damages
recoverable by the liquidator included the dividends, the costs
of recovering the tax, and any tax not recoverable.

Until recently, however, it was clear that he was not liable to
third parties with whom he had no contract, since at common law
there was no tortious liability for negligent mis-statements: to
establish liability for a mis-statement it was necessary to prove
fraud, which might well be impossible.

As a result of the decision in *Hedley Byrne & Co., Ltd.* v
Heller & Partners, Ltd. (1963), however, it was established that a
person may be liable for a negligent mis-statement even where
there is no contractual relationship between him and the party to
whom he makes it, provided there is some "special relationship"
between them, and provided he does not expressly disclaim responsibility. The House of Lords did not define the expression
"special relationship", but thought that it arose wherever one
person relies on the skill or knowledge of another who is using it
responsibly, though gratuitously, to assist him. This would seem
to cover an auditor who, for example, makes a negligent mis-
statement to a potential investor.

19. Duties of auditors.
  (*a*) *An auditor must act honestly*, and with *reasonable skill, care
and caution*.
  (*b*) *He must show the true financial position as shown by the
books*. If proper accounting records have not been kept, or they
do not, in his opinion, show a true and fair view of the com

pany's affairs, he must state that fact in his report and even refuse to certify the accounts and resign.

(*c*) *He must know his duties* under the articles and the Companies Acts, and his report must comply with s. 14 Companies Act 1967.

(*d*) *He must verify the existence of the company's securities* and see that they are in safe custody. Thus he should actually see the securities unless they have been deposited with a third party with whom securities would normally be deposited in the ordinary course of business, e.g. a bank.

(*e*) He must check the *cash in hand* and *the bank balance*.

(*f*) *He is not concerned with policy or management*. He must simply state the effect of what has been done, and the remedy for bad management will lie with the shareholders, who can remove the directors or at least raise the matter at a meeting.

(*g*) *He is not under a duty to take stock*, unless there are suspicious circumstances, but he should make sure that the amount of stock stated to exist is a reasonably probable figure. In practice, an auditor often thinks it prudent to exceed his legal duty with regard to stock-taking.

(*h*) *A watchdog but not a bloodhound.* Although the famous words of Lopes L.J. in *Re Kingston Cotton Mill Co.* (1896), that an auditor "is a watchdog but not a bloodhound" are invariably remembered by students and are often the only remark which they can make when asked for the duties of an auditor, constant repetition of even such a delightful phrase tends to depress the examiner. Lopes L.J. also said that "an auditor is not bound to be a detective", which is another way of expressing the same idea and at least makes a change.

20. Relief from liability. Section 205 applies not only to officers of the company but also to auditors. Section 205(1) states that any provision in the articles or in any contract exempting them from, or indemnifying them against, liability for negligence or breach of duty towards the company is *void*. Thus it is impossible for an auditor to limit or exclude liability for negligence by the terms of his contract.

If, however, the court thinks that, though liable, the auditor has acted honestly and reasonably and ought fairly to be excused, it may, under s. 448(1), relieve him from liability on such terms as it thinks fit. This compassionate section, like s. 205, applies also to defaulting officers, and not only to auditors.

21. Share valuations by auditors. The valuation of shares is not an easy matter. It is not just a question of valuing the entire undertaking of the company and then dividing the figure reached by the number of shares issued, i.e. estimating what is called the "break-up" value. A share in a going concern will be affected by many factors: the dividend yield, the number of times the dividend was covered, the marketability of the shares, the existence of reserves, the possibility of expansion and the making of "rights" issues, and the hope of a takeover bid.

Auditors, therefore, are often required to make such valuations under the articles of a private company where there are no dealings in the shares and some price must be attached to them. When they perform this function they must of course act honestly, but they *need not give reasons for their valuation.* Indeed, the less said the better, for if they give reasons the court can inquire into the accuracy of the valuation and set it aside. Their position here is similar to that of directors who refuse to register a transfer of shares under an article conferring on them an unrestricted discretion.

In valuing shares an auditor is not normally acting in a judicial or arbitral capacity and is therefore not entitled to the immunity from liability for negligence possessed by a judge or arbitrator. He is exercising a professional function, not settling a dispute, and will therefore be liable to the person who employs him for any loss caused to that person by his negligence: *Arenson* v. *Casson Beckman Rutley and Co.* (1975).

He will, of course, also be liable for fraud or collusion if he acts dishonestly.

PROGRESS TEST 17

1. Who appoints:

(*a*) the first auditors of a company? (**1**)

(*b*) auditors to fill casual vacancies? (**2**)

(*c*) auditors at the general meeting before which the accounts are laid? (**3**)

2. Under what circumstances may the Secretary of State appoint an auditor? (**4**)

3. How is the remuneration of auditors fixed? (**5**)

4. How may an auditor be removed before the expiration of his term of office and what are his rights in respect of meetings? (**6, 9**)

5. What resolutions regarding auditors require special notice? **(7)**

6. Describe the statutory requirements and possible consequences when special notice is given of a resolution to appoint an auditor other than the retiring auditor, or to remove an auditor before the expiration of his term of office. **(8)**

7. Give the statutory provisions relating to the resignation of auditors and the resigning auditor's rights. **(10, 11)**

8. Give the statutory provisions relating to:

(a) the qualifications of an auditor; **(12)**
(b) the disqualifications of an auditor. **(13)**

9. What rights has an auditor to attend and speak at general meetings? **(14)**

10. How far is an auditor:

(a) an officer of the company?
(b) a servant of the company?
(c) an agent of the company? **(17)**

11. Discuss the duties of an auditor. **(14, 15, 19)**

12. Give an account of the auditor's powers relating to subsidiary companies. **(15)**

13. Can an auditor exclude liability for negligence by the terms of his contract? **(20)**

CHAPTER XVIII

Investigations and Inspection of Documents

There are three types of investigation which can be carried out by the Department of Trade:

(a) An investigation of the company's *affairs*;
(b) An investigation of the company's *ownership*;
(c) An investigation of *share dealings*.

Section 42 Companies Act 1967 provides that ss. 165–171 and s. 175 apply not only to companies registered under the 1948 Act, but also to companies incorporated outside Great Britain which are carrying on business in Great Britain.

INVESTIGATION OF AFFAIRS

1. Power of Department to investigate affairs of company. Section 164(1) states that the Department *may* appoint inspectors to investigate and report on a company's affairs:

(a) Where it has a share capital, on the application of:
    (i) at least 200 members, *or*
    (ii) members holding at least one-tenth of the shares issued.
(b) Where it has no share capital, on the application of at least one-fifth of the members.

Section 164(2) states that the application must be supported by such evidence as the Department may require, showing good reason for the investigation, and the Department may also require security for costs not exceeding £100 from the applicants.

Section 165 has been considerably amended by para. 21 of the 3rd Schedule to the Companies Act 1980. It now states in subsection (1)(b) that the Department *may* appoint inspectors to investigate the company's affairs if it appears:

(a) That its affairs are being or have been conducted:
    (i) with intent to defraud creditors; *or*
    (ii) for a fraudulent or unlawful purpose; *or*
    (iii) in a manner unfairly prejudicial to any of its members;

(b) That any actual or proposed act or omission of the company is or would be unfairly prejudicial to any of its members;

(c) That the business was formed for a fraudulent or unlawful purpose;

(d) That the persons concerned with formation or management have been guilty of fraud, misfeasance or other misconduct towards the company or its members;

(e) That its members have not been given all the information about its affairs which they might reasonably expect.

Section 165(2) provides that the power of the Department under s. 165(1)(b) is exercisable even if the company is in voluntary liquidation, and that the word "member" in (a) and (b) above includes a person who is not a member but to whom shares have been transferred or transmitted by operation of law (e.g. a personal representative).

2. Duty of Department to investigate affairs of company. Section 165(1)(a) states that the Department *must* appoint inspectors to investigate and report on a company's affairs if:

(a) the company by special resolution, *or*
(b) the court

declares that its affairs require it.

3. Investigation into affairs of related companies. Section 166 states that if an inspector appointed under either s. 164 or s. 165 thinks it necessary, he may also investigate and report on the affairs of any other company which is or has been within the same group.

Note that this section provides another example of "lifting the veil of incorporation", for in order to discover whether or not a group exists, it is essential to establish the identity of the *members*.

4. Powers of the inspector. Section 167(1), as amended by s. 39 Companies Act 1967, states that all officers and agents of the company (and an *auditor* is an agent for this purpose) must produce to the inspectors all books and documents, attend before the inspectors when required, and give all the assistance that they can.

Section 167(2) empowers the inspector to examine them on oath.

Section 167(3) states that if they refuse to comply with s.

167(1), the inspector may certify their refusal to the court, and they then become punishable as if guilty of contempt of court.

Section 167(4) empowers the inspector to apply to the court for an order for the examination before it on oath of any other persons whom he thinks it necessary to examine.

Section 41 Companies Act 1967 empowers the inspector at any time in the course of his investigation to inform the Department of matters tending to show the commission of an offence, without the necessity of making an interim report (*see* **5**).

5. The inspector's report. Section 168(1) states that the inspector may, and, if directed to do so by the Department, must make interim reports to the Department, and at the end of the investigation must make a final report. Reports must be either written or printed, as the Department directs.

Section 168(2) requires the Department to send a copy of any report:

(*a*) to the registered office of the company;

(*b*) if it thinks fit, on request and at the prescribed fee, to any member of the company, or of any company within the group, or to any person whose interests as a creditor are affected;

(*c*) to the applicants specified in s. 164, on request; and

(*d*) to the court, where the court required an investigation under s. 165.

Section 171 states that a copy of an inspector's report is admissible in any legal proceedings as evidence of the inspector's opinion concerning anything in it.

6. Powers of the Department arising from investigation. The Companies Act 1967 repealed s. 169 and provides in s. 35(1) and s. 37 for the consequences of an investigation. Section 75 Companies Act 1980 repeals and replaces s. 35(2) in this connection.

Section 35(1) Companies Act 1967 states that if it appears to the Department from any inspector's report or from any information or document obtained under s. 109 Companies Act 1967 (*see* **13**) that it is expedient in the public interest that the company should be wound up, it may, unless the company is already being wound up by the court, *present a petition for it to be so wound up* if the court thinks it just and equitable (*see* s. 222(*f*)).

Section 75(2) Companies Act 1980 states that if it appears to the Secretary of State from any inspector's report or from any information or document obtained under s. 109 Companies Act 1967 that there is any ground for a petition by a member under s. 75(1), he may, as well as or instead of presenting a winding up petition, present a petition for an *order under s. 75 (see* XXXI).

Finally, s. 37(1) Companies Act 1967 empowers the Department itself to bring *civil proceedings* in the name of any company wherever it appears in the public interest to do so.

INVESTIGATION OF OWNERSHIP

7. Power of Department to investigate ownership of company. Section 172(1) states that where there appears to be good reason to do so, the Department *may* appoint inspectors to investigate and report on the membership of any company in order to determine the true persons financially interested in its success or failure, or able to control its policy.

8. Duty of Department to investigate ownership of company. Section 172(3) states that where members falling within the requirements of s. 164 as to numbers of shareholdings apply to the Department for the appointment of an inspector to make an investigation of ownership, it *must* appoint an inspector unless the application is vexatious.

Students should note carefully, when they have learnt the figures relating to the applicants under s. 164, that while s. 164 gives the Department a *power* to appoint an inspector, s. 172(3) imposes a *duty* to do so. This is an important practical and academic distinction which, if not accurately made, leads to confused answers to examination questions.

9. Powers of inspector in an investigation of ownership. Section 172(4) empowers the inspector to investigate arrangements which, though not legally binding, are observed in practice.

The provisions of s. 166, s. 167, and s. 168 also apply to an investigation of ownership.

10. Power of Department to require information. Section 173 applies where it appears to the Department that the ownership should be investigated, but it is unnecessary to appoint an inspector. It empowers the Department to require any person interested in the shares or debentures of the company, or their solicitor or agent, to give information.

Section 175, however, places limits on the amount of information which the Department or its inspectors may require from solicitors or bankers. It provides:

- (*a*) that solicitors need not disclose any privileged communication made to them in that capacity, except the name and address of their client; and
- (*b*) that the company's bankers need not disclose any information about the affairs of their customers other than the company.

11. Power of Department to impose restrictions on shares or debentures. Where the Department makes an investigation under either s. 172 or s. 173, and it finds difficulty in obtaining information because the persons concerned are unwilling to assist it, s. 174 empowers it to impose restrictions on the shares and debentures as follows:

- (*a*) Transfers shall be void.
- (*b*) Voting rights shall not be exercisable.
- (*c*) No further issues may be made in right of those shares or debentures.
- (*d*) No payment, either of capital or dividend, shall be made, except in a liquidation.

(*See* s. 174(2) and (8).)

INVESTIGATION OF SHARE DEALINGS

12. Power of Department to investigate share dealings. Section 32(1) Companies Act 1967 authorises the Department, if circumstances suggest that contravention of s. 25 Companies Act 1967 (*see* XXII, **57**) or s. 27 Companies Act 1967 (*see* XXII, **13**), or s. 31(2) Companies Act 1967 (*see* XXII, **14**) has occurred regarding a company's shares or debentures, to appoint an inspector to investigate in order to establish whether this is the case, and to report the result of his investigation to the Department.

Section 32(3) states that for the purposes of such an investigation, s. 167 (*see* **4**) applies. Section 32(4) and (5) state that the inspector may, and, if so directed by the Department, must, make interim reports to the Department, and must make a final report at the end of the investigation. The reports may be written or printed, as the Department directs, and the Department may have them published.

INSPECTION OF COMPANY'S DOCUMENTS

13. Inspection of company's books and papers. Section 109(1) and (2) Companies Act 1967 empower the Department, if it thinks there is good reason to do so, to require the production of any specified books or papers from the company or from any person who appears in possession of them, without prejudice to that person's lien on them, if any.

Section 109(3) states that the power conferred by the section includes power:

(a) if the books or papers are produced
  (i) to take copies of or extracts from them; and
  (ii) to require the person producing them, or any employee, or past or present officer of the company in question, to explain them;

(b) if they are not produced, to require the person required to produce them to state, to the best of his knowledge and belief, where they are.

Section 114(1) states that if such person gives an explanation or makes a statement which he *knows to be false*, or gives a false explanation or makes a false statement *recklessly*, he is guilty of an offence.

Section 110(1) authorises a justice of the peace, if satisfied by the Department that there are reasonable grounds for suspecting that there are on any premises books or papers which have been required but not produced, to issue a warrant authorising any constable to enter (using such force as is reasonably necessary) and search the premises, and to take possession of the books or papers, or take any steps necessary for preserving them.

Section 109, like ss. 165–171 and s. 175 Companies Act 1948 applies not only to companies registered in Great Britain, but also to companies incorporated outside Great Britain which carry on business in Great Britain.

14. Security of information. Section 111(1) states that no information or document obtained under ss. 109 or 110 shall be published or disclosed without the company's previous consent in writing, except to a competent authority, unless publication or disclosure is required:

(*a*) for the purpose of any criminal proceedings arising out of the Companies Acts 1948 and 1967, or for an offence involving misconduct in management or misapplication of property;

(*b*) for the purpose of complying with any requirements imposed or exercising any power given by the Companies Act 1948 with regard to inspectors' reports;

(*c*) with a view to the institution of civil proceedings by the Department under s. 37 Companies Act 1967 (*see* **6**);

(*d*) with a view to the institution of winding up proceedings by the Department.

Section 111(3) states that for the purposes of this section, each of the following is a competent authority:

(*a*) The Department of Trade.

(*b*) An officer of the Department of Trade.

(*c*) An inspector appointed under the Companies Act 1948 by the Department of Trade.

15. Destruction of documents. Section 113(1) Companies Act 1967 makes it an offence for an officer of a company to destroy, mutilate or falsify a document relating to the company's property or affairs, or to make a false entry in it, unless he proves that he did not intend to conceal the state of affairs or defeat the law.

Section 113(2) makes it an offence for him fraudulently to part with, alter or make an omission in any such document.

PROGRESS TEST 18

1. When may the Department of Trade investigate the affairs of a company, and when must it do so? (**1, 2**)

2. What are the powers and duties of an inspector appointed by the Department of Trade to investigate the affairs of a company? (**4, 5**)

3. What steps can be taken by the Department of Trade after an investigation of affairs has been carried out? (**6**)

4. When may the Department of Trade investigate the ownership of a company, and when must it do so? (**7, 8**)

5. What steps may be taken by the Department of Trade during an investigation of ownership if it finds difficulty in

obtaining information because the persons concerned are unwilling to assist it? **(11)**

6. In what circumstances can the Department of Trade investigate share dealings? **(12 and XXII, 13, 14, 57)**

7. What power has the Department of Trade to inspect the company's books and documents? **(13)**

8. What provisions exist for ensuring the security of the information so obtained? **(14)**

CHAPTER XIX

Private Companies

1. Definition of a private company. The Companies Act 1980 repealed s. 28, s. 29 and s. 30 Companies Act 1948 and in s. 1(1) defined a private company simply as "a company which is not a public company" (*see* II, **2**).

In s. 15 it makes it a criminal offence for a private company to offer its shares or debentures to the public, whether for cash or otherwise, and whether directly or by means of an offer for sale (*see* VII, **1**). It would thus be unlawful for a private company to make a share exchange offer to the members of a public company with a view to obtaining control of it. However, s. 15(4) makes it clear that if an unlawful allotment is made, its validity is not affected by the section.

Apart from these two provisions, the Companies Act 1980 contains nothing more about a private company as such, although it deals extensively with the procedure whereby a private company converts into a public company, and vice versa.

2. Capital requirements for conversion to public company. Section 6(1) Companies Act 1980 imposes strict initial rules regarding the share capital of any private company seeking conversion. Before it can be re-registered as a public company, it must satisfy two of the same conditions required of a company registered as a public company on its original incorporation when such a company applies for a trading certificate, namely:

(*a*) the nominal value of its allotted share capital must be not less than the authorised minimum (*see* II, **41**); and

(*b*) not less than one quarter of the nominal value of each allotted share, together with the whole of any premium on it, must have been paid up (*see* V, **2** and IX, **15**).

There are, however, two further conditions to be satisfied under s. 6(1) owing to the fact that s. 20(2) and s. 23(1) Companies Act 1980 do not apply to private companies (see XII, **1** and IX, **16**). Thus safeguards are required when conversion is sought:

(*c*) where any share in the company, or any premium on it, has been paid up by *an undertaking to do work or perform services* for the company, that undertaking must have been performed; and

(*d*) where shares have been allotted as paid up as to their nominal value or any premium on them *otherwise than in cash*, and the consideration for the allotment includes an undertaking to the company which *does not fall within* (*c*) *above*, then *either*:
  (*i*) that undertaking must have been performed; *or*
  (*ii*) there must be a contract between the company and some person under which that undertaking must have been performed *within five years*.

Under s. 6(2), where (*b*) above has not been complied with as regards shares allotted under a share scheme for employees, those shares may be disregarded for the purpose of compliance with (*b*)–(*d*), but must then be treated for the purpose of (*a*) as though they were not part of the allotted share capital.

In addition to the four requirements of s. 6(1), s. 5(5) imposes two more conditions which apply where, between the date of the balance sheet and the passing of the special resolution, shares are allotted as paid up as to their nominal value or any premium on them *otherwise than in cash*. In these circumstances the company may not apply for re-registration as a public company unless:

(*a*) the consideration has been valued in accordance with s. 24; and

(*b*) a report has been made on its value during the six months immediately preceding the allotment (*see* IX, **18** and **19**).

3. Procedure for re-registration of private company as public company. Section 5 Companies Act 1980 governs the procedure to be followed for the re-registration of a private company with a share capital as a public company.

The first step is for the company to pass a special resolution for re-registration which:

(*a*) alters its memorandum so that it states that the company is to be a public company; and

(*b*) makes all other necessary alterations in both its memorandum and articles.

Next, an application for re-registration, signed by a director or secretary, must be delivered to the registrar along with the following documents:

(*a*) a printed copy of the *altered memorandum and articles*;

(*b*) a copy of a written *statement by the company's auditors* that in their opinion the relevant balance sheet shows that the amount of the company's net assets at the date of the balance sheet was not less than the aggregate of its called-up capital and undistributable reserves;

(*c*) a copy of the *relevant balance sheet*, i.e. one prepared as at a date not more than seven months before the company's application, together with a copy of an *unqualified report by the auditors*;

(*d*) a copy of any *report* prepared under s. 5(5)(*b*) (*see* **2** *above*); and

(*e*) a *statutory declaration* by a director or secretary:

(*i*) that the special resolution for re-registration has been passed and the conditions specified in s. 5(5) and s. 6(1) have been satisfied (*see* **2** *above*); and

(*ii*) that between the date of the balance sheet and the application for re-registration there has been no change in the company's financial position resulting in the amount of its net assets falling below the aggregate of its called-up capital and undistributable reserves.

Under s. 5(4) the registrar may accept this declaration as sufficient evidence that the special resolution has been passed and the conditions satisfied. Under s. 5(6) he then retains the application and other documents and issues the company with a certificate of incorporation stating that it is a public company. Section 5(8) states that on the issue of the certificate the company becomes a public company and the alterations in its memorandum and articles take effect, while under s. 5(9) the certificate is conclusive evidence that all the requirements of the Act regarding re-registration have been complied with, and that the company is a public company. Under Statutory Instrument No. 1749 of 1980 there is a re-registration fee of £50.

It should be noted that under s. 7 Companies Act 1980 the same procedure, with slight and obvious modifications, is required for the re-registration of an *unlimited* (and therefore necessarily private) company as a public company. Furthermore, although s. 44 Companies Act 1967 now applies only to private companies, s. 7(4) expressly extends the application of s. 44(7), which protects the interests of creditors where an unlimited company re-registers as a limited company and then goes into liquidation, to cover the case of conversion to a *public* limited company under s. 7 (*see* XXVI, **4**).

4. Procedure for re-registration of public company as private company. Section 10 Companies Act 1980 prescribes the procedure for the converse operation, namely, the re-registration of a public company as a private company. Although this is a far less common occurrence, it is sometimes seen where one company has taken over another and the holding company wishes to alter the status of its subsidiary (*see* XI, **14**).

The first step, once again, is the passing of a special resolution for re-registration by the company which:

(*a*) alters its memorandum so that it no longer states that the company is a public company; and

(*b*) makes all other necessary alterations in both its memorandum and articles.

Next, an application for re-registration, signed by a director or secretary, must be delivered to the registrar together with a printed copy of the altered memorandum and articles. Furthermore, either the period for making an application to the court under s. 11 to cancel the resolution must have expired without such an application having been made or, if such an application has been made, it must have been withdrawn or a court order made confirming the resolution and a copy of that order delivered to the registrar.

Under s. 10(3) the registrar then retains the application and other documents and issues the company with an appropriate certificate of incorporation. On the issue of the certificate the company, under s. 10(4), becomes a private company and the alterations in its memorandum and articles take effect, while under s. 10(5) the certificate is conclusive evidence that all the requirements of the section regarding re-registration have been complied with, and that the company is a private company. Under Statutory Instrument No. 1749 of 1980 there is a re-registration fee of £5.

5. Provision for dissentient members. It can be seen from **4** above that an application can be made to the court to cancel a resolution passed by a public company for re-registration as a private company. Section 11 Companies Act 1980 governs such an application, dealing with the applicants, the period of time allowed and the powers of the court.

Section 11(3) states that such an application may be made:

(*a*) by the holders of not less than 5% in nominal value of the company's issued share capital or any class thereof;

(*b*) if the company is not limited by shares, by not less than 5% of its members; *or*

(*c*) by not less than 50 of the company's members.

No person who has voted in favour of the resolution can apply.

Section 11(4) requires the application to be made within twenty-eight days of the passing of the resolution. The court, under s. 11(6), must then make an order either cancelling or confirming the resolution on such terms as it thinks fit, and may adjourn the proceedings in order that an arrangement may be made for the purchase of the interests of the dissentient members.

Section 11(7) states that the court order may provide for the purchase by the company of the shares of any members and for the resulting reduction of capital (*see* XI, **9**). It can also make any alterations to the memorandum or articles which are thereby rendered necessary and, under s. 11(8), prohibit the company from making subsequent alterations to these documents. The company may then make such alterations only with the leave of the court (*see* III, **9**(*d*)).

Finally, the registrar must be kept informed. As soon as an application to the court is made, s. 11(5)(*a*) requires the company to notify him. Then, when the court order is made, the company must deliver to him within fifteen days an office copy of it.

6. Differences between public and private company. Private companies have a number of advantages which can sometimes be *dis*advantageous according to whose interests are being considered. Thus a 96-year-old director may cling to office with obvious enjoyment even though there is a point at which efficiency outweighs experience. It can at least be said, however, that a private company differs from a public company in the following ways:

(*a*) The statutory minimum of directors is one: s. 176.

(*b*) Two or more directors can be appointed by a single resolution of a general meeting: s. 183.

(*c*) A director holding office for life on 18th July 1945 (now almost extinct) cannot be removed by ordinary resolution under s. 184.

(*d*) There is no statutory age-limit on the directors unless the company is a subsidiary of a public company: s. 185.

(*e*) There is no requirement that the secretary shall have qualifications: s. 79 Companies Act 1980.

(*f*) A private company can convert from a limited company to an unlimited company: s. 43 Companies Act 1967 and para. 43 of the 3rd Schedule to the Companies Act 1980.

(*g*) A private company may continue to apply for and be granted a licence under s. 19 to be registered as a limited company without the addition of the word "limited" to its name: para. 5 of the 3rd Schedule to the Companies Act 1980.

(*h*) A proxy may speak at general meetings: s. 136.

(*i*) The directors are not required to convene an extraordinary general meeting where the company's net assets fall to half or less of its called-up capital: s. 34 Companies Act 1980.

(*j*) No minimum authorised capital is required on registration: s. 3 Companies Act 1980.

(*k*) No minimum subscription is required before the first allotment: s. 47.

(*l*) A private company can commence business immediately on registration and requires no trading certificate: s. 4 Companies Act 1980.

(*m*) It is an offence for a private company to offer its shares or debentures to the public: s. 15 Companies Act 1980.

(*n*) Shares issued by a private company to a subscriber to the memorandum are not required to be paid up in cash: s. 29 Companies Act 1980.

(*o*) Where a subscriber to the memorandum of a private company sells non-cash assets to the company, there is no requirement that those assets shall be valued by an expert: s. 26 Companies Act 1980.

(*p*) It is unnecessary for 25% of the nominal value of the shares in a private company to be paid up on allotment: s. 22 Companies Act 1980.

(*q*) A private company is not prohibited from accepting payment for its shares in the form of an undertaking to do work or perform services for the company: s. 20 Companies Act 1980.

(*r*) Non-cash consideration to be furnished to a private company in respect of an allotment of shares need not be so furnished within five years: s. 23 Companies Act 1980.

(*s*) Non-cash consideration furnished to a private company in respect of an allotment of shares need not be valued by an expert: s. 24 Companies Act 1980.

(*t*) The statutory pre-emption rights can be totally excluded by the memorandum or articles of a private company: s. 17 Companies Act 1980.

(*u*) A private company may declare a dividend even though the amount of its net assets is less than the aggregate of its called-up share capital and its undistributable reserves: s. 40 Companies Act 1980.

(*v*) A private company is not required to file interim accounts to support a proposed interim dividend: s. 43 Companies Act 1980.

(*w*) The strict rules applicable to shares in which the company itself has a beneficial interest do not apply to private companies: s. 37 Companies Act 1980.

(*x*) A private company is not subject to the statutory restrictions on the taking of a lien or charge on its own shares: s. 38 Companies Act 1980.

(*y*) A private company which is not in the same group as a public company is not prohibited from making quasi-loans to its directors or entering into credit transactions with them: s. 49 Companies Act 1980.

(*z*) A private company which is not in the same group as a public company is not prohibited from making loans to persons connected with a director: s. 49 Companies Act 1980.

It can be seen from the length of this list that the Companies Act 1980 very greatly accentuated the difference between a public and a private company. Accordingly it is considerably more advantageous to register as a private company than was formerly the case before that Act was passed.

PROGRESS TEST 19

1. Define a private company. (**1**)
2. With what conditions must a private company comply as regards share capital when it seeks conversion to a public company? (**2**)
3. How does a private company convert into a public company? (**3**)
4. By what procedure does a public company convert into a private company? (**4**)
5. In what ways does a private company differ from a public company? (**6**)

CHAPTER XX

Shares

1. The nature of a share. Section 73 provides that shares are personal property and that they are transferable in the manner laid down by the articles. Section 74, as was explained in XV, **20**, requires each share to be numbered, except where all the shares in a company, or all those of a particular class, are fully paid up and rank *pari passu* for all purposes. The remainder of the sections on shares deal with transfer, share certificates and share warrants, and will be discussed later in this chapter.

None of these provisions is very helpful in telling us what a share is. It follows from s. 73, of course, that a share is a chose in action, since personal property consists of chattels real (leaseholds) and chattels personal, and chattels personal in their turn consist of choses in possession (tangible things such as goods) and choses in action (intangible things such as debts, contractual rights and patents). Clearly a share is intangible, its ownership being evidenced by a document called a *share certificate*. But if we were to try to describe it in these terms, no-one would have much conception of what we were discussing.

Probably the best description of a share is not given in the Act at all, but in *Borland's Trustees* v. *Steel* (1901), by Farwell J.: "A share is the interest of a shareholder in the company measured by a sum of money, for the purpose of liability in the first place, and of interest in the second". This definition indicates the true position of the member: he is under a *liability* to the company, namely to pay for his shares either on application, allotment, or when called upon to do so; but also he has an *interest* in the company which confers upon him certain rights, such as voting and dividend rights, and attendance at meetings. His interest is something he *owns*, so that he owns in reality a non-identified part of the company's undertaking. This is sometimes expressed by saying that the shareholders own the company, but of course no legal person can own another legal person. What the shareholders really own, collectively, is the entire undertaking of the company which, for convenience, is vested in the person of the company as soon as it is incorporated. It will readily be seen why it is sometimes said that the company is the *agent* of the shareholders.

2. Transfer of shares. A transfer of shares is simply a *voluntary assignment* and occurs, for example, where the shareholder sells his shares to another person or where he gives them away. In all cases of transfer s. 75 requires that a *proper instrument of transfer* must be delivered to the company. The word "instrument" simply means a document, i.e. the transfer must be in writing. A deed is not necessary unless the articles require one, and Table A, Article 23, does not do so.

The effect of s. 75 is that an instrument of transfer is essential. An article, therefore, which attempts to provide for the *automatic* transfer of shares in the company to any particular person on the death of a member is illegal and void, for on death the legal ownership of the shares passes automatically to the personal representatives by transmission: *Re Greene* (1949). On the other hand an article which provides that on the death of a member his shares must be offered to certain other persons is valid, and will bind the personal representatives accordingly, for no avoidance of s. 75 is involved: *Jarvis Motors (Harrow) Ltd.* v. *Carabott* (1964).

3. Form of transfer. At one time the instrument of transfer had to be executed both by the transferor and the transferee and their signatures had to be witnessed. Table A, Article 22, contains a requirement to this effect. Now, however, under the Stock Transfer Act 1963, the transfer of fully paid shares need only be signed by the transferor and no attestation is required. The Act overrides any provision to the contrary in the articles.

Table A, Article 25, provides that the directors may refuse to recognise an instrument of transfer unless:

(*a*) a transfer fee of 2*s.* 6*d.* (13p) is paid to the company;
(*b*) the instrument of transfer is accompanied by the share certificate; and
(*c*) the instrument of transfer is in respect of only one class of share.

In the case of listed companies, however, Stock Exchange rules require that the company's articles should provide for registration of a transfer without payment of any fee.

Section 77 states that on the application of the *transferor* of shares the company must enter the name of the transferee in the register of members in the same way as if the application for entry were made by the *transferee*.

4. Certification of transfers. Where a shareholder transfers only *some* of his shares in a company, it would be unsafe for him to part with the share certificate for his entire holding to the transferee. He therefore sends it to the company, which endorses the instrument of transfer with the words "certificate lodged", returns it to the transferor, but retains the share certificate. This process is known as certification of the transfer.

The transferor then sends the certified instrument of transfer to the transferee, who applies to the company for registration. The company issues two new share certificates, one to the transferor to cover the shares which he continues to own, and one to the transferee to cover the shares he has acquired.

If the company is negligent and sends the transferor's original certificate for the entire holding back to him, it is not liable for any fraudulent act which he is able to do as a result, for that is *his* act and not that of the company.

5. The legal effect of certification. Section 79(1) states that the certification of a transfer amounts simply to a representation by the company that documents have been produced to it showing that the transferor has a *prima facie* title to the shares. The section carefully amplifies this by going on to say what certification is not: it is not a representation that the transferor has a title.

Thus, when the certification of a transfer is effected, the company is merely saying that it has seen a share certificate which appears to be in order, though it is *not* saying that it is in order. For the company to guarantee the title of the transferor would be to put altogether too heavy a burden on it.

NOTE: Naturally, if the company makes a *fraudulent* certification, i.e. with the intention to deceive, it will be liable for deceit. If, however, it makes a false certification *negligently*, there was at one time no liability at common law for negligent mis-statements. Section 79(2) covered this possibility by providing that a company should be under the same liability for a negligent certification as for a fraudulent one. Possibly today this provision is no longer necessary, for it is arguable that the company and the transferee are in a "special relationship" within the principle laid down in *Hedley Byrne & Co., Ltd.* v. *Heller & Partners, Ltd.* (1963), and that the common law would now cover the position.

6. Restrictions on transfer. Subject to the articles, shares may be freely transferred to any person provided the correct stamp duty is paid. Under the Finance Act 1974, the stamp duty is £2% of the price, and the Stamp Act 1891, imposes a fine of £10 for registration of a transfer which is not correctly stamped. For administrative convenience, however, the articles sometimes provide for the suspension of the registration of transfers for a short time each year in order to enable dividend lists to be prepared. Table A, Article 27, contains such a provision, which must necessarily be within the period laid down by s. 115, i.e. not more than thirty days in the year. But not all companies take advantage of s. 115, and there are many which do not close their books at all.

(1) *Private companies.* Formerly, a company could not satisfy the definition of a private company in s. 28 unless its articles contained a restriction of some kind on the transfer of its shares. Despite the repeal of s. 28 by the Companies Act 1980 (*see* XIX, 1), it is probable that private companies will normally find it desirable to continue to include restrictions on the transfer of shares in their articles.

(2) *Public companies.* Often there are restrictions on transfer in *public* companies, although in this case the Stock Exchange will not grant a listing for the shares if they are fully paid. Table A, Article 24, provides that the directors may refuse to register the transfer of *partly paid* shares to a person of whom they do not approve. Were it not for such a restriction, a member could transfer his shares to a "man of straw" simply for the purpose of avoiding liability for the next call on them. Article 24 also provides that the directors may refuse to register a transfer of any share on which the company has a lien.

7. The exercise of the company's power to refuse registration. The company's power to refuse registration of a transfer is, under Article 24 of Table A, exercised by the board of directors, but unless they actively exercise it the transferee must be registered. Thus there must be a *majority* of the board *opposing* the registration in order to constitute exercise of the power.

It follows that if the board are evenly divided with no casting vote, the transfer must be registered: *Re Hackney Pavilion, Ltd.* (1924). And if one of two directors intentionally fails to attend a board meeting so that the quorum of two will not be reached and accordingly transfers cannot be passed for registration, the transferee must, again, be registered: *Re Copal Varnish Co.* (1917). Moreover, the board's power to refuse registration of a transfer must be exercised within a reasonable time, or it will be lost: *Re Swaledale Cleaners, Ltd.* (1968).

So long as the directors act within the scope of the article, their decision cannot be challenged except on the grounds of bad faith. Since the onus of proving bad faith rests on the plaintiff, the directors' refusal to register the transfer can seldom be successfully attacked, for while a state of mind may be a fact, it is a fact which is exceedingly difficult to prove.

Thus in *Charles Forte Investments* v. *Amanda* (1963), the articles gave the directors power to refuse to register transfers "in their absolute discretion and without assigning any reason". They refused, giving no reason, to register a transfer by a former employee and minor shareholder who had quarrelled with one of the directors. He threatened to present a petition for winding up the company, whereupon the company applied for an injunction to prevent him from doing so. HELD: (*i*) the injunction should be granted, since the winding up would injure other members who were in no way responsible for the situation; (*ii*) the directors were acting within the scope of the articles, unless bad faith could be proved, which it could not.

The articles may, of course, be more specific than they were in the Forte case; they may empower the directors to refuse to register transfers on certain specified grounds. The directors can then be interrogated as to the grounds for their refusal. But whether the article is widely phrased or narrowly expressed, they need only show that they were acting within its terms. They need give no reasons for their decision beyond this. If, on the other hand, they are foolish enough to give their reasons, then the court may consider whether those reasons were adequate. This is one of many legal situations in which the less that is said the less likelihood there is of liability.

Section 78 and Table A, Article 26, both provide that notice of a refusal to register a transfer must be sent to the transferee within two months from the date when the transfer was lodged with the company. If the transferee wishes to challenge the refusal, he should apply to the court for rectification of the register under s. 116.

3. Forged transfers. A forged document never has any legal effect. It can never move ownership from one person to another, however genuine it may appear. Thus a forged instrument of transfer leaves the ownership of the shares exactly where it always was: in the so-called transferor.

It follows that if the company registers a forged transfer, the true owner can apply to be replaced on the register. At the same time if the company has issued a new share certificate to a subsequent purchaser, it cannot, as will be seen later, deny his title to the shares, for the certificate estops it from doing so. It will therefore be under a liability to compensate him for his loss: *Re Bahia and San Francisco Railway* (1868).

In order to avoid this result, companies normally notify the transferor of the transfer so that he can object if he wishes, but such a notification does not enable the company to escape liability if in fact it registers a forged transfer and causes loss to a transferee. Nor is it always of much use to the company, for the transferor may be abroad at the time, or not trouble to reply.

The Forged Transfers Acts 1891–2, however, permit the company to form a fund out of which to pay compensation for forged transfers, and it is always possible for a company to insure against the risk.

If the company is compelled to pay compensation, it can claim an indemnity from the person who sent it the forged transfer even though that person was unaware of the forgery: *Sheffield Corporation* v. *Barclay* (1905). Moreover, that person, however innocent, cannot rely on a share certificate issued to him as an estoppel preventing the company from denying his title.

9. Share certificates. Section 80(1) states that a company must have the share certificate ready for delivery within two months after the allotment or the lodging of the transfer, unless the terms of issue of the shares otherwise provide. It imposes no requirements as regards the form of the certificate. In the case of listed companies, Stock Exchange rules require certificates to be ready for delivery within two weeks.

Table A, Article 8, however, while repeating the provisions of s. 80, requires the certificate to be under seal and to specify both the shares to which it relates and the amount paid up on them. Article 9 provides that if a share certificate is defaced, lost or destroyed, it may be renewed on payment of 2*s*. 6*d*. (13p) and on such terms as to evidence and indemnity as the directors think fit.

10. Legal effect of share certificates. Section 81 states that a share certificate under the common seal of the company specifying the shares held by the member is *prima facie evidence of his title to them*. It is important to understand the legal effect of this provision:

(*a*) *A share certificate is not a negotiable instrument*, for its transfer from one person to another does not move the ownership of the shares. To move the ownership, as we have seen, an instrument of transfer must be completed, lodged with the company, and approved by the directors, after which the transferee must be entered on the register. It is this final act of entry on the register which completes the shift of ownership. The physical whereabouts of the share *certificate* is legally immaterial even though it may be administratively inconvenient. If lost, it must be found. If damaged, it must be replaced. If destroyed, it must be renewed. But whatever has happened to it and wherever it is, the legal title to the shares is in the registered holder.

(*b*) *Evidence of title*. All that the share certificate amounts to, then, is a statement by the company that *at the moment when it was issued* the person named on it was the legal owner of the shares specified in it, and that those shares were paid up to the extent stated. It does not constitute title but is merely evidence of title. It is, however, a statement of considerable importance for it is made with the knowledge that other persons may act upon it in the belief that it is true, and this fact brings into operation the doctrine of *estoppel*.

(*c*) *Estoppel* is not a principle of substantive law. It is a *rule of evidence which prevents a person from denying the legal implications of his conduct*. If he has behaved in a certain way, and if other persons have drawn certain natural and reasonable deductions from that behaviour as to his legal position, then he is not allowed to give evidence to show that his legal position is not in fact what it appeared to be. A company, therefore, is not allowed to deny the facts which it has stated to be true when it issued the share certificate.

This rule is expressed by saying that the share certificate acts as an estoppel against the company as regards:

(*i*) the title of the member; and

(*ii*) the amount paid up on the shares.

The company, once it has issued the certificate, may not deny these facts, except, as stated above, against a person who sent up a forged transfer, or where the certificate itself is a forgery: *Ruben* v. *Great Fingall Consolidated* (1906).

11. The rights of a transferee. It will be apparent from the preceding pages of this chapter that there is of necessity a certain interval of time between the *contract* to sell a shareholding and the *registration* of the transferee. During this period the transferee clearly has certain rights, but his exact legal position is far from clear. It can be most easily considered if a transfer is divided into stages.

The first stage in a sale of shares is the *contract of sale*. If the vendor breaks this contract, the would-be purchaser has a right to damages for breach of contract, calculated on the normal basis, wherever damages would be an adequate remedy. However, if he is trying to buy shares in a private company, or if the shares in question are not readily available on the market, damages will be quite useless. In this case he may seek a decree of specific performance: *Duncuft* v. *Albrecht* (1841). He is then often said to have an *equitable interest* in the shares and indeed he has an interest which equity protects; nevertheless, it is an equitable interest of a qualified nature, for the only right which it confers on the purchaser is the "right to enforce the contract in proceedings for specific performance": *Oughtred* v. *Inland Revenue Commissioners* (1959).

The second stage in a sale of shares—and the first stage of a gift—is the completion of an instrument of transfer by the transferor. This in itself confers no further rights on a purchaser, at least where the vendor is still unpaid: *Musselwhite* v. *Musselwhite & Son, Ltd.* (1962). A donee has no rights at all.

The third stage in a sale—and the second stage of a gift—is the delivery of an executed instrument of transfer accompanied by the relevant share certificate to the purchaser or donee, as the case may be. At this point the transferor has done all that he can do. The only remaining thing to be done in order to perfect the transferee's title is an act of the *company*, not of the transferor—namely, the entry of the transferee's name in the register of members. It has been held that the completion of this stage is the true moment of gift: *Re Rose* (1952). From this moment onwards the transferee has a full beneficial interest in the shares and the transferor holds them on trust for him until registration is effected. Thus the benefits attached to the shares, such as dividends, belong in equity to the transferee, while the exercise of the transferor's voting rights are controlled by the transferee.

The parties to the transaction can of course modify these rules as they wish. They can, for instance, agree that the shares are to be sold "cum" (with) dividend or "ex" (without) dividend, and the price paid for the shares will vary accordingly. The vendor can also agree to sell "with registration guaranteed", the effect of which is to make the eventual registration of the purchaser a *condition* of the contract, failure of which gives the purchaser the right to recover his money. If registration is not expressly guaranteed in this way, the purchaser has no remedy against the vendor if the company, under the appropriate provisions in its articles, lawfully refuses to register the transfer. He will simply continue to own the *equitable interest* in the shares while the *legal title* remains in the vendor. Moreover, it should be borne in mind that all the rules concerning equitable interests which were explained in XIII, **8–14** are relevant here.

The final stage of a transfer, whether by sale or gift, is the company's entry of the transferee in its register of members. This is the moment at which the *legal title* to the shares passes from the transferor to the transferee, and the transaction is now complete.

12. Duty to notify company of interests in voting share capital. Section 33(1) Companies Act 1967, as amended by s. 26 Companies Act 1976, requires any of the following persons to notify the company of their interests in the relevant share capital:

(*a*) A person who either had *no interests* in it, or else was interested in *less than* 5% *of it* in nominal value, and who then, as the result of an event, acquires interests so that he is interested in 5% *or more of it* in nominal value;

(*b*) A person who was interested in 5% *or more of it* in nominal value, and who, as the result of an event, either acquires *further interests*, or loses some but *remains interested in* 5% *or more*;

(*c*) A person who was interested in 5% *or more of it* in nominal value, but as the result of an event is interested in *less than* 5% or has *no interests* at all.

Any of these persons must, within five days, notify the company in writing of:

(*a*) the occurrence of the event concerned;

(*b*) the date on which it occurred;

(*c*) the number of shares in the relevant share capital in which he is interested immediately after the event, or the fact that he has no interests at all.

Section 33(7) requires the notice to identify him and to give his address.

Section 33(10) states that this section applies only to companies with a stock exchange listing for the whole or part of their share capital. It also defines "relevant share capital" as the "issued share capital of a class carrying rights to vote in all circumstances at general meetings". The definition, which has caused difficulty, has been clarified by s. 26(10) Companies Act 1976. This subsection thoughtfully states that, "for the avoidance of doubt", where the relevant share capital of a company is divided into different classes of shares, the stated percentage refers to a percentage of the issued shares of *each class taken separately*. This was probably the original intention, but the language of the 1967 Act was far from clear. Moreover, s. 26(2) Companies Act 1976 authorises the Secretary of State to prescribe a different notifiable percentage at any time by statutory instrument.

Section 33(4) states that in computing the five days, Saturdays, Sundays, and bank holidays must be disregarded.

Finally, s. 33(4) states that "interest" has the same meaning as is given by s. 28 (*see* XXII, **16**), except that the interest of a person whose ordinary business includes the lending of money, and who holds the shares by way of security in the ordinary course of that business, is to be disregarded.

13. The register of interests in voting share capital. Section 34(1) and (3) Companies Act 1967 require every company to which s. 33 applies to keep a register for the purpose of recording the information furnished under that section (*see* **12**). Whenever it obtains such information, it must within three days inscribe it in the register against the name of the person concerned, together with the date of the inscription. In computing the three days, Saturdays, Sundays and bank holidays are to be disregarded.

Section 34(2) requires the register to be made up so that the entries against each name are in chronological order.

Section 34(4) prevents the company becoming concerned in any question regarding the rights of any person to any shares. The section is imposing merely an administrative duty, and the company must be protected from further involvement: cf. s. 117 (*see* XIII, **12**).

Section 34(5) requires the register to be kept at the registered office or at the same place as the company's register of members (*see* XIII, **3**), and to be open for at least two hours a day during business hours to the inspection of any member without charge, and of any other persons on payment of the prescibed fee (£1 under Statutory Instrument No. 1749 of 1980).

Section 34(7) authorises any person to require a copy of the register, or of any part of it, on payment of 30p. per page: Statutory Instrument No. 1749 of 1980. The copy must be supplied within ten days.

Lastly, s. 34(9) states that if inspection is refused, or a copy not sent within the ten days, the court may order that inspection be allowed or that the copy be sent.

14. Power of company to require disclosure of beneficial interests in voting share capital. Section 27(1) Companies Act 1976 empowers any listed company by written notice to require any member to indicate in writing:

(*a*) the *capacity* in which he holds any shares forming part of the relevant share capital; and

(*b*) if he does not hold them as beneficial owner, the *persons* who have an interest in them and the *nature of their interest*, so far as it lies within his knowledge.

Section 27(2) provides that where a company is informed that *any other person* has an interest in shares forming part of the relevant share capital, it may by written notice require that other person to indicate in writing:

(*a*) the *capacity* in which he holds that interest; and

(*b*) if he holds it otherwise than as beneficial owner, the *persons* who have an interest in it and the *nature of their interest*, so far as it lies within his knowledge.

Section 27(5) requires the company, whenever it receives information under these rules, to inscribe against the name of the member in question, in a separate part of the register of interests in voting share capital:

(*a*) the fact that a requirement was imposed on him under the section and its date; and

(*b*) the information received as a result.

15. Power of company to require disclosure of voting agreements. Section 27(3) Companies Act 1976 empowers any listed company by written notice to require any member to indicate in writing whether any voting rights carried by any shares forming part of the relevant share capital and held by him are the subject of any *agreement or arrangement* by which some other person is entitled to control the exercise of those rights. If so, he must give written particulars of the agreement and the parties to it, so far as it lies within his knowledge.

Section 27(4) provides that where a company is informed that any other person is a party to such a voting agreement, it may by written notice require that other person to give written particulars of the agreement and the parties to it, so far as it lies within his knowledge.

Section 27(5) (*see* **14**) applies also to information regarding voting agreements which is received by the company.

16. Share warrants. Section 83(1) permits a company limited by shares to issue share warrants under its common seal provided:

(*a*) there is authority in the articles, and
(*b*) the shares are fully paid.

It also permits the company to provide for the payment of dividends on the shares included in the warrant by means of coupons.

Section 83(3) states that a share warrant entitles the bearer to the shares specified in it, and that the shares may be transferred by delivery of the warrant. It follows, therefore, that a share warrant, unlike a share certificate, *is a negotiable instrument*, and thus may be issued only by companies without restrictions on transfer in their articles.

Section 112(1) provides that on the issue of a share warrant the company must strike out of the register of members the name of the person who held the shares now comprised in the warrant, and enter in the register:

(*a*) the fact of the issue of the warrant;
(*b*) a statement of the shares included in the warrant, with distinguishing numbers, if any; and
(*c*) the date of the issue of the warrant.

Section 112(2) entitles the bearer of a share warrant to surrender it for cancellation and to have his name entered in the register in respect of the shares which were included in it.

Section 112(5) provides that the bearer of a share warrant may, if the articles so provide, be deemed to be a member of the company either to the full extent or for any purposes defined in the articles.

Section 182(2) states that a share warrant will not constitute the share qualification of a director, where one is imposed by the articles.

We have already seen in XIV that the annual return must give particulars of share warrants. These are:

(a) The amount of shares for which warrants are outstanding.

(b) The amount of share warrants issued and surrendered since the date of the last return.

(c) The number of shares comprised in each share warrant.

Where a company has converted its shares into stock, stock warrants may be issued in exactly the same way. In practice neither share nor stock warrants are common.

17. Personation of a shareholder. Section 84, concerning personation of a shareholder or holder of a share warrant, has been repealed and superseded by the Theft Act 1968, ss. 15 and 20 of which are sufficiently widely drawn to embrace this offence.

18. Mortgage of shares. Shares, like any other form of property, may be mortgaged as security for a loan. The mortgage may be legal or equitable.

(a) *Legal mortgage*. Here the shares are *actually transferred* to the lender so that he becomes the registered holder with full membership rights. When the loan is repaid he transfers them back again to the borrower, with whom he has made an agreement to this effect.

Clearly this type of mortgage gives the lender complete security. He obtains the *legal* title to the shares, not merely an equitable interest in them. But it is cumbersome, stamp duty will be paid on each transfer, and if the shares are only partly paid the lender becomes personally liable for calls while his name is on the register.

(b) *Equitable mortgage*. Here the shares are not transferred to the lender, but the share certificate is merely deposited with him, sometimes accompanied by a *blank transfer*, i.e. an instrument of transfer signed by the borrower but with the name of the transferee left "blank".

In this case the lender's security is not complete, for he has merely an *equitable* interest in the shares unless he fills in the blank transfer when the borrower defaults and becomes the registered holder. He cannot, as we have already seen in XIII, inform the company that he has an equitable interest in the shares, for s. 117 states that the company may not take notice of trusts. The only way in which he can protect his interest, then, is by serving a stop notice on the company.

Equitable mortgages are more common, however, than legal mortgages, for they do not have the same disadvantages.

19. Calls. A call in the strict sense is a demand by the company for money due on the shares *excluding* the amounts payable on application, allotment or by instalments. Often the full amount of the share is payable on application, in which case the member is never liable to pay any more (with the exception of those rare cases when his liability can become unlimited). Sometimes a certain amount is payable on application and the balance on allotment or by instalments, i.e. at certain fixed dates. The date of a call, however, is not fixed until the call is made, and it will not be made until the company requires more capital.

Despite this distinction, Table A, Article 19, provides that for the purposes of Table A sums payable on allotment or at a fixed date, i.e. by instalments, shall be deemed to be calls, and all the rules relating to calls apply to them as well.

The method of making calls depends entirely on the articles. Table A, Article 15, empowers the directors to make calls provided:

(a) no call exceeds a quarter of the nominal value of the share;
(b) no call is payable at less than one month from the date fixed for payment of the last call; and
(c) each member is given at least fourteen days' notice of the time and place of payment.

It also authorises the directors to revoke or postpone a call if they wish.

Table A, Article 18, provides that if the member does not pay the call he must pay interest not exceeding 5% on the sum due from the date fixed for payment until he actually pays it, though the directors may waive the payment of interest. Under s. 20, as was explained in III, **10**, a call is a specialty debt.

The directors' power to make calls must, like all their other powers, be exercised *bona fide* for the benefit of the company, and they may not abuse it. Thus they may not make calls on all the shareholders except themselves: *Alexander* v. *Automatic Telephone Co.* (1900), nor on one particular shareholder alone because he happens to annoy them: *Galloway* v. *Hallé Concerts Society* (1915).

Section 59, however, permits a company, with authority in its articles, to arrange on the issue of the shares for a difference between the shareholders in the amounts and times of payment of calls, and Table A, Article 20, gives the necessary authority. It is important to remember, however, that such an arrangement must be made *on issue*, and so is a term of the contract between the shareholder and the company, and that even when it exists the directors cannot avoid their duty to act in *good faith*.

Under the Finance Act 1973 capital duty of £1 per cent is payable on the amount of the calls received.

20. Payment of calls in advance. Section 59 also permits a company, with authority in its articles, to accept from a member the whole or part of the amount unpaid on his shares, even though it has not been called up. Table A, Article 21, again gives the necessary authority, and allows the directors to pay interest not exceeding 5% on the money so advanced until it would have become payable.

The advance payment, although in reality share capital, is treated as a *loan* to the company, for interest is a debt payable regardless of whether profits are available (*see* XVI, **2**). Moreover, in liquidation (*see* IV, **5**) it must be repaid to the appropriate shareholders *after* the debts have been paid, but *before* the share capital is repaid to the shareholders generally. It cannot, however, be repaid to the shareholders while the company is a going concern, except under a reduction of capital complying with s. 66, so that in this respect it is treated as capital.

Table A, Article 118, makes it clear that the advance payment does *not* count as paid-up capital for dividend purposes. This, of course, follows from Article 21, for it would be inequitable if the advance payment carried a right to dividend as well as to interest. Once again, the directors' power to accept calls in advance must be exercised *bona fide*.

In *Sykes' Case* (1872), the directors, who knew that the company was insolvent, paid up the amount unpaid on their own shares in advance, and then at once applied it in payment of their own fees. HELD: They were still liable for the amount unpaid on their shares.

21. Lien. A lien, like a mortgage or pledge, is a form of security. It can arise at common law, such as the possessory lien of a repairer on the article repaired, or in equity, or under the maritime law. The lien of a company on the shares of a member is an example of an equitable lien, giving the company an *equitable* interest in the shares of the member.

Apart from s. 38 Companies Act 1980 (see below) the Acts contain no reference to lien, but the articles of companies frequently give the company a lien on the shares of a member for money owed by him to the company. Table A, Article 11, as amended by the Companies Act 1980, gives the company a lien on all *partly paid* shares in respect of *money due on the shares*. This lien extends to the dividends as well.

If the member does not pay the sum which he owes to the company, the lien can be enforced by applying to the court for an order for the sale of the shares. Possibly, under the Law of Property Act 1925, this power of sale is exercisable without application to the court, but in any case the articles of the company usually give a power of sale in such circumstances. Table A, Article 12, accordingly gives the company *power to sell* any shares on which a lien exists provided:

(*a*) the sum in respect of which the lien exists is presently payable;

(*b*) written notice demanding payment has been given to the registered holder; and

(*c*) fourteen days after the notice have expired.

Article 13 permits the directors to authorise a transfer of the shares to the purchaser, who can then be registered in respect of them, but is not bound to see to the application of the purchase-money, and cannot have his title affected by any irregularity in the proceedings.

Article 14 states that the proceeds of the sale are to be received by the company, and applied in payment of the amount due to it, the balance being paid to the original owner.

Since, as stated above, a lien gives the company an equitable interest, students should make sure that they have fully grasped the rules relating to the priority of equitable interests explained in XIII.

Section 38(1) Companies Act 1980 greatly restricts the taking of a lien or other charge on its own shares by a *public* company. Such a lien or charge is *void* unless authorised by s. 38(2) which expressly permits a public company to take:

(*a*) a charge on its own *partly paid* shares for an amount payable in respect of them; and

(*b*) if it is a money-lending company, a charge on its own shares, *whether fully or partly paid*, as security in connection with a transaction entered into in the ordinary course of its business.

22. Forfeiture. When shares are forfeited the company *takes them away* from the member. This is obviously a serious step to take, for not only does it deprive the shareholder of his property but, unless the shares are re-issued, it involves a *reduction of capital* without the consent of the court and is the only example of this apart from surrender.

It is unlawful to forfeit shares unless the articles authorise it. Table A, Article 33, authorises forfeiture for non-payment of calls and Article 39 for non-payment of sums payable at a fixed time, i.e. by instalments. Forfeiture of shares for any debt which does not arise from the shares is invalid. Consequently it has a much narrower scope than a lien.

Article 33 empowers the directors to serve a notice on the defaulting member requiring him to pay the company. Article 34 states that this notice must name a day at least fourteen days ahead on or before which payment must be made, and must inform the member that unless he makes the required payment his shares will be forfeited. Article 35 empowers the directors to forfeit the shares concerned by resolution if the member does not comply with the notice.

Article 36 permits the directors to sell the forfeited shares or otherwise dispose of them as they wish. It also allows them to cancel the forfeiture up to the time when they have disposed of the shares. Article 38 authorises the company to receive the purchase-money if the shares are sold, and to execute a transfer to the purchaser, who then becomes the registered holder and is not bound to see to the application of the purchase-money; nor is his title affected by any irregularity in the proceedings. This article is similar to Article 13 relating to sale of the shares on exercise of the company's lien.

As stated above, unless the shares are re-issued forfeiture results in a reduction of capital. Normally, therefore, the company re-issues them. It can re-issue at any price provided that the total of the *sum paid by the former holder* of the shares, together with the *amount paid on re-issue* and the *amount for which the purchaser is liable in the future* is not less than the par value for, if it were, this would be an issue at a discount. Usually it is *more* than the par value, and the excess is of course a *premium* and must go into the share premium account.

The shares are forfeited in the condition in which they then are. Thus if they are £1 shares 50p paid up, and the shareholder is unable to pay a call of 25p, the shares will be re-issued 50p paid up, and the new holder becomes liable for the whole amount unpaid on the shares, including the call of 25p which resulted in the forfeiture. In this case the price the purchaser pays for the re-issued shares is a *premium*.

Meanwhile the original holder is discharged from all liability on the shares, except that he will go on the "B" list if the company goes into liquidation within a year. To preserve his liability, an express provision in the articles is required, and Table A, Article 37, has this effect. Such an article makes him liable as a *debtor* for, as stated above, he is liable as a *contributory* in a liquidation in any case. The debt, as we have seen, is under s. 20 a specialty debt, and accordingly he will be liable for twelve years: *Ladies' Dress Association* v. *Pulbrook* (1900).

23. Lien and forfeiture compared. Students are sometimes asked to compare the enforcement of the company's lien with forfeiture. The following points should then be borne in mind:

(*a*) A lien *never involves a reduction of capital*, for the shares are necessarily sold. Forfeiture *will involve a reduction of capital* unless the shares are re-issued.

(*b*) A lien is enforced by *sale*. Forfeiture is effected by *depriving the member of his shares*.

(*c*) Lien is a form of *security* for a debt. Forfeiture is a *penal proceeding*.

(*d*) In the case of lien, the liability of the former owner is only as a "B" list *contributory* in a liquidation. After forfeiture an article similar to Table A, Article 37, can impose the liability of a *debtor* upon him.

(*e*) In the case of lien, the former owner *receives*, on the sale of the shares, the difference between *the amount received for them* and *the amount of his debt*. After forfeiture, he receives *nothing* and never recovers what he has already paid on the shares.

24. Surrender. The surrender of shares, like forfeiture, is lawful only where the articles authorise it, and Table A does not do so. Sometimes, however, a company's articles authorise the directors to accept a surrender of shares where it would be proper to do so.

Surrender is permissible only in two cases:

(*a*) As a short cut to forfeiture, to avoid the formalities.

(*b*) Where shares are surrendered in exchange for new shares of the same nominal value (but with different rights).

Surrendered shares may be re-issued in the same way as forfeited shares, and if this is done no reduction of capital occurs in (*a*) above. In (*b*) there is of course no reduction because the capital is replaced.

25. Cancellation of shares after forfeiture or surrender. Section 37 Companies Act 1980 gives two further rules applicable only to *public* companies:

(*a*) Where shares are forfeited or surrendered, then unless the company has disposed of them (by re-issue) within the following three years, it must:
  (*i*) cancel them and diminish the amount of its share capital accordingly; and
  (*ii*) where the cancellation brings the nominal value of the allotted share capital below the authorised minimum, apply for *re-registration as a private company*.

In s. 37(2) that Act makes it clear that it is not necessary to comply with the rules in s. 66 Companies Act 1948 governing reduction of capital, although a board resolution altering the company's memorandum is required.

(*b*) Section 37(3) prohibits the company from exercising any voting rights in respect of shares which have been forfeited or surrendered.

PROGRESS TEST 20

1. What is a share? (**1**)
2. By what method must shares be transferred? Discuss the form of transfer. (**2, 3**)
3. What do you understand by certification of transfers? What is the legal effect of certification? (**4, 5**)
4. How far can a company refuse to register a transfer of shares? (**6, 7**)
5. What is the legal effect of a forged transfer? What steps can a company take to minimise losses which it may sustain due to forged transfers? (**8**)
6. What are the requirements of the Act and Table A with regard to the completion and the form of the share certificate? (**9**)
7. What is the legal effect of a share certificate? (**10**)
8. What is the legal position with regard to shares during the period of time from the making of the contract of sale until the registration of the transfer? (**11**)
9. Give the statutory provisions regarding the register of interests in voting share capital. (**12, 13**)

10. Give the statutory provisions regarding the disclosure of beneficial interests in voting share capital. (**14**)

11. Give the statutory provisions regarding voting agreements. (**15**)

12. Give the statutory provisions with regard to share warrants. (**16**)

13. How far is the bearer of a share warrant a member of the company? (**16**)

14. In what ways may a mortgage of shares be effected? (**18**)

15. What is a call? What are the provisions of Table A regarding calls? (**19**)

16. Under what circumstances may a company accept payment of calls in advance from a member? How should the advance payment be treated? (**20**)

17. Give the provisions of Table A regarding the lien of a company on the shares of its members. (**21**)

18. Give the provisions of Table A regarding the forfeiture of shares. (**22**)

19. Compare and contrast the company's enforcement of its lien with its power of forfeiture. (**23**)

20. Under what circumstances is a surrender of shares lawful? (**24**)

21. What special rules were introduced by the Companies Act 1980 relating to liens in public companies? (**21**)

22. What special rules were introduced by the Companies Act 1980 to apply in public companies when shares have been forfeited or surrendered? (**25**)

CHAPTER XXI

Debentures

1. Power of company to borrow. The power of a company to borrow money is implied in the case of all trading companies. Non-trading companies, however, must be expressly authorised to borrow by their memorandum.

A power to borrow money, whether express or implied, includes the power to charge the assets of the company by way of security to the lender. Charges have already been discussed in II, and it will by this time be clear that the company can charge any type of property which it happens to own. It can also charge its uncalled capital (*see* II, **18**), though not its reserve capital (*see* XV, **3**).

Borrowing powers are not exercisable until the company can *commence business.* Public companies, therefore, must first obtain their trading certificate by complying with the requirements of s. 4 Companies Act 1980 which are set out in V, **2**. Moreover, the memorandum may restrict the amount of money which the company may borrow.

The power of the company to borrow is exercised by the directors, who cannot of course borrow more than the sum authorised. Sometimes, however, the power of the *company* to borrow is *unrestricted*, but the authority of the *directors* acting as its agents is *limited* to a certain figure. For instance, Table A, Article 79, prohibits the directors from borrowing a sum which exceeds the nominal amount of the issued share capital unless they have first obtained the sanction of a general meeting of the company. It is naturally very important to distinguish between borrowing which is *ultra vires the company*, and borrowing which is *intra vires the company* but *outside the scope of the directors' authority*.

The European Communities Act 1972 has made an important change here and it is therefore necessary to consider the position before that Act in order to understand its effect.

2. Ultra vires borrowing before the European Communities Act 1972. Any act which was *ultra vires* the company was void. Here the behaviour of the directors, as the company's agents, could have no effect whatsoever on the validity of the loan, for no agent can ever have more capacity than his principal. If, therefore, the borrowing was *ultra vires* so that the company had no capacity to undertake it, the lender could have no right of action against the company in respect of it, nor could he enforce any security granted to him. This was so even where the company's memorandum empowered it to borrow if the loan, to the lender's knowledge, was to be used for an *ultra vires* purpose: *Introductions, Ltd.* v. *National Provincial Bank, Ltd.* (1969), (*see* II, **25**).

The lender might, however, have the following remedies against the company:

(*a*) If he could *identify* the money lent, or any property which the company had bought with it, he could at common law recover the money or the property, as the case might be, since he was still regarded as its owner.

(*b*) If he could *not identify* the money lent, he might in equity be able to obtain a "tracing order" giving him an equitable charge on a mixed mass of assets: *Sinclair* v. *Brougham* (1914), (*see* II, **27**).

(*c*) If the company had used the borrowed money to pay off any of its *intra vires* debts, the lender ranked as a creditor up to the amount so used. He did not here obtain the security or the priority, if any, of the *intra vires* creditors, but he was able to enforce any security granted *to him*.

This remedy appeared to be based on the fact that the company still owed the same amount of money; it merely owed it to a different person. Its liabilities remained constant, but there was a change of creditor.

Finally, although the lender had no right of action on the contract of loan against the *company*, he might be able to sue the *directors* for *breach of warranty of authority*. If their lack of authority was obvious from the memorandum and articles, it must be remembered that these are public documents the contents of which the lender was *deemed to know*. He might therefore be met by the argument that he knew the directors had no authority, and so could not have been misled by their warranty. On the other hand, if the directors deliberately misrepresented their authority the lender ought in principle to have had a right of action. An analogy could perhaps have been drawn between this situation and that in *Curtis* v. *Chemical Cleaning and Dyeing Co.*

(1951), where the document by its terms denied the plaintiff a remedy, but the plaintiff nevertheless sued successfully because the terms of the document had been misrepresented to her.

3. Intra vires borrowing outside the agent's authority before the European Communities Act 1972. This type of borrowing was often described as being "*ultra vires* the directors", but this was confusing. Strictly speaking, the terms "*intra vires*" and "*ultra vires*" should be reserved for describing the *company's capacity*, and should not be used to describe the *agent's authority*.

The legal position here, however, was quite simple. The company had the *power* to borrow, but it had restricted the authority of the agent to a certain sum which had been exceeded. There was no lack of *capacity*. It followed that the company might, if it wished, ratify the agent's act, in which case the loan bound both the lender and the company as if it had been made with the company's authority in the first place.

On the other hand, the company might refuse to ratify the agent's act. Here the normal principles of agency applied. A third party who deals with an agent knowing that the agent is exceeding his authority has no right of action against the principal. Bearing in mind that the memorandum and articles are public documents *the contents of which the third party was deemed to know*, he had no right of action against the company if the agent's lack of authority was obvious from reading them. A third party, however, is not affected by *secret* restrictions of the agent's authority, so that if the lack of authority was not clear from the public documents and the lender did not know of it from some other source, the company was bound (*see* XXII, **24, 25**).

4. The provisions of the European Communities Act 1972. The relevant provision of the European Communities Act 1972 is s. 9(1). This has been set out and fully discussed in II, **30**, where *ultra vires* contracts in general, and not merely *ultra vires* borrowings, are considered.

Students are advised at this point to re-read II, **26–30**.

5. The nature of a debenture. The statutory definition of a debenture in s. 455 is very wide. The Act here states that debenture includes debenture stock, bonds, and any other securities of a company whether constituting a charge on the assets or not.

The definition is juristically confused, for a debenture is strictly speaking a *document*, while debenture stock is not. The word "securities" also sometimes misleads students here. It is used to mean the *undertaking to repay* the money borrowed, and the definition goes on to state that this undertaking may or may not be accompanied by a charge on the company's assets. Thus a mortgage of the company's property to a single individual as security is a debenture within the definition.

Usually, however, a debenture is *one of a series* issued to a number of lenders. It is often accompanied by a charge on the assets which, as was explained in II, may be either fixed or floating. But sometimes no charge is given, and then the debenture is described as "naked" or "unsecured". Moreover, the term "mortgage debenture" is restricted by the Stock Exchange to debentures with *fixed* charges, although its legal meaning would appear to cover charges of both types.

Shares and debentures are commonly mentioned, even in the Act, as though they were similar, but their legal nature is entirely different. *A share is a chose in action, evidenced by a document* called a share certificate. *A debenture is a document which is evidence of a chose in action*, i.e. the debt. *Debenture stock*, however, is similar to *stock*, for it is evidenced by a document called a *debenture stock certificate*, while stockholders receive a *stock certificate*. Moreover, a debenture can be transferred only *as a whole*, i.e. if it is evidence of a debt from the company of £500, then the *whole debt* must be transferred. Debenture stock, on the other hand, is *divisible* into any amounts required, in the same way as stock.

Sometimes the debenture-holders are given a right, by the terms of the debenture, to convert their debentures into shares at some future date. Such debentures are called *convertible*, and if the holders exercise their right of conversion they cease to be lenders to the company and become members instead. The convertible debentures cannot, however, be issued at a discount entitling the holder to exchange them immediately for shares of the same par value, as this would be an indirect method of issuing shares at a discount and therefore unlawful under s. 21 Companies Act 1980.

6. Trust deeds. When a *series of debentures* is issued to numerous debenture-holders, a trust deed is normally drawn up. Under the terms of the deed the company undertakes to pay the debenture-holders their principal and interest, and normally charges its property to the trustees (usually a trust corporation) as security.

If the charge is to be a *legal fixed* charge such a deed is essential, for a legal estate in land cannot be owned by more than four persons, and therefore could not be granted to a large number of debenture-holders.

The deed usually empowers the trustees to appoint a receiver to protect the property charged if the company defaults in payment of the principal or interest, and may contain other provisions concerning meetings of the debenture-holders, supervision of the assets charged, and the keeping of a register of debenture-holders.

A similar deed can be drawn up for debenture stock.

7. Advantages of a trust deed. A trust deed has two main advantages:

(*a*) As stated above, it makes it possible for the company to give the debenture-holders (through the trustees) a *legal fixed charge* over property of a permanent nature such as land.

(*b*) The rights of the debenture-holders and the company's covenants for payment of principal and interest and for the care and insurance of the property charged to them can be enforced by the trustees against the company.

It would be much more difficult for a large and fluctuating body of individual debenture-holders to do this.

The Act does not impose any specific statutory duties on the trustees, but s. 88 renders *void* any provision in the trust deed exempting them from, or indemnifying them against, liability for breach of trust.

8. Forms of debenture. A debenture may be either:

(*a*) a registered debenture, *or*
(*b*) a bearer debenture.

It is usually, though not necessarily, under the company's seal.

9. Registered debentures. These are subject to many of the same rules as shares. A register of debenture-holders is kept in the same way as a register of members, and must under s. 86 be kept at the registered office of the company (*see* II, **14**). Section 75 applies to debentures as well as to shares, requiring a *proper instrument of transfer* to be delivered to the company before a transfer can be registered. Section 80 applies to debentures and debenture stock certificates in the same way as it applies to share certificates (*see* XX, **9**) and so also does s. 78 concerning notice of the company's refusal to register a transfer (*see* XX, **7**).

The debenture itself consists of two parts:

(*a*) the covenants by the company to pay the principal and interest, and

(*b*) the endorsed conditions, i.e. the terms of the loan.

The endorsed conditions vary, but they normally contain a provision that the debenture is one of a series all ranking *pari passu*. This is necessary because without such a clause the debentures would rank *in the order of issue* regarding the assets charged by the company, and if a large issue of debentures is made it is obviously essential that the debenture-holders should all have the same rights as regards security.

Another usual endorsed condition is a provision keeping the trusts off the register. This is required because s. 117 (*see* XIII, **7**) applies only to the register of members and not to the register of debenture-holders.

10. Bearer debentures. Bearer debentures are similar to share warrants in that they too are negotiable instruments, transferable by delivery. The interest on them is paid by means of attached coupons, as are dividends on share warrants (*see* XX, **16**).

11. Perpetual debentures. As a general rule when a mortgage is made by an individual, *equity will not permit it to be irredeemable*. The purpose of the transaction has been to borrow money: anything, therefore, which prevents the borrower from repaying the loan and recovering his security will be void in equity. This will be the position right up to the moment when the mortgagee has obtained an order for the sale or foreclosure of the mortgaged property, even if the legal or contractual right to redeem has long since expired. Equity expresses this rule in the maxim: "Once a mortgage, always a mortgage".

Thus the mortgagor normally has a *legal or contractual* right to repay the loan and redeem his property on the date specified in the contract of loan. Once this date has passed, he has an *equitable* right to redeem his property on payment of the loan and accrued interest. From the moment the mortgage is created, he has an *equitable interest* in the mortgaged property which remains in him so long as the mortgage endures, and which is called the *equity of redemption*. Equity will hold invalid any provision which "clogs" the equity of redemption, i.e. fetters the rights of the mortgagor, and his most important right is his equitable right to redeem.

This rule, however, is subject to an exception in the case of companies. Section 89 expressly states that a condition in a *debenture* is *not invalid* on the grounds that it is *irredeemable* or *redeemable only* on the occurrence of an event, however remote, or on the expiration of a period of time, however long. It follows that debentures can be made *perpetual*, i.e. the loan is repayable only on winding up, or after a long period of time.

12. The company's power to re-issue redeemed debentures. Although in the last paragraph we saw that debentures may be perpetual or irredeemable, they are, unlike shares, normally redeemable at a certain specified future date. The company may then lawfully effect an economy by redeeming them, i.e. buying them back from any willing seller, *before* the specified redemption date has arrived.

When debentures are redeemed they are, at common law, extinguished and the company would therefore be unable to re-issue them were it not for the provisions of s. 90. This section permits the company to re-issue them, or to issue others in their place, *with the priority of the original series* provided:

   (a) there is no provision to the contrary, express or implied, in the articles or in any contract made by the company; and
   (b) the company has not shown an intention to cancel them, e.g. by passing a resolution to that effect.

13. The remedies of debenture-holders. The remedies of a debenture-holder vary according to whether he is secured or unsecured. He will naturally have wider protection in the former case.

An *unsecured* debenture-holder is in exactly the same position as an ordinary trade creditor. The fact that his debt arises from a loan to the company rather than the supply of goods to it or the performance of services for it is quite immaterial. He is owed money and he has no security. Like any other unsecured creditor, therefore, he has *only two remedies*:

   (a) He can *sue* for his principal and interest, obtain judgment, and, if the judgment debt is not paid, levy execution against the company's property.
   (b) He can, if he wishes, *petition under s. 224 for a winding up* of the company by the court on the grounds specified in s. 222(e), namely, that the company is unable to pay its debts.

A *secured* debenture-holder has *both the above remedies*, but in addition he also has the following courses open to him:

(*c*) He can *exercise any of the powers* which are given to him by the *debenture or the trust deed*, as the case may be, without applying to the court. Usually these include a power to appoint a receiver, and a power to sell the company's property.

(*d*) He can *apply to the court* for the appointment of a *receiver* or for an order for the *sale or foreclosure* of the property.

When the company defaults in payment of principal or interest, any debenture-holder may sue, but he normally brings the action on behalf of himself and the other debenture-holders of the same class. This is known as a *debenture-holders' action*, and if several individuals start to sue separately, the court can consolidate their actions into one.

14. Receivers. A receiver may be appointed:

(*a*) by the court, *or*

(*b*) under the terms of the debenture or the trust deed.

Section 366 disqualifies a corporation from appointment as a receiver, and s. 367 disqualifies an undischarged bankrupt unless he is acting under a court order. If the company is in compulsory liquidation when the debenture-holders apply to the court to appoint a receiver, s. 368 states that the official receiver may be appointed.

Once the appointment is made, every invoice, order for goods or business letter on which the company's name appears is required by s. 370 to contain a statement that a receiver has been appointed.

Further, s. 102(1) states that if any person obtains an order for the appointment of a receiver, or appoints a receiver under the terms of a document, he must notify the registrar within seven days from the order or the appointment, and the registrar must enter the fact in the register of charges. Notice of the fact that the receiver has ceased to act must likewise be given to the registrar under s. 102(2), and the registrar must make the appropriate entry in the register of charges.

15. A receiver appointed by the court. When a receiver is appointed by the court, he is not the agent either of the debenture-holders or of the company, but is an *officer of the court*. He must therefore act according to the court's directions. The court may appoint a receiver:

(*a*) if the principal or interest is in arrears, *or*

(*b*) if the security is in jeopardy, *i.e.* where the company or its other creditors are about to take steps which will put the assets charged beyond the reach of the debenture-holders.

A receiver appointed by the court is personally liable on contracts, but has a right of indemnity out of the company's assets. His remuneration is fixed by the court.

16. A receiver appointed under a power in the debenture or trust deed. When a receiver is appointed under the terms of the debenture or trust deed, he would naturally be the agent of the *debenture-holders* if it were not for the terms of the debenture itself and of the Act. In fact, however, the debenture or trust deed normally provides that he shall be the agent of the *company*, while s. 369(2) makes him personally liable on contracts in the same way as a receiver appointed by the court. It also gives him a similar right of indemnity out of the company's assets. Section 369(1) entitles him to apply to the court for directions whenever he wishes, so that as a result his legal position is equivalent to that of a receiver appointed by the court. His remuneration, however, is fixed by agreement.

17. Provisions as to information when receiver is appointed. Section 372 applies whenever a receiver of the whole, or substantially the whole, of the company's property is appointed on behalf of the holders of any debentures secured by a floating charge.

It provides that:

(*a*) The receiver must notify the company of his appointment at once.

(*b*) Within fourteen days of the receipt of that notice, a statement of affairs must be made out and submitted to the receiver. This statement of affairs must, under s. 373, be submitted by the same persons and contain the same information as is required in a compulsory liquidation by s. 235, which is discussed in **XXVII, 13**.

(*c*) Within two months after receipt of the statement of affairs, the receiver must send:

(*i*) a copy of the statement of affairs and of his comments on it, if any, to the registrar and, if he is appointed by the court, to the court; in the case of the registrar he must also send a summary of both;

(*ii*) a copy of his comments, if any, to the company, or if none, a notice to that effect;

(*iii*) a copy of the summary to any trustees for the debenture-holders and to the debenture-holders.

The section also requires the receiver to send an abstract of his receipts and payments to the registrar, the company, the debenture-holders and any trustees for the debenture-holders, within two months after the end of each year or after he ceases to act.

When s. 372 is not applicable, s. 374 requires a receiver appointed under the terms of the debenture or trust deed to send an abstract of his receipts and payments to the registrar within one month after the end of each half-year or after he ceases to act.

18. Priority of preferential debts. Where a receiver is appointed on behalf of the holders of debentures secured by a floating charge and the company is *not in liquidation*, s. 94 requires him to pay all preferential debts of the company out of the assets in his hands before meeting any claim for principal or interest in respect of the debentures.

(Note that if the company *is in liquidation*, the priority of the preferential debts is preserved by s. 319 (*see* IV, **5**).)

PROGRESS TEST 21

1. What was the position prior to the European Communities Act 1972 of a person who had lent money to the company where the borrowing was *ultra vires* the company?   (**1, 2**)

2. What was the position prior to the European Communities Act 1972 of a person who had lent money to the company where the borrowing was *intra vires* the company but outside the scope of the directors' authority?   (**3**)

3. How has s. 9(1) European Communities Act 1972 affected (*a*) *ultra vires* borrowings by the company, and (*b*) *intra vires* borrowings which are outside the scope of the directors' authority?   (**4** and II, **30**)

4. What is a debenture? Discuss the various types of debenture. (**5, 8, 9, 10, 11**)

5. What is a trust deed in relation to debentures? What are its advantages?   (**6, 7**)

6. What is meant by:

(*a*) a registered debenture?   (**9**)

(*b*) a bearer debenture?   (**10**)

(*c*) a perpetual debenture?   (**11**)

7. Under what circumstances may a company re-issue redeemed debentures? **(12)**

8. Give an account of the remedies of debenture-holders. **(13)**

9. What is the legal position of a receiver appointed by the court? When may the court appoint a receiver? **(14, 15)**

10. What is the legal position of a receiver appointed under the terms of the debenture or the trust deed? **(16)**

CHAPTER XXII

Directors

1. Definition of a director. Section 455 defines a director as including "any person occupying the position of director, by whatever name called". This is a definition based purely on *function*: a person is a director if he does whatever a director normally does. But the Act gives no further guidance on the function and duties of a director.

A director is an *officer* of the company, for s. 455, as we saw in II, **8**, states that officer "includes a director, manager or secretary". He is also an *agent* of the company, though the Act does not say so. But he is *not a servant* and is therefore not entitled to preferential payment when the company goes into liquidation.

2. Shadow directors. In previous legislation a person in accordance with whose directions or instructions the directors of a company are accustomed to act has, for the purposes of certain sections, been deemed to be a director.

Section 63(1) Companies Act 1980, however, is the first statutory provision to confer on such a person the name of "shadow director". For the purposes of Part IV of the Act, i.e. s. 46–s. 67, a shadow director must be treated as a director unless the directors are accustomed to act as he directs merely because they are following the advice which he has given them in a professional capacity.

3. The number of directors required. Section 176 states that every public company must have at least two directors, and every private company must have at least one.

The Act also contains a number of provisions designed to ensure that the offices of director and secretary do not fall into the same hands in companies with only one director.

Thus s. 177(1) states that every company must have a secretary, but then provides that a sole director may not be the secretary. Of course, if there are two or more directors, one of them may be the secretary and in practice often is.

Section 178, in language which students find a parody of legal expression, is designed to prevent evasion of s. 177 by using the device of the corporate person. Section 178(*a*) provides that where two companies have the same person as sole director, neither company may be the secretary of the other. Section 178(*b*) provides that where the same person is sole director of X company and secretary of Y company, X company may not be the sole director of Y company.

Finally, s. 179 provides that anything which must be done by the secretary and a director must be done by *two separate individuals*, and not by one person acting in both capacities.

NOTE: Students who are still mystified by s. 178 in spite of the attempted simplification above are advised to make a pictorial representation of the forbidden situation. They will then see the purpose of the section, having regard to s. 177(1).

4. Appointment of the first directors. Section 21(5) Companies Act 1976 provides that the persons named in the statement required by that section (*see* IV, **1**) as the directors of the company shall, on incorporation, be deemed to have been appointed the first directors. In practice, the articles often name the first directors, but s. 21(5) invalidates any such appointment unless the persons mentioned have also been named as directors in the statement.

Table A, Article 75, states that the number of the directors and the names of the first directors shall be determined in writing by the subscribers to the memorandum (*see* III, **8**).

5. Subsequent appointments. Table A, Article 89, states that at the first annual general meeting all the directors retire, and at every subsequent annual general meeting one-third or the number nearest one-third, retire. This is *retirement by rotation*.

Article 90 states that those to retire are those who have been longest in office, but if they all took office on the same day, those to retire must be determined by lot.

Article 91 provides that retiring directors are eligible for re-election.

Article 92 empowers the company, at the meeting at which a director retires, to fill the vacated office by electing a person to it, but then provides that if the company fails to do this the retiring director shall be *automatically re-elected*, unless:

(*a*) it is resolved not to fill the vacancy; *or*
(*b*) a resolution for his re-election is lost.

Article 93 provides that if it is desired to propose a person other than a retiring director or a person recommended by the directors for election as a director, then at least three and not more than twenty-one days before the meeting a written notice must be left at the registered office. It must be signed by a member entitled to attend and vote, and give notice of his intention to propose that person for election. It must be accompanied by that person's written consent to stand.

Article 94 empowers the company to increase or reduce the number of directors by ordinary resolution.

6. Appointment of directors to fill casual vacancies. Article 95 states that if a vacancy on the board occurs in between two annual general meetings, the remaining directors may appoint a person to fill it. It also authorises the directors to appoint additional directors, so long as the maximum number permitted by the regulations is not exceeded.

In both cases the directors so appointed hold office only until the next annual general meeting. They are then eligible for re-election, but are not taken into account in determining those who are to retire by rotation at that meeting.

7. Voting on the appointment of directors. Section 183(1) provides that in a *public* company (*see* XIX, **6**) directors must be elected *individually*, unless the meeting has first resolved *nem. con.* (*nemine contradicente* = with no vote cast *against* the resolution) to vote on them together.

The purpose of this section is to ensure that the will of the meeting is expressed on each director as an individual. If two or more directors could be elected by a single resolution, this would be impossible. Accordingly s. 183(2) invalidates any resolution which contravenes the section by attempting to apply to more than one director.

8. Permanent directors. Sometimes the articles appoint a person a permanent director, i.e. for life. In such a case it is not necessary to re-elect him, and the articles usually expressly exclude him from the operation of the clauses relating to retirement by rotation. He is normally given wide powers of management, and in practice he will probably be a major shareholder in the company.

It should not, however, be thought that he is truly "permanent". He is, like any other director, removable under s. 184, the provisions of which will be discussed later in this chapter. It follows that unless he has voting control, he can be removed at any time. We have already seen (*see* III, **10**) that the articles never constitute a *contract* between the company and any person in a capacity other than that of *member*. But even if a permanent director has taken care to see that, quite apart from the appropriate clause in the articles, he has entered into a valid service contract with the company as, for example, its managing director, he can still be removed. He will in this case have a right of action for breach of contract, but no right to continue in office.

9. Assignment of office by directors. If the articles or any agreement empower a director to assign his office to another person, s. 204 states that the assignment will be void unless approved by a special resolution of the company.

10. Alternate directors. Alternate directors are entirely different from assignees of office, and are not affected by s. 204. The main distinction between them is that in the case of alternate directors there is only a *temporary* delegation of authority and function.

An alternate director cannot be appointed unless there is authority in the articles to that effect. Most articles nowadays contain the necessary authority, although Table A does not. The articles should go on to define the alternate director's legal position with the utmost clarity, so as to avoid difficulty in the future. They should specify whether a share qualification is required, provide for his remuneration, and state whether the approval of the other members of the board of his appointment is to be obtained. Most important of all is the clause stating whether or not the alternate director is the *agent* of his appointer, for if this is the case then the appointing director will be responsible for all acts done by the alternate.

Most of the statutory provisions apply to alternate directors in the same way as to ordinary directors. Thus s. 180, s. 182 and s. 187 are applicable. So also are s. 193, s. 194, s. 199, s. 200 and s. 201. All these sections are considered later in this chapter. Section 176, however, requiring a minimum of two directors in a public company, is not satisfied by the company having one director with his alternate, for an alternate director is essentially a *substitute*.

11. The register of directors and secretaries. Section 200(1) requires every company to keep a register of its directors and secretaries at its registered office (*see* II, **14, 15**).

Section 200(2) states that this register must contain the following particulars with respect to each director:

(a) His name and former name, if any.

(b) His address.

(c) His nationality.

(d) His business occupation, if any.

(e) Particulars of any other directorships held by him, except of companies within the same group where the subsidiary companies are wholly owned.

(f) His date of birth, where the company is subject to s. 185.

Where the director is a corporation, the register must specify its corporate name and its registered office.

NOTE

(1) *Particulars of other directorships.* These requirements are all quite simple, except for (e). The Act states that particulars of directorships of other companies are to be entered in the register of directors and secretaries, but it then exempts from this provision directorships of *certain* other companies. If it merely exempted directorships of other companies *within the same group*, this would be easy to understand: we should then know that in the register of directors it would not be necessary to give particulars of directorships held of the company's holding company, or its subsidiary company, or any co-subsidiary company (*see* XI, **14**). But in fact it only exempts directorships of *wholly owned* subsidiaries, or of companies of which the company in question is a *wholly owned* subsidiary, or of companies which are the *wholly owned* subsidiaries of the holding company of which the company in question is a *wholly owned* subsidiary.

It is therefore necessary to try to understand what a wholly owned subsidiary is. The Act defines it for us: s. 200(2) (*ii*) states that a company is the wholly owned subsidiary of another if its *members consist entirely of that other company and its wholly owned subsidiaries* and its or their nominees. But this is not simple to grasp. Nothing can be defined by reference to itself, and this definition does exactly that. Perhaps what is meant is that a company is a wholly owned subsidiary where its only members are the holding company and the co-subsidiaries, whose members likewise consist entirely of the holding company and their co-subsidiaries. In such a closely-knit group as this it would undoubtedly be superfluous to include in the register of directors of any one company the directorships held by the directors in other companies within the same group.

(2) *Notification to registrar, publication and inspection of register.* Section 200(4) and (5) have been repealed and replaced by s. 22(1) Companies Act 1976 which requires the company to notify the registrar of any change among its directors or in its secretary, or any change in the particulars contained in the register, within fourteen days. Any notification of a person having become a director or secretary must contain a signed consent by that person to act in the relevant capacity. If the company fails to notify him of any change among its directors, and cannot show that it was known at the time to the person concerned, then it cannot rely on the change against that person: s. 9(4)(c) European Communities Act 1972.

Section 9(3)(c) European Communities Act 1972 requires the registrar to publish in the *Gazette* the receipt by him of any return relating to a company's register of directors, or notification of any change among its directors.

Finally, s. 200(6) requires the register to be kept open for at least two hours a day during business hours to members free, and to other persons on payment of the prescribed fee (£1 under Statutory Instrument No. 1749 of 1980) (*see* II, **14**).

12. Particulars of directors on documents. Section 201 provides that, unless exemption is obtained from the Department of Trade, every company must state on all catalogues, circulars, showcards and business letters on which the company's name appears the following particulars with respect to each director:

(*a*) His name and former name, if any.
(*b*) His nationality, if not British.

13. Directors' interests in shares or debentures. Section 195 was repealed by the Companies Act 1967 which, in ss. 27, 28, 29 and 31 contains much more detailed provisions on a director's duty to notify the company of his interests in shares or debentures, and the company's obligation to keep a register in which to record them. These sections have now been slightly amended by s. 24 Companies Act 1976.

Section 27(1)(a) and (3)(a) Companies Act 1967, as amended, require a director within five days to notify the company in writing of his interests in shares or debentures of the company or any other company within the group, giving particulars of the amount of shares or debentures of each class held by him.

Section 27(1)(*b*) and (3)(*b*), as amended, require him within five days to notify the company in writing of any of the following events:

(*a*) an event as a result of which he becomes, or ceases to be, interested in such shares or debentures;

(*b*) the making by him of a contract to sell such shares or debentures;

(*c*) the assignment by him of any right granted to him by the company to subscribe for shares or debentures;

(*d*) the grant to him by any other company within the group of a right to subscribe for shares or debentures of that company, and his exercise or assignment of it.

In each case the amount and class of shares or debentures involved must be stated.

Section 27(12), as amended, states that in computing the five days, Saturdays, Sundays and bank holidays must be disregarded.

Section 27(13) states that there is no duty under the section to disclose interests in shares in a company which is the wholly owned subsidiary of another company (*see* **11**).

14. Extension of s. 27 to spouses and children. Section 31 Companies Act 1967 extends the application of s. 27 by providing in s. 31(1)(*a*) that an interest of a director's spouse or infant child in shares or debentures must be treated as being the director's interest.

Section 31(1)(*b*) states that a contract, assignment or right of subscription exercised or made by a director's spouse or infant child must be treated as having been exercised or made by the director, and a grant made to a director's spouse or infant child must be treated as having been made to the director.

Section 31(2), as amended, requires a director within five days to notify the company in writing of the occurrence of either of the following events:

(*a*) the grant by the company to the director's spouse or infant child of a right to subscribe for shares or debentures of the company; and

(*b*) the exercise of that right by the director's spouse or infant child.

15. Duty of company to notify stock exchange of directors' interests. Section 25(1) and (2) Companies Act 1976 state that whenever a *listed* company is notified by a director under ss. 27 or 31 of any matter relating to *listed* shares or debentures, it must, before the end of the following day, notify the stock exchange which may publish the information received.

16. The nature of an interest. Section 28 Companies Act 1967, explains what constitutes an interest within s. 27.

Section 28(2) and (8) state that a person who has an *interest under a trust* where the trust property includes shares or debentures is to be deemed interested in them, but a person who is a *bare trustee* of shares or debentures is not.

Section 28(3) states that a person is deemed interested in shares or debentures if a *company* is interested in them and:

(*a*) that company or its directors are accustomed to act according to his instructions; *or*

(*b*) he exercises or controls the exercise of *one-third or more* of the voting power at a general meeting of that company.

Section 28(4) states that a person is deemed interested in shares or debentures if:

(*a*) he enters into a contract to buy them; *or*

(*b*) he has a right (other than an interest under a trust) to call for delivery of them; or

(*c*) although not a registered holder, he is entitled (other than as a proxy or corporation representative) to exercise or control the exercise of any right conferred by the holding.

Section 28(5) states that persons with a joint interest shall be deemed each to have that interest, and s. 28(6) states that it is immaterial if the shares or debentures in which a person has an interest are unidentifiable.

17. The register of directors' interests. Section 29(1) and (4) Companies Act 1967 require every company to keep a register for the purpose of recording the information furnished under s. 27 (*see* **13** and **14**). Whenever it obtains such information, it must within three days inscribe it in the register against the name of the director concerned, together with the date of the inscription. In computing the three days, Saturdays, Sundays and bank holidays are to be disregarded.

Section 29(2) and (4) require every company:

(*a*) whenever it *grants to a director a right to subscribe* for shares or debentures of the company, within three days to inscribe in the register against his name:

    (*i*) the date on which the right is granted;

    (*ii*) the period during which it is exercisable;

    (*iii*) the consideration for the grant or, if none, that fact;

    (*iv*) the description of the shares or debentures involved;

    (*v*) the amount of shares or debentures involved;

    (*vi*) the price to be paid for them.

  (*b*) whenever *a right to subscribe* for shares or debentures of the company is *exercised* by a director, within three days to inscribe in the register against his name:

    (*i*) the fact that the right was exercised;

    (*ii*) the amount of shares or debentures involved;

    (*iii*) if they were registered in his name, that fact, and if not, the name of the registered holder.

Section 29(3) requires the register to be made up so that the entries against each name appear in chronological order.

Section 29(6) is a provision similar to s. 34(4) (*see* XX, **13**), except that it applies to debentures as well as to shares.

Section 29(7) requires the register to be kept at the registered office or at the same place as the company's register of members (*see* XIII, **3**), and to be open for at least two hours a day during business hours to the inspection of any member without charge, and of any other person on payment of the prescribed fee (£1 under Statutory Instrument No. 1749 of 1980).

Section 29(8) requires the company to notify the registrar of the place where the register is kept, unless it is kept at the registered office.

Section 29(10) authorises any person to require a copy of the register, or of any part of it, on payment of 30p. per page Statutory Instrument No. 1749 of 1980. The copy must be supplied within ten days. Section 29(13) states that if inspection is refused, or a copy not sent within the ten days, the court may order that inspection be allowed or that the copy be sent.

Finally, s. 29(11) requires the register to be produced at the company's annual general meeting, and to remain accessible to any person throughout the meeting.

18. Qualification shares. There is a widespread misconception that a director is necessarily a member of the company. This is not so. The Act imposes no share qualification on the directors, so that unless the company's *articles* contain a requirement to that effect, a director need not be a shareholder unless he wishes. While the articles of many companies provide that the directors must hold a specified number of shares in the company, those of many other companies do not. Table A, Article 77, for instance, states that no share qualification for directors shall be required unless and until one is fixed by the company in general meeting.

If the articles impose a share qualification on the directors, s. 182 applies. Section 182(1) requires them to obtain their share qualification within a maximum period of two months after appointment. The articles may fix a shorter period. Section 182(2) states that the holding of a *share warrant* will not suffice for this purpose. Section 182(3) states that if a director fails to obtain his share qualification within the specified time after his appointment, or at any time after appointment ceases to hold it, he vacates office.

NOTE: Care must be taken in computing the period of time when a poll is demanded on the election of a director and there is an interval between the taking of the poll and the declaration of the result. The period of time is calculated as running from the date when the result of the poll is *ascertained*: *Holmes* v. *Keyes* (1958).

Where a share qualification is imposed by the articles, a joint holding will suffice unless the articles provide otherwise. The holding of stock instead of shares is also permissible. The shares or stock need not necessarily have been allotted to the director by the company; he may have acquired them by transfer from another member. Moreover, as long as his name appears on the register of members as the holder of the shares, it is immaterial that he is a mere trustee and does not own the *equitable* interest in them. This is so even where the articles provide, as they sometimes do, that he shall own them "in his own right", though this curious expression has been held not to cover the case where a director held the shares as liquidator of another company.

9. The age limit for directors. Section 185 contains provisions regarding age limit, but s. 185(8) states that the section applies only to *public* companies or to private companies which are *subsidiaries of public companies*.

Section 185(1) provides that a person cannot be appointed a director of such a company if he has attained the age of seventy. Section 185(2) further provides that an existing director of such a company must vacate office at the end of the next annual general meeting held after he attains the age of seventy.

These stringent provisions, however, are rendered considerably less harsh by the remainder of the section. Section 185(7) states that the articles may alter or entirely remove the age limit, and s. 185(5) states that a director may be appointed at any age if the appointment is approved by the company in general meeting, so long as *special notice* of the resolution is given, stating his age. It also contains a similar provision regarding existing directors who attain the age of seventy.

Section 186 requires any person who is appointed, or is proposed to be appointed, director of such a company to give notice of his age to the company when he has attained the age limit either under the Act or the company's articles.

20. Other disqualifications. Section 187(1) makes it a criminal offence for an undischarged bankrupt to act as director or take part in the management of any company, except with the leave of the court.

Section 188 has been fully discussed in VI, **4**, but should be very carefully revised at this point since it has quite as much application to directors as to promoters. It should be noted that the period of disqualification under this section runs from the *date of conviction*, and not from the date of release from any sentence of imprisonment imposed: *R.* v. *Bradley* (1961).

Section 9 Insolvency Act 1976 and s. 28 Companies Act 1976 contain similar provisions relating to directors of insolvent companies and defaulting directors respectively.

Section 9(1) Insolvency Act 1976 states that where, on an application under the section, it appears to the court:

(*a*) that a person
  (*i*) is or has been a director of a company which has at any time gone into liquidation (whether while he was a director or afterwards) and was insolvent at the time; and
  (*ii*) is or has been a director of another such company which has gone into liquidation within five years of the date on which the first company went into liquidation; and
(*b*) that his conduct as director of any of those companies makes him unfit to be concerned in the management of a company,

the court may order that he shall not be a director of or take part in the management of a company for a period not exceeding five years without the leave of the court.

Section 9(2) states that where the company in question is being wound up by the court, the application must be made by the official receiver and the power to make an order is exercisable by the court by which the company is being wound up. In any other case the application must be made by the Secretary of State and the power to make an order is exercisable by the High Court.

Section 9(3) requires the applicant to give at least ten days' notice of his intention to the person concerned.

Finally, s. 28(1) Companies Act 1976 provides that where, on an application by the Secretary of State, it appears to the High Court that a person has been *persistently in default* as regards relevant requirements of the Companies Acts, the court may order that he shall not be a director of or take part in the management of a company for a period not exceeding five years without the leave of the court.

The relevant requirements are interpreted by s. 28(2) to mean any provision of the Acts which requires any return, account or other document to be filed with or delivered, or notice of any matter to be given, to the registrar.

Section 28(3) states that for the purposes of the section it is conclusive evidence that a person has been persistently in default if it is shown that in the previous five years he has been adjudged guilty of *three or more* defaults as regards such requirements.

21. The register of disqualification orders. Section 29(1) Companies Act 1976 requires the prescribed officer of any court which makes an order under s. 188 Companies Act 1948, s. 9 Insolvency Act 1976, or s. 28 Companies Act 1976, or which grants leave in respect of it, to notify the Secretary of State.

Section 29(2) requires the Secretary of State to keep a register of such disqualification orders and of cases in which a court has granted leave. The register is open to inspection.

22. Vacation of office. Apart from the sections mentioned above, and s. 184 which is discussed in the next paragraph, the articles usually contain a clause setting out the events which will cause a director to vacate office.

Thus Table A, Article 88, as amended by the Companies Act 1976, states that the office of director shall be vacated in the following cases:

(*a*) Under s. 182.

(*b*) Under s. 185.

(*c*) Under s. 188 Companies Act 1948 or s. 28 Companies Act 1976. An order under s. 188 includes, under s. 9(8) Insolvency Act 1976, an order under s. 9 of that Act.

(*d*) On bankruptcy or entering into an arrangement with creditors.

(e) On becoming of unsound mind.
(f) On resigning by notice in writing.
(g) On absence from board meetings for more than six months without permission.

Where the clause contains a provision similar to (g) above, vacation of office does not occur if the director cannot avoid being absent, e.g. if he is unwell, unless his illness is of a prolonged nature.

Directors must always resign in accordance with the articles. Thus if the articles provide that a director may resign by notice in writing, as does Article 88 above, a director who wishes to resign should comply. If, however, he merely resigns orally, his resignation will still be valid provided it is accepted by a resolution in *general meeting*, and he cannot afterwards withdraw it: *Latchford Premier Cinema* v. *Ennion* (1931). Acceptance by a *board meeting* would not suffice.

23. Removal of directors. Section 184 gives the company its ultimate power of control over the directors. While they are in office there is very little which the company can do to influence the way in which the directors choose to manage the company's affairs. But if the company disapproves strongly enough of the method of management, it can resort to removing the board under this section. The only time this will be impossible is where the directors themselves have voting control.

The section does not, however, prevent the company from weighting the votes (*see* XI, **14**), i.e. attaching greater voting rights to certain shares for certain matters, e.g. to directors' shares on any resolution for their removal: *Bushell* v. *Faith* (1970).

Section 184(1) states that a company may by ordinary resolution remove a director before the expiration of his period of office and despite anything in the company's articles or in any contract between the company and the director. There is one exception for certain directors of private companies (*see* XIX, **6**).

The intention of the section is clear: the shareholders must have power to remove the board. But the director so removed is not without his remedy. Section 184(6) provides that the section does not deprive him of his right to sue for damages for breach of contract, if in fact he has one.

Section 184(2) requires *special notice* to be given of any resolution to *remove a director*, or to *appoint another director in his place*. From this point onwards, under s. 184(2) and (3), the procedure is exactly the same as in the case of the removal of an auditor under s. 15(3)–(5) Companies Act 1976. These provisions of s. 15 have been fully set out in XVII, **8** and should now be revised. The language of the sections is identical.

Finally, it should be noted that difficulties may arise regarding the use of the provisions of s. 184. It appears from *Pedley* v. *Inland Waterways Association Ltd.* (1977) that an *individual* member has no right to compel the inclusion of a resolution in the agenda of a company meeting unless the provisions of s. 140 (*see* XXIII, **40**) have also been complied with. He can serve special notice under s. 142, but that is as far as he can go. If this decision represents the law, it would appear that the same problem would arise with the procedure for the removal of an auditor which, as stated above, is exactly the same.

24. Validity of directors' acts. Section 180 states that the acts of a director are valid despite any defect which may afterwards be discovered in his appointment or qualification. Table A, Article 105, repeats this provision.

The effect of this section must not be over-stated. It does *not* permit an improperly appointed or unqualified director to do whatever he likes. It simply means that provided the director's act is in other respects *a proper act*, the mere fact that he has not been properly appointed, or is not qualified is immaterial and does not invalidate that act. This can be clearly seen in *Craven-Ellis* v. *Canons, Ltd.* (1936), the facts of which are given in III, **12**, and where the act which the improperly qualified directors were trying to do, namely to appoint another improperly qualified director, was an *improper act* in itself and therefore not protected by s. 180.

The section is stating in a narrow form what is really a well-known and fundamental rule of *agency*, namely, that a principal is always bound by the act of his agent provided the agent is acting within the scope of his *actual or apparent authority*. This rule applies to companies and their agents in the same way as it applies to natural legal persons and their agents, and has been enunciated in the famous decision in *Royal British Bank* v. *Turquand* (1856).

25. The rule in Royal British Bank v. Turquand. By the time a decision of the courts has become familiar even to beginners of a subject, the facts which gave rise to it have usually become lost in the same way as basic assumptions tend to get overlooked. The facts should never be disregarded.

In *Royal British Bank* v. *Turquand* (1856), the company's deed of settlement (corresponding to a modern memorandum and articles) empowered the directors to borrow such sums as were authorised by an ordinary resolution of a general meeting. The directors issued a bond to T, from whom they borrowed money. The bond was under the company's seal, but no resolution was passed by the company authorising it. HELD: The company was bound.

It should be remembered that a third party has no means of knowing whether an *ordinary* resolution has been passed by the company. He can read the memorandum and study the *vires*, or inspect the register of charges, or discover whether a *special* or *extraordinary* resolution has been passed. He can read the articles and obtain particulars of the directors. But he cannot know, unless he has been told, whether an ordinary resolution such as was required in this case has been passed by a general meeting. The loan was clearly within the *vires* of the company. The company therefore had the necessary *capacity*. It was also clear from the articles that the directors had the necessary *authority*. A third party need go no further: he need not make sure that the rules of internal management have been observed. If a principal places secret restrictions on the apparent authority of his agent, they do not affect the third party: the third party need not take steps to ensure that there are no such restrictions, for this would make the carrying on of business a practical impossibility.

NOTE: There are two further points which should be borne in mind in connection with this case:

(1) If a document apparently issued by a company in a regular manner turns out to be a forgery, it can never bind the company. This is the basic principle applicable to all forgeries: they are totally ineffectual.

(2) If the authority of the company's agent is based on *estoppel*, i.e. on the *behaviour* of the company, which has "held him out" as having authority, then the public documents are not regarded as "holding out" for this purpose, whatever they say, *unless the third party has actually read them*.

This is because estoppel is always based on the effect which the behaviour of one person has on the mind of another, and if that other has not seen the behaviour he cannot have been affected by it.

Despite the tremendous amount of material which has been written concerning this formerly important case, it seems that the decision is entirely in accordance with the usual principles of the law of agency, and that it enunciated nothing new. It has now been deprived of much of its significance by s. 9(1) European Communities Act 1972 which destroys the doctrine of constructive notice of a company's memorandum and articles both as regards the *vires* of the company and the *authority* of the directors (*see* II, **30**).

26. Remuneration of directors. We have already seen in **1** that directors are officers and agents, but not servants. They have not, as directors, any contract with the company and are not employed by it, though often they are employed by it in another capacity and are then termed "service directors".

As directors, they accordingly have no right to remuneration. The articles, however, normally make provision for them, and Table A, Article 76, states that their remuneration shall be fixed by the company in general meeting. It also allows them travelling and hotel expenses for meetings and for attending to the company's business: these would not otherwise be allowed. The articles are not, of course, a contract, but they make it proper for the company to make such payments as are authorised by them.

Section 189(1) makes it unlawful for a company to pay a director his remuneration tax-free, and s. 189(2) states that if a provision for tax-free payment is made, it will take effect as if the *net* sum payable were a *gross* sum subject to tax.

As stated in **1**, a director is not entitled to preferential payment when the company goes into liquidation, for he is not a "clerk or servant" within s. 319.

27. Apportionment of directors' remuneration. The Apportionment Act 1870, provides that all salaries are apportionable, but it is undecided whether this Act applies to directors. If it does not, and the articles provide for payment "at the rate of" a certain sum per annum, or are expressed in such a way as to indicate that the annual sum is to be apportioned, then a director who holds office for less than a year is entitled to a proportion of that annual sum. If, however, the articles provide for payment of an annual sum on an annual basis, the remuneration is not apportionable. Table A, Article 76, provides that it shall *accrue from* day to day, making the position quite clear wherever Table A is applicable.

Probably, however, the Apportionment Act applies, so that the wording of the articles is immaterial.

28. Right of inspection of directors' service contracts. In the case of a "service director" (*see* **26**) s. 26 Companies Act 1967 gives the members of the company a right to inspect any director's contract of service. Under s. 63(4) Companies Act 1980 a shadow director (*see* **2**) must be treated as a director for the purposes of this section.

Section 26(1), as amended by s. 61 Companies Act 1980, requires every company to keep at an appropriate place:

(*a*) in the case of a director whose contract of service is in writing, *a copy of the contract*;

(*b*) in the case of a director whose contract of service is not in writing, *a written memorandum* setting out its terms;

(*c*) in the case of a director employed under a contract of service with a *subsidiary* of the company, *a copy of the contract* or, if it is not in writing, *a written memorandum* setting out its terms.

All the copies and memoranda must be kept at the same place.

Section 26(2) states that the following places are appropriate:

(*a*) the registered office;

(*b*) the place where the register of members is kept, if elsewhere;

(*c*) the principal place of business.

Section 26(3) requires every company to give notice to the registrar of the place where the copies and memoranda are kept, and of any change in that place, except where they have always been kept at the registered office.

Section 26(4) requires every copy and memorandum to be open to the inspection of any member without charge for at least two hours a day during business hours.

Section 26(6) states that if inspection is refused, the court may by order compel an immediate inspection.

Finally, there are two provisions which apply in special circumstances. Section 26(8), as amended by s. 61 Companies Act 1980, states that the section does not apply where the unexpired term of the contract is *less than a year*, or when the contract can be terminated by the company within the next year without payment of compensation. Section 26(3A)—a subsection added by s.

61 Companies Act 1980—states that s. 26(1) does not apply if the director's contract requires him to work wholly or mainly *outside the United Kingdom*. Instead it requires the company to keep a *memorandum* which sets out:

   (*a*) the *name* of the director;
   (*b*) the provisions of the contract relating to its *duration*; and
   (*c*) in the case of a contract of service with a *subsidiary* of the company, the *name and place of incorporation* of that subsidiary.

29. Directors' contracts of employment exceeding five years. Section 47 Companies Act 1980 for the first time requires long-term contracts of employment of directors to be approved by the company in general meeting. It should be noted that the meaning of "contract of employment" is somewhat wider than "contract of service" since, under s. 47(7)(*a*), it includes a *contract for services*, e.g. a consultancy agreement. "Services", according to s. 65(1), means anything other than goods or land.

Section 47(2) provides that the section applies to any term by which a director's employment with the company of which he is a director or, where he is the director of a holding company, his employment within the group, is to continue for a period of *more than five years* during which:

   (*a*) it cannot be terminated by the company by notice; *or*
   (*b*) can be so terminated only in specified circumstances.

Section 47(1) prohibits a company from incorporating such a term in any agreement unless it is first approved by a resolution of the company in general meeting and, in the case of a director of a holding company, by a resolution of the holding company in general meeting as well. The only exception to this rule is in the case of a wholly owned subsidiary where no approval by its members is required: s. 47(6).

Under s. 47(4) the resolution may not be passed unless a *written memorandum* setting out the proposed agreement incorporating the term is available for inspection by members of the company both:

   (*a*) at the registered office for not less than fifteen days ending with the date of the meeting; and
   (*b*) at the meeting itself.

If a term is incorporated in an agreement in contravention of the section, it is *void* and the agreement, the rest of which remains valid, is deemed to contain a term entitling the company to terminate it at any time by giving reasonable notice: s. 47(5).

30. Connected persons. The Companies Act 1980 contains a number of provisions which refer to "a person connected with a director". The meaning of these words is found in s. 64 and should be borne in mind whenever the expression appears.

Section 64(1) states that, unless a person is himself a director of the company, he is connected with a director if he is:

(a) that director's *spouse, child* or *step-child* (this includes illegitimate children but not any person over eighteen years of age: s. 64(2));

(b) a *body corporate* with which the director is associated (surely the first time a corporate person has been given a gender!);

Under s. 64(3)(a) a director is associated with a body corporate if he and the persons connected with him together are *either*:

    (i) interested in at least one fifth in nominal value of its equity share capital (*see* XI, **15**); *or*

    (ii) entitled to exercise or control the exercise of more than one fifth of the voting power at any general meeting.

(c) a person acting in his capacity as the *trustee* of any trust under which the beneficiaries include the director or any person falling under (a) or (b) above; *or*

(d) a person acting in his capacity as *partner* of that director or of any person falling under (a), (b) or (c) above.

Under s. 64(4)(b) references to voting power the exercise of which is controlled by a director include references to voting power the exercise of which is controlled by a *body corporate* controlled by that director (a neat example of "veil-lifting" (*see* XXXII, **10**)).

Under s. 64(3)(b) a director is deemed to control a body corporate if:

(a) he or a person connected with him is interested in any part of its equity share capital or is entitled to exercise or control the exercise of any part of the voting power at any general meeting; and

(b) he, the persons connected with him, and the other directors of the company together are interested in more than half the equity share capital or are entitled to exercise or control the exercise of more than half of that voting power.

31. Substantial property transactions involving directors. Section 48 Companies Act 1980 is in principle very much the same as s.

47. It too requires the approval by the company in general meeting—this time where a director acquires substantial non-cash assets from the company, or vice versa (*see* XII, **1**).

Section 48(1) prohibits a company from making any arrangement by which a director of the company or of its holding company, or a person connected with such a director (*see* **30**), is to acquire *a non-cash asset of the requisite value* from the company, or vice versa, unless that arrangement is first approved by a resolution of the company in general meeting. If the director or connected person is a director of the holding company or a person connected with such a director, approval by a resolution in general meeting of the holding company is required as well.

Under s. 48(2) a non-cash asset is of the requisite value if its value exceeds £50,000 or 10% of the amount of the company's net assets normally determined by reference to the last annual accounts, and is not less than £1,000. These amounts can be increased at any time by order of the Secretary of State under s. 62(1).

As in s. 47, there is one exception to this rule, namely, that in the case of a wholly owned subsidiary no approval by its members is required: s. 48(6).

32. Effect of contravention of s. 48. Section 48(3) deals with the effect of contravention of the section. Any unlawful arrangement, and any transaction entered into in pursuance of it, is *voidable by the company* unless:

(*a*) *restitution* of the subject-matter is *impossible*; *or*

(*b*) the company has been *indemnified* (see below) for the loss suffered; *or*

(*c*) *rights* acquired by a *third party* bona fide, for value, and without notice of the contravention would be affected by the avoidance; *or*

(*d*) the arrangement is, within a reasonable time, *affirmed* by the company in general meeting and, where applicable, by a resolution of its holding company in general meeting as well.

Contravention of the section not only has an effect on the arrangement or transaction in question but, under s. 48(4), it renders the director, any person connected with him and any other director of the company who authorised it liable:

(*a*) to *account to the company for any gain* which he made by it, directly or indirectly; and

(*b*) jointly and severally with any other person liable, to *indemnify the company* for any resulting loss.

Whether or not the unlawful arrangement or transaction has been avoided under s. 48(3) is immaterial.

Where an unlawful arrangement is made by a company and a person connected with a director, that director will not be liable if he shows that he took all reasonable steps to secure the company's compliance with the section, while the connected person and the other directors who authorised it can escape liability if they can show that at the time it was made, they did not know of the contravention: s. 48(5).

33. Legislation on loans to directors. Section 190 Companies Act 1948, which formerly dealt with loans made by a company to its directors, was repealed by s. 66(1) Companies Act 1980. Its comparatively simple provisions have been replaced by highly technical and sophisticated rules contained in s. 49–53 Companies Act 1980.

Before embarking on these, it is essential to understand the meaning given by the Act to three expressions:

(*a*) a relevant company;
(*b*) a quasi-loan;
(*c*) a credit transaction.

34. Meaning of "relevant company". Section 65 Companies Act 1980, the interpretation section for Part IV of the Act, defines a "relevant company" in subsection (1).

This provides that "relevant company" means any company which:

(*a*) is not a private company; *or*
(*b*) is a subsidiary of a company which either is itself not a private company or has another subsidiary which is not a private company; *or*
(*c*) has a subsidiary which is not a private company.

The gist of this definition is that a relevant company is *either*:

(*a*) a public company; *or*
(*b*) a private company which is in a group containing a public company.

35. Meaning of "quasi-loan". Section 65(2) defines a quasi-loan as a transaction under which one party ("the creditor") pays or agrees to pay a sum for another ("the borrower"), or reimburses or agrees to reimburse expenditure incurred by another party for another ("the borrower"):

(*a*) on terms that the borrower will reimburse the creditor; *or*

(*b*) in circumstances giving rise to a liability on the borrower to reimburse the creditor.

An example of a quasi-loan is where the company pays a debt which is owed by a director to a third party on terms that the director will repay the company over a period of time at his convenience.

36. Meaning of "credit transaction". Section 65(3) defines a credit transaction as a transaction under which one party ("the creditor"):

(*a*) sells any land or supplies any goods under a hire-purchase or conditional sale agreement;

(*b*) leases or hires any land or goods in return for periodical payments;

(*c*) otherwise disposes of land or supplies goods or services on the understanding that payment (however made) is to be deferred.

37. Loans to directors. Section 49(1)(*a*) Companies Act 1980 provides that, with certain exceptions, no *company* may:

(*i*) make a *loan* to any of its directors or to any director of its holding company;

(*ii*) enter into any *guarantee* or provide any *security* in connection with a loan made by any other person to such a director.

This comprehensive prohibition applicable to all companies is followed by one which applies only to *relevant companies* (*see* **34**).

Section 49(1)(*b*) and (2) provide that, again with certain exceptions, no *relevant company* may:

(*i*) make a *quasi-loan* to any of its directors or to any director of its holding company (*see* **35**);

(*ii*) make a *loan or quasi-loan* to a person connected with such a director (*see* **30**);

(*iii*) enter into a *guarantee* or provide any *security* in connection with a loan or quasi-loan made by any other person for such a director or connected person: s. 49(1)(*b*)

(*iv*) enter into a *credit transaction* as creditor for such a director or connected person (*see* **36**);

(*v*) enter into any *guarantee* or provide any *security* in connection with a credit transaction made by any other person for such a director or connected person: s. 49(2).

38. Extension of prohibitions in s. 49 to indirect arrangements. Section 49(3) and (4) extend to indirect arrangements by which a company may try to evade the rules stated above.

Section 49(3) provides that no company may arrange for the assignment to it of rights, or the assumption by it of obligations, under a transaction which would have contravened subsections (1) or (2) if it had been entered into by the company itself.

Section 49(4) provides that no company may take part in an arrangement by which:

(*a*) another person enters into a transaction which would have contravened subsections (1), (2) or (3) if it had been entered into by the company itself; and

(*b*) under which that other person obtains a benefit from the company or any company within the group.

39. Exceptions from s. 49. Section 50 Companies Act 1980 gives a large number of exceptions from the rules laid down in s. 49. In subsection (4), which is the simplest place to start, it gives four cases where s. 49 does not apply:

(*a*) a *loan* or *quasi-loan* by a company to its *holding company* or a *guarantee* or *security* given by a company in connection with a loan or quasi-loan given by any other person to its holding company;

(*b*) a company's entering into a *credit transaction* as creditor for its *holding company*, or giving a *guarantee* or *security* in connection with any credit transaction made by any other person for its holding company;

(*c*) a company's doing anything to provide any of its directors with funds to meet *expenditure incurred for the purposes of the company* or to enable him *properly to perform his duties as an officer*, or anything to enable any of its directors to avoid incurring such expenditure, provided *either*:

  (*i*) that thing is done with the *prior approval of the company in general meeting* at which all the details are disclosed; *or*

  (*ii*) it is done on the condition that if the approval of the company is not so obtained before the next annual general meeting, the loan must be repaid or the liability discharged *within six months* from the end of that meeting: s. 50(5)

Even if one of these conditions is satisfied, the exception is subject to a financial limit in the case of any *relevant company*. Such a company may not enter into any transaction under (*c*) if the *aggregate of the relevant amounts* exceeds £10,000.

(*d*) a loan or quasi-loan made by a *money-lending company* to any person, or a guarantee given by a money-lending company in connection with any other loan or quasi-loan, provided:

   (*i*) the loan or quasi-loan is made, or the guarantee given, in the *ordinary course of its business*; and

   (*ii*) the amount of the loan, quasi-loan or guarantee is not greater, and the terms not more favourable, than the company could reasonably be expected to offer to a person of the *same financial standing but unconnected with the company*.

Even if these two conditions are satisfied, this exception is also subject to a financial limit in the case of *any relevant company which is not a recognised bank* (i.e. not recognised as a bank for the purposes of the Banking Act 1979: s. 65(1)). Such a company may not enter into any transaction under (*d*) if the *aggregate of the relevant amounts* exceeds £50,000: s. 50(6).

The second condition, however, is itself subject to an exception regarding a *dwelling-house*. Section 50(7) provides that (*d*) (*ii*) above does not prevent a company from making a loan to one of its directors or a director of its holding company:

   (*i*) for the purpose of the *purchase of a dwelling-house*, together with any land to be occupied with it, for use as that director's *only or main residence*;

   (*ii*) for the purpose of *improving* such a dwelling-house or land;

   (*iii*) in substitution for any loan made by any other person for either of the above purposes;

if loans of that description are ordinarily made by the company to its employees on terms which are no less favourable, and if the *aggregate of the relevant amounts* does not exceed £50,000.

40. Exceptions from s. 49(2). Section 50(3) gives an exception from s. 49(2): *see* **37**, (*iv*) and (*v*) *above*. The prohibitions in s. 49(2) do not prevent a *company* from entering into any transaction for any person if:

(*a*) the *aggregate of the relevant amounts* does not exceed £5,000; or

(*b*) (*i*) the company enters into the transaction in the *ordinary course of its business*; and

   (*ii*) its value is not greater, and its terms not more favour-

able, than the company could reasonably be expected to
offer to a person of the *same financial standing but
unconnected
with the company*.

41. Exception from s. 49(1)(*b*). Section 50(2) gives an exception
from s. 49(1)(*b*): *see* **37**, (*i*), (*ii*) and (*iii*) *above*. The prohibitions in s.
49(1)(*b*) do not prevent a *relevant company* from making a quasi-
loan to one of its directors or a director of its holding company if:

(*a*) the quasi-loan contains a term requiring the director to
    reimburse the creditor within two months; and
(*b*) the aggregate of the amount of that quasi-loan and the
    amount outstanding on any other quasi-loans does not
    exceed £1,000.

42. Exception from s. 49(1)(*b*)(*ii*) and (*iii*). Section 50(1) gives an
exception from s. 49(1)(*b*)(*ii*) and (*iii*): *see* **37**.

Where a director of a *relevant company* or of its holding company is associated with a subsidiary of either of those companies
(*see* **30**(*b*)), the prohibitions in s. 49(1)(*b*)(*ii*) and (*iii*) do not prevent the relevant company from:

(*a*) making a loan or quasi-loan to that subsidiary; *or*
(*b*) giving a guarantee or security in connection with a loan or
    quasi-loan made by any other person to that subsidiary.

43. Relevant amounts. It can be seen from **37–42** above that the
rules relating to loans by a company to its directors are not easy
to master. It is probably best to acquire a thorough knowledge of
37 and then, given a transaction which appears to be prohibited
by it, see which, if any, of the exceptions are applicable.

Further, it should be borne in mind that any of the amounts
specified in s. 50 can be increased at any time by order of the
Secretary of State under s. 62(1).

In many of the rules governing the exceptions, however, the
expression "aggregate of the relevant amounts" appears and this
too requires explanation. Its meaning is given in s. 51 but unfortunately, again, not without tears. Before "relevant amounts"
can be understood, it is necessary to understand the meaning of
"relevant arrangement" and "relevant transaction".

Section 51(3) provides that a *transaction* is relevant if it was
made:

(*a*) for the director for whom the proposed transaction or
arrangement is to be made, or for any person connected with
him; *or*

(*b*) where the proposed transaction or arrangement is to be made for a person connected with a director, for that director or any person connected with him.

It concludes by stating that an *arrangement* is relevant if it relates to a relevant transaction.

Section 51(2) provides that the *relevant amounts* in relation to a proposed transaction or arrangement are:

(*a*) the value of the *proposed transaction or arrangement*;

(*b*) the value of any *existing relevant arrangement* falling under s. 49(3) or (4) (*see* **38**) but covered by one of the exceptions in s. 50;

(*c*) the amount outstanding under *any other relevant transaction* covered by one of the exceptions in s. 50.

The amounts to be included under (*b*) and (*c*) comprise not only those provided by the company, but also those provided by any of its subsidiaries or, where the proposed transaction or arrangement is to be made for a director of its holding company or a person connected with him, by any of its co-subsidiaries (*see* **XI, 17**).

44. Civil remedies for breach of s. 49. The provisions of s. 52 Companies Act 1980 regarding the effect of contravention of s. 49 on the transaction or arrangement in question are, with one exception, *exactly the same* as those relating to substantial property transactions involving directors which are described in **32** above.

Thus s. 52(1), (2) and (3) correspond to s. 48(3), (4) and (5).

The single difference is that the provision in s. 48(3)(*c*) regarding affirmation by the company does not appear in s. 52.

45. Criminal penalties for breach of s. 49. Section 53 Companies Act 1980, which deals with the penalties for contravention of s. 49, applies only to *relevant companies*.

Under s. 53(1) a *director* of a relevant company who authorises or permits the company to enter into a transaction or arrangement, knowing or having reasonable cause to believe that the company was thereby contravening s. 49, is guilty of an offence.

Under s. 53(2) and (4) a *relevant company* which enters into a transaction or arrangement for one of its directors or for a director of its holding company in contravention of s. 49 is also guilty of an offence, unless it shows that at the time the transaction was entered into it did not know of the contravention.

Under s. 53(3) a person who *procures* a relevant company to enter into a transaction or arrangement, knowing or having reasonable cause to believe that the company was thereby contravening s. 49, is guilty of an offence.

Finally, s. 53(5) states the penalties. A person guilty of an offence under the section is liable:

(a) on conviction on indictment, to imprisonment not exceeding two years or a fine, or both;

(b) on summary conviction, to imprisonment not exceeding six months or a fine not exceeding the statutory maximum, or both.

46. Disclosure in accounts of transactions involving directors. Section 197 Companies Act 1948, which required disclosure in the company's accounts of loans made to its officers, and s. 16(1)(c) Companies Act 1967, which required disclosure in the directors' report of directors' material interests in contracts of significance, were both repealed by s. 66(2) Companies Act 1980. They were replaced by much more detailed provisions contained in s. 54–56 Companies Act 1980 which require, in both cases, disclosure in the *accounts*.

Section 54(2) Companies Act 1980 requires the accounts of *any company other than a holding company* to contain *specified particulars* (*see* **47**) of:

(a) any transaction or arrangement *of a kind described in s. 49* entered into by the company for any of its directors, or a director of its holding company, or for any person connected with such a director;

(b) an agreement by the company to enter into any such transaction or arrangement; and

(c) any other transaction or arrangement with the company in which any of its directors, or a director of its holding company, had, directly or indirectly, a *material interest*.

Section 54(1) requires disclosure in the *group accounts of a holding company* of specified particulars of the same transactions or arrangements, except that those entered into by any subsidiary of the company must also be included.

Section 54(4) enlarges on (c) above, stating that:

(a) a transaction or arrangement between a company and any of its directors, or a director of its holding company, or a person connected with such a director, must be treated, if it would not otherwise be so, as one in which that director is interested; and (*b*) an interest is not material if it is not material in the opinion of the majority of the directors, other than that director, of the company which is preparing the accounts in question.

47. The specified particulars. Section 55 Companies Act 1980 gives details of the specified particulars which are to be disclosed under s. 54. It states that these consist of particulars of the *principal terms* of the transaction, arrangement or agreement and:

(*a*) a statement of the fact that it either was made or subsisted during the financial year in question;

(*b*) the name of the person for whom it was made and, where that person is connected with a director of the company or its holding company, the name of that director;

(*c*) the name of any director with a material interest and the nature of that interest;

(*d*) in the case of a loan, agreement for a loan, or arrangement within s. 49(3) or (4) relating to a loan (*see* **38**):

(*i*) the amount of the liability of the person to whom the loan was made or agreed to be made, in respect of principal and interest, at the beginning and at the end of the financial year in question;

(*ii*) the maximum amount of that liability during that financial year;

(*iii*) the amount of any interest which has fallen due but not been paid; and

(*iv*) the amount of any provision made in respect of any failure by the borrower to repay the loan or any interest on it.

(*e*) in the case of a guarantee, security, or arrangement within s. 49(3) relating to a guarantee or security (*see* **38**):

(*i*) the amount for which the company or its subsidiary was liable both at the beginning and at the end of the financial year in question;

(*ii*) the maximum amount for which the company or its subsidiary may become so liable; and

(*iii*) any amount paid or liability incurred by the company or its subsidiary in fulfilling the guarantee or discharging the security.

(*f*) in the case of any other transaction, arrangement or agreement, the value of the transaction or arrangement in question.

48. Types of transaction excepted from s. 54. Certain types of transaction are excepted from the disclosure requirements of s. 54. In s. 54(6) these are stated to be:

(*a*) a transaction, arrangement or agreement between one company and another in which a director of the first company, or of its subsidiary or holding company, is interested only by virtue of his being a director of the other;

(*b*) a contract of service between a company and any of its directors or a director of its holding company;

(*c*) a transaction, arrangement or agreement which was not entered into during the financial year in question or which did not subsist at any time during that year.

49. Exception of small transactions from s. 54. Even where a transaction does not fall within the types excepted by s. 54(6), s. 58(1), (2) and (3) provide that no disclosure is required if:

(*a*) it is made by a company or its subsidiary for a person who at any time during the financial year in question was a director of the company or of its holding company, or connected with such a director; and

(*b*) *either:*

(*i*) it is a *credit transaction*, agreement to enter into a credit transaction, a guarantee or security given in connection with a credit transaction, or an arrangement within s. 49(3) or (4) (*see* **38**) relating to a credit transaction, and the *outstanding aggregate value* of each such transaction made for that person did not at any time during that year exceed £5,000; *or*

(*ii*) it is a transaction or arrangement with the company or its subsidiary in which the director in question had a *material interest*, and the *outstanding aggregate value* of each such transaction made for that person did not at any time during that year exceed £1,000 or, if more, did not exceed £5,000 or 1% of the company's net assets, whichever is the less.

The amounts specified in s. 58 can, like any other amount specified in Part IV of the Act, be increased at any time by order of the Secretary of State under s. 62(1).

50. Disclosure in accounts of transactions involving officers other than directors. Section 56 Companies Act 1980 applies only to officers of the company other than directors. In subsection (2) it provides that the group accounts of a holding company and the accounts of any other company must contain a *statement* relating to transactions, arrangements and agreements made by the company and, in the case of a holding company, its subsidiary, for persons who at any time during the financial year were *officers but not directors.*

The statement must give details of the aggregate amounts outstanding at the end of the financial year under transactions listed in subsection (1), and the number of officers for whom such transactions were made.

Section 56(1) lists the transactions in question as consisting of *loans, quasi-loans and credit transactions*, guarantees and securities relating to them, arrangements within s. 49(3) or (4) (*see* **38**) relating to them, and agreements to enter into any of these transactions or arrangements.

51. Duty of auditors regarding non-compliance with disclosure requirements. Section 59 Companies Act 1980 provides that if a company fails to comply with the requirements of s. 54 or s. 56 regarding disclosure in the accounts, the auditors must include in their report a statement giving the required particulars, in so far as they are reasonably able to do so.

52. Compensation for loss of office. Section 191 states that it is unlawful for a company to pay a director compensation for loss of office or to make any payment to him in connection with his retirement, unless the amount of the proposed payment is disclosed to the members and approved by the company. If it is not so disclosed and approved the directors responsible for making it are liable to the company for misapplication of the company's funds: *Re Duomatic* (1969).

Section 192(1) contains an exactly similar provision regarding payments to directors when the undertaking or property of the company is being transferred, and s. 192(2) states that if such an illegal payment is in fact made, the director must hold the amount which he received on trust for the company.

Section 193(1) requires the amount of the payment to be stated in any notice given to shareholders of an offer for their shares wherever a transfer of all or any of the shares in the company results from:

(*a*) an offer to the general body of shareholders;

(*b*) an offer by some other company with a view to making the company its subsidiary;

(*c*) an offer by an individual with a view to his acquiring at least one-third of the voting power; *or*

(*d*) any other offer conditional on acceptance to a given extent; (i.e. the offer stands *provided* a specified fraction of the members accept it).

Offers for the shares of a company often result in its directors being virtually paid to go quietly, and the Act is merely making sure that the members know what is happening. Section 193(3) further provides that if the above rules are not complied with, the director must hold the amount which he has received on trust for any persons who have sold their shares as a result of the offer.

NOTE: The provisions of these three sections are also very important and must be studied carefully. It should be noted, however, that they apply only to payments *which the company is not legally obliged to make*. Payments made in fulfilment of the terms of a service contract are thus not subject to the requirement of approval by the company: *Taupo Totara Timber Co. Ltd.* v. *Rowe* (1977).

53. Disclosure in accounts of payments to directors. Section 196(1) requires the accounts which must be laid before the company in general meeting to show:

(*a*) the aggregate amount of the directors' emoluments, distinguishing between those received by him *qua director* and those received *qua employee* if in fact he has a service contract with the company;

(*b*) the aggregate amount of directors' or past directors' pensions; and

(*c*) the aggregate amount of any compensation to directors or past directors for loss of office.

Section 198(1) requires a director to disclose to the company all the information necessary for the purposes of s. 196, and s. 6(5) Companies Act 1967 extends its application to cover information necessary for the purposes of ss. 6 and 7 of that Act.

Section 6(1) and (2) Companies Act 1967, as amended by Statutory Instrument No. 1618 of 1979, require the accounts to show also the *emoluments of the chairman*, and of the most highly paid director if he is paid *more than the chairman*. In addition, they must show the number of directors who had *no emoluments* and those who received £5,000 or less. They must then proceed to show the number of directors receiving more than £5,000 but not more than £10,000, the number receiving more than £10,000 but not more than £15,000, and so on up a scale of multiples of £5,000.

Section 7 Companies Act 1967 requires the accounts to show the number of directors who have *waived* their rights to emoluments, and the aggregate amount of the emoluments concerned.

These two sections do not apply to any company which is neither a holding nor a subsidiary company if the amount shown in its accounts under s. 196(1)(*a*) above does not exceed £40,000: s. 6(6), as amended by Statutory Instrument 1618 of 1979.

54. The legal position of directors. We have already seen that directors are officers of the company and agents of it. All the normal rules of agency apply, e.g. a director may not make a *secret profit*.

Sometimes, however, the directors are in the position of agents of *the shareholders* as well. This can arise where the shareholders *expressly appoint* them to act as their agents: *Briess* v. *Woolley* (1954), or where by their own *behaviour* they render themselves agents for the shareholders: *Allen* v. *Hyatt* (1914). But this is not the normal legal position and arises only in exceptional circumstances.

Directors are also sometimes said to be *trustees* for the company, but this is not truly the case. A trustee is the *legal owner* of property which he holds on trust for a beneficiary; a director does not hold property on trust for the company, for the company itself is the legal owner. Moreover, the duties of a trustee are well defined by law, e.g. under a will or a settlement, but a director's duties are not capable of precise definition.

On the other hand a director, like a trustee, is in a *fiduciary relation* towards the company. He is, of course, in a fiduciary relation towards the company in any case where he is acting as the company's agent, for an agent is always in a fiduciary relation with his principal. But the fiduciary relation of the director towards the company covers not only his activities as its agent, i.e. the making of contracts on its behalf, but the entire field of operation. There is nothing he can do in his capacity of director which is *not* required to be done *in good faith*, for the *benefit of the company as a whole*. The care and control of its assets, the making of calls, the forfeiture of shares, the approval of transfers—all these things and any other things which are done by the directors as directors must be done in good faith. It is this that is meant when they are said to be trustees of their powers.

55. Directors' duties of good faith and care. These can best be summed up by saying that a director is permitted to be very stupid so long as he is honest. In fact, if one were to draw any conclusions from the state of the law, one would imagine that the business world was full of honest, stupid men.

The courts have imposed two duties upon directors:

(*a*) the *fiduciary* duty, and
(*b*) the duty of *care*.

Statute law is almost silent concerning both, so that the source of all but one of the following rules is the decided cases.

(*a*) *The fiduciary duty*. We have already seen in **54** that directors must always act *bona fide* for the benefit of the company as a whole, but here there are a number of points which must be borne in mind:

(*i*) The directors owe their duty to the *company*, not to individual members.

Thus in *Percival* v. *Wright* (1902), the directors bought some shares in the company from a member who wished to sell them. The directors knew at the time that negotiations were in progress for the sale of all the shares in the company at a higher price than they were paying, but they did not disclose this fact to the member. HELD: The sale should not be set aside. The directors owed no duty to that individual member.

It should be borne in mind, however, that today the directors in question would have committed a criminal offence under the "insider dealing" rules (*see* Chapter XXXI).

(*ii*) Their duty to the company as *directors* does not prevent them from voting as *members* at general meetings in any way that they wish: *North-West Transportation Co., Ltd.* v. *Beatty* (1887).

They may not, however, use their voting control to ratify their own fraud: *Cook* v. *Deeks* (1916).

(*iii*) They must exercise their powers not only in good faith, but for a proper purpose: *Hogg* v. *Cramphorn, Ltd.* (1966).

Thus in *Howard Smith Ltd.* v. *Ampol Petroleum Ltd.* (1974), where the directors of R. W. Miller (Holdings) Ltd. issued shares to Howard Smith with a view to diluting the majority voting power of two large existing shareholders, Ampol and Bulkships, and so facilitating a take-over bid from Howard Smith, the Privy Council dismissed Howard Smith's appeal from the decision of the Supreme Court of New South Wales setting aside the issue. The directors had used their fiduciary power "solely for the purposes of shifting the power to decide to whom and at what price shares are to be sold", and this could not be "related to any purpose for which the power over the share capital was conferred on them".

(*iv*) They must not place themselves in a position where their interest conflicts with their duty without making full disclosure to the general meeting. If they fail to make full disclosure, any contract made in these circumstances may be *voidable* by the company in equity; and the director will be accountable to the company for any profits made out of the transaction: *Hely Hutchinson* v. *Brayhead, Ltd.* (1967).

The liability to account for the profit to the company "arises from the mere fact of a profit having been made", and it is irrelevant that the profit could not have been obtained by the company: *Regal (Hastings), Ltd.* v. *Gulliver* (1942). Thus in *Industrial Development Consultants, Ltd.* v. *Cooley* (1972) where Cooley obtained for himself the benefit of a contract which could not have been obtained by the company, but failed to make any disclosure to the company although he was a director at the time, he was held accountable for the profit.

(*v*) They must have regard in the performance of their functions to the interests of the company's *employees* in general, as well as those of the members.

This is the single statutory rule in the midst of well-developed case-law relating to fiduciary duties. It is found in s. 46(1) Companies Act 1980 and the section makes in clear in subsection (2) that, like any other fiduciary duty, the duty of directors to consider the employees is owed to the *company* and thus enforceable by the company alone. The provision has been much criticised as being ineffective and indeed is illustrative, along with certain other sections of the 1980 Act, of the truth of the ancient proverb that barking dogs seldom bite.

(*b*) *The duty of care.* This was considered at length by Romer. in *Re City Equitable Fire Insurance Co., Ltd.* (1925) where the following propositions were stated:

(*i*) "A director need not exhibit in the performance of his duties a greater degree of skill than may reasonably be expected from a person of his knowledge and experience. . . ."

He may, however, have no knowledge of the company's business, and little experience, so that a reasonable standard of skill may be a very low one.

(*ii*) "Directors are not liable for mere errors of judgment." Brett L.J. had stated many years earlier in *Marzetti's Case* (1880): "Mere imprudence is not negligence. Want of judgment is not".

(*iii*) "A director is not bound to give continuous attention

to the affairs of his company. He is not bound to attend all
(board) meetings, though he ought to attend whenever he is reasonably able to do so."

(*iv*) "In respect of all duties that may properly be left to
some other official, a director is, in the absence of grounds for
suspicion, justified in trusting that official to perform such duties
honestly."

It is clear that the standard of care required from a director is
subjective, i.e. it is a variable standard depending on the skill and
knowledge of the particular director in question. In law a director
may safely be ignorant, inexperienced and lacking in judgment so
long as he is honest and careful.

56. Disclosure by directors of interests in contracts. Section 199(1)
requires a director who is in any way interested in a contract with
the company to declare the nature of his interest at a *board meeting*. Unless the articles state otherwise, this duty to disclose to the
board is in addition to, and not instead of, the duty to disclose to
the general meeting imposed by the rules of equity considered in
55 and expressly preserved by s. 199(5).

Section 199(2) states that the declaration must be made at the
board meeting at which the question of entering into the contract
is first considered, or, if the director was not interested in it at
that date, at the next board meeting held after he became interested. If he became interested in the contract only after it was
made, he must declare his interest at the first board meeting held
after he became so interested.

Section 199(3) states that if a director gives a *general notice* to
the board that he is a member of a specified company or firm
and is to be regarded as interested in any contract which is made
with it, this is a sufficient declaration of interest. Such a notice,
however, must either be given at a board meeting, or brought up
and read at the next board meeting after it is given.

If proper disclosure as required by the section is not made, the
director is liable, under s. 199(4), as amended by s. 80 and the
2nd Schedule to the Companies Act 1980, to a fine of an unspecified amount on conviction on indictment, and on summary
conviction to a fine not exceeding the statutory maximum.

The articles often exclude the equitable duty to disclose an interest to the general meeting provided the director complies with
s. 199. It appears that this is the intended effect of Article 84 of
Table A, although the wording is far from clear.

It should be noted that the meaning of the word "contract" in s. 199 is extended by s. 60(1) Companies Act 1980 to include any transaction or arrangement, whether constituting a contract or not. Moreover, under s. 60(2) a transaction or arrangement within s. 49 (*see* **37** and **38**) made by a company for any of its directors, or for a person connected with such director, must be treated, for the purposes of s. 199, as one in which that director is interested.

Lastly, s. 63(3) Companies Act 1980 provides that s. 199 applies to a *shadow director* (*see* **2**) in the same way that it applies to a director, except that a shadow director must declare his interest, not at a board meeting, but by a *written notice* to the directors which is *either*:

(*a*) a *specific* notice given before the meeting at which, if he had been a director, the declaration would be required by s. 199(2) to be made; *or*

(*b*) a *general* notice which is sufficient under s. 199(3), disregarding the proviso.

For the purpose of minutes, the declaration is treated as if it had formed part of the proceedings at the meeting in question.

57. Dealings in options by directors. Section 25(1) and (2) Companies Act 1967, as amended by the Companies Act 1976, prohibits a director from purchasing any option, whether a "call" option, a "put" option or a "double" option, with regard to shares or debentures of the company or any other company within the group if a stock exchange listing has been granted in respect of them.

Section 25(4) nevertheless permits him to buy an option to *subscribe* for the shares or debentures of a company, or to buy debentures entitling the holder to subscribe for shares or convert the debentures into shares.

Section 30(1) Companies Act 1967 extends the application of s. 25 to a director's spouse or infant child, though it is a defence for such a person to prove that he had no reason to believe that his spouse or parent, as the case may be, was a director of the company in question.

58. Liability for acts of co-directors. A director is the agent of the *company* and not of the other members of the board. It follows that nothing done by the *board* can impose liability on a director who did not know of their action and did not participate in it, even if he attends the subsequent board meeting at which the minutes recording the wrongful action of the earlier meeting are confirmed. To incur liability he must either be a party to the wrongful act, or later acquiesce in it.

Where the directors have misappropriated the company's money, any director against whom an action is brought is entitled to *contribution* from as many of his co-directors as were parties to the misapplication.

Section 205 and s. 448 apply to directors as to auditors (*see* XVII, **20**).

59. Powers of directors. The directors' powers are normally set out in the articles. Once these powers are vested in the directors, only they may exercise them. Thus the shareholders cannot control the way in which the directors choose to act, provided their actions are within the scope of the powers given to them. If the shareholders disapprove of the board's actions strongly enough, they can alter the articles to restrict the board's powers, or they can remove the directors under s. 184, but they cannot themselves try to perform the very functions which they have entrusted to the directors: *Salmon* v. *Quin and Axtens, Ltd.* (1909).

Table A, Article 80, states that the business of the company shall be managed by the directors, who may pay all expenses incurred in promoting and registering the company, and may exercise all such powers of the company as are not required to be exercised by the company in general meeting.

The effect of this article is to vest in the directors all the powers *except* those which the Act or the articles specifically state must be exercised by the company in general meeting. It could not, therefore, be more widely expressed.

60. Delegation of directors' powers. The maxim "*delegatus non potest delegare*" applies to directors in the same way as to all agents. A person to whom a function has been delegated may not himself delegate it further without the consent of his principal.

Table A, Article 102, however, specifically permits delegation, stating that the directors may delegate any of their powers to committees consisting of such member or members of their body as they think fit. Thus a committee may consist of a single director under this article.

61. The managing director. The directors may not appoint a managing director unless the articles authorise them to do so

Table A, Article 107, empowers them to *appoint one of their body* to the office of managing director for such period and on such terms as they think fit and, subject to any agreement entered into, to revoke such appointment. The managing director is not subject to retirement by rotation, but his appointment is automatically determined if he ceases from any cause to be a director.

The managing director is normally a service director with a contract setting out his powers and duties and terms of employment. Table A, Article 108, states that he shall receive such remuneration as the directors may determine, and Article 109 that the directors may entrust to him any of the powers exercisable by them, and may revoke or vary such powers. He is not, however, a servant of the company for the purposes of preferential payment in a liquidation.

If he has a service contract, the revocation of his appointment by the directors under Article 107, or an alteration of the articles, or his removal under s. 184 from the office of director, cannot deprive him of his right to damages for breach of contract, if indeed a breach has been committed. But it is for him to prove, as plaintiff, that his dismissal was contrary to the terms of his service agreement.

62. The secretary. A secretary, as we have already seen in **1**, is an officer of the company under s. 455, and s. 177 (*see* **3**) requires every company to have one.

Nevertheless, until very recently, his important status was not recognised by the courts. In 1887 Lord Esher said: "A secretary is a mere servant; his position is that he is to do what he is told, and no person can assume that he has any authority to represent anything at all": *Barnett, Hoares & Co.* v. *South London Tramways Co.* (1887). In 1902 Lord Macnaghten described his duties as "of a limited and of a somewhat humble character": *George Whitechurch Ltd.* v. *Cavanagh* (1902).

In *Panorama Developments, Ltd.* v. *Fidelis Furnishing Fabrics Ltd.* (1971), however, the Court of Appeal were of the opinion that times have changed. The secretary is no longer a mere clerk, but the chief administrative officer of the company, and as regards *matters of administration* has ostensible authority to sign contracts on behalf of the company.

This change in the secretary's status is reflected in s. 79 Companies Act 1980 which for the first time deals with his qualifications. Section 79(1) provides that in a *public* company it is the directors' duty to take all reasonable steps to secure that the secretary is a person who appears to them to have the requisite *knowledge and experience* to discharge his functions *and*:

(*a*) held office as secretary, assistant secretary, or deputy secretary of the company when the section came into operation; *or*

(*b*) for at least three out of the five years immediately preceding his appointment as secretary held office as secretary of a public company; *or*

(*c*) is a member of any of the bodies listed in subsection (2); (i.e. the Institute of Chartered Accountants, the Association of Certified Accountants, the Institute of Chartered Secretaries and Administrators, the Institute of Cost and Management Accountants, and the Chartered Institute of Public Finance and Accountancy) *or*

(*d*) is a barrister, advocate or solicitor; *or*

(*e*) is a person who, by virtue of his having held some other position or being a member of some other body, appears to the directors to be capable of discharging those functions.

PROGRESS TEST 22

1. Define a director. How far is he:

(*a*) an officer of the company?

(*b*) an agent of the company?

(*c*) a servant of the company? (**1**)

2. What do you understand by the expression "shadow director"? (**2**)

3. How many directors are required by law in any company? Can a director also be the secretary of the company? (**3**)

4. Who appoints:

(*a*) the first directors of a company? (**4**)

(*b*) the subsequent directors? (**5**)

(*c*) persons to fill casual vacancies of directors? (**6**)

5. Under what circumstances, according to Table A, are retiring directors automatically re-elected? (**5**)

6. What is meant by retirement by rotation? (**5**)

7. Give the statutory provision regarding voting on the appointment of directors. (**7**)

8. Under what circumstances may a director assign his office? Compare the legal position of an assignee of office with that of an alternate director. (**9, 10**)

9. What details must be contained in the register of directors and secretaries as regards directors? (**11**)

10. Give the statutory provisions as to the contents and right of inspection of the register of directors' interests. (**13, 14, 17**)

11. Give the provisions of Table A and of the Act regarding the share qualification of directors. (**18**)

12. It is said that a director must hold his qualification shares, if any, "in his own right". What does this expression mean? (**18**)

13. Give the statutory provisions regarding the age limit for directors. (**19**)

14. Give the statutory provisions relating to directors of insolvent companies. (**20**)

15. What is the purpose of the register of disqualification orders? (**20, 21**)

16. Give the provisions of Table A regarding vacation of office by directors. (**22**)

17. How may a director be removed from office? (**23**)

18. Outline the Rule in *Royal British Bank* v. *Turquand*. (**24**)

19. Give the provisions of Table A and of the Companies Act 1948 regarding the remuneration of directors and its apportionment. (**26, 27**).

20. Give the statutory provisions relating to the inspection of directors' service contracts. What special rules apply if a director's contract requires him to work outside the United Kingdom? (**28**)

21. What do you understand by the expression "contract of employment" within the Companies Act 1980? What special rules apply to long-term contracts of employment of directors? (**29**)

22. What do you understand by the expression "person connected with a director"? (**30**)

23. What special rules apply to substantial property transactions between a company and any of its directors? (**31**)

24. What is the legal effect of contravention of the rules applying to substantial property transactions between a company and any of its directors? (**32**)

25. What do you understand by the expressions:

(*a*) relevant company;
(*b*) quasi-loan;
(*c*) credit transaction? (**33–36**)

26. State the rules prohibiting a company from lending

money, or assisting some other person to lend money, to any of its directors or persons connected with him.   (**37, 38**)

27. Give the exceptions to the rules which prohibit a company from lending money, or assisting some other person to lend money, to any of its directors.   (**39–42**)

28. What do you understand by the expressions:

(*a*) relevant transaction;

(*b*) relevant arrangement;

(*c*) relevant amount;

as they are used in the rules relating to loans to directors?   (**43**)

29. What is the legal effect of contravention of the rules relating to loans to directors? Are there any criminal penalties?   (**44, 45**)

30. State the rules relating to disclosure in the accounts of transactions between a company and any of its directors. What do you understand by the expression "specified particulars" in relation to these rules?   (**46, 47**)

31. State the transactions which are excepted from the rules of disclosure.   (**48, 49**)

32. State the rules relating to disclosure in the accounts of transactions between a company and any of its officers other than a director.   (**50**)

33. What is the duty of the company's auditors if the disclosure requirements are not complied with?   (**51**)

34. Give the statutory provisions regarding payment to a director of compensation for loss of office.   (**52**)

35. Give the statutory provisions regarding disclosure in the accounts of payments to directors.   (**53**)

36. How far can it be said that a director:

(*a*) is an agent of the *shareholders*?

(*b*) is a trustee for the company?   (**54**)

37. Outline the fiduciary duty of directors. How far do they owe such a duty to the employees of the company?   (**55**)

38. Describe a director's duty of care.   (**55**)

39. Give the statutory provisions regarding disclosure by directors of their interests in contracts. How were these rules extended by the Companies Act 1980?   (**56**)

40. How far is it lawful for a director to purchase an option regarding shares or debentures?   (**57**)

41. How far is a director liable for an action by the board in which he had no part?   (**58**)

42. How far is a director who is found liable for misappropriation of the company's money a right to contribution from the other directors?   (**58**)

43. What is the extent of the powers of directors? Can they delegate such powers?   (**59, 60**)

44. Give the provisions of Table A regarding the managing director and outline his legal position.   (**61**)

45. What is the legal position of a company's secretary? What qualifications is he required to have?   (**62**)

CHAPTER XXIII

Company Meetings

1. Types of company meeting. Section 130, dealing with the statutory meeting of a public company, was repealed by the Companies Act 1980. There are now accordingly only three types of meeting attended by shareholders:

(*a*) Annual general meetings.
(*b*) Extraordinary general meetings.
(*c*) Class meetings.

2. Annual general meetings. Section 131(1) requires every company in each year (i.e. calendar year) to hold a general meeting as its annual general meeting, and to specify it as such in the notices calling it. There must not be more than fifteen months between the meetings.

If, however, the *first* annual general meeting is held *within eighteen months of incorporation*, none need be held in the year of incorporation or the following year (*see* XIV, 1).

Table A, Article 47, states that the annual general meeting must be held at the time and place appointed by the directors.

3. Default in holding the annual general meeting. Section 131(2) states that if the company does not comply with s. 131(1), any member may apply to the Department of Trade, which may then itself call a general meeting and give such directions as it thinks fit, including a direction that *one member present in person or by proxy* shall be deemed to constitute a meeting.

Such a meeting is deemed to be the annual general meeting for the current year, under s. 131(3), unless it is not held in the year in which the default occurred. In the latter case it will be deemed to be the annual general meeting for the previous year unless the company resolves otherwise.

4. The business transacted at an annual general meeting. The Act does not state what business must be transacted at the annual general meeting. Thus although the usual business at an annual general meeting is the *ordinary business* as defined by the articles, any other type of business can be transacted there as well. All business other than ordinary business is called *special business*.

Table A, Article 52, states that at an *extraordinary general* meeting *all business is special business,* and at an *annual general* meeting all business is special business *except*:

- (*a*) declaring a dividend;
- (*b*) the consideration of the accounts, balance sheets, and directors' and auditors' reports;
- (*c*) the election of directors; and
- (*d*) the appointment and remuneration of the auditors.

These four items are therefore the *ordinary* business of an annual general meeting. It is essential to know them.

5. The documents accompanying the notice of the annual general meeting. As stated in **4** above, the annual general meeting is normally the occasion on which the directors lay before the company the profit and loss account and balance sheet.

Section 158(1), as amended by the Companies Act 1976, states that a copy of the balance sheet, including every document required by law to be annexed to it (i.e. profit and loss account and group accounts: s. 156(1)), of which a copy is to be laid before the company in general meeting, together with a copy of the auditors' report, must, at least twenty-one days before the meeting, be sent to every member, every debenture-holder, and all other persons entitled to receive notice of general meetings. Section 24 Companies Act 1967 now requires a copy of the directors' report to be sent as well.

If these documents are sent less than twenty-one days before the meeting, they are still deemed to have been duly sent if it is so agreed by all the members entitled to attend and vote.

Thus the documents normally sent out by a company are:

- (*a*) The balance sheet.
- (*b*) The profit and loss account (*annexed* to balance sheet).
- (*c*) Group accounts where appropriate (*annexed* to balance sheet).
- (*d*) Directors' report (*attached* to balance sheet).
- (*e*) Auditors' report (*attached* to balance sheet).

At this point it is advisable to re-read XIV, **6–9**.

In addition to the profit and loss account and group accounts, the following documents may also be annexed to the balance sheet:

(*a*) Any information required by the Act to be disclosed, but allowed to be given in annexed documents, e.g. the directors' emoluments, pensions and compensation for loss of office under s. 196(1) (*see* XXII, **53**).

(*b*) Certified translations of any documents required to be comprised in the accounts if they are in a foreign language, under s. 1(7) Companies Act 1976.

(*c*) The directors' report if, *and only if*, it contains such information as is required to be given in the accounts or in an annexed statement, under s. 163.

The directors' report is not normally an annexed document, but in this exceptional case it becomes one. As a rule it is required to be *attached to the balance sheet* under s. 157(1).

6. The contents of the directors' report. Section 157(1), as amended by the Companies Act 1976, states that there must be attached to every balance sheet prepared under s. 1 Companies Act 1976 a report by the directors on the company's affairs, the amount, if any, which they recommend should be paid by way of dividend, and the amount, if any, which they propose to carry to reserves.

The rest of this section is repealed by the Companies Act 1967 which deals at length with the contents of the directors' report. In ss. 16, 17, 18, 19, 20 and 22 it requires disclosure of many matters of which the Companies Act 1948 makes no mention.

Section 19 has already been discussed fully in II, **31**. Section 22 merely states that where the directors' report is a document annexed to the accounts under the proviso to s. 163 Companies Act 1948 (*see* **5**), it must now also state the *corresponding information for the preceding year*.

Section 16, dealing with a variety of matters but concerning mainly the names and interests in the company of the directors, the activities of the company, the fixed assets and the issue of shares or debentures, is set out below in **7**. Section 17, requiring disclosure of turnover, s. 18, requiring disclosure of the number of employees and the amount of their wages, and s. 20, requiring disclosure of exports, are set out in **8**, **9** and **10** respectively.

These miscellaneous requirements are so numerous that a simple list is given below for revision purposes:

(*a*) Dividend (s. 157).
(*b*) Reserves (s. 157).
(*c*) Names of directors (s. 16 Companies Act 1967).

(*d*) Activities of company and subsidiaries (s. 16 Companies Act 1967).

(*e*) Changes in fixed assets (s. 16 Companies Act 1967).

(*f*) Issues of shares or debentures (s. 16 Companies Act 1967).

(*g*) Arrangements enabling directors to acquire shares or debentures (s. 16 Companies Act 1967).

(*h*) Directors' interests in shares or debentures (s. 16 Companies Act 1967).

(*i*) Health and safety arrangements (s. 16 Companies Act 1967).

(*j*) Any other material matters (s. 16 Companies Act 1967).

(*k*) Turnover (s. 17 Companies Act 1967).

(*l*) Employees and wages (s. 18 Companies Act 1967).

(*m*) Contributions for political and charitable purposes (s. 19 Companies Act 1967).

(*n*) Exports (s. 20 Companies Act 1967).

(*o*) Corresponding information for previous year where directors' report is annexed to accounts (s. 22 Companies Act 1967).

7. Matters of general nature to be stated in directors' report. Section 16(1) Companies Act 1967 as amended by the Companies Act 1980 requires the directors' report to state:

(*a*) the *names of the persons who were directors* at any time during the financial year;

(*b*) the *principal activities* of the company and its subsidiaries during that year;

(*c*) any *significant change in those activities* in that year;

(*d*) particulars of any *significant changes in the fixed assets* of the company or its subsidiaries in that year and, in the case of land, any significant difference between the market value and the amount at which it is included in the balance sheet;

(*e*) if in that year the company has *issued any shares or debentures*, the *reason* for making the issue, the *classes* issued, the *number* issued, and the *consideration* received by the company for the issue;

(*f*) the effect of any *arrangements* to enable directors *to acquire shares or debentures* in the company or in any other company, and the names of the directors who held, or whose nominees held, shares or debentures acquired by means of the arrangements;

(*g*) the *interest*, if any, according to the register, of each director *in shares or debentures* of the company or any other company within the group (*see* XXII, **13–17**);

(*h*) *any other matters* material for the appreciation of the state of the company's affairs by the members so long as they can, in the directors' opinion, be disclosed without harming the company's business;

(*i*) in companies prescribed by the Secretary of State, the arrangements for securing the *health, safety and welfare* at work of *employees* of the company and its subsidiaries, and for protecting *other persons* against risk to health or safety arising out of those employees' activities at work: (*see* s. 79 Health and Safety at Work Act 1974).

8. Statement of turnover in directors' report. Section 17(1) Companies Act 1967 provides that if, during the financial year, a company has carried on business of *two or more classes* which, in the directors' opinion, differ substantially from each other, the directors' report must state:

(*a*) the proportions in which the turnover for the year is divided amongst those classes; and

(*b*) the extent, expressed in monetary terms, to which, in the directors' opinion, the business of each class contributed to or restricted the company's profit or loss.

Section 17(2) requires the same details to be disclosed where a company has subsidiaries and between them they carry on business of two or more classes.

A company is not subject to this section if it is not subject to para. 13A of the 8th Schedule, as amended by Statutory Instrument No. 1618 of 1979, i.e. if it is neither a holding nor a subsidiary company, and its turnover does not exceed £1,000,000.

9. Statement of employees and wages in directors' report. Section 18(1) Companies Act 1967 requires the directors' report to state:

(*a*) the *average number of employees* in each week in the year; and

(*b*) the *aggregate remuneration* paid or payable to them for that year.

Section 18(2) states that if the company has subsidiaries, the directors' report must give the same details regarding the persons employed between them.

Section 18(3) gives instruction on the calculation of the average.

Section 18(4) states that it is the *gross* remuneration which must be disclosed, and that "remuneration" includes bonuses, whether payable under contract or not.

Lastly, s. 18(5) states that the section does not apply if the average number of employees per week is *less than 100* or if the company is a *wholly-owned subsidiary* of a company incorporated in Great Britain.

10. Statement of exports in directors' report. Section 20(1) Companies Act 1967 provides that where the company's business consists in or includes the *supplying of goods,* and the *turnover exceeds £50,000* the directors' report must give:

    (*a*) the value of any goods exported from the United Kingdom during the financial year;

    (*b*) if no goods were exported, a statement to that effect.

Section 20(2) requires the same details where the company has subsidiaries and the business of any one of them consists in or includes the supplying of goods.

Section 20(4) states that the directors' report need not comply with this section if the directors of the company satisfy the Department of Trade that it is in the national interest that the information should not be disclosed.

A company is not subject to this section if it is not subject to para. 13A of the 8th Schedule, as amended by Statutory Instrument No. 1618 of 1979, i.e. if it is neither a holding nor a subsidiary company, and its turnover does not exceed £1,000,000.

11. Extraordinary general meetings. All general meetings other than the annual general meeting are extraordinary general meetings. The directors may convene one whenever they wish.

Table A, Article 49, authorises the directors to convene an extraordinary general meeting whenever they think fit. It then states that if at any time there are not within the United Kingdom enough directors to form a quorum any director or any two members may convene one.

12. Convening of extraordinary general meeting on requisition. Section 132(1) states that despite anything in the articles, the directors *must* convene an extraordinary general meeting on the requisition of members holding *not less than one-tenth of the paid up capital carrying the right to vote* (if some shares have more than one vote this is disregarded) or, if the company has no share capital, members representing not less than one-tenth of the total voting rights.

Section 132(2) requires the requisition to state the objects of the meeting, to be signed by the requisitionists, and deposited at the registered office.

Section 132(3) states that if the directors do not proceed to convene a meeting within twenty-one days from the deposit of the requisition, the requisitionists, or those representing more than half their total voting rights, may themselves convene a meeting. This meeting must not be held more than three months after the date of the deposit. Section 132(4) requires it to be convened in the same manner as meetings convened by the directors.

Section 132(5) states that any reasonable expenses incurred by the requisitionists must be repaid to them by the company, and that sum retained by the company out of the remuneration due to the defaulting directors.

13. The business transacted at an extraordinary general meeting. This can comprise anything which under the Act or the articles is required to be done by the company in general meeeting. Under Table A, Article 52, however, it will all be *special business* (*see* **4**).

14. Provisions enabling members to call a meeting. Section 134(*b*) states that unless the articles otherwise provide, *two or more members holding not less than one-tenth of the issued share capital* (whether with voting rights or not), or if no share capital, not less than 5% of the members, may call a meeting.

15. Power of court to order a meeting. Section 135(1) provides that if for any reason it is impracticable to call or conduct a meeting, the court may, either of its own motion or on the application of any director or any member who would be entitled to vote, order a meeting to be called, held and conducted in such manner as the court thinks fit, and may give such directions as it thinks expedient, including a direction that *one member present in person or by proxy* shall be deemed to constitute a meeting.

16. Class meetings. Sometimes a meeting of a particular class of shareholders is held. At a class meeting the holders of the remainder of the company's shares have no right to be present.

The usual business of a class meeting is to consider a variation of class rights. This topic has been extensively treated in Chapter XV but, in relation to meetings, XV, **17** is of special relevance here since it deals with the provisions of s. 32(6) Companies Act 1980 and Table A, Article 4.

17. The requisites of a valid meeting. For a meeting to be valid the following conditions must be satisfied:

    (*a*) It must be properly convened. This means:
        (*i*) the persons entitled to attend must have been summoned by the proper authority, i.e. the board of directors, and
        (*ii*) proper and adequate notice must have been sent to all those entitled to attend.

In convening the meeting the directors must act as a valid board meeting, and in good faith in the interests of the company as a whole, as always. Thus they must not convene a general meeting at an unreasonable hour or inconvenient place, or with the deliberate intention of making it impossible for certain members to attend.

    (*b*) It must be legally constituted. This means:
        (*i*) the proper person must be in the chair;
        (*ii*) the rules as to quorum must be observed;
        (*iii*) the Act and the articles must be complied with.

    (*c*) The business at the meeting must be validly transacted.

These three conditions are considered below.

18. Persons entitled to notice of meetings. Section 134(*a*) states that unless the articles otherwise provide, notice of meetings must be served on *every member* in the manner required by the *Table A of the 1948 Act* (*see* III, **6**).

Table A, Article 134, requires notice to be sent to:

    (*a*) every member, except those who have neither got a registered address within the United Kingdom nor supplied the company with an address for the purpose;
    (*b*) the personal representative of a deceased member who, but for his death, would have been entitled to notice; (XI, **5**)
    (*c*) the trustee in bankruptcy of a bankrupt member who, but for his bankruptcy, would have been entitled to notice; (XI, **7**)
    (*d*) the auditor.

At common law, notice of meetings may be excused if a person is beyond summoning distance or, perhaps, if he is too unwell to attend. But in the case of registered companies, this rule does not apply, for s. 136, considered below, allows members to appoint *proxies* to attend and vote on their behalf if they are unable to do so themselves. All members, therefore, should receive notice.

Again, at common law failure to give notice, even if it is quite accidental, will invalidate the meeting. Nor can a member waive his right to notice by saying, for example, that he is unable to attend and therefore notice need not be served on him. Table A, Article 51, accordingly contains a provision which prevents this result, by stating that the accidental omission to give notice, or the non-receipt of notice, shall not invalidate the proceedings at the meeting.

Thus in *Re West Canadian Collieries* (1961), in sending to members notice of a special resolution for a proposed reduction of capital, the company by an error omitted to send notice to nine of its members. The special resolution was passed at the meeting. The articles contained a clause identical with Article 51 above, HELD: The omission was "accidental" within the article, and notice was deemed to have been duly given so that the proceedings were valid.

It should be noted that under Table A, Article 134, *every member* is entitled to notice and therefore to attend the meeting. This is so even if he holds non-voting shares and thus cannot vote when he gets there. Probably a member without a vote would not be entitled to attend meetings unless the articles expressly provide to that effect: *Re Mackenzie and Co., Ltd.* (1916).

19. Method of service of notice. Table A, Article 131, states that notice may be given to any member either personally, or by sending it by post to him or to his registered address, or, if none within the United Kingdom, to any address within the United Kingdom supplied by him for the purpose.

Where the notice is sent by post, service is effected by properly addressing, pre-paying and posting it, and takes effect at the expiration of twenty-four hours after posting.

Article 132 states that notice may be given to joint holders by giving it to the joint holder first named in the register.

20. The contents of the notice. Table A, Article 50, states that the notice must specify the place, day and hour of the meeting and, in the case of special business, the general nature of that business.

It is unnecessary to give details of the ordinary business in the notice convening the annual general meeting, though often companies do so.

A resolution which is not covered by the terms of the notice cannot validly be passed, and if it is an *extraordinary* or *special resolution the exact wording* of the resolution must be given.

Thus in *Re Moorgate Mercantile Holdings Ltd.* (1980) Slade J. held, with respect to a special resolution, that "there must be absolute identity, at least in substance, between the intended resolution referred to in the notice and the resolution actually passed".

Furthermore, s. 141(1) and (2) require the notice to state that it is intended to propose the resolution as an extraordinary or special one, as the case may be.

Finally, s. 136(2) requires the notice to state that a member entitled to attend and vote is entitled to appoint a proxy to attend and vote instead of him, and that the proxy need not also be a member.

21. Statutory requirements as to length of notice. Table A, Article 50, states that the number of days' notice specified always means *clear days*, i.e. the number is exclusive of the day on which the notice is served and the day of the meeting. The Act contains important provisions on the number of days' notice required.

Section 133(1) states that any article is *void* in so far as it provides for the calling of a meeting by a *shorter* notice than:

(*a*) twenty-one days' notice in writing for the annual general meeting;

(*b*) fourteen days' notice in writing for all other meetings, except those for the passing of a special resolution.

Section 133(2) states that unless the articles otherwise provide by a clause which is not avoided by s. 133(1), a meeting may be called:

(*a*) by twenty-one days' notice in writing for the annual general meeting;

(*b*) by fourteen days' notice in writing for all other meetings, except those for the passing of a special resolution.

The effect of these two sub-sections is that the articles may provide for *longer* periods of notice than the stated twenty-one or fourteen days, but may *not* provide for *shorter* periods.

The section does not state specifically the period of notice required when a special resolution is to be passed at a meeting other than the annual general meeting. The period is in fact twenty-one days, as is clear from s. 141(2) (*see below*).

Section 133(3) states when a *shorter* notice is permissible. It provides that a meeting shall be deemed to have been duly called, even though the period of notice is shorter than the required twenty-one or fourteen days or the period required by the articles, if it is so agreed:

(*a*) in the case of the *annual general meeting,* by *all the members entitled to attend and vote*;

(*b*) in the case of *any other meeting*, by a *majority in number of* the members with the right to attend and vote *holding not less than 95%* in nominal value of the shares giving the right to attend and vote.

If the company has no share capital, the majority must represent not less than 95% of the total voting rights.

The consent to shorter notice may be given either at or before the meeting. It is usual to obtain it in writing by asking the shareholders to sign a form of consent, but presumably oral consent would suffice since s. 133(3) does not require it to be in writing.

The members cannot entirely dispense with notice: there must be some notice, however short. This follows from the wording of the sub-section.

Section 141(2), mentioned above, states that where a *special resolution* is to be passed, not less than *twenty-one days' notice* of the meeting must be given, specifying the intention to propose the resolution as a special resolution. Shorter notice is again permissible here where agreed to by the same majority as required by s. 133(3)(*b*) above.

22. Special notice. Certain *ordinary* resolutions require *special* notice, in which case s. 142 states that such a resolution is not effective unless notice of the intention to move it has been given *to* the company at least *twenty-eight days before the meeting*.

The company must then give the members notice of the resolution at the same time and in the same manner as it gives notice of the meeting, or, if that is not practicable, by advertisement or in any other mode allowed by the articles, not less than twenty-one days before the meeting.

If a meeting is called for a date twenty-eight days or less after the notice has been given, the notice, though not given within the time required by the section, is still deemed to have been properly given. This useful little proviso is intended to defeat deliberately obstructive directors.

When a company receives special notice, it is not necessary to convene a meeting specially to enable the resolution to be considered. It can be deferred until the next annual general meeting or extraordinary general meeting which is convened.

It should also be noted that if the resolution is considered at an extraordinary general meeting, fourteen days' notice is adequate provided it is given at the same time and in the same manner as the notice of the meeting.

The following are the resolutions requiring special notice:

(a) A resolution to remove a director: s. 184(2). (XXII, **23**.)

(b) A resolution to appoint another director in his place: s. 184(2).

(c) A resolution appointing a director over the age limit: s. 185(5). (XXII, **19**.)

(d) A resolution to appoint as auditor a person other than a retiring auditor: s. 15(1) Companies Act 1976. (XVII, **7**.)

(e) A resolution to fill a casual vacancy in the office of auditor: s. 15(1).

(f) A resolution to reappoint as auditor a retiring auditor who was appointed by the directors to fill a casual vacancy: s. 15(1).

(g) a resolution to remove an auditor before the expiration of his term of office: s. 15(1).

Students should be careful to observe that *special notice* (s. 142) has no connection whatever with *special business* (Article 52) or with *special resolutions* (s. 141). The terminology is confusing, but once it is understood that these three things are quite unconnected, there is less likelihood of error.

23. The chairman. Section 134(*d*) states that unless the articles otherwise provide, *any member* elected by the members present at a meeting may be the chairman. Normally, however, the articles in fact provide otherwise, and Table A, Article 55, states that the *chairman of the board of directors* shall preside as chairman at every general meeting. It also states that if the chairman is not present within *fifteen minutes* of the time appointed for the commencement of the meeting, or is unwilling to act, the directors present shall elect one of their number to be chairman.

Article 56 states that if no director is willing to act as chairman, or if no director is present within fifteen minutes, the members present shall choose one of their number to be chairman.

At common law a chairman has no casting vote, but Table A, Article 60, gives him one in the case of an *equality of votes*, either on a show of hands or on a poll. If he is not also a shareholder in the company, this will be his only vote, and he is not bound to exercise it.

24. Duties of the chairman. The chairman's position is of great importance, and his many duties include the following:

(*a*) He must act at all times *bona fide* and in the interests of the company as a whole.

(*b*) He must ensure that the meeting is properly convened and constituted, i.e. that proper notice has been given, that the rules as to quorum are observed, and that his own appointment is in order.

(*c*) He must ensure that the provisions of the Act and the articles are observed, that the business is taken in the order set out in the agenda, and that the business is within the scope of the meeting.

(*d*) He must preserve order.

(*e*) He must take the sense of the meeting by putting the motions in their proper form, and declare the result of the voting.

(*f*) He must exercise his casting vote *bona fide* in the interests of the company. This probably involves voting *against* the motion.

(*g*) He must exercise correctly his powers of adjournment and of demanding a poll.

25. Quorum. A quorum is the minimum number of persons whose presence is necessary for the transaction of business. At *common law*, *one* person cannot constitute a meeting, even though he holds proxies for several other persons, and the minimum quorum is therefore two persons entitled to vote and present in person: *Sharp* v. *Dawes* (1876).

In the case of registered companies s. 134(*c*), as amended by the Companies Act 1980, adopts the common law rule and states that, unless the articles otherwise provide, the quorum shall be *two members personally present*. Table A, Article 53, was also amended to repeat this provision with recognition for proxies, stating that *two members present in person or by proxy* shall be a quorum.

An interesting construction was put on an article similar to the former Article 53 which required *three members present in person* in the Scottish case of *Neil McLeod and Sons, Petitioners* (1967). There two shareholders attended the meeting, one of them in the dual capacity of individual and trustee. It was held that the required quorum was present. A different result might well have been reached in England where s. 117 applies (*see* XIII, **12**).

At one time it was essential that the required quorum should remain present *throughout the proceedings*. But in *Re Hartley Baird, Ltd.* (1954), it was held that where the company's articles were similar to Table A, a quorum need be present only when the meeting *commenced*, and it was immaterial that there was no quorum at the time when the vote was taken. This decision follows from the wording of Article 53, which states that no business shall be transacted unless a quorum is present when the meeting proceeds to business.

Article 54 states that if within half an hour a quorum is not present, the meeting, if convened on the requisition of members, shall be dissolved. In any other case, it shall stand adjourned to the same day in the next week, at the same time and place, or to such day, time and place as the directors may determine. If at the *adjourned* meeting a quorum is not present within half an hour, the *members present* shall be a quorum.

26. Exceptions to the rule in Sharp v. Dawes. There are certain exceptional cases where, despite the rule in *Sharp* v. *Dawes, one* person may constitute a meeting. These are as follows:

(*a*) Under s. 131: *see* **3** above.

(*b*) Under s. 135: *see* **15** above.

(*c*) Possibly, under Article 54 above, at an adjourned meeting, though this depends on the interpretation given to *members present*.

(*d*) Where there is a committee of one (*see* XXII, **60**).

(*e*) Where there is a class meeting of shareholders, and all the shares of that class are held by one person: *East* v. *Bennett Bros. Ltd.* (1911).

(*f*) Under Article 99, where the directors fix the quorum for board meetings at one.

(*g*) Under s. 293, where one creditor has lodged a proof of a debt in a winding up.

27. Adjournments. Table A, Article 57, states that the chairman may, with the consent of any meeting at which a quorum is present, and shall if so directed by the meeting, adjourn the meeting.

Under such an article a chairman has no power to adjourn the meeting without its consent, unless there is disorder, and if he wrongly adjourns it, the meeting may appoint another chairman and continue the business.

At *common law* no notice is required of an adjourned meeting unless the original meeting is adjourned *sine die* (without a day being fixed for the holding of the adjourned meeting) or unless *fresh business* is to be discussed. Articles often vary this rule, and Table A, Article 57, prevents fresh business at an adjourned meeting and restricts it to *unfinished business*, i.e. the business left unfinished at the original meeting. Moreover, when the meeting is adjourned for thirty days or more, Article 57 requires notice of the adjourned meeting to be given.

A properly convened meeting *cannot be postponed* by subsequent notice to that effect. It should be held and then immediately adjourned without transacting any business.

28. Resolutions passed at adjourned meetings. Section 144 provides that resolutions passed at adjourned meetings are to be treated as having been passed on the date on which they were in fact passed.

This provision is necessary because in law an adjourned meeting is merely a continuation of the original meeting, so that a resolution passed at an adjourned meeting would otherwise take effect as if passed at the *original* meeting.

29. Voting. The common law method of taking a vote is on a *show of hands*, and this is adopted by registered companies.

Table A, Article 58, states that a resolution shall be decided on a show of hands unless a poll is demanded by the proper persons, and Article 62 states that on a show of hands *every member present shall have one vote*. It follows that under Article 62 *proxies* cannot vote on a show of hands.

Section 136)1((*c*) states that unless the articles otherwise provide, a proxy is not entitled to vote on a show of hands, but even where the articles confer this right, a member present who holds proxies for several other absent members still has only one vote.

Section 139(2) states that a representative appointed by a corporation to attend and vote at meetings of a company of which it is a member or creditor has the same powers as it would have if it were an individual. Thus he can vote on a show of hands, and is not a proxy.

Section 141(3) states that at a meeting at which an extraordinary or special resolution is to be passed, a declaration by the chairman that it is carried shall, unless a poll is demanded, be conclusive evidence of that fact without proof of the number of votes recorded for or against the resolution. Table A, Article 58, contains an even stronger provision to the same effect, stating that unless a poll is demanded, a declaration by the chairman that a resolution has been carried, or carried unanimously, or by a particular majority, or lost and an entry in the minutes to that effect, is conclusive evidence of the fact without proof of the number of votes recorded for or against the resolution.

NOTE: Article 32 (XI, 5), Article 63 (X, 3), and Article 64 (XI, 3) are all relevant here, but have already been discussed. Article 65 states that a member may not vote unless all calls or other sums presently payable by him in respect of his shares have been paid. Lastly, Article 66 states that no objection may be raised to the qualification of any voter *except at the meeting* or adjourned meeting at which the vote objected to is given, and every vote not disallowed at such meeting is valid. Any objection made in due time must be referred to the chairman, whose decision is final.

30. Voting on a poll. Voting on a show of hands ceases to have any effect once a poll has been properly demanded; indeed, a poll can be demanded without going through the formality of a show of hands at all: *Holmes* v. *Keyes* (1958). The chairman must then allow a poll and decide when and where it is to be taken.

Table A, Article 61, provides that a poll demanded on the *election of a chairman* or on a *question of adjournment* must be taken forthwith. A poll demanded on *any other question* must be taken at such time as the chairman directs, and meanwhile any other business may be proceeded with.

On a poll, members have the number of votes attached to their shares. Table A, Article 62, states that a member has one vote for each share, and s. 134(e) states that unless the articles otherwise provide, every member has one vote for each share or each £10 of stock. Article 67 states that on a poll votes may be given either *personally* or *by proxy*.

Section 138 states that on a poll, a member entitled to more than one vote need not use all his votes, nor cast all those used in the same way. This enables a nominee shareholder holding shares on trust for more than one beneficial owner to exercise the votes as the beneficial owners direct.

If the chairman decides that a poll should be taken at some future date, the question arises as to whether proxies lodged between the date of the meeting and the date of the poll can be accepted. A poll is an enlargement or *continuation* of the meeting at which it was demanded, and *not an adjournment* of it, so that in *Shaw* v. *Tati Concessions, Ltd.* (1913), where the articles allowed lodgement of proxies forty-eight hours before *a meeting or any adjournment thereof*, it was held that fresh proxies could *not* be lodged between the meeting and the poll.

Table A, Article 69, however, resolves this difficulty by providing that proxies must be lodged at least forty-eight hours before the time of the meeting or any adjournment thereof, or, in the case of a poll, at least twenty-four hours before the time appointed for the taking of the poll. Thus under such an article fresh proxies can be accepted between the date of the meeting and that of the poll.

31. The right to demand a poll. The right to demand a poll is a *common law* right which normally may be excluded by the regulations of any association. In the case of registered companies, however, s. 137(1)(*a*) gives members a *statutory right* to demand a poll on any question *except*:

(*a*) the election of the chairman, and

(*b*) the adjournment of the meeting.

This statutory right cannot be excluded by the articles.

Section 137(1)(*b*) states that an article which *makes ineffective* a demand for a poll by any of the following is *void*:

(*a*) by five or more members having the right to vote;

(*b*) by members having at least one-tenth of the total voting rights of members having the right to vote at the meeting;

(*c*) by members holding voting shares on which one-tenth of the sum paid up on all voting shares has been paid up.

Students often find this provision difficult, especially (*a*). Perhaps this can be more simply expressed by saying that *any five or more members have a right to demand a poll, no matter what the articles may say*. In fact, Table A, Article 58, as amended by the Companies Act 1980, gives *wider rights* than the section, for it states that a poll may be demanded by:

(*a*) the chairman; *or*

(*b*) at least two members present in person or by proxy; *or*

(*c*) members present in person or by proxy and representing at least one-tenth of the total voting rights of all members having the right to vote at the meeting; *or* (*d*) members holding voting shares on which one-tenth of the total sum paid up on all voting shares has been paid up.

It is important to understand that there is no conflict between s. 137(1)(*b*) and Article 58. The Act is merely ensuring that the articles do not insist on a poll being demanded by, e.g., twenty persons before the demand is valid. There is nothing to prevent the articles from stating that a poll may be validly demanded by *one* member, if this is thought desirable.

Section 137(2) states that an instrument appointing a proxy to vote is deemed also to confer authority to demand a poll, and Table A, Article 72, also contains this provision.

Finally, Article 58 states that a demand for a poll may be withdrawn. Probably without such a provision withdrawal is not possible except with the unanimous consent of all persons present when the demand was made.

32. Proxies. The term "proxy" covers not only the *person* who is appointed to act on behalf of a member at a meeting, but also the *instrument* by which the appointment is made. There is no right to appoint a proxy at *common law*, but s. 136 gives members a statutory right to do so.

Section 136(1) states that any member entitled to attend and vote is entitled to appoint another person (*whether a member or not*) as his proxy to attend and vote instead of him. In a *private* company a proxy also has the same right as the member to *speak*.

However, unless the articles otherwise provide:

(*a*) This subsection applies only to companies with share capital.

(*b*) A member of a *private* company may appoint only one proxy on each occasion.

(*c*) A proxy may vote only on a poll.

Section 136(2) has already been discussed (*see* **20**).

Section 136(3) states that any provision in the articles is *void* if it requires the instrument appointing the proxy to be received by the company more than forty-eight hours before a meeting or adjourned meeting. Table A, Article 69, specifies the maximum period permitted by the subsection, i.e. forty-eight hours.

A member who has appointed a proxy, however, may still attend the meeting and exercise his vote if he wishes, though this will revoke his proxy. Proxies may also be revoked by notice to the company at any time before they are acted upon, or by the death of the member. Accordingly Table A, Article 73, states that a vote of a proxy is valid despite the previous death or insanity of the principal, or revocation of the proxy, or the transfer of the share in respect of which the proxy is given, provided that no notice in writing of the death, insanity, revocation or transfer has been received by the company before the commencement of the meeting.

33. Specified proxies. Many companies send along with the notice of the meeting a form of proxy in favour of the directors. Members who cannot attend the meeting merely have to complete the form and send it back to the company. These proxy forms may be sent at the expense of the company, but some control is obviously necessary to prevent the directors sending them only to persons who will support their policy.

Section 136(4) accordingly provides that if invitations to appoint as proxy a person *specified in the invitations* are issued at the company's expense to *some only* of the members, every officer who knowingly and wilfully authorises their issue is liable to a fine not exceeding one-fifth of the statutory maximum, unless he does so at the written request of the member, and the form would be available to every member on his written request.

34. Form of proxy. Table A, Article 68, states that the instrument appointing a proxy shall be in writing under the hand of the appointer or of his attorney duly authorised in writing, or if the appointer is a corporation, either under the seal, or under the hand of an officer or attorney duly authorised. *A proxy need not be a member.*

Two forms of proxy are in use:

(*a*) The *ordinary* form, as shown in Table A, Article 70, which simply authorises the proxy to *vote on behalf of the member* (a *general* proxy).

(*b*) The *two-way* form, as shown in Table A, Article 71, which directs the proxy to *vote for or against the resolution*; here only if the member fails to give the proxy express directions how to vote may he exercise his discretion (a *special* proxy).

35. Minutes. In II, **15** we saw that s. 145(1) requires every company to keep minutes of the proceedings at both general and board meetings.

Section 145(2) provides that minutes, if signed by the chairman of the meeting or the next succeeding meeting, are evidence of the proceedings. They are normally only *prima facie* evidence, though Article 58 (*see* **29**) gives an exception to this.

Section 145(3) states that where minutes have been made in accordance with the section, the meeting is deemed duly held and convened, the proceedings duly had, and appointments of directors or liquidators valid, until the contrary is proved.

Section 146(1) requires the minute books of proceedings at general meetings to be kept at the registered office (*see* II, **14**), and to be open to inspection for at least two hours a day during business hours to any member free. Section 146(2) entitles any member to a copy of the minutes within seven days on payment of a small charge, and s. 146(4) empowers the court to order inspection or the provision of copies if the company fails to comply with the section.

36. Resolutions. In II, **10** the three types of resolution at company meetings were discussed and the differences between them noted. It is important to understand that unless an Act or the articles expressly require a special or extraordinary resolution, an ordinary resolution will suffice.

It is therefore essential to know the occasions on which any Act requires a special or extraordinary resolution.

37. Purposes for which a special resolution is required.

(*a*) Under s. 5, to alter the objects clause of the memorandum.

(*b*) Under s. 10, to alter the articles.

(*c*) Under s. 18, to alter the name of the company with the sanction of the Department of Trade.

(*d*) Under s. 23, to alter any condition in the memorandum other than the compulsory clauses and class rights.

(*e*) Under s. 60, to create reserve capital.

(*f*) Under s. 66, to reduce capital, with the consent of the court.

(*g*) Under s. 165, to declare that the affairs of the company ought to be investigated by the Department of Trade.

(*h*) Under s. 203, to make the liability of the directors unlimited.

(*i*) Under s. 204, to approve the assignment of office by a director.

(*j*) Under s. 222, to effect a winding up by the court.

(*k*) Under s. 278, to wind up voluntarily.

(*l*) Under s. 287, to sanction the sale of the company's property by the liquidator in a voluntary winding up for shares in another company.

(*m*) Under s. 44 Companies Act 1967, to re-register an unlimited (private) company as limited.

(*n*) Under s. 5 Companies Act 1980, to re-register a private company with a share capital as a public company.

(*o*) Under s. 7 Companies Act 1980, to re-register an unlimited private company as a public company.

(*p*) Under s. 10 Companies Act 1980, to re-register a public company as a private company.

(*q*) Under s. 18 Companies Act 1980, to withdraw or modify the statutory pre-emption rights.

38. Purposes for which an extraordinary resolution is required.
(*a*) Under s. 278, to wind up the company voluntarily because it cannot continue its business due to its liabilities.

(*b*) Under s. 303, in a members' voluntary winding up, to sanction the exercise by the liquidator of the following powers:

    (*i*) To pay any class of creditors in full;

    (*ii*) To make a compromise or arrangement with creditors;

    (*iii*) To compromise all calls, debts and claims between the company and a contributory or other debtor.

(*c*) Under s. 306, in a voluntary winding up, to sanction any arrangement between a company and its creditors.

(*d*) Under s. 341, in a members' voluntary winding up, to dispose of the company's and the liquidator's books and papers.

(*e*) Under s. 32 Companies Act 1980, at a class meeting to sanction a variation of class rights in certain circumstances.

39. The filing of resolutions. Section 143(1) requires a copy of the resolutions or agreements listed in s. 143(4), as amended by para. 17 of the 3rd Schedule to the Companies Act 1980, to be sent to the registrar within fifteen days. These are:

(*a*) *Special* resolutions.

(*b*) *Extraordinary* resolutions.

(*c*) Resolutions which have been agreed to by *all the members*, but which would not otherwise have been effective unless they had been passed as special or extraordinary resolutions.

(*d*) Resolutions or agreements which have been agreed to by *all the members of some class* of shareholders, but which would not otherwise have been effective unless passed by some *particular majority* or in some *particular manner*, and all resolutions

r agreements which *bind all the members of a class* of share-
olders though not agreed to by all of them.

(*e*) *Ordinary resolutions passed under s. 278(1)(a)* requiring a
ompany to be wound up voluntarily when the period fixed by
he articles for its duration expires.

(*f*) Resolutions of the directors passed under s. 37(2) Com-
anies Act 1980 (*see* XX, **25**).

Since the Companies Act 1967 abolished the status of exempt
rivate company, the proviso to s. 143(1) has been repealed.
urther, s. 51 Companies Act 1967 made it no longer obligatory
o print copies of the specified resolutions and agreements, pro-
ided they are in some other form approved by the registrar.

Section 143(2) states that where articles have been registered, a
opy of every resolution and agreement to which the section ap-
lies must be annexed to every future copy of the articles. If the
lterations to the articles become too numerous, reprinting may
e desirable, but the section does not require it. Note, however,
he provisions of s. 9(5) European Communities Act 1972 (*see*
II, **9**).

Section 143(3) states that where articles have not been regis-
ered, a copy of every resolution and agreement to which the
ection applies must be sent to any member at his request, on
ayment of a small fee.

Finally, s. 9(3) European Communities Act 1972, as amended
y para. 45 of the 3rd Schedule to the Companies Act 1980,
equires the registrar to publish in the *Gazette* a copy of any
esolution or agreement to which s. 143 applies and which:

(*a*) *states the rights attached to any shares in a public company*,
ther than shares which are in all respects uniform with those
reviously allotted;

(*b*) *varies rights* attached to any shares in a public company; *or*

(*c*) *assigns a name or other designation*, or a new name or de-
gnation, to any class of shares in a public company.

0. Circulation of members' resolutions. Section 140(1) and (2)
ate that on the requisition in writing of:

(*a*) *any number of members* representing *at least one-twentieth
f the total voting rights* of all the members with a right to vote at
e date of the requisition; *or*

(*b*) *at least 100 members* (whether entitled to vote or not)
ho have *paid up* on their shares *an average sum of at least £100
er member*.

the company must, at the requisitionists' expense unless the company otherwise resolves, give members entitled to receive notice of the next *annual* general meeting notice of any resolution which may properly be moved and is intended to be moved thereat.

It must also circulate to members entitled to notice of *any* general meeting any statement of not more than 1,000 words concerning the subject-matter of the proposed resolution or the business to be dealt with at that meeting.

Section 140(3) requires the notice of the resolution to be given and the statement to be circulated, in the same manner and, as far as is practicable, at the same time as the notice of the meeting through under s. 140(5) it need not circulate any statement if, on the application of the company or any aggrieved person, the court is satisfied that these rights are being abused to secure *needless publicity for defamatory matter*.

Section 140(4) states that a company need not comply with this section unless:

(*a*) a copy of the requisition signed by the requisitionists deposited at the registered office:

    (*i*) in the case of a requisition requiring notice of a resolution, at least *six weeks* before the meeting, and

    (*ii*) in the case of any other requisition, at least *one week* before the meeting, *and*

(*b*) there is deposited or tendered with the requisition a sum reasonably sufficient to meet the company's expenses.

However, if after a copy of a requisition requiring notice of resolution has been deposited at the registered office, an annual general meeting is called for a date six weeks or less afterward the copy is still deemed to have been properly deposited.

41. Power to dispense with general meeting. When any particular act of the company requires the assent of the shareholders general meeting, it was at one time doubtful whether there could ever be any effective substitute for the holding of a meeting and the passing of a resolution in a formal manner.

The courts, however, became progressively more lenient their view, and in *Re Duomatic* (1969), Buckley J. held that when *all* the shareholders with the right to attend and vote at a general meeting assent to some matter which a general meeting of the company could carry into effect, that assent is as binding as resolution in general meeting.

The Companies Act 1980 gives formal expression to this rule

ara. 36(4) of the 3rd Schedule. This adds to Table A a new
lause—Article 73A—which states that a resolution in writing
igned by all the members entitled to attend and vote is as valid
nd effective as if passed at a general meeting.

PROGRESS TEST 23

1. What are the statutory provisions regarding the holding of
he annual general meeting? **(2)**

2. Under what circumstances may the Department of Trade
all a general meeting of a company? **(3)**

3. What type of business may be transacted at an annual gen-
ral meeting? What is the ordinary business transacted
here? **(4)**

4. What do you understand by special business? **(4)**

5. What are the contents of the directors' report? **(6, 7, 8, 9,
0)**

6. What documents accompany the notice of the annual
eneral meeting when it is sent out to the members? **(5)**

7. Give the statutory provisions regarding requisitioned meet-
ags. **(12)**

8. Under what circumstances may the court call a meet-
ag? **(15)**

9. In what manner must notice of meetings be served? Under
able A, on whom must it be served? **(18, 19)**

10. What is the legal effect of:

(a) waiver of his right to notice by a member?

(b) the accidental failure to give notice to a member? **(18)**

11. What are the statutory requirements as to length of notice?
/ho may validly consent to shorter notice being given? **(21)**

12. What is special notice, and for which resolutions is it re-
uired? **(22)**

13. What do you understand by a quorum? Must a quorum be
resent throughout the meeting? What is the correct procedure if
quorum is never formed? **(25)**

14. Under what circumstances may one person constitute a
eeting? **(26)**

15. What are the statutory provisions regarding the right to
mand a poll? **(31)**

16. What are the provisions in Table A regarding the right to
mand a poll? Can a demand for a poll be withdrawn? **(31)**

17. What do you understand by the term "proxy"? What are the statutory provisions regarding proxies? (**32**)

18. What is:

(*a*) a specified proxy?

(*b*) a general proxy?

(*c*) a special proxy? (**33, 34**)

19. For what purposes is a special resolution required? (**37**)

20. For what purposes is an extraordinary resolution required? (**38**)

21. Which resolutions are required to be filed with the registrar? (**39**)

22. What rights are given by the Act regarding the circulation of members' resolutions? (**40**)

23. Is it ever possible to dispense with the holding of a meeting? (**41**)

CHAPTER XXIV

Board Meetings

1. The holding of board meetings. Table A, Article 98, states that the directors may meet for the despatch of business, adjourn, and regulate their meetings, as they think fit. Questions shall be decided *by a majority of votes*, and the chairman has a *casting vote*. A director may, and the secretary on the requisition of a director shall, at any time summon a meeting. It is not necessary to give notice of a meeting to any director absent from the United Kingdom.

2. Notice of board meetings. Board meetings are often held regularly on the same day in each week or month, and in such cases notice is not required though it may be given in practice. If they are not held regularly in this way, then either *the period of notice prescribed by the articles* or, if none, *reasonable* notice must be given. Table A does not specify any particular period.

The notice need not be in writing, and oral notice will therefore suffice. If all the directors are assembled together and no-one objects, no notice at all is necessary and a meeting may be held then and there, but it is essential that they all consent to the holding of the meeting.

Thus in *Barron* v. *Potter* (1914), B. and P, who were both directors of the company, disliked each other and refused to meet at board meetings. One day they met by chance at Paddington station, whereupon P insisted on holding a board meeting on the spot, claiming that he had proposed a motion and carried it with his chairman's casting vote. HELD: B had not consented to the holding of the meeting, and his mere physical presence without consent did not constitute a valid meeting.

3. The chairman of board meetings. Table A, Article 101, states that the *directors may elect a chairman* of their meetings, and determine the period for which he is to hold office. If no chairman is elected, or if at any meeting he is not present *within five minutes* after the time appointed for the holding of the meeting,

307

the directors present may choose one of their number to be chairman.

This article may be compared with Article 55 (*see* XXIII, **23**) which contains a similar provision but requires less promptitude.

4. Quorum at board meetings. Table A, Article 99, states that the quorum necessary for the transaction of business may be fixed by the directors, and unless so fixed shall be two (*see* XXIII, **26** (*f*)).

If the articles *empower the directors* to fix the quorum, but fail to specify what the quorum shall be if they do not fix it, then the *number of directors who usually act* will form the quorum. If the articles make no provision concerning quorum at all, then the *majority* of the directors must be present to constitute a valid meeting.

The quorum at a board meeting must be a *disinterested quorum*. This means that directors who are disqualified from voting on a resolution because they have an interest in it (*see* XXII, **56**) must not be counted in ascertaining whether a quorum is present, though they cannot be excluded from the meeting. Article 84 should be re-read at this point.

Table A, Article 100, permits the continuing directors to act in spite of any vacancies on the board so long as there are enough of them to form a quorum. Once, however, their number falls below that required for a quorum, *they may act only for two purposes*:

(*a*) To increase the number of directors to that required for a quorum; and

(*b*) To call a general meeting of the company.

The wording of Article 99 should be carefully noted. It requires a quorum for the *transaction of business,* and is not worded in the same way as Article 53 concerning general meetings, which requires a quorum to be present only when the meeting *proceeds to business*. The rule in *Re Hartley Baird, Ltd.* (1954) (*see* XXIII, **25**) therefore does not apply to board meetings, and business can thus not be validly transacted unless the quorum is present throughout the meeting.

5. Power to dispense with board meeting. Table A, Article 106, states that a resolution in writing signed by all the directors entitled to receive notice of a board meeting shall be as valid as if it had been passed at a board meeting.

PROGRESS TEST 24

1. What are the provisions of Table A regarding the holding of board meetings? What period of notice is required? **(1, 2)**

2. What, under Table A, is the quorum for a board meeting? Must a quorum be present throughout the board meeting? **(4)**

CHAPTER XXV

Dissolution

1. Methods of dissolution. A company is like a contract in th having been created by a legal process, it can only be destroye by a legal process. It will not evaporate or disappear. A contra is created by agreement supported by consideration, and d stroyed by one of the four methods of discharge familiar to st dents of Commercial Law. A company is created by registratio and destroyed by one of the four methods of dissolution whic we are about to consider. They are as follows:

(*a*) A company which has been re-registered with *illegal* objec can be dissolved by the taking of proceedings by the Attorne General for *cancellation of the registration.*

Thus in *Attorney-General v. Lindi St. Claire (Person Services) Ltd.* (1980). Miss St. Claire, who was engaged in t business of prostitution, was advised to register a limited cor pany for the purposes of her business. The registrar rejecte the names of Prostitutes Limited., Hookers Ltd., and Lindi $ Claire French Lessons Ltd., but finally accepted the name Lindi St. Claire (Personal Services) Ltd. and the company w duly registered. The Attorney-General successfully applied have the registration cancelled on the grounds that the purpo of the company was unlawful.

(*b*) A company which is transferring its undertaking to a other company under a scheme for reconstruction or amalgam tion may, according to *s. 208(1)(d),* be *dissolved without windi up,* if the court so orders.

(*c*) A company which is *defunct* may be *struck off the regist* by the registrar, under s. 353, and will then be *dissolved.*
This is now a very common method of dissolution, as it is bo cheap and easy.

(*d*) A company may be *wound up,* i.e. *liquidated.*

It is unnecessary to say more about (*a*), and there is very little be learnt about (*b*) and (*c*), both of which will be discussed lat Liquidation, however, is a lengthy topic and it must now studied in detail.

. **Methods of winding up and sections to be studied.** There are three methods of winding up, according to s. 211(1):

(a) Winding up *by the court*1, i.e. *compulsory* liquidation.

(b) *Voluntary* winding up, which may be either:

   (i) *a members'* voluntary winding up, *or*

   (ii) a *creditors'* voluntary winding up.

(c) Winding up *subject to the supervision of the court.*

The main problem in studying liquidation is not its difficulty, but is length. Students find it an unmanageable topic, and do not now where to start. Here an attempt has been made to simplify so that they will not feel too aware of the size of the subject, nd it is hoped that they will then be able to read the many etailed books on it without losing their way.

The sections to be studied range from s. 211 to s. 355. This eed cause no alarm, for there are many which can be omitted (it vas not a Scot who once exclaimed "Thank God for Scotland"), nd there are many to which a very short reference is enough. It s helpful if they are grouped so the student knows where he is:

ections 211–216	These are general sections applying to all three methods of winding-up, and concerning *contributories*.
ections 218–274	These sections deal with winding up *by the court*.
ections 278–310	These sections deal with *voluntary* winding up, but are subdivided:
	ss. 278–283 General sections.
	ss. 284–291 *Members'* voluntary winding up.
	ss. 292–300 *Creditors'* voluntary winding up.
	ss. 301–310 General sections.
ections 311–315	These sections deal with winding up subject to the *supervision of the court*.
ections 316–355	These again are general sections applying to all three methods of winding up.

Detailed regulartions regarding the winding up of companies re set out in the Companies (Winding-Up) Rules, 1949, as subequently amended, and references to them will be made where ecessary in subsequent chapters.

PROGRESS TEST 25

1. In what ways may a registered company be dissolved? **(1)**

2. In what ways may a registered company be wound up? **(2)**

CHAPTER XXVI

Contributories

1. Definition of a contributory. Section 213 defines a contributor as *every person liable to contribute to the assets of a company o winding up*.

Section 215(1) states that if a contributory dies, his person representatives become liable to contribute to the assets and s become contributories. Moreover, s. 215(2) states that if they de fault in paying any money due, the company may take admini stration proceedings in order to compel payment out of the estat (*see* XI, **6**).

Section 216(*a*) states that if a contributory becomes bankrup his trustee in bankruptcy represents him and becomes a con tributory, and s. 216(*b*) states that the estimated value of his lia bility to future calls, as well as calls already made, may be prove against the bankrupt's estate.

2. Liability of a contributory. Section 214 states that the liabilit of a contributory creates a *specialty debt* accruing due from hir at the time when his liability commenced (i.e. when he acquire the shares), but *payable when calls are made*.

Section 212 is a lengthy section, giving the details of the liabilit of the contributories. It does not refer to the terms "A list" an "B list" so that these require some explanation. The term "/ list" denotes the list of all those persons whose names were o the company's register of members at the time of the liquidation The term "B list" denotes the list of all those persons who wer members *within the year preceding the liquidation,* but who ha transferred their shares before liquidation commenced. The tw lists together form the contributories, i.e. persons who are liabl to contribute to the assets in accordance with s. 212.

Section 212(1) provides first in a general statement that ever present and past member is liable to contribute to the assets o the company on liquidation an amount sufficient to pay its debts It then proceeds to qualify this statement in the following way (s 212(1)(*f*) has been omitted):

(*a*) A *past* member (B list) is not liable to contribute if he ceased to be a member a year or more before the commencement of the winding up, i.e. he is liable *only* if he ceased to be a member *within a year* preceding the winding up.

(*b*) A *past* member is not liable in respect of any debt contracted after he ceased to be a member.

(*c*) A *past* member is not liable unless the *existing* members (A list) are unable to satisfy the contributions required from them.

(*d*) In a company limited by shares, no contribution is required from *any member*, past or present, exceeding the amount, if any, *unpaid on the shares* in respect of which he is liable (limited liability).

(*e*) In a company limited by guarantee, no amount is required from any member exceeding the amount of the guarantee. Section 212(3), however, adds that if such a company also has a share capital, then the member will be liable not only up to the amount of the guarantee, but also up to the amount unpaid on the shares, so that he has a double, if limited, liability.

(*f*) A sum due to a member *in his character of member*, by way of dividends, profits or otherwise, shall not be deemed a debt of the company payable to that member in the case of competition between himself and any other creditor not a member, though it may be taken into account in adjusting the rights of the contributories among themselves (*see* IV, **5**).

This curiously worded little paragraph is, of course, a reference to the order of distribution of assets which has been fully discussed in IV, **5**. Students are often puzzled by it, asking what is the position if a trade creditor is also a member. Does the fact that he is a member deprive him of his priority, since the Act says "creditor not a member"? Probably the correct view to take is that the Act means "creditor regarding a debt which has *not arisen* in respect of his shares".

. Contribution and distribution. The rules given above, apart from *f*), relate to *contribution*. They do not affect *distribution* by the liquidator of the assets on which he can lay his hands: these are distributed in accordance with the rules set out in IV, **5**. But this can have some odd practical results.

Thus the liquidator must first call upon persons on the A list (*see* (*c*) above). Only if the individual A list member cannot pay the amount due on his shares may the liquidator resort to the person on the B list, if any, in respect of those shares. If the A list member has owned the shares for a year or more, there is then no one to whom the liquidator can resort in respect of those shares.

Having received such A list assets as he can collect, the liquidator applies those assets to *all the debts of the company, pari passu,* in the *order of distribution of assets, irrespective of the date when any particular debt was contracted.* Thus he will dispose of the creditors with fixed charges first, set aside a sum for costs, pay the preferential creditors next, and then the creditors with floating charges. Finally he will reach the unsecured creditors. Let us suppose that at this point he has not enough money to pay them all in full: he will then pay them, *pari passu,* as much as he can, e.g. 50p in £1.

Only then can he resort to the B list, and even when he does so he can only claim from a B list member when the corresponding A list member has been unable to pay. Moreover, he is now restricted by (*b*) above. If all the outstanding debts were contracted *after* the persons on the B list had transferred their shares, he cannot claim contribution from any of them. But let us suppose that there is one debt of £500 contracted *before* six B list members had transferred their shares. There are many other debts amounting to £10,000 in all contracted *after* all the B list members had transferred their shares. The total liability on the shares of the six B list members is £1,000. In such a case the liquidator can demand from them *only £500,* (*b*), and he must apply this £500 *pari passu* towards *all the debts.* It is clear that if he has £500 to apply towards debts of £10,500, each creditor will receive only one-twenty-first of the amount which he is owed. The single B list creditor will therefore receive one-twenty-first of £500, yet there is still a liability on the B list shares of £500.

4. Special rules where unlimited private company re-registers as limited. Section 44(7) Companies Act 1967 lays down special rules which apply where an unlimited private company has re-registered as limited (*see* II, **39**) and then goes into liquidation. Under s. 7(4) Companies Act 1980 these rules also apply where an unlimited private company re-registers as a public (and therefore necessarily limited) company. They are as follows:

(*a*) Despite s. 212(1)(*a*) (*see* **2**), (which imposes a time limit of one year on the liability of a past member), a past member who was a member of the company *at the time of re-registration* is liable to contribute to the assets in respect of debts contracted *before* that time if the winding up commences within *three years* from re-registration.

(*b*) Despite s. 212(1)(*c*) (*see* **2**), (which exonerates past members entirely unless the existing members are unable to meet their obligations), where *all* the existing members have become members *since* the time of re-registration, a person who was a past or present member *at that time* is liable to contribute to the assets in respect of debts contracted *before* that time, even though the existing members have satisfied the contributions required from them. This rule is subject to the time limits imposed on liability both by s. 212(1)(*a*) and s. 44(7)(*a*).

(*c*) Despite s. 212(1)(*d*) and (*e*) (*see* **2**), (which impose a limit on the liability of a member of a company limited by shares or guarantee), the liability of any person who was a *past or present member* of the company *at the time of re-registration* in respect of debts contracted *before* that time is *unlimited.*

The intention of the section is clearly to ensure that the members of an unlimited company do not escape their obligations by re-registering the company as limited. No provision, however, seems to have been made for *distribution,* and it seems a little hard on the creditors who dealt with an unlimited company that they should receive exactly the same proportion of the distributed assets as those creditors who dealt with the company after it re-registered as limited. This is especially the case where the distributed assets are greatly increased by the rules of *contribution* given above.

PROGRESS TEST 26

1. Define a contributory. Give the statutory provisions regarding the death and bankruptcy of a contributory.   (**1**)

2. Give the statutory provisions regarding the liability of a contributory. What do you understand by the terms "A list" and "B list"?   (**2**)

CHAPTER XXVII

Winding Up by the Court

1. Cases in which a company may be wound up by the court. Section 222, as amended by the Companies Act 1980, states that a company may be wound up by the court if:

(*a*) the company has passed a special resolution to that effect;

(*b*) a public company registered as such on its original incorporation has not been issued with its trading certificate within a year from registration (*see* V, **3**);

(*c*) the company does not commence business within one year from incorporation or suspends business for a year;

(*d*) the number of members is reduced below two (*see* the 4th Schedule to the Companies Act 1980);

(*e*) the company is unable to pay its debts;

(*f*) the court is of the opinion that it is just and equitable that the company should be wound up.

2. Definition of inability to pay debts. Section 223, as amended by s. 1 Insolvency Act 1976, explains what is meant by s. 222(*e*), and states that a company is deemed unable to pay its debts if:

(*a*) a creditor for more than £200 has served on the company a demand for the sum due, and the company has for three weeks neglected to pay it or to secure or compound for it to his satisfaction; *or*

(*b*) execution is unsatisfied; *or*

(*c*) it is proved to the court's satisfaction that the company is unable to pay its debts, taking into account its contingent and prospective liabilities.

3. The meaning of "just and equitable". The court's power under s. 222(*f*) to wind a company up on the grounds that it is just and equitable to do so is purely discretionary. There is therefore no definite number of occasions on which the court will exercise its power, but it has done so in the following cases:

(*a*) Where the substratum or main object has failed: *Re German Date Coffee Co.* (1882), (*see* II, **25**).

[b] Where there was deadlock in the management: *Re Yenidje Tobacco Co.* (1916).

(c) Where the company was formed for a fraudulent purpose.

(d) Where the company was a "bubble", i.e. it never in fact had any business or property.

(e) Where a director had voting control and refused to hold meetings, produce accounts or pay dividends: *Loch* v. *John Blackwood Ltd.* (1924).

(f) Where, in a private company which distributed its profits as directors' remuneration and paid no dividends, all three of the members were directors, and one of them was removed from office as director under s. 184 by the other two: *Ebrahimi* v. *Westbourne Galleries, Ltd.* (1972).

Here the House of Lords held that the words "just and equitable" are *general words* of wide application and must not be restricted:

> (i) to particular instances; nor
> (ii) by the previous clauses of s. 222; nor
> (iii) to cases where *mala fides* can be proved; nor
> (iv) to circumstances where the petitioner is wronged in his capacity of *shareholder*.

Further, while the concepts of probity, good faith and mutual confidence, and the remedies where these are absent, developed in the law of partnership, they apply in the same way to registered companies, and it is merely confusing to refer to small companies of this kind as "quasi-partnerships". Individuals in companies have rights and obligations *inter se* which are not submerged in the company structure, and the "just and equitable" provision enables the court to subject the exercise of legal rights (such as the right to remove a director under s. 184) to equitable considerations.

The court will not, however, grant an injunction to *prevent* the exercise of legal rights, even though it may give a remedy for the inequitable use of them: *Bentley-Stevens* v. *Jones* (1974).

Where the entitlement to management participation is the basis of the relationship between the members, it appears that exclusion from management will be a ground for winding up whether it arises from the inequitable exercise of legal rights or a total disregard of the legal rights of others: *Re A & BC Chewing Gum* (1975).

4. The presentation of the winding up petition. While s. 222 (*see* **1**) gives the *grounds* on which a company may be wound up by the court, s. 224 gives the *persons* by whom the petition for winding up may be brought.

Under s. 224(1) and (2) there are *the following possible petitioners*:

(*a*) The *company*, after passing a special resolution (*see* **1**).

(*b*) A *creditor*, including a contingent or prospective creditor who must, under s. 224(1)(*c*), give security for costs and establish a *prima facie* case before he may petition.

A judgment creditor has a right to a winding up order even though the company has a disputed claim for a larger sum against him: *Re Douglas Griggs Engineering Co.* (1962).

(*c*) A *contributory*, whether A list or B list. Despite the definition of a contributory in s. 213, the term includes for the purposes of s. 224 a holder of *fully paid shares* (*see* **XXVI**, **1**, **2**).

A contributory, however, may petition only if one of the following conditions is fulfilled:

   (*i*) If the memerbership is reduced below the statutory minimum (*see* II, **40**); *or*
   (*ii*) If he is an original allottee; *or*
   (*iii*) If he has held his shares for any six out of the previous eighteen months; *or*
   (*iv*) If the shares devolved on him through the death of a former holder.

The last three provisions are designed to prevent a person from buying shares in a company with the sole intention of qualifying himself to bring a winding up petition.

A *personal representative* of a *deceased* contributory, even though he is not registered as a member in respect of the shares, is a contributory for the purposes of s. 224: *Re Bayswater Trading Co., Ltd.* (1970). An *unregistered* allottee of shares is likewise a contributory for the purposes of s. 224 since there is nothing in that section which expressly requires registration: *Re JN2 Ltd.* (1977). An unregistered *trustee in bankruptcy* of a *bankrupt* contributory, however, is not: *Re Bolton Engineering Co., Ltd.* (1956). The Jenkins Committee recommended that s. 224 should be amended expressly to empower both the trustee in bankruptcy and the personal representative of a contributory to present a winding up petition.

(*d*) The Secretary of State, if the ground of the petition is that specified in s. 222(*b*). (See **1** above and para. 28 of the 3rd Schedule to the Companies Act 1980.)

(*e*) The *Department of Trade*, in the cases specified in s. 35(1) Companies Act 1967 (*see* XVIII, **6**), and on the grounds that it is just and equitable that the company should be wound up.

(*f*) The *official receiver*, where the company is already in voluntary liquidation, or being wound up subject to the supervision of the court, and the interests of the creditors or contributories are not adequately protected.

An example of this occurred in *Re Ryder Installations* (1966), where the voluntary liquidator's conduct was irregular and his accounts unsatisfactory.

The statutory right to present a winding up petition in accordance with the section cannot in any way be restricted or excluded by provisions to that effect in the articles.

5. Non-statutory rules concerning petitioners. Apart from the possible petitioners under s. 224, there are decisions establishing that the following persons may present a winding up petition:

(*a*) A secured creditor (who will not lose his security by doing so).
(*b*) A creditor's executor.
(*c*) An assignee of a debt or part of a debt, including an equitable assignee.
(*d*) A holder of bearer debentures.
(*e*) A mortgagee who intends to exercise his power of sale (but he will be restrained from so doing until his petition is heard).
(*f*) A shareholder whose calls are in arrear (but he must first pay the amount of the call into court).

Conversely, the holder of a share warrant cannot present a petition.

6. Powers of court on hearing petition. Section 225(1) empowers the court to dismiss the petition, or adjourn the hearing, or make any order that it thinks fit, but states that it *must not refuse* to make a winding up order merely because the assets have been fully mortgaged or because there are no assets at all. Despite this provision, however, a fully paid shareholder is not entitled to a winding up order unless he can show that he, as a member of the company, will achieve some advantage or avoid or minimise some disadvantage which would accrue to him by virtue of his membership: *Re Chesterfield Catering Co., Ltd.* (1976).

Section 225(2) states that where the petition is presented by members on the grounds that it is just and equitable that the company should be wound up, the court must make a winding up order unless it is of the opinion that the petitioners have some other remedy available to them, and that they are acting unreasonably in failing to pursue it. A good example of this situation occurred in *Charles Forte Investments* v. *Amanda* (1963), *see* XX, 7.

7. Power of court to stay proceedings against the company. Section 226 is a section applying only to the period of time *after* the presentation of the petition and *before* a winding up order has been made.

It states that during this period the company, or any creditor or contributory, may apply to the appropriate court to stay any proceedings which are pending against the company, and the court may do so.

8. The commencement of winding up by the court. As in bankruptcy, the *moment of commencement* of the winding up is of great legal importance. Section 229(1) states that where *before the presentation of a petition* for winding up by the court, the company has passed a resolution for *voluntary* winding up, the winding up is deemed to have commenced *at the time of the passing of the resolution*.

Section 229(2) states that in all other cases (i.e. where the company has *not* previously resolved to wind up voluntarily) a winding up by the court commences *at the time of the presentation of the petition*.

It is helpful at this point to look at s. 280, which deals with the moment of commencement of a voluntary winding up, stating that it is the time of the passing of the resolution to wind up. This explains the provisions of s. 229(1), and the two sections should always be studied together.

9. The consequences of a winding up order. Once the winding up order is made, its consequences *date back* to the commencement of the winding up. This is the reason why it is essential to know exactly when the moment of commencement is. Section 229(2), as we have just seen, states that as a rule it is *the time of the presentation of the petition*, so that in the normal case the consequences of the winding up order will date back to that time.

These consequences are:

(*a*) Under s. 227, any disposition of the company's property, any transfer of shares, and any alteration in the status of members is void.

(*b*) Under s. 228(1), any execution against the company's property is void.

(*c*) Under s. 230, a copy of the winding up order must be sent at once by the company to the registrar who, under s. 9(3)(*f*) European Communities Act 1972, must publish notice of its receipt by him in the *Gazette*.

If the company fails to notify him of the making of the winding up order and cannot show that it was known at the time to the person concerned, then, under s. 9(4)(*a*) European Communities Act 1972, it cannot rely on the making of the order against that person.

(*d*) Under s. 231, actions against the company are stayed. (This section does not come into operation until the winding up order is made, and s. 226 no longer applies.)

(*e*) Under s. 239(*a*) the official receiver automatically becomes provisional liquidator.

(*f*) The powers of the directors cease.

(*g*) The servants of the company are dismissed.

10. The official receiver. Section 233(1) states that the term "official receiver" means the official receiver attached to the court for bankruptcy purposes, although s. 234 empowers the court to appoint some other person if it thinks it desirable.

The official receiver is an official of the Department of Trade who is attached to the court.

11. The provisional liquidator. Section 238(1) and (2) empower the court to appoint a provisional liquidator at any time *after* the presentation of the petition and *before* the making of the winding up order. Section 238(2) states that either the official receiver or any other fit person may be appointed.

This is a purely *temporary* appointment, for as soon as the winding up order is made the official receiver automatically becomes provisional liquidator (*see* **9**(*e*)) in a *totally different sense of the word*. It is not made in every case, but only where proof by affidavit is given that there are sufficient grounds for the appointment, usually that the assets are in jeopardy.

To secure the appointment, application must be made to the court by a creditor, a contributory, or the company. If the court grants the application, it must notify the official receiver who is usually, though not necessarily, the person appointed.

Section 238(4) makes it clear that the powers of the provisional liquidator depend on the order appointing him. He is merely a receiver, his function being to protect the assets of the company; thus he cannot sell the assets unless they are perishable.

12. The appointment of the liquidator. Section 237 empowers the court to appoint a liquidator. Section 239, however, contains further details regarding the appointment.

Section 239(*a*), as we have already seen in **9**(*e*), states that as soon as the winding up order is made, the *official receiver* automatically becomes *provisional liquidator* and acts as such until a liquidator is appointed. This occurs in *every* compulsory liquidation and is in no way connected with the appointment of a provisional liquidator under s. 238 between the time of the presentation of the petition and the making of the winding up order.

Section 239(*b*) requires the official receiver to summon separate meetings of the creditors and contributories to decide whether or not to apply to the court to appoint a liquidator in his place.

Section 239(*c*) empowers the court to make any appointment required to give effect to their decision, and if the two meetings disagree, the court must decide the difference and make such order as it thinks fit.

Section 239(*d*) states that if the court makes no appointment, then the *official receiver* becomes *the liquidator*. Section 239(*e*) provides that in any case he is automatically the liquidator where there is any vacancy.

Finally, s. 240 states that where a person *other than the official receiver* is appointed liquidator:

(*a*) He may not act until he has notified his appointment to the registrar and given security to the satisfaction of the Department of Trade.

(*b*) He must give the official receiver such information, aid, and access to books and documents as are necessary to enable him to perform his statutory duties.

13. The statement of affairs. Section 235(1) states that where the court has made a winding up order, a statement of the company's affairs must, unless the court orders otherwise, be made out and *submitted to the official receiver*.

It must be in the prescribed form, verified by affidavit, and show:

(*a*) Particulars of assets, debts and liabilities.

(b) Names, residences and occupations of creditors.
(c) Securities held by them, and the dates when these were given.
(d) Any further information which the official receiver may require.

Section 235(2) states that the statement must be submitted and verified by *one or more of the directors and the secretary*, or by such of the following persons as the official receiver may require:

(a) Past or present officers of the company.
(b) Persons who have taken part in its formation within one year before the winding up order.
(c) Persons who are, or have been within that year, employed by the company and who are capable of giving the required information.
(d) Persons who are, or have been within that year, officers or employees of another company which is, or has been within that year, an officer of the company now in liquidation.

Section 235(3) requires the statement to be submitted *within fourteen days* from the making of the winding up order.

Lastly, s. 235(6) entitles any person stating himself in writing to be a creditor or contributory to inspect the statement at reasonable times on payment of the prescribed fee, and to a copy of it.

14. The official receiver's report. Section 236(1) requires the official receiver, as soon as possible after receiving the statement of affairs, to submit to the court a *preliminary report*:

(a) as to the amount of capital issued, subscribed and paid up and the estimated amount of assets and liabilities; and
(b) if the company has failed, as to the causes of its failure; and
(c) whether in his opinion further inquiry is desirable into the promotion or failure or the conduct of the business.

Section 236(2) states that he may also, if he thinks fit, make a *further report* stating the manner in which the company was formed, and whether in his opinion any *fraud* has been committed by any person in its promotion or by any officer since formation, and any other matters which should be brought to the court's notice.

Section 236(3) provides that if in any such further report the official receiver states that *fraud* has been committed, the court has the powers conferred on it by s. 270 (public examination of promoters and officers).

15. Summary of the duties of the official receiver.

(*a*) He may be appointed *provisional liquidator after* the presentation of the petition and *before* the winding up order is made, under s. 238. He is then merely a receiver and his function is to protect the assets during this intervening period.

(*b*) He becomes the *provisional liquidator* automatically in all cases and in a different sense to (*a*) above as soon as the winding up order is made, under s. 239. He acts as liquidator until a liquidator is appointed.

(*c*) He must summon separate *meetings* of creditors and contributories, under s. 239(*b*), to decide whether to apply to the court to appoint a liquidator in his place.

(*d*) If the court makes no appointment, then the official receiver becomes the *liquidator*, under s. 239(*d*).

(*e*) He is, by virtue of his office, the *liquidator* during any *vacancy*, under s. 239(*e*).

(*f*) He receives and considers the *statement of affairs*, under s. 235.

(*g*) He *must make a preliminary report* to the court, under s. 236(1).

(*h*) He *may* also, if he thinks fit, make a *further report* to the court, under s. 236(2), which may result in a public examination of promoters and officers under s. 270.

(*i*) He must take part in any public examination, under s. 270.

(*j*) He may apply in an appropriate case for a disqualification order under s. 9 Insolvency Act 1976 (*see* XXII, **20**).

16. Resignation of liquidator. Section 242(1) permits a liquidator appointed by the court to resign.

Winding Up Rule 167 states that a liquidator who wishes to resign must summon separate meetings of creditors and contributories to decide whether or not to accept his resignation. If the meetings by ordinary resolution both agree to accept it, he must notify the court and the official receiver, whereupon it takes effect.

If either of the meetings does not accept his resignation, he must report the result of the meetings to the court and the official receiver, and the court then decides the matter.

Section 242(3) provides that a vacancy in the office of a liquidator appointed by the court must be filled by the court and, as we have already seen (**12**), the official receiver acts as liquidator until the court makes the necessary appointment.

17. Removal of liquidator. Section 242(1) empowers the court to remove a liquidator appointed by the court "*on cause shown*".

This widely worded subsection is clearly intended to give the court an unfettered discretion in the matter, and the expression "on cause shown" certainly includes insanity, bias, dishonesty, and undesirability on any ground.

Under s. 248(2) a liquidator may also be removed by the Department of Trade under certain circumstances, but this section will be considered later.

18. Remuneration of liquidator. Section 242(2) states that where a person other than the official receiver is appointed liquidator, he receives such remuneration as the court directs.

Winding Up Rule 159 states that, unless the court orders otherwise, his remuneration must be fixed by the committee of inspection, and be in the form of a commission or percentage based partly on the assets *realised*, and partly on those *distributed*.

If the Department of Trade is of the opinion that the committee of inspection has fixed the remuneration at too large a figure, it may apply to the court, which will then itself fix the sum to be paid to the liquidator.

If there is no committee of inspection, the liquidator's remuneration must be based on the scale payable to the official receiver when he acts as liquidator.

19. Validity of liquidator's acts. Section 242(5) makes the same provision regarding liquidators as is made by s. 180 regarding directors (*see* XXII, **24**). It states that the acts of a liquidator are valid despite defects in his appointment or qualification. It gives, however, *one exception* to this rule: nothing will validate an act done by a liquidator whose appointment contravenes s. 335.

Section 335, which will be considered later, disqualifies a *corporation* from appointment as liquidator and makes such an appointment *void*. Section 242(5), therefore, would not operate to validate the acts of a corporation which had unlawfully been appointed liquidator in contravention of the section.

(A corporation can, of course, lawfully be appointed a *director* of another company, provided there is no contravention of s. 178 (*see* XXII, **3**).)

20. The position of the liquidator regarding the company's property. Section 243(1) states that the liquidator obtains *custody and control* of the company's property. It is important to notice that he does not obtain *title* to it, i.e. *ownership*, unless he applies to the court under s. 244 for a *vesting order* to be made and the court makes an order to that effect.

This is one of the ways in which a liquidation differs from a bankruptcy, for in a bankruptcy the property of the debtor (with minor exceptions) vests in the trustee in bankruptcy.

21. The powers of the liquidator. Section 245 is an important section setting out the powers of the liquidator. There are fourteen powers in all, six of them requiring sanction and eight of them freely exercisable. They have been shortened and rearranged below in order to make it easier to learn them.

(*a*) *Powers exercisable with permission.* Section 245(1) empowers the liquidator, with the *sanction of the court or the committee of inspection*, to:

- (*i*) conduct legal proceedings in the company's name;
- (*ii*) carry on the company's business so far as is necessary;
- (*iii*) appoint a solicitor;
- (*iv*) pay any class of creditors in full;
- (*v*) make compromises or arrangements with creditors;
- (*vi*) compromise calls, debts and claims between the company and a contributory or other debtor.

(*b*) *Powers exercisable without permission.* Section 245(2) empowers the liquidator, *without sanction*, to:

- (*i*) sell the company's property by public auction or private contract;
- (*ii*) execute documents in the company's name and use the seal;
- (*iii*) sign negotiable instruments in the company's name;
- (*iv*) raise money on the security of the assets;
- (*v*) prove in the bankruptcy of a contributory;
- (*vi*) take out letters of administration to a deceased contributory;
- (*vii*) appoint an agent;
- (*viii*) do anything else necessary to wind up the company and distribute its assets.

Section 245(3) provides that the liquidator, in exercising any of these fourteen powers, is subject to the control of the court, and empowers any creditor or contributory to apply to the court regarding them.

22. Exercise and control of liquidator's powers. Section 246(1) states that the liquidator must have regard to any directions given by resolution of the meetings of creditors or contributories or by the committee of inspection. In case of *conflict*, the directions given by the *creditors or contributories* at a general meeting override those given by the *committee of inspection*.

Section 246(2) empowers the liquidator to call meetings of creditors or contributories in order to ascertain their wishes, and requires him to do so whenever the creditors or contributories *by resolution so direct*, or whenever *requested in writing* to do so by *one-tenth in value* of the creditors or contributories.

Section 246(3) empowers the liquidator to apply to the court for directions in any matter which arises in the winding up, and s. 246(5) enables any person who is aggrieved by an act of the liquidator to apply to the court, which may then make such order as it thinks just.

23. The liquidator's books. Section 247 requires the liquidator to keep *proper books*, and gives any creditor or contributory a right of inspection.

Details of the proper books are given in the Winding Up Rules. They are as follows:

(*a*) Rule 171 requires a *record book* containing the minutes, proceedings and resolutions of the meetings of creditors, contributories, and the committee of inspection.

(*b*) Rule 172 requirds a *cash book* containing receipts and payments.

(*c*) Rule 176 applies only where the liquidator carries on the company's business, when it requires a *trading account*.

24. Payments of liquidator into bank. Section 248(1), as amended by s. 3 Insolvency Act 1976, requires the liquidator to pay the money which he receives into the Insolvency Services Account at the Bank of England. The Department of Trade must give him a receipt for it.

If, however, the committee of inspection satisfy the Department that it is to the advantage of the creditors or contributories that the account should be at another bank, they may apply to the Department to authorise the liquidator to make his payments there.

Section 248(2), as amended by s. 1 Insolvency Act 1976, states that if the liquidator retains for more than ten days a sum exceeding £100 without a satisfactory explanation, he must pay interest on the excess at 20%, is liable to have some or all of his remuneration disallowed, and may be *removed from office by the Department* (*see* **17**).

Finally, s. 248(3) makes it unlawful for a liquidator to pay any money which he has received as liquidator into his private banking account.

25. The liquidator's accounts. Section 249(1) requires the liquidator at the prescribed times, but at least twice a year, to send to the Department of Trade an account of his receipts and payments.

Section 2(1) Insolvency Act 1976 relieves the Secretary of State of his former obligation under s. 249(3) to have the liquidator's account *audited*, although he may do so if he wishes. Whether he does so or not, s. 249(3), as amended by the Insolvency Act 1976, requires the liquidator to provide the Department with all required information, and authorises the Department to inspect his books and accounts at any time.

Section 249(4), as amended by s. 2(3) and (4) Insolvency Act 1976, states that when the account has been audited or, if not audited, when the liquidator has been notified of the decision not to have it audited, one copy of it must be filed and kept by the Department, and the other delivered to the court. The copy filed with the court is open to the inspection of any person.

Section 249(5) requires the liquidator to have the account printed, and to send a printed copy to every creditor and contributory.

26. Control of Department of Trade over liquidators. Section 250(1) states that the Department of Trade must take cognisance of the liquidator's conduct, and if he does not perform his duties or if any complaint is made to the Department by a creditor or contributory, it must inquire into it.

Section 250(2) empowers the Department to require the liquidator to answer any inquiry concerning the liquidation, and to apply to the court to examine him or any other person on oath. It may also, under s. 250(3), direct an investigation to be made of his books and vouchers.

27. Release of liquidators. Section 251(1) states that when the liquidator has realised the property, and distributed the final dividend, if any, to the creditors, and adjusted the rights of the contributories *inter se* and made a final return, if any, to them, *or when he has resigned, or been removed from office, he may apply to the Department of Trade for his release.*

The Department must then have a report on his accounts prepared, and must either grant or withhold his release, subject to an appeal to the High Court.

Section 251(3) states that *a release discharges the liquidator from all liability*, though it can be revoked on proof that it was obtained by fraud or concealment of a material fact. Under s. 251(4), where the liquidator has not already resigned or been removed, the release operates as a removal from office.

Section 251(2) states that where the release is withheld, any creditor or contributory, or any person interested, may apply to the court, which may then make such order as it thinks just, charging the liquidator with the consequences of any breach of duty.

28. Liability of the liquidator. We have already seen that the ownership of the company's property remains in the company and does not pass to the liquidator on the making of the winding up order (**20**). He is not, therefore, a *trustee* either for the company or for the creditors or contributories, any more than a director is (*see* XXII, **54**).

He is, however, in a *fiduciary relation* towards the company and the creditors, and for *breach of the many statutory duties* imposed on him he will be liable to pay damages to any creditor or contributory who has been injured by the breach. Moreover, if he is *negligent* in his application of the company's assets, he will likewise incur liability to any person who suffers as a result, and proceedings can be taken against him, as against a promoter, director, or any officer of the company under s. 333 for *misfeasance* (*see* XXX, **13**).

In *Pulsford* v. *Devenish* (1903), the liquidator advertised in the usual way for creditors to make their claims against the company, but took no further steps to notify a creditor whose debt appeared in the company's books, but who did not know of the liquidation. HELD: The liquidator was liable to compensate him.

29. The committee of inspection. Section 252(1) states that the meetings of the creditors and contributories summoned by the official receiver under s. 239(*b*) (*see* **12**) must decide whether or not to apply to the court for the appointment of a committee of inspection to act with the liquidator, and who are to be members of it, if appointed.

Section 252(3) empowers the court to make an order to give effect to their decision, and, if they disagree, to decide the difference.

Section 253(1) states that the committee of inspection must consist of *creditors and contributories in the proportions agreed on by the meetings* or, if they disagreed, in the proportions fixed by the court.

Section 253(2) requires the committee to meet whenever they appoint, and failing appointment at least once a month. The liquidator or any member of the committee may also call a meeting when he thinks it necessary.

Section 253(3) states that the committee may act by a *majority of the members present, provided a majority of the committee are present.*

Section 253(4) states that a member of the committee may resign by giving written notice to the liquidator, and s. 253(5) states that he vacates office if he:

(*a*) becomes bankrupt; *or*

(*b*) compounds or arranges with his creditors; *or*

(*c*) is absent from five consecutive meetings without permission.

Under s. 253(6) he can be removed by an ordinary resolution of a meeting of the creditors, if he is a creditor, or of contributories, if he is a contributory. Seven days' notice of the meeting must be given, stating its objects.

If there is a vacancy on the committee, s. 253(7) requires the liquidator to summon a meeting of creditors or contributories, as the case may be, to fill the vacancy. The meeting may then by resolution appoint the same or another creditor or contributory.

If, however, the liquidator thinks it unnecessary to fill the vacancy, he may apply to the court for an order to that effect. In any case s. 253(8) authorises the continuing members of the committee to act despite any vacancy, provided there are at least two of them.

Winding Up Rule 161 prohibits a member of the committee from buying any of the company's property without the leave of the court.

30. Power of Department of Trade where no committee of inspection. Section 254 states that if there is no committee of inspection, the liquidator may apply to the Department of Trade to do any act or give any permission which the Act requires to be done or given by the committee (*see* **21**).

31. General powers of the court. The remainder of the sections on compulsory winding up deal with the powers of the court. Some of these powers must be considered in detail, and the rest of this chapter is concerned with them, but others require no explanation, and a short list of them will suffice:

(*a*) Section 256 empowers the court to *stay the winding up proceedings* at any time in a proper case, on the application of the liquidator, the official receiver, any creditor or contributory.

(*b*) Section 257 requires the court to *settle a list of contributories*, and empowers it to *rectify the register*. It also requires it to *collect the company's assets and apply them towards its liabilities*. A list of contributories is not necessary where calls need not be made on them.

(*c*) Section 258 empowers the court to require any contributory on the list, and any trustee, receiver, banker, agent or officer of the company to *pay or transfer to the liquidator any of the company's money, property, books or papers*.

(*d*) Section 260 empowers the court to *make calls* on the contributories on the list.

(*e*) Section 264 empowers the court to *fix a time within which creditors must prove their debts*, or be excluded from the benefit of any distribution made before proof.

Under s. 273 the powers of the court conferred by ss. 257, 258, 260, and 264 may be *delegated to the liquidator* as an officer of the court and subject to the control of the court, though he may not, without the special leave of the court, *rectify the register of members*. Nor can he *make a call* without either the special leave of the court or the sanction of the committee of inspection.

32. Extent to which set-off allowed. Section 259(1) empowers the court to order any contributory to pay any money which he owes to the company, exclusive of calls. If, however, the company at the same time owes money to the contributory, s. 259(3) allows the debts to be set off against each other *when all the creditors have been paid in full*.

Further, it has been held that set-off must be allowed when the contributory *becomes bankrupt* after the commencement of the winding up.

33. Appointment of special manager. Section 263(1) states that where the official receiver becomes the liquidator, he may apply to the court for the appointment of a special manager if the *nature of the company's business* or the *interests of the creditors or contributories* make it desirable.

The court will specify the period during which the special manager is to act, and the powers which he will have. Under s. 263(3) it also fixes his remuneration.

34. The court's power of private examination. Section 268(1) empowers the court to summon before it any officer of the company, or any person known or suspected to have in his possession any property of the company, or to be indebted to the company, or capable of giving information about its promotion, trade, affairs or property.

The power of the court under this section is purely discretionary, and it can make an order for private examination either of its own motion, or on the application of a contributory, or, as is usually the case, on the application of the liquidator.

Section 268(2) empowers the court to examine the person concerned *on oath*, either orally or by written interrogatories, to reduce his answers to writing, and to require him to sign them. The examination is conducted *in private*. Under s. 268(3) the person concerned may be required to produce any books or papers relating to the company, without prejudice to any lien which he may claim on them.

If, after being tendered his expenses, he refuses to appear, s. 268(4) empowers the court to apprehend him.

35. The court's power of public examination. Section 270(1) states that where the official receiver has made a further report under s. 236(2) and (3) alleging *fraud* (*see* **14**), the court may direct that the person or officer concerned shall attend the court for a *public examination*.

Section 270(2) states that the official receiver must take part in the examination and may, if authorised by the Department of Trade, employ a solicitor and counsel. Section 270(3) states that the liquidator, where the official receiver is not acting as such, and any creditor or contributory may also take part, either personally or by a solicitor or counsel.

Section 270(4) authorises the court to put such questions as it thinks fit, and s. 270(5) requires the examination to be *on oath*, and the person concerned to answer all questions put to him. He may, however, under s. 270(6), employ a solicitor and counsel, and must be provided with a copy of the official receiver's report.

36. The court's power to arrest an absconding contributory. By far the most delightful section in the Act is s. 271, giving the court power to arrest a contributory. It states that on proof that a contributory is about to quit the United Kingdom or to abscond or to remove or conceal his property in order to evade payment of calls or avoid examination, the court may have him arrested, and his books, papers and movable personal property seized, and him and them safely kept for such time as the court may order.

NOTE: The meaning is clear, but the language picturesque, conjuring up an image of a disconsolate contributory incarcerated along with and entirely surrounded by his books, papers, and movable personal property, while acres of good arable land (unaffected by the section) lie abandoned.

No examiner has ever set a question on this section, which therefore remains a modest gem of legal literature.

37. Dissolution. Section 274(1) states that when the winding up is completed, the liquidator may apply to the court which then makes a *dissolution order*. The company is then *dissolved from the date of the order*.

Section 274(2) requires the liquidator to send a copy of the order within fourteen days to the registrar who, under s. 9(3)(*g*) European Communities Act 1972, must publish its receipt by him in the *Gazette*.

NOTE: The company has now ceased to exist but we shall see later that, unlike a natural legal person, it can be restored to life if necessary.

PROGRESS TEST 27

1. In what cases may a company be wound up by the court? **(1)**

2. Discuss the court's power to wind up a company when it thinks it just and equitable to do so. **(3)**

3. Who may present a winding up petition? **(4)**

4. At what moment does a winding up by the court commence? **(8)**

5. What are the consequences of a winding up order? **(9)**

6. Under what circumstances may a provisional liquidator be appointed after the presentation of the winding up petition and

before the making of the winding up order? Who may apply for his appointment, and what are his powers? (**11**)

7. Give the statutory provisions on the appointment of a liquidator in a winding up by the court. (**12**)

8. What are the contents of the statement of affairs? Who submits it, and to whom is it submitted? (**13**)

9. Who is the official receiver? What are his duties? (**10, 11, 12, 13, 14, 15**)

10. In what manner may a liquidator resign? (**16**)

11. When may a liquidator be removed from office by the court? (**17**)

12. How is a liquidator remunerated? (**18**)

13. What is the legal position of the liquidator with regard to the company's property? (**20**)

14. What are the powers of the liquidator in a winding up by the court? (**21**)

15. If there is conflict between the directions given to the liquidator by the meetings of the creditors or contributories and those given to him by the committee of inspection, which should he observe? (**22**)

16. When is the liquidator required to call a meeting of creditors or contributories? (**22**)

17. What books is the liquidator required to keep? (**23**)

18. What are the statutory provisions regarding the payment by the liquidator into a bank of money which he has received as liquidator? (**24**)

19. Give the statutory provisions regarding the liquidator's accounts. (**25**)

20. Discuss the liability of the liquidator. (**28**)

21. Give the statutory provisions regarding the committee of inspection in a winding up by the court. (**29**)

22. Where there is no committee of inspection, who may do any act or give any permission which the Act requires to be done or given by the committee? (**30**)

23. How far is a set-off allowed between a company and its contributories? (**32**)

24. Give the statutory provisions regarding the appointment of a special manager. (**33**)

25. Give an account of the court's power of private examination. (**34**)

26. Give an account of the court's power of public examination. (**35**)

CHAPTER XXVIII

Voluntary Winding Up

1. Resolutions for voluntary winding up. Section 278(1) provides that a company may be wound up voluntarily:

(a) when the *period*, if any, fixed for its duration by the articles *expires*, or the *event*, if any, *occurs*, on the occurrence of which the articles provide that it is to be dissolved, and the company has passed an *ordinary resolution* to be wound up voluntarily;

(b) if the company passes a *special resolution* to be wound up voluntarily;

(c) if the company passes an *extraordinary resolution* to the effect that it cannot continue its business *by reason of its liabilities*, and that it is advisable to wind up.

Section 279(1) requires notice of any of the above resolutions to be given by the company within fourteen days by advertisement in the *Gazette*.

2. The commencement of voluntary winding up. Section 280 states that the moment of commencement of a voluntary winding up is the time of the *passing of the resolution* (*see* XXVII, **8**).

3. The consequences of a voluntary winding up. These are:

(a) Under s. 281, the company ceases to carry on business, except so far as is required for its beneficial winding up.

(b) Under s. 281, the company's corporate state and powers continue until dissolution.

(c) Under s. 282, any transfer of shares without the sanction of the liquidator, and any alteration in the status of members, is void.

(d) Under s. 285(2) and s. 296(2), the powers of the directors cease on the appointment of a liquidator. But the company in general meeting or the liquidator in a *members'* voluntary winding up, and the committee of inspection or, if none, the creditors in a *creditors'* voluntary winding up, can sanction their continuance.

(*e*) If the liquidation occurs because of insolvency, the company's servants are dismissed. The liquidator may continue the employment of the servants, but this will be a *new* contract.

(*f*) There is no provision similar to s. 231 (*see* XXVII, **9**), but the court may stay proceedings under s. 307(1) (*see* **20**).

4. The declaration of solvency. Section 283(1) states that where it is proposed to wind up a company voluntarily, the *directors* or, *if more than two, the majority of them*, may at a board meeting make a statutory declaration that they have inquired into the company's affairs and have formed the opinion that it will be able to pay its debts in full within a specified period not exceeding twelve months from the commencement of the winding up.

Section 283(2) states that this declaration is ineffective unless:

(*a*) it is made, *within the five weeks preceding* the date of the passing of the resolution for winding up, and is *delivered to the registrar before that date*; and

(*b*) it contains a *statement of assets and liabilities* at the latest practicable date.

Section 283(3), as amended by s. 80 Companies Act 1980 and the 2nd Schedule, provides that a director who makes this declaration without reasonable grounds for his opinion is liable to imprisonment or a fine or both. Further, it states that if the company is duly wound up but its debts are not paid in full within the specified period, it is presumed that the director did not have reasonable grounds for his opinion. This provision puts the burden of proof on the director concerned.

The declaration of solvency is extremely important, for it *determines the nature of the winding up*. Section 283(4) states that when such a declaration *is* made and delivered as above, the winding up is a *members' voluntary winding up*. When it is *not* made and delivered, the winding up is a *creditors' voluntary winding up*.

Accordingly we must now see first what the Act provides regarding a members' voluntary winding up, and then what it provides regarding a creditors' voluntary winding up.

5. Appointment and remuneration of liquidator in members' voluntary winding up. Section 285(1) empowers the *company* in general meeting to appoint a liquidator and fix his remuneration.

Section 286(1) empowers the *company* in general meeting also to fill any casual vacancy in the office of liquidator, subject to any arrangement with its creditors.

6. Power of liquidator to sell the company's property for shares.
Usually the liquidator sells the undertaking and all the property
of the company for *cash*, which is then distributed in the normal
way to creditors and members. But sometimes he sells them
for *shares* in another company, so that the members, instead of
receiving their capital and any surplus assets in the form of money,
become *shareholders in another company*.

In the final chapter we shall consider the various methods of
company reconstruction and amalgamation, of which this is one.
At this point, however, we must consider the provisions of s. 287
which enable the liquidator to make this arrangement.

Section 287(1) states that when a company is in *voluntary liquidation*, and the whole or part of its property is to be transferred to
another company, the liquidator may, with the sanction of a
special resolution, accept in compensation *shares in the transferee
company* for distribution among the members of the transferor
company.

Section 287(2) states that such an arrangement is binding on
the members of the transferor company, but s. 287(3) protects
dissentients. It permits any member who did not vote in favour
of the special resolution to dissent in writing to the liquidator at
the registered office within seven days of the passing of the resolution, and to require the liquidator *either* to abstain from implementing the arrangement *or* to purchase his shares.

If, as is usually the case, the liquidator decides to purchase his
shares, s. 287(4) states that the purchase-money must be paid
before the company is dissolved, and that it must be raised by the
liquidator in such way as is determined by special resolution.

The provisions of s. 287 apply in exactly the same way in a
creditors' voluntary winding up, except that s. 298 prevents the
liquidator from exercising his powers without the *sanction of the
court or the committee of inspection*.

**7. Liquidator's duty to call meetings in members' voluntary wind-
ing up.** Section 289(1) requires the liquidator to summon a general meeting of the company at the end of the first year from the
commencement of the winding up, and of each succeeding year if
it continues, and to lay before the meeting an account of the
winding up during the preceding year.

8. Final meeting and dissolution in members' voluntary winding up.
Section 290(1) and (2) state that as soon as the winding up is
completed, the liquidator must make up an account of the

winding up, showing how it has been conducted and the property disposed of, and must call a general meeting by advertisement in the *Gazette*, stating the time, place and object of the meeting, and published at least one month before the meeting. He must lay the account before this meeting.

Section 290(3) states that within a week after the meeting, he must send a copy of the account to the registrar, and make a return to him of the holding and date of the meeting. If, however, a quorum is not present at the meeting, he must make a return that the meeting was duly called, and that no quorum was present.

The registrar, under s. 9(3)(*h*) European Communities Act 1972, must publish in the *Gazette* the receipt by him of the return. Section 290(4) requires him to register both the account and the return, and on the expiration of three months from their registration the company is *deemed dissolved*.

9. Insolvency of company in members' voluntary winding up. If in a *members'* voluntary winding up the liquidator is at any time of the opinion that the company will not be able to pay its debts in full within the period stated in the declaration of solvency, s. 288 requires him to call a *meeting of the creditors*, and lay before it a statement of the company's assets and liabilities.

If insolvency should occur in this way, despite the making of the declaration of solvency, *ss. 289 and 290 above do not apply*. Section 291 provides that *ss. 299 and 300 shall apply instead*, as if the winding up were a *creditors'* voluntary winding up, though in fact it is not. We shall consider these two sections later in this chapter.

10. Creditors' meeting in a creditors' voluntary winding up. In a creditors' voluntary winding up s. 293(1) requires the company to call a creditors' meeting either for the day of the meeting at which the resolution for voluntary winding up is to be proposed, or for the following day.

Notice of the creditors' meeting must be sent by post to the creditors at the same time as notice of the company meeting is sent out.

Section 293(2) requires the company to advertise notice of the creditors' meeting once in the *Gazette* and at least once in two local newspapers.

Section 293(3) states that the directors must:

(*a*) lay before the creditors' meeting a full statement of the company's affairs, a list of creditors, and the estimated amount of their claims, and

(b) appoint one of themselves to preside at the meeting.

Section 293(4) requires the director so appointed to attend and preside at the meeting.

11. Appointment of liquidator in creditors' voluntary winding up.
Section 294 states that both the creditors and the company at their respective meetings may nominate a liquidator. If they nominate different persons, the *creditors'* choice prevails. If the creditors do not make a nomination, then the *company's* nominee becomes the liquidator.

If two different persons are nominated so that the creditors' nominee becomes the liquidator, any director, member or creditor may apply to the court within seven days for an order either that the company's nominee shall be the liquidator instead of or together with him, or appointing some other person.

If a vacancy occurs in the office of liquidator, s. 297 states that, unless the liquidator was appointed by the court, the creditors may fill the vacancy.

12. Remuneration of liquidator in creditors' voluntary winding up.
Section 296(1) states that the remuneration of the liquidator is fixed by the committee of inspection, or, if none, by the creditors.

13. Committee of inspection in creditors' voluntary winding up.
Section 295(1) states that the creditors at their first or any subsequent meeting may appoint a committee of inspection consisting of *not more than five* persons. If they do so, the company may also appoint *not more than five* persons to act as members of the committee.

If, however, the creditors resolve that all or any of the persons appointed by the company ought not to be members, then those persons are not qualified to act unless the court directs otherwise, and the court may appoint other persons to act as members instead of those appointed by the company.

Section 295(2) states that the provisions of s. 253 (*see* **XXVII, 29**) regarding the committee of inspection in a winding up by the court also apply to the committee of inspection in a creditors' voluntary winding up, except for s. 253(1) dealing with its composition.

NOTE: Thus the *only difference* between the rules relating to a committee of inspection in a winding up *by the court* and those relating to a committee in a *creditors' voluntary* winding up is that in the latter case a *maximum number of members is prescribed* by s. 295(1).

14. Liquidator's duty to call meetings in creditors' voluntary winding up. Section 299(1) makes exactly the same provision for the holding of general meetings of the company as is made by s. 289, relating to a members' voluntary winding up (**7**), but adds that *creditors' meetings* must also be held at the same times.

15. Final meeting and dissolution in creditors' voluntary winding up. Section 300 makes exactly the same provision for the holding of a final general meeting of the company and for dissolution as is made by s. 290, relating to a members' voluntary winding up, but adds that a final *creditors' meeting* must also be held.

Section 9(3)(*h*) European Communities Act 1972 also applies in the same way (*see* **8**).

16. Powers of liquidator in voluntary winding up. The remaining sections of the Act dealt with in this chapter apply to *every* voluntary winding up, whether it is a members' or creditors' winding up.

Section 303(1) sets out the powers of the liquidator, which must be studied with reference to s. 245 (*see* **XXVII, 26**), dealing with his powers in a winding up by the court.

It states that the liquidator may:

(*a*) Exercise the powers given by s. 245(1)(*d*), (*e*) and (*f*) with the sanction of an *extraordinary resolution* in a *members'* voluntary winding up, and with the sanction of the *court* or the *committee of inspection,* or, if none, a *creditors' meeting* in a *creditors'* voluntary winding up (*see* **XXVII, 21**).

(*b*) Exercise without sanction any of the other powers given to him by the Act in a winding up by the court (*see* **XXVII, 21**).

(*c*) Exercise the court's power under the Act of settling the list of contributories (*see* s. 257).

(*d*) Exercise the court's power of making calls (*see* s. 260).

(*e*) Summon general meetings of the company to obtain the company's sanction or for any other purpose.

17. Court's power to appoint and remove liquidator in voluntary winding up. Section 304(1) empowers the court to appoint a liquidator in a voluntary winding up if from any cause whatever there is no liquidator acting.

Section 304(2) empowers the court to remove a liquidator *on cause shown* (*see* XXVII, **17**), and to appoint another.

18. Notice by liquidator of his appointment. Regardless of the manner in which he is appointed, the liquidator is required within fourteen days in every case by s. 305 to publish in the *Gazette* and deliver to the registrar a notice of his appointment.

If the appointment is not duly notified and is not shown by the company to have been known at the time to the person concerned then, under s. 9(4)(*a*) European Communities Act 1972, it cannot be relied on by the company against that person.

19. Arrangements with creditors. Section 306(1) states that an arrangement made between a company in voluntary liquidation and its creditors is binding on the *company* if sanctioned by an *extraordinary resolution*, and on the *creditors* if agreed to by *three-quarters in number and value*.

However, s. 306(2) empowers any dissenting creditor or contributory to appeal to the court against the arrangement within three weeks from its completion, whereupon the court may either vary or confirm it, but cannot set it entirely aside.

NOTE: In practice this section is not frequently used, for the majority of creditors required to agree to the arrangement is very high (note that it is *not* a majority of those *present and voting*, as is usually the case, but of *all* the creditors). Moreover, the section cannot be used in order to avoid liquidation: the winding up must be completed.

20. Power to apply to court in voluntary liquidation. Section 307(1) entitles the liquidator, or any contributory, or any creditor to apply to the court to decide any question arising in the winding up, or to exercise any power which it would have in a winding up by the court.

Under s. 307(2) the court may then make such order as it thinks just. If it should stay the winding up proceedings, the company must under s. 307(3) at once notify the registrar.

21. Right of creditor or contributory to winding up by the court. Section 310 states that the fact that a company is in voluntary liquidation does not bar the right of a creditor or contributory to have it wound up *by the court*, if there are proper grounds. If a contributory should apply, however, the court will not make an order for winding up by the court unless it is satisfied that the rights of the contributories are prejudiced by a voluntary winding up.

In the same way, although a creditor has a right to have the company wound up by the court, he will not succeed in his application if the other creditors wish the voluntary winding up to continue, unless he can show that his position would be prejudiced by it.

PROGRESS TEST 28

1. When may a company be wound up voluntarily? **(1)**

2. At what moment does a voluntary winding up commence? **(2)**

3. What are the consequences of a voluntary winding up? **(3)**

4. What is the importance of the declaration of solvency? By whom is it made, and to whom is it submitted? **(4)**

5. In a members' voluntary liquidation, who appoints the liquidator, and by whom is his remuneration fixed? **(5)**

6. Give the statutory provisions regarding the power of the liquidator to sell the company's undertaking and property for shares in another company instead of for cash. **(6)**

7. Give an account of the liquidator's duty to call meetings in a members' voluntary winding up. **(7, 8)**

8. If, in a members' voluntary winding up, the liquidator suddenly realises that the company is not solvent after all, what should he do? **(9)**

9. Give the statutory provisions relating to the first meeting of creditors in a creditors' voluntary winding up. **(10)**

10. In a creditors' voluntary liquidation, who appoints the liquidator, and by whom is his remuneration fixed? **(11, 12)**

11. State the rules which apply to the committee of inspection in a creditors' voluntary winding up. **(13)**

12. Give an account of the liquidator's duty to call meetings in a creditors' voluntary winding up. **(10, 14, 15)**

13. What are the powers of the liquidator in a voluntary winding up? **(16)**

14. What are the powers of the court regarding appointment and removal of the liquidator in a voluntary winding up? **(17)**

15. Discuss the power of a company in voluntary liquidation to make an arrangement with its creditors. **(19)**

CHAPTER XXIX

Winding Up Subject to the Supervision of the Court

1. Court's power to order winding up subject to court's supervision. Section 311 states that when a company has passed a resolution for voluntary winding up, the court may order that the winding up shall continue subject to the supervision of the court. Such orders are, however, extremely rare.

Since a supervision order can be made only after a voluntary winding up has already commenced, the *moment of the commencement* of the winding up is the *date of the passing of the resolution* for voluntary winding up.

2. The effect of a petition for a supervision order. Section 312 states that as soon as a petition for a supervision order is made, the court has the same jurisdiction over actions as in a winding up by the court, under ss. 226 and 231 (*see* XXVII, **7** and **9**).

3. Court's power to appoint or remove liquidator. Section 314(1) empowers the court to appoint an additional liquidator when a supervision order is made. Such a liquidator, under s. 314(2), has the same powers and duties, and is in the same legal position, as in a *voluntary* winding up.

Section 314(3) empowers the court to remove any of the liquidators, and to fill any vacancy caused by the removal, or by death or resignation.

4. Powers of the liquidator. Section 315(1) states that the liquidator may exercise all his powers without the sanction of the court and in the same way as if the winding up were voluntary, except for the powers specified in s. 245(1)(*d*), (*e*) and (*f*) (*see* XXVII, **21**).

These three powers he may not exercise without *the sanction of the court*, or, where the winding up was a creditors' voluntary winding up, without the sanction of the *court*, or the *committee of inspection*, or, if none, a *creditors' meeting*.

5. The effect of a supervision order. Section 313 states that ss. 227 and 228 (*see* XXVII, **9**) apply as in the case of a winding up by the court.

Further, s. 315(2) states that except for the statutory provisions specified in the 11th Schedule, this type of winding up is deemed to be a winding up by the court.

6. The provisions specified in the 11th Schedule. These are as follows:

Section 235.   The statement of affairs.
Section 236.   The official receiver's report.
Section 237.   Power of court to appoint liquidator.
Section 238.   Appointment of provisional liquidator.
Section 239.   Appointment of liquidator.
Section 240.   Provisions where a person other than the official receiver is liquidator.
Section 242(1)–(4).   General provisions as to liquidators.
Section 246.   Exercise and control of liquidator's powers.
Section 247.   Liquidator's books.
Section 248.   Payments of liquidator into bank.
Section 249.   The liquidator's accounts.
Section 250.   Control of Department of Trade over liquidators.
Section 251.   Release of liquidators.
Section 252.   Meetings of creditors and contributories.
Section 253.   The committee of inspection.
Section 254.   Powers of Department of Trade where no committee of inspection.
Section 263.   Appointment of special manager.
Section 270.   Public examination of promoters and officers.
Section 273.   Delegation to liquidator of powers of the court.

These sections were all considered in detail in XXVII, so that they should be familiar to students at this stage. They are so numerous that, despite s. 315(2), this type of winding up resembles a *voluntary* winding up rather than a compulsory one.

PROGRESS TEST 29

1. When may the court order that a winding up shall be subject to the supervision of the court?   (**1**)

2. Discuss the court's power to appoint or remove a liquidator in a winding up subject to the supervision of the court.   (**3**)

3. Give an account of the powers of the liquidator in a winding up subject to the supervision of the court.   (**4**)

CHAPTER XXX

Statutory Provisions Applicable to All Modes of Winding Up

1. Proof of debts. Section 316 states that when the company is *solvent, all debts*, present or future, certain or contingent, ascertained or sounding in damages, may be proved against it in liquidation. This includes unliquidated damages for torts, but will not, of course, include a debt which has become statute-barred under the Limitation Act 1980, or any other statute.

Section 317 states that when the company is *insolvent*, the bankruptcy rules apply with regard to provable debts. Thus *all debts*, present or future, certain or contingent, which are *owing at the date of the commencement of the winding up* may be proved. This does *not* include damages for torts which are still unliquidated at the time when the claimant proves for them: *Re Berkeley Securities (Property)* (1980).

Where there have been mutual dealings between the company and a creditor, an account must be taken and the balance paid or claimed, as the case may be.

2. Preferential debts. Section 319(5) states that these rank equally among themselves, abate in equal proportions, and have priority over creditors with a floating charge (*see* IV, **5**).

Section 319(1) states that they consist of:

(*a*) *Rates and taxes* payable within the last year. Note, however, that:

> (*i*) only *one* year's assessment of tax may be proved as a *preferential* debt, although *any* year may be taken; and
> (*ii*) *foreign* tax is not a provable debt in a liquidation: *Government of India* v. *Taylor* (1955).

(*b*) *Wages or salary* of clerks, servants, workmen or labourers for services rendered during the last *four months*, not exceeding £800 per person: *see* s. 319(2) as amended by s. 1 Insolvency Act 1976.

(A secretary is a servant for this purpose, but not a director or managing director, unless employed in some other salaried position.)

(c) Accrued *holiday remuneration* to clerks, servants, workmen or labourers.

(d) Contributions payable within the last year under the *Insurance Acts*.

(e) Sums due on account of *P.A.Y.E.* during the last year.

Section 319(4) states that where payments of wages, salary or holiday remuneration have been made out of money *advanced by some person for that purpose*, then that person has the *same priority* to repayment as the persons to whom the money was paid. For example, a bank which lent money to a company to enable it to pay its servants would be a preferential creditor for that amount in a liquidation.

Section 319(7) states that when a landlord has distrained on the company's property *within three months* before the winding up order, the preferential debts are a *first charge* on the goods distrained on, or the proceeds of sale, but the landlord will have the *same priority* as the person to whom the payment is made. Thus a landlord must return the goods distrained on, or the proceeds of sale, if he exercised his rights within the previous three months, but he then ranks equally with the other preferential creditors, over whom he would otherwise have an advantage.

In addition to the debts which are preferential under s. 319, further preferential debts were created by s. 63 Employment Protection Act 1975. This section was later repealed and replaced by s. 121 Employment Protection (Consolidation) Act 1978.

3. Fraudulent preference. Section 320(1) states that the bankruptcy rules concerning fraudulent preferences apply to companies, and affect transactions made *within six months* before the commencement of the winding up.

The details of fraudulent preferences are outside the scope of this book, but it should be remembered that a transfer of property or payment of money will be a fraudulent preference and therefore *void* if:

(a) it is made with the *primary intention* of giving a particular creditor a preference over others; *and*

(b) it is an entirely *voluntary* act, and not made under any pressure.

Thus in *Re Kushler, Ltd.* (1943), Mr and Mrs K. were the only directors and members of the company, which had an overdraft at the bank guaranteed by Mr K. They knew that the company was insolvent, but nevertheless arranged for the company to repay the bank, extinguishing the overdraft, just before winding up commenced. The company had not paid any of its other creditors at that time. HELD: The payment was a fraudulent preference, and therefore void.

Section 321(1) states that where any transaction is void under s. 320 as a fraudulent preference of a person interested in *property charged to secure the company's debt*, then the person so preferred is regarded as a *surety* for the debt to the extent of his charge. For instance, if a person has deposited securities at a bank in order to secure the company's overdraft, the company may fraudulently prefer that person by paying money into the bank in reduction of the overdraft instead of paying its other creditors in the normal course of business. The bank may then have to return the money to the liquidator, since the payment is void as a fraudulent preference. If the bank has retained the securities deposited with it, its position is satisfactory, but if it returned them to the owner when the company's overdraft was extinguished, it will have no remedy apart from that given by s. 321(1), i.e. it can now proceed against him *as though he had been a guarantor* of the company's overdraft.

4. Avoidance of floating charges. Section 322 prevents a company from selecting one of its existing unsecured creditors and, by giving him a floating charge on its assets, enabling him to claim a priority over the others (*see* IV, **5**). It is similar in principle to the rules regarding fraudulent preferences.

Section 322(1) states that a floating charge on the company's property created *within twelve months* before the commencement of the winding up, *unless the company was solvent immediately after its creation*, is *void except to* the amount of *sums paid* to the company *at the time of or after and in consideration for* the charge.

Students often find this section difficult. First, it should be noted that a floating charge created *a year or more* before the commencement of the winding up can never be invalidated by this rule. Secondly, even if the floating charge is created *within a year* before the commencement of the winding up, it cannot be invalidated if the company was *solvent* immediately afterwards.

Assuming, however, that the floating charge was created within the year, and that the company cannot be proved to have been solvent immediately afterwards, then the charge is *void*, *except* in so far as it was given to a creditor *before* or *at the same time as* he paid money to the company, *and in consideration* for his payment. In the latter case it is valid in so far as it secures that payment, but it cannot constitute security for earlier debts. In other words, it is only when the charge is given to secure a *past* debt with which it is unconnected that it is void. Moreover, even where the section invalidates it, the *debt* is unaffected, and the creditor retains his right to prove as an unsecured creditor in the liquidation.

A very liberal interpretation is given by the courts to the words of the section.

Thus in *Re Stanton Ltd.* (1929), the payments made by the creditor to an insolvent company were made shortly *before* the charge was created, though in consideration for it. HELD: The charge was valid.

In *Re Yeovil Glove Co., Ltd.* (1965), a company had an account with a bank which refused further credit unless it was secured by a floating charge. The company accordingly gave the bank a floating charge, but within a year went into liquidation. The bank had paid cheques drawn on this account *after* the charge was created, although they were not bound to do so under the terms of the charge. The liquidator claimed that the charge was void under s. 322, since these later payments were not made *in consideration for* the charge. HELD: (*a*) The words "in consideration for" mean "in consideration of the fact that the charge exists", i.e. having regard to the charge. (*b*) Cash paid by the bank on cheques drawn by the company in favour of third parties was "cash paid to the company" within s. 322. Therefore the charge was valid.

5. Transfer of property by company to trustees for creditors. Unlike a natural legal person, a company is not permitted to transfer all its property to trustees for its creditors. Section 320(2) renders any such transfer *void*, for a company must comply with the rules for winding up.

6. Disclaimer of onerous property by liquidator. Section 323 gives the liquidator of a company a similar right of disclaimer to that of the trustee in bankruptcy of an individual.

Section 323(1) states that where any of the company's property consists of:

(*a*) land burdened with onerous covenants;

(*b*) shares or stock;

(*c*) unprofitable contracts; *or*

(*d*) any other property which is unsaleable or not readily saleable because it binds the owner to an onerous act or payment of money,

the liquidator may, *with the leave of the court, disclaim it in writing* at any time *within twelve months* after the commencement of the winding up.

If such property has not come to his knowledge *within one month* of the commencement of the winding up, he may disclaim within twelve months of *becoming aware of it.*

Section 323(2) states that the effect of the disclaimer is to *determine* all the company's rights, interest and liabilities in respect of the property.

Section 323(4) states that the liquidator may not disclaim any property where a written application has been made to him by any persons interested in it requiring him to decide whether or not he will disclaim, unless within twenty-eight days from the receipt of the application he has informed the applicants that he intends to disclaim. In the case of a contract, if he does not disclaim it within the twenty-eight days, the company is deemed to have adopted it.

Section 323(5) states that where a person who has a contract with the company applies to the court, it may make an order rescinding that contract on such terms as to damages as it thinks just. Any damages payable to the applicant may be proved by him as a debt in the winding up.

Section 323(6) states that where a person claiming an interest in the disclaimed property, or under a liability in respect of it, applies to the court, the court may make an order vesting the property in any persons entitled to it. The property passes on the vesting order without any conveyance or assignment.

Where the property disclaimed is leasehold, the court may make a vesting order in favour of a person claiming under the company *only* if it makes that person:

(*a*) subject to the same obligations as the company under the lease; *or*

(*b*) subject to the same obligations as if the lease had been assigned to him.

Finally, s. 323(7) states that *any person injured by the disclaimer* shall be deemed a *creditor* of the company to the amount of the injury, and may *prove that amount as a debt* in the winding up.

7. Rights of creditors as to execution or attachment. Section 325(1) states that where a creditor has issued execution against the company's goods or land, or has attached any debt due to the company, he may not keep the benefit of the execution or attachment against the liquidator unless he completed it before *the commencement of the winding up.*

However, where a creditor has had notice of a meeting at which a resolution for voluntary winding up is to be proposed, he must complete the execution or attachment *before the date on which he had the notice.*

A person who buys under a sale by the sheriff any of the company's goods on which execution has been levied acquires a good title against the liquidator provided he buys in good faith. Further, the court may set aside the liquidator's rights in favour of the creditor if it thinks fit.

Section 325(2) explains what is meant by "completion". It states that execution against goods is completed by seizure and sale, attachment by receipt of the debt, and execution against land by seizure and, in the case of an equitable interest, by the appointment of a receiver.

8. Duties of sheriff as to goods taken in execution. Section 326(1) states that where a company's goods are taken in execution, and *before their sale* notice is served on the sheriff that a provisional liquidator has been appointed, a winding up order made, or a resolution for voluntary winding up passed, he must if required deliver the goods and any money seized or received in part satisfaction of the execution to the liquidator.

The costs of the execution are a first charge on the goods or money, and the liquidator may sell those goods to satisfy that charge.

Section 326(2), as amended by s. 1 Insolvency Act 1976, states that where under an execution for a sum of more than £250 goods are sold or money paid to avoid sale, the sheriff must deduct the costs of the execution from the proceeds of sale or the money paid, and *hold the balance for fourteen days.* If within that time notice is served on him of the presentation of a petition for winding up, or a meeting called at which a resolution for voluntary winding up is to be proposed, and then a winding up order is in fact made, or the resolution for voluntary winding up passed, he *must pay the balance to the liquidator*, who may retain it as against the execution creditor. Notice of a meeting of *credi-*

tors, however, will not defeat the execution creditors. The words of the subsection must be strictly construed, and the execution creditors will only be defeated by notice of a meeting of the *company* to pass a winding up resolution: *Re T. D. Walton* (1966).

Section 326(3) states again that the court may set aside the liquidator's rights in favour of the creditor if it thinks fit.

9. Falsification of books. There are many offences of which an officer of a company in liquidation can be found guilty under s. 328. Section 328(1)(*m*) and (*n*) have now been repealed and superseded by the Theft Act 1968, but the remainder of the offences concern the company's property and its books or documents, the sums mentioned in s. 328(1)(*d*) and (*e*) having been raised to £120 by s. 1 Insolvency Act 1976.

Apart from these, however, s. 329 makes it an offence to falsify the books. It states that if an officer or contributory of a company in liquidation destroys, mutilates, alters or falsifies any books, papers or securities, or makes false or fraudulent entries in any register, account book or document, with intent to defraud, he is guilty of an offence.

10. Frauds by officers of companies in liquidation. Section 330(*a*) has also been repealed and superseded by the Theft Act 1968. The remainder of the section states that if any officer of a company which is subsequently wound up:

(*a*) with intent to defraud the company's creditors, has transferred or charged the company's property, or has caused the levying of execution against it; *or*

(*b*) with intent to defraud the company's creditors, has concealed or removed any of the company's property since, or within two months before, an unsatisfied judgment was obtained against the company,

he is guilty of an offence.

Section 331 has been repealed by s. 12(12) Companies Act 1976.

11. Fraudulent trading. Section 332 deals with fraudulent trading, and has already been discussed in II, **40** in connection with liability. Here it need only be noted that this section in s. 332(3) imposes criminal liability on the persons knowingly parties to the fraudulent trading, in addition to their civil liability for the company's debts.

12. Misfeasance. Section 333(1) is an important provision. It states that if it appears in liquidation that any promoter, past or present director, liquidator, or officer has misapplied or retained any of the company's money or property, or been guilty of any misfeasance, or breach of trust towards the company, the court may examine into his conduct on the application of:

- (*a*) the official receiver; *or*
- (*b*) the liquidator; *or*
- (*c*) any creditor; *or*
- (*d*) any contributory.

The court may then compel him to *restore the money or property*, or to *contribute such sum as the court thinks just* to the company's assets *by way of compensation*.

For the purposes of this section, an auditor is an officer of the company (*see* XVII, **17**).

13. Disqualification for appointment as liquidator. Section 335 states that a corporation may not be appointed liquidator, and if such an appointment is made, it will be *void* (*see* XXVII, **19**).

14. Corruption regarding appointment as liquidator. Section 336 states that any person who gives, or agrees or offers to give, to any member or creditor of a company any consideration with a view to securing his own appointment or nomination as liquidator, or securing or preventing the appointment of some other person is liable to a fine.

15. Rules concerning liquidator's conduct. Winding Up Rule 160 states that the liquidator may not make any arrangement under which he receives any gift, remuneration or other benefit beyond his permitted remuneration.

Rule 161 states that he may not purchase any of the company's assets without the leave of the court, and Rule 162 states that where he is carrying on the company's business, he cannot buy goods for that purpose from any person whose connection with him would result in his making any profit out of the transaction.

16. Notification of liquidation. Section 338(1) states that where a company is in liquidation, every business document on which the company's name appears must contain a statement that the company is being wound up.

17. Disposal of books and papers. Section 341(1) states that when a company has been wound up and is about to be dissolved, its books and papers and those of the liquidator may be disposed of as follows:

(*a*) in a winding up by or subject to the supervision of the court as the court directs;

(*b*) in a members' voluntary winding up, as the company by extraordinary resolution directs;

(*c*) in a creditors' voluntary winding up, as the committee of inspection, or, if none, as the creditors direct.

Section 341(2) states that *after five years from the company's dissolution* there is no responsibility on the company, the liquidator, or any other person for the books or papers not being available. Winding Up Rule 206, however, in pursuance of s. 341(3), empowers the Department of Trade to order that the books and papers shall not be destroyed for such period as the Department thinks proper, but *not exceeding five years from the dissolution*.

18. Unclaimed assets. Section 343(1), as amended by s. 3 Insolvency Act 1976, states that if the liquidator has any money representing unclaimed or undistributed assets of the company which have so remained for *six months after receipt*, or any money held by the company in trust in respect of dividends or other sums due to a person as member, he must pay that money into the Insolvency Services Account at the Bank of England.

He is then entitled to a receipt for it, which discharges him in respect of it.

Section 343(3) states that any person claiming to be entitled to such money may apply to the Department of Trade, which, on the liquidator's certificate that the person claiming is entitled to it, may make an order for payment. Section 343(4) permits any person who is dissatisfied with the decision of the Department to appeal to the court.

19. Court's power to declare dissolution void. In XXVII, **37** it was mentioned that a dissolved company can be revived if necessary. Section 352 gives details of the process of resurrection, which is sometimes advisable if the company is subsequently found to have had either unpaid debts or undistributed property.

Section 352(1) states that on an application by the liquidator or any other interested person, the court at any time *within two* years from the date of dissolution may by order declare that the dissolution was *void*.

Section 352(2) then requires the applicant to deliver to the registrar within seven days an office copy of the order.

Despite the wording of the section, the court will declare the dissolution void *after* the two-year period has expired provided the *application* is made within the two years.

20. Defunct companies. A company can also be restored to life under s. 353, the main purpose of which is to enable a company which is no longer carrying on business, but which has not been wound up, to be dissolved by removal from the register (*see* XXV, 1).

Section 353(1) states that where the registrar has reasonable cause to believe that a company is not carrying on business, he may send a letter inquiring whether it is doing so.

Section 353(2) states that if *within one month* he does not receive an answer, he must *within the next fourteen days* send a registered letter referring to the first letter, and saying that if an answer is not received within one month a notice will be published in the *Gazette* with a view to striking the company off the register.

Section 353(3) states that if he receives an answer saying that the company is not carrying on business, or does not receive any answer within the prescribed time, he may publish in the *Gazette* and send to the company a notice that *after three months* the name of the company will be struck off the register and the company dissolved.

Section 353(4) requires the registrar to publish and send to the company a notice similar to that specified in s. 353(3) where a company is in *liquidation*, but he has reasonable cause to believe either that no liquidator is acting, or that the affairs of the company have been fully wound up, and the returns required to be made by the liquidator have not been made *for six consecutive months*.

Section 353(5) states that after the prescribed time the registrar may strike the company's name off the register, and must publish notice of the fact in the *Gazette*, whereupon the company is *dissolved*. This does not affect, however, either the liability, if any, of the directors, officers, or members, or the power of the court to wind up the company.

Finally, s. 353(6) states that if the company, or any member or creditor, feels aggrieved by the company having been struck off, it or he may apply to the court *within twenty years*. If the court is satisfied that the company was carrying on business when it was struck off, or that it is just and equitable to restore it to the register, it may order the company's name to be restored. In order to qualify as an applicant the petitioner must show that he was a member or creditor *at the date of dissolution.* The words "any member", however, extend to the personal representative of a deceased member, even though he was never on the register of members, since it is not unlikely that in the course of the twenty years a registered member might die: *Re Bayswater Trading Co., Ltd.* (1970).

A copy of the court order must be delivered to the registrar, and the company is then *deemed to have continued to exist as if its name had not been struck off.* The court may place it and other persons in their original position. The effect of this provision is that all acts done by the company during the period between dissolution and restoration are validated, and this period is ignored for the purposes of the Limitation Act.

21. The property of a dissolved company. Section 354 states that where a company is dissolved, all its property, except that which it holds on trust for another person, is deemed to be *bona vacantia*, and accordingly belongs to the Crown.

Section 355 empowers the Crown to *disclaim it* by a notice signed by the Treasury Solicitor.

PROGRESS TEST 30

1. What debts may be proved against the company in liquidation? **(1)**

2. What are preferential debts? **(2)**

3. Give the statutory provisions with regard to fraudulent preferences. **(3)**

4. Under what circumstances will a floating charge on the company's assets be void? **(4)**

5. Give an account of the liquidator's right of disclaimer. **(6)**

6. What is the position of a person who suffers loss as a result of the exercise by the liquidator of his right of disclaimer? **(6)**

7. What are the rights of a creditor who has issued execution against a company which is in liquidation? **(7)**

8. What do you understand by "falsification of books"? **(9)**

9. Discuss the statutory provisions with regard to fraudulent trading.   (**11**; II, **40**)

10. State what you understand by misfeasance proceedings. Who may apply to the court in connection with such proceedings?   (**12**)

11. Give the statutory provisions regarding bribery in connection with the appointment of a liquidator.   (**14**)

12. Explain how the conduct of the liquidator is regulated by the Winding Up Rules.   (**15**)

13. Give the statutory provisions regarding the disposal of the company's books and papers.   (**17**)

14. What should the liquidator do with unclaimed dividends?   (**18**)

15. Discuss the court's power to declare a dissolution void.   (**19**)

16. Give the statutory provisions regarding the removal from the register of defunct companies.   (**20**)

17. Once a defunct company has been removed from the register, who can apply, and within what period of time, for its restoration?   (**20**)

18. To whom does any property of a dissolved company belong?   (**21**)

CHAPTER XXXI

Shareholder Protection

1. Areas of Statutory Intervention. In some areas it is the courts which have evolved rules for the protection of shareholders. Thus it is in these cases that there are found the development of the minority shareholders' action (*see* IV, **9**) and the principles relating to the lifting of the corporate veil where the concept of the corporate entity is being abused (*see* IV, **6** and XXXII, **9–10**).

There are other areas, however, in which the fundamental role is played by legislation. Lengthy provisions exist, as explained in Chapter VII, regarding the issue of a prospectus or the making of an offer for sale. Statutory rules safeguarding the capital of the company abound and have been considered in Chapters XV and XVI, while innumerable provisions in the Acts relating to company meetings serve their intended purpose of arming the shareholder so that he may resist unwarranted interference with his rights.

It is against this background that there must now be considered two further areas in which recent legislation plays a basic and innovative part. They are:

(*a*) unfair prejudice; and
(*b*) insider dealing.

UNFAIR PREJUDICE

2. Former legislation. The first statutory provision in this area was s. 210 Companies Act 1948 which authorised any shareholder who complained that the company's affairs were being conducted in an *oppressive* manner to petition the court for an order to deal with the position.

Although this provision received a considerable amount of academic attention, it was in practice of very little value. It had two major weaknesses, as the Jenkins Committee pointed out. First, it had no application to isolated acts—the petitioner had to show that there had been an oppressive *course of conduct*. Secondly, the petitioner was required to convince the court that the facts of which he complained would *justify the making of a winding up order* by the court on the ground that it was *just and equitable* to wind the company up (*see* XXVII, 1 and 3). Often he could not establish this and accordingly orders under the section were a rarity.

3. Present legislation. Section 75 Companies Act 1980 repealed and replaced s. 210 and removed both of the weaknesses mentioned above. Under s. 75(1) any member may petition the court for an order on the ground that the company's affairs are being or have been conducted in a manner which is *unfairly prejudicial* to the interests of some part of the members, including himself, or that any actual or proposed act or omission of the company is or would be so prejudicial.

This provision clearly enlarges the scope of the remedy in several respects. It covers the past conduct of affairs as well as the present. It covers not only an isolated act but also an isolated omission or failure to act; and it extends to a proposed or contemplated act or omission.

Further, under s. 75(3) the court may make such order as it thinks fit if it is satisfied that the petition is *well founded*. No mention is made of a winding up order being justified.

4. Petitioners under s. 75. The Jenkins Committee recommended that it should be made possible for personal representatives of deceased members and others to whom shares are transmitted by operation of law, but who are not on the company's register of members, to petition under s. 210. This recommendation was in part given judicial approval in *Re Jermyn Street Turkish Baths Ltd.* (1971) where it was held that the personal representatives of a deceased member, even if not registered in respect of the shares, were members of the company for the purposes of that section.

Section 75(9) removes all doubts as to the position by stating that the remedy is available to a person who is not a member but to whom shares have been transferred (i.e. an unregistered transferee) or transmitted by operation of law (i.e. a personal representative or trustee in bankruptcy).

Finally, s. 75(2) states that in certain circumstances, mentioned in XVIII, 6, the Secretary of State may petition under the section.

5. The court order. As stated in 3 above, the court may make such order as it thinks fit to give relief to the petitioner under the section: s. 75(3).

Section 75(4), however, provides that, without prejudice to the generality of subsection (3), a court order may:

(a) regulate the conduct of the company's affairs in the future;
(b) require the company to refrain from doing an act complained of by the petitioner or to do an act which he has complained it has omitted to do;
(c) authorise civil proceedings to be brought in the name and on behalf of the company by such person as the court directs;
(d) provide for the purchase of the shares of any members of the company by other members or by the company itself, and in the latter case for the resulting reduction of capital (*see* XI, **9**).

It should be noted that (c) authorises a *derivative action*—the first time that such a course has been given a statutory basis in English law (*see* IV, **10**). Nothing is said, however, about the costs of such an action. Presumably the plaintiff would be entitled to be indemnified by the company against all costs reasonably incurred in the proceedings: *Wallersteiner* v. *Moir* (1975) (*see* IV, **9**).

Lastly, it is clear from s. 75(6) that the court may alter the company's memorandum or articles if it so desires, while under s. 75(5) it can prohibit the company from altering these documents without the court's consent (*see* III, **9**(*e*)).

6. Judicial decisions. It is difficult to know how far the courts will employ the same approach to the interpretation of s. 75 as to its predecessor. In each of the two only reported cases where orders under s. 210 were made—*Re Harmer* (1959) and *Scottish C.W.S. Ltd.* v. *Meyer* (1959)—the court was concerned with the nature of "oppressive conduct of the company's affairs". It remains to be seen whether there is some essential distinction to be drawn by the courts between conduct which is oppressive and that which is unfairly prejudicial.

It would appear that if these words are given their ordinary meaning conduct could be unfairly prejudicial, i.e. injurious or detrimental, without necessarily being oppressive—a word already interpreted by the court in *Scottish C.W.S. Ltd.* v. *Meyer* as meaning "burdensome, harsh and wrongful" and by the dictionary as meaning "tyrannical" or "severe". If this is so, then the term of *unfair prejudice* is of much wider application than that of *oppression* and could well lead to the remedy under s. 75 becoming widely available in many circumstances where s. 210 would have been inappropriate.

In some cases where unsuccessful petitions under s. 210 were brought, however, the court was concerned with the capacity in which the petitioner was applying.

Thus in *Elder* v. *Elder and Watson* (1952) the applicants claimed that they had been wrongfully removed from office as directors and from employment as secretary and manager.
HELD: The remedy under s. 210 was not available to them, for no wrong had been done to them *as members*.

Further, there were cases in which the purpose of the petition was not to seek relief from oppression, but to achieve some different object.

Thus in *Re Bellador Silk* (1965) a director applied for relief under s. 210 alleging oppressive conduct by the other two members of the board with whom he was not on good terms. His real purpose, however, was to obtain repayment of a loan which he had made the company.
HELD: The remedy under s. 210 was not available to him.

It would appear that the principles evolved by the courts in these circumstances could well apply to petitions under s. 75 since there is nothing in the section to indicate otherwise.

INSIDER DEALING

7. Meaning of expression "insider dealing". The expression "insider trading" or "insider dealing" is used to mean the dealing in the securities of a company for the purpose of private gain by a person who has inside information about them which would affect their price if it were generally known.

The topic was not covered by the Companies Act 1948 at all. The earliest English legislation on it was contained in the Companies Act 1967 which made it a criminal offence in certain circumstances for a director to deal in options (*see* XXII, **57**).

After that Act was passed repeated attempts were made to draft comprehensive provisions on the topic which would trap the culpable without at the same time punishing the blameless. The result of these efforts can now be seen in s. 68–73 Companies Act 1980 where English drafting is found in its most intense form. It remains to be seen whether these detailed and thorough provisions achieve their purpose or whether they merely present yet another challenge to the ingenuity of English lawyers.

Broadly speaking, the Act creates three types of offence:

(a) *dealing* in securities;
(b) *counselling or procuring* another person to deal in securities;
(c) *communicating information* knowing that the recipient will use it for the purpose of dealing in securities.

8. Definition of "insider". In order to understand the intricacies of the insider dealing legislation it is necessary first to grasp the meaning given by the Act to the language normally associated with this type of activity. The word of primary importance is clearly the word "insider"—a term which the Act uses only in the heading to Part V and never in the statutory provisions themselves. Section 73, the interpretation section, is the best place to start on the trail.

Instead of the term "insider" the Act employs the phrase "individual connected with a company". This would appear to indicate that a *company*, being a corporation, cannot be affected by the Act at all in this respect. Only "individuals", i.e. people, can be insiders.

Section 73(1) provides that an individual is connected with a company, i.e. he is an insider, if:

(a) he is a director of that company or a related company; *or*
(b) he occupies a position:
  (i) as an officer (other than director) or employee of that company or a related company; *or*
  (ii) involving a professional or business relationship between himself (or his employer or a company of which he is a director) and that company or a related company which may reasonably be expected to give him access to unpublished price sensitive information relating to the securities of either company, and which it would be reasonable to expect a person in his position not to disclose except for the proper performance of his functions.

Even this initial definition is somewhat indigestible and requires some study. First, there is the expression "related company". In order to understand the nature of a related company we must turn to s. 73(5) which defines it as "any body corporate which is that company's subsidiary or holding company, or a subsidiary of that company's holding company". Rather than to memorise this cumbersome definition, it is simpler merely to regard a related company as one *within the same group*.

Secondly, while the persons who would fall under (a) and (b) (i) are obvious, those who would be caught by (b) (ii) are almost infinitely various. The words used would clearly cover persons in the professions commonly associated with corporate activities— i.e. solicitors and accountants—but would also cover financial advisers, management consultants, printers of securities or indeed almost anyone who managed by any lawful method to *obtain* unpublished price sensitive information, since it is difficult to see how one can lawfully obtain something to which one cannot reasonably be expected to have access.

Accordingly a shareholder in his capacity of shareholder is not an insider since he has no access to information of this kind.

9. Definition of "unpublished price sensitive information". Section 73(2) defines unpublished price sensitive information in relation to a company's securities as information which:

(a) relates to *specific matters* relating or of concern (directly or indirectly) to the company, i.e. is not of a general nature; and

(b) is *not generally known* to those persons who are accustomed or would be likely to deal in those securities but which would be likely materially to affect their price if it were.

10. Offences created by s. 68. Section 68(1) prohibits any individual who is knowingly connected with a company, or has been so connected at any time within the last six months, from dealing on a recognised stock exchange in that company's securities if he has information which:

(a) he holds by virtue of being connected with the company;

(b) it would be reasonable to expect him not to disclose except for the proper performance of his functions; and

(c) he knows is unpublished price sensitive information.

Under s. 68(2) this same individual is also prohibited from dealing in the securities of *any other company* if he has information which:

(a) he holds by virtue of being connected with the first company;

(b) it would be reasonable to expect him not to disclose except for the proper performance of his functions;

(c) he knows is unpublished price sensitive information in relation to the securities of that other company; and

(d) relates to any transaction (actual or contemplated) involving both companies, or one of them and the securities of the other, or to the fact that any such transaction is no longer contemplated.

It can be seen that under both these subsections a *present or recent insider* is prohibited from dealing. Under s. 68(3), however, any individual who is given a "tip" by the insider, commonly known as a "tippee", is also prohibited from dealing. Section 68(3) provides that where an individual:

(*a*) has information which he knowingly obtained (directly or indirectly) from a present or recent insider who he knows or has reasonable cause to believe held it by virtue of his connection with a particular company; and

(*b*) knows or has reasonable cause to believe that it would be reasonable to expect the insider not to disclose the information except for the proper performance of his functions;

he is prohibited from dealing on a recognised stock exchange:

(*a*) in securities of that company if he knows that the information is unpublished price sensitive information in relation to them; and

(*b*) in securities of any other company if he knows that the information is unpublished price sensitive information in relation to them, and it relates to any transaction (actual or contemplated) involving both companies, or one of them and the securities of the other, or to the fact that any such transaction is no longer contemplated.

Since s. 68 covers the "tippee" it is not surprising that it also covers the "tippor", i.e. the individual who gives a "tip" to another person. Section 68(7) prohibits any individual who is forbidden by the section from dealing on a recognised stock exchange in any securities owing to the fact that he has certain information from *communicating* that information to any other person if he knows or has reasonable cause to believe that that person or some other person will use it for the purpose of dealing, or counselling or procuring any other person to deal, on a recognised stock exchange in those securities.

Two more subsections in s. 68 cover the position where a takeover bid is being considered. Section 68(4) prohibits any individual who is contemplating or has contemplated making a takeover offer for a company in a particular capacity from dealing on a recognised stock exchange in securities of that company in another capacity if he knows that information that the offer is, or is no longer, contemplated is unpublished price sensitive information in relation to them.

Section 68(5) prohibits that individual's "tippee" from dealing in them if he knowingly obtained (directly or indirectly) the information in question and knows that it is unpublished price sensitive information in relation to them.

Lastly, s. 68(6) prohibits any individual who is forbidden *by any provision in the section* from dealing on a recognised stock exchange in any securities from *counselling or procuring* any other person to deal in them, knowing or having reasonable cause to believe that he would do so.

It should be noted that the expression "recognised stock exchange" wherever it occurs in the Act includes an investment exchange, i.e. an organisation maintaining a system whereby an offer to deal in securities made by a subscriber to the organisation is communicated, without his identity being revealed, to other subscribers, and any acceptance of that offer is recorded and confirmed: s. 73(5).

It should also be noted that all these prohibited activities require positive action of some kind to constitute an offence. Thus it can never be an offence to *refrain* from dealing, however profitable that may sometimes be.

11. Offences created by s. 69 and s. 70. It is clear that s. 68 covers insider dealing in great detail. Whether it is also exhaustive remains to be seen. However, it is supplemented by s. 69 which contains similar provisions applicable to present and former *Crown servants* who hold unpublished price sensitive information concerning a company's securities by virtue of their position, and to individuals who knowingly obtain it from them (directly or indirectly). Further, s. 70(1) extends the provisions of both s. 68 and s. 69 to *off-market deals*, i.e. deals in the advertised securities of a company otherwise than on a recognised stock exchange.

Lastly, s. 70(2) prohibits an individual who is subject to any prohibition under s. 68 or s. 69 from:

(*a*) *counselling or procuring* any other person to deal in the securities in question in the knowledge or with reasonable cause to believe that he would deal in them *outside Great Britain*; *or*

(*b*) *communicating* the information in question to any other person in the knowledge or with reasonable cause to believe that that person or some other person will use it for the purpose of dealing, or counselling or procuring any other person to deal, in the securities in question *outside Great Britain.*

It appears that the insider is not *himself* prohibited by this provision from dealing on a foreign stock exchange.

12. Summary of offences. The offences which can be committed under the head of insider dealing are so numerous that a summary may perhaps be helpful even though brevity necessarily imports a degree of inaccuracy where the rules are of such a technical nature.

The offences fall into the following categories:

(a) Dealing by the insider in the securities of his own company.

(b) Dealing by the insider in the securities of another company.

(c) Communicating information by the insider, i.e. insider acting as "tippor".

(d) Dealing by insider's "tippee".

(e) Dealing by person contemplating a take-over bid.

(f) Dealing by "tippee" of person contemplating take-over bid.

(g) Counselling or procuring another person to deal.

(h) Crown servants.

(i) Off-market deals.

(j) Foreign stock exchanges.

13. Exceptions to the prohibitions in s. 68, s. 69 and s. 70. Section 68(8) and (11) contain provisions which expressly exempt certain transactions from the prohibitions imposed by that section. Under s. 69(4) and s. 70(1) and (2) these provisions are made applicable also to the prohibitions in those sections.

Section 68(8) states that an individual is not prohibited by reason of his having any information from:

(a) doing any particular thing *otherwise than with a view to making a profit or avoiding a loss* by the use of that information (e.g. realising securities because he is in immediate need of money);

(b) entering into a transaction in the course of the exercise in good faith of his functions as *liquidator, receiver* or *trustee in bankruptcy;* or

(c) doing any particular thing in good faith in the course of his business as a *jobber* if the information:

(*i*) was obtained by him in the course of that business; and

(*ii*) was of a description which it would be reasonable to expect him to obtain in the ordinary course of that business.

Section 68(11) states that a trustee or personal representative who would otherwise be subject to the prohibitions in the section is *presumed* to have acted within the terms of s. 68(8)(*a*) above provided he acted on the advice of a person who:

(*a*) appeared to him to be an appropriate person from whom to seek such advice; and

(*b*) did not appear to him to be prohibited by the section from dealing in the securities in question.

This subsection would protect, for instance, a trustee who seeks the advice of an investment consultant.

Finally, s. 71 gives exemption in certain circumstances from the prohibitions in s. 70 to issue managers acting in good faith in connection with an issue of *international bonds* (e.g. Eurobonds).

14. Penalties. The penalties for committing any of the statutory offences are found in s. 72. Section 72(1) states that an individual who contravenes the provisions of s. 68 or s. 69 is liable:

(*a*) on conviction on indictment to imprisonment for a term not exceeding two years or a fine, or both; and

(*b*) on summary conviction to imprisonment for a term not exceeding six months or a fine not exceeding the statutory maximum, or both.

The sting is taken out of this subsection, however, by s. 72(2) which states that proceedings for an offence cannot be instituted except by the Secretary of State or by or with the consent of the Director of Public Prosecutions. It is unlikely, therefore, that such proceedings will be a frequent occurrence.

15. Legal effect of unlawful transaction. Section 72(3) makes it clear that the illegality of a transaction prohibited by s. 68 or s. 69 has no effect on its validity. It provides that no transaction shall be void or voidable merely because it contravenes either of these sections.

Another important feature of the statutory provisions is that they give no remedy to anyone who has suffered loss as a result of an offence having been committed. The courts, however, have not always been averse to the awarding of damages for loss suffered as the result of the commission of a statutory offence: *see Re South of England Natural Gas Co.* (1911) in VII, **8**.

PROGRESS TEST 31

1. In what circumstances may a shareholder petition the court for an order under s. 75 Companies Act 1980? [**3**]

2. State what persons other than those on the register of members may petition the court under s. 75. (**4**)

3. State what remedies are available to the petitioner under a court order. (**5**)

4. What do you understand by the expression "insider dealing"? (**7**)

5. Define an "insider". (**8**)

6. Define "unpublished price sensitive information". (**9**)

7. What offences relating to insider dealing have been created by the Companies Act 1980? (**10–12**)

8. Give the exceptions to the criminal liability imposed by the Companies Act 1980 with respect to insider dealing. (**13**)

9. What penalties have been imposed by the Companies Act 1980 for insider dealing? Who may bring proceedings against an individual alleged to have committed an offence of this kind? (**14**)

10. What is the legal effect of a transaction prohibited by the Companies Act 1980 by reason of the fact that it constitutes an insider dealing offence? What remedy does the Act give to a person who has suffered loss as a result of the commission of an offence by an insider? (**15**)

CHAPTER XXXII

Arrangements and Reconstructions

1. The scope of s. 206. We have already seen in XXVIII, **19** that a company in voluntary liquidation may make an arrangement with its creditors under s. 306. A company which is *not* in liquidation, however, cannot proceed under that section. It must instead enter into a scheme of arrangement under s. 206, under which almost any type of compromise, arrangement or reorganisation of the company's capital can be effected.

Section 206 has been mentioned before in connection with the alteration of rights attached to shares (*see* XV, **14**). But it has a far wider scope than this. Since, as we shall see below, the consent of the court has to be obtained, the section permits the company to enter into any type of scheme regarding either its creditors or its members which does not conflict with the general law or with any particular statutory provision. Thus the company could not under this section be empowered to do an *ultra vires* act, or to convert its issued share capital into redeemable preference shares (*see* XV, **10**) but only to do acts which are lawful in themselves.

Moreover, the section does not enable the company to avoid a prescribed statutory procedure where there is one, e.g. for the reduction of capital.

2. Power to compromise with creditors and members. Section 206(1) states that where a compromise or arrangement is proposed between a company and its creditors or any class of them, or its members or any class of them, the court may, on the application of the company, or any creditor, or member, or liquidator, *order a meeting* of the creditors or members, or any class of them, as the case may be.

Section 206(2) states that if a *majority in number* representing *three-quarters in value* of the creditors or members or any class of them, present and voting either in person or by proxy, agree to any compromise or arrangement, it is *binding if sanctioned by the court*.

The court will refuse to sanction the arrangement unless the class meetings are properly constituted. Thus where one of the members was the wholly-owned subsidiary of a company which was to purchase all the shares under the arrangement, Templeman J. held that that member formed a class on its own, separate from the other members, since it had different interests, and accordingly he refused to sanction the arrangement: *Re Hellenic & General Trust, Ltd.* (1975).

Section 206(3) states that the court order has no effect until a copy has been delivered to the registrar for registration. Further, a copy of the order must be annexed to every copy of the memorandum subsequently issued.

3. Information to be sent with notice of the meeting. Section 207(1) requires the company to send with the notice of the meeting called under s. 206 a *statement* explaining the *effect of the scheme*, and stating in particular the *material interests of the directors* and the effect of the scheme on them.

If the notice is given by advertisement, such a statement must be included, or a place notified where creditors or members may obtain copies of one.

Where the scheme affects the rights of debenture-holders, the statement must give a similar explanation with regard to the trustees of any deed for securing the issue as is required with regard to the directors.

4. Matters for which the court may provide. Section 208(1) states that where an application is made to the court under s. 206 for the sanction of a scheme, and that scheme is one under which the whole or part of the company's undertaking or property is to be *transferred to another company*, the court may provide for the following matters:

(*a*) The transfer of the whole or part of the undertaking, property or liabilities of the transferor company to the transferee company.

(*b*) The allotting or appropriation by the transferee company of shares or debentures in that company.

(*c*) The continuation by or against the transferee company of legal proceedings which are pending by or against the transferor company.

(*d*) The dissolution, without winding up, of the transferor company (*see* XXV, **1**).

(*e*) Dissenting persons.

(*f*) Any other incidental matters.

Section 208(3) requires a copy of the court order to be delivered to the registrar within seven days.

5. Comparison with a reconstruction under s. 287. It is clear from s. 208 that it is possible under ss. 206–208 for companies to amalgamate, so that the undertaking and property of one is transferred to another. This may, as is obvious from s. 208(1)(*d*), involve the dissolution of the transferor company without a winding up (i.e. a "merger").

In XXVIII, **6** we saw that much the same sort of result can be achieved under s. 287, and it is therefore interesting to compare and contrast the two types of reconstruction:

(*a*) Section 287 is a much *narrower* section than s. 206. It permits only one type of reconstruction, by which a company in voluntary liquidation sells its undertaking for shares in another company. Section 206 covers a wide variety of activities, as was mentioned in **1**.

(*b*) Section 287 can be used only by a company in *voluntary liquidation*. Section 206 is frequently used by a company which is a going concern, even though the court may provide, under s. 208, for the dissolution of the transferor company in appropriate circumstances.

(*c*) Section 287 can be used without obtaining the *sanction of the court*, unless the winding up is a *creditors'* voluntary winding up, when either the sanction of the court or of the committee of inspection must be obtained. Section 206 invariably requires the sanction of the court.

(*d*) A dissentient under s. 287 can require the liquidator either to purchase his interest or to abandon the whole scheme. Under s. 206 the scheme will bind all the members once it is sanctioned by the court, though the court may make provision for dissentients under s. 208(1)(*e*).

6. Power of company to acquire shares of dissentients. In the type of scheme popularly known as the "take-over bid", s. 209 empowers a company which has made an offer for the shares of another company to "buy out" the dissenting shareholders provided a sufficient majority of the members accept the offer. The principle of the section is simple. The arithmetic is sometimes perplexing to students, and requires careful study because frequent

mistakes are made. In order to avoid the use of the cumbersome expressions "transferor" and "transferee" company, in this
paragraph the transferor company (i.e. the company being
"taken over") is called Company A, and the transferee company
(i.e. the company making the take-over bid) is called Company B.

Section 209(1) states that where a scheme involving the transfer of shares in one company to another company has, *within
four months of the making of the offer* by Company B, been approved by the *holders of not less than nine-tenths in value* of the
shares in Company A whose transfer is involved, then Company
B may, at any time *within two months from the expiration of the
four months*, give notice to any dissenting shareholder in Company A that it wishes to acquire his shares.

> NOTE: In calculating the *nine-tenths in value*, shares in Com-
> pany A which are *already held* by Company B at the date of
> the offer are disregarded. Approval must be by the holders of
> nine-tenths in value of the shares *whose transfer is involved*, i.e.
> the shares which Company B is hoping to acquire.

Once this notice is given to the dissenting shareholder, then
unless he applies to the court within one month and the court
orders otherwise, Company B becomes *entitled and bound to
acquire his shares* on the same terms as apply to the approving
shareholders under the scheme. Thus although he will be compelled to sell his shares, he will receive the same price for them as
other shareholders who supported the scheme.

**7. Position where transferee company already holds shares in
transferor company.** Section 209(1) lays down special rules where
Company B at the date of its offer to the shareholders of Company A already holds a considerable number of shares in Company A.

It states that where Company B *already holds* shares in Company A of the *same class* as those involved in the transfer *to a
value greater than one-tenth of the aggregate of their value and of
those involved in the transfer* the provisions of s. 209(1) given
above will apply only provided:

(*a*) Company B offers the same terms to *all holders* of the
shares involved in the transfer, or each class of them, *and*

(*b*) The holders approving the scheme not only hold nine-
tenths in value of the shares whose transfer is involved, but *also
are three-quarters in number* of the holders of those shares.

The date on which a count must be made to ascertain whether the approving shareholders amount to three-quarters in number of the total holders of the relevant shares is *the date when the offer is made: In re Simo Securities Trust Ltd.* (1971).

One may well wonder why these further requirements are imposed by the section only where Company B already has a fairly large holding in Company A. It would seem more reasonable if they applied to every take-over bid, or to none at all. It is interesting to note, therefore, that the Jenkins Committee recommended the repeal of these special rules laid down in the proviso to s. 209(1), while advocating that the wording of the section should be amended to make it clear that it applies only to offers for *all the outstanding shares* of a company, and on the *same terms* to all the shareholders concerned.

The effect of this recommendation, if adopted, would be to make (*a*) above apply *in every case*, and to repeal (*b*) entirely—a much more logical position.

NOTE: Students sometimes find the arithmetic in the proviso difficult. If an example is given with figures, therefore, it is sometimes helpful. Let us assume that the share capital of Company A is 1,000 shares, of which Company B already holds 100, and is making an offer for the other 900. We must first find the *aggregate* of those it *already holds* (100) and of those it is *hoping to acquire* (900). $100 + 900 = 1,000$. Now we must divide this aggregate by 10. $1,000 \div 10 = 100$. Now we must see if the number of shares already held by Company B in Company A *exceeds this figure*, for if it does, the provisions of s. 209 do not apply unless Company B complies with conditions (*a*) and (*b*). We have said in our example that Company B already holds 100 shares in Company A, which does *not* exceed one-tenth of the aggregate, so that it is *not* here necessary to comply with (*a*) and (*b*).

Supposing, however, that the share capital of Company A is 200 preference shares with no voting rights, and 800 ordinary voting shares, and Company B *already holds* 100 ordinary shares and is making an offer for the remaining 700. The aggregate of those it already holds (100) and of those it is hoping to acquire (700) is 800. One-tenth of 800 is 80. The number of shares already held (100) exceeds this figure, and therefore the provisions of s. 209 will apply only if Company B complies with conditions (*a*) and (*b*).

8. Opportunity for dissentients to change their minds. Sometimes Company B does not trouble to serve notice on the dissentients under s. 209(1). It is content to have had its offer accepted by nearly all the shareholders in Company A, and knows very well that a small minority of the remaining members can do nothing to stop it implementing its policies so long as it does not oppress them. Meanwhile the dissenting shareholders find themselves a helpless minority, and perhaps wish that they had accepted the offer when it was first made to them. In this case, s. 209(2), which has been slightly amended by the Companies Act 1976, sympathetically allows them to change their minds.

It states that where under the scheme shares in Company A are transferred to Company B so that the *entire shareholding* of Company B in Company A amounts to *nine-tenths in value of the shares in Company A* or of any class of them, then:

(*a*) Company B must *within one month* from the date of the transfer give notice of that fact to the holders of the remaining shares in Company A who have not assented to the scheme, and

(*b*) any such holder may *within three months* from the giving of the notice himself give notice requiring Company B to acquire his shares.

Company B then becomes entitled and bound to acquire them on the *same terms as apply under the scheme*.

9. View taken by court on application of dissenting shareholder. We have seen in **6** that a dissenting shareholder has the right to apply to the court under s. 209(1) if he thinks that the offer made by Company B is unfair. In such a case, the court will normally take the view that since the required majority have approved the scheme, it is up to the dissenting shareholder to show grounds for his disapproval of it. Thus the offer will be treated as *prima facie* a fair one, and the burden of showing otherwise is on the dissentient who seeks relief. In discharging it he must show unfairness to the shareholders *as a body*, so that while the market price of the shares is a relevant factor, the personal circumstances of the dissentient are not: *Re Grierson, Oldham and Adams* (1967).

Where, however, the offer is in reality being made by the same majority shareholders who have accepted it, the burden of proof is *reversed* and it is up to the offeror to *show that the scheme is fair*. This is a perfect example of what is meant by "lifting the veil" of incorporation, and the facts of *Re Bugle Press, Ltd.* (1960), are interesting in this connection.

B.P. Ltd. had an issued capital of 10,000 £1 shares, of which Jackson held 4,500, Shaw held 4,500, and Treby held 1,000. Jackson and Shaw then incorporated a new company, called Jackson and Shaw (Holdings), Ltd., with an issued capital of 100 shares, of which each of them held 50. This company then made an offer under s. 209 to the shareholders of B.P. Ltd. Jackson and Shaw naturally accepted the offer, but Treby refused it on the grounds that the price was too low. HELD: He was not bound to sell at that price. Where "as a matter of substance the persons who are putting forward the offer are the majority shareholders", it is up to them to show that the scheme is fair and not to the dissenting shareholder to show that it is unfair.

NOTE: Here the corporate personality of Jackson and Shaw (Holdings), Ltd., has been disregarded. The "veil" has been lifted to reveal, behind the corporate person, the natural persons of Jackson and Shaw—those same natural persons who are accepting the offer made, in substance, by themselves.

10. Lifting the veil of incorporation. Throughout the study of Company Law much emphasis is given to the *separate legal personality* of the corporation. The fundamental principle, so clearly laid down in *Salomon's case*, still stands. But *Re Bugle Press* shows us one occasion when the demands of justice require it to be set aside. The principle is then reversed; the corporation is pierced; the identity of the members is revealed.

We cannot here investigate all the occasions on which the law will lift the corporate veil, for on this topic alone much has already been written both in this country and in the United States. We ought at least to note, however, some of the sections of the Companies Acts which have this effect.

(*a*) Section 31 (*see* II, **40**). Under this section the members can lose the protective shield of the company as regards its debts.

(*b*) Section 108(4) (*see* II, **8**). Under this subsection an officer of the company or any person on its behalf who omits to place the company's name on a negotiable instrument which he signs on behalf of the company may be personally liable to the holder for the specified amount.

(*c*) Section 166 (*see* XVIII, **3**). This concerns the power of an inspector appointed by the Department of Trade to investigate the affairs of any company within the same group as the company primarily under investigation.

(*d*) Section 172 (*see* XVIII, **7**). This concerns the power of the Department of Trade to investigate membership.

(*e*) Section 178 (*see* XXII, **3**). The device of the corporation can be used to evade s. 177(1).

(*f*) Section 206, in circumstances similar to those in *Re Hellenic & General Trust*.

(*g*) Section 209, in circumstances similar to those in *Re Bugle Press*.

(*h*) Section 332 (*see* II, **40**). Here again, as under s. 31, the protective shield of the corporation is removed as regards its debts.

(*i*) Section 28(3)(*b*) Companies Act 1967. Here a person is deemed interested in shares or debentures if he has a certain degree of control over the company which holds them.

(*j*) Section 8(1) Companies Act 1976. This section requires group accounts to be laid before the general meeting of the holding company, disregarding the separate corporate personalities of the companies in the group and emphasising their economic unity.

(*k*) Section 64(4)(*b*) Companies Act 1980 (*see* XXII, **30**). Under this provision a director is identified with a body corporate controlled by him.

If these examples are examined closely, it will be seen that the expression is used in more than one way. In its strict sense, it is applied to cases where the personality of the corporation is penetrated to reveal the *members* of the company as individuals, e.g. in *Re Bugle Press* or under s. 31. In these cases it is as though one were looking at the bricks rather than the building. The emphasis is on the composition, not the structure. In a wider sense, however, the expression covers in a loose and academically unsatisfactory way cases where the personality of the corporation is swept aside in order to reach the *officers* of the company, e.g. under s. 108(4), or even quite nebulous characters such as the *persons knowingly parties* to a prohibited activity, e.g. under s. 332. Here it is not a matter of the law substituting composition for structure, since the officers do not compose the corporation, but rather enabling an injured outsider to pursue his remedy against the persons responsible for his injury, whether they are members or not. If there is any rationale behind these cases, it may be that the *corporation* ought not to be made liable for wrongful acts done by *individuals* purporting to act on its behalf or in its name. This leads to the province of criminal and tortious liability where general principles regarding corporations are still in any event confused.

All one can say with certainty about the topic is that it has not yet evolved into a general doctrine, but remains in the form of unconnected and dissimilar departures from the normal principle—cases where, in the words of the Vice-Chancellor in *Foss* v. *Harbottle*, "the claims of justice would be superior to any difficulties arising out of technical rules".

11. The meaning of "reconstruction" and "amalgamation". In his celebrated speech in *Liversidge* v. *Anderson* (1914), Lord Atkin quoted a passage from Lewis Carroll's *Through the Looking-Glass*: " 'When I use a word,' Humpty Dumpty said, 'it means just what I choose it to mean, neither more nor less.' 'The question is,' said Alice, 'whether you can make words mean so many different things.' "

Unfortunately, you can. And the longer the word, the safer you are, for while people sometimes ask you what you mean by a *short* word, they rarely have the courage to inquire what a *long* word means.

Words such as "reconstruction" and "amalgamation" have *no fixed technical legal significance*, but are used loosely to indicate some sort of re-arrangement or re-organisation entered into by companies. Examiners who ask students to explain what these words mean, therefore, are in effect asking for an account of procedures which can be adopted under ss. 206–208, 209 and 287. All that can be said about the *meaning* of the words is that a "reconstruction" can cover, for instance, a reorganisation of share or loan capital which is purely *internal* affecting *one company only* (s. 206), or the formation of a *new* company to carry on the business of the old one, with the same shareholders (s. 287). The word "amalgamation" necessarily involves *two companies*, but can cover the transfer of the whole undertaking from one company to another under ss. 206–208, or the absorption of one company by another under s. 287, or even extend to the *economic*, though not the legal, unity obtainable under s. 209.

Humpty Dumpty clearly had the right idea, but it is very important for examination purposes not to be drawn into prolonged and inconclusive discussion, and instead to show a detailed knowledge of the procedures which can be adopted under the various sections. Too many students take refuge in complexity, no doubt believing with Oscar Wilde that "to be intelligible is to be found out". Examiners are not unaware of this, and the best marks will always go to the student who understands what he knows, knows what he means, and means what he says.

PROGRESS TEST 31

1. Discuss the company's power to enter into a scheme of arrangement with its creditors or members. **(2)**

2. When a meeting of creditors or members is called in connection with a scheme of arrangement, what information must be sent out with the notice of the meeting? **(3)**

3. When application is made to the court to sanction a scheme of arrangement, and the scheme is one under which the whole or part of the company's undertaking is to be transferred to another company, for what matters may the court provide? **(4)**

4. Compare and contrast a reconstruction under s. 287 with a reconstruction under ss. 206–208. **(5; XXVIII, 6)**

5. What do you understand by a "take-over bid"? Give an account of the statutory provisions which permit a company making an offer for the shares of another company to acquire the shares of the dissenting minority. **(6)**

6. Give an account of the further statutory provisions which apply in a take-over bid where the company making the offer already holds a considerable number of shares in the company whose shares it wishes to acquire. **(7)**

7. What is the position in a take-over bid of a dissenting shareholder whose shares are *not* acquired by the company making the offer? **(8)**

8. Where a dissenting shareholder in a take-over bid applies to the court for relief, what principles guide the court in making its decision? **(9)**

9. What do you understand by "lifting the veil of incorporation"? Give examples of where this occurs. **(10)**

10. Discuss the various types of reconstruction and amalgamation which may be effected by companies. **(11)**

Examination Technique

Throughout this book an attempt has been made to anticipate and so prevent some of the mistakes commonly made by students, though often a candidate's main difficulty is not lack of knowledge, but his failure to identify the questions asked. If he knew what they were about, he could answer them. This is especially likely where the candidate is a foreigner, or where he has little previous experience of academic work, and some advice here may perhaps be useful.

(*a*) If the student has read and learnt the contents of this book, and also understands them, he should *assume that he knows the answer* to any examination question.

He should not feel any sense of arrogance or over-optimism in doing this, for the majority of examination questions set by any professional body are now within the scope of his knowledge. Sometimes the examiner is playfully original; sometimes he is obscure; but most of the time he conforms to a particular standard and pattern.

(*b*) Having assumed that he knows the answer, the student should next try to isolate and identify the question asked. What is it about? Which particular bit of knowledge does it require to be shown? Time spent in doing this is not wasted, because *unless the question is identified it should not be answered.* If after five minutes the student still cannot see what the question is about, he should temporarily abandon it and answer other questions which he understands. Another period of contemplation later on during the examination may produce an answer.

(*c*) The student should remember that *the form of the question does not affect the form of the answer.* Various forms of question are discussed below, and it will be seen that there are several in use. But an answer should consist of *a clear account of the legal principles and statutory provisions involved*, followed, in the case of a "problem" question, by a short application of those principles and provisions to the facts given.

An examiner does not require the numbers of the sections of the Acts to be stated, but a student who can do this accurately improves the general tone of his paper. The invaluable expression "The Act provides" can always be used where memory fails.

The names of cases (though not the dates) should be memorised and cited where appropriate, and a student should *never invent a case*. He may give hypothetical facts to explain the workings of a particular legal rule, but he must do this honestly, stating that his facts are imaginary. If he knows that there is a decided case on a particular point, but cannot remember its name, he should simply write "In a decided case it was held that . . ."

(*d*) The student should make an effort to *disregard* the advice almost certainly given to him at school *not to write irrelevant material*. The paralysing effect of this negative instruction is seen all too often in examination scripts, as where a particularly gifted student, in answering a question setting out some facts and ending "Can A sue B?", wrote simply: "No". His explanation was that as the examiner knew the law, there was no point in saying more.

The student who exclaimed in desperation: "But everything I know is irrelevant" was suffering from a common malady—the inability to identify questions described above. *Everything is relevant to something*, and the student's task is to decide to what. He cannot answer any question with any material, but he can bear in mind that the examiner *wants to know how much he knows*, and that unless he answers the question *fully* and displays his knowledge, he cannot expect good marks.

Far more candidates fail through writing too little than through writing too much.

(*e*) The student should not be influenced by people who try to alleviate his nervousness with sympathy, sedatives or pep-pills. *There is nothing wrong with being nervous*. Equally disastrous are people who tell him not to overwork. *He should overwork if he wants to*. If he is nervous, or cannot eat or sleep, he should accept the fact that *this is normal*, and he is no different from anyone else. A glance round the examination room will convince him that he does not need a psychiatrist. He should, however, try to eat something before the examination. The author on one occasion when invigilating had to supply a particularly promising candidate with an entirely irregular bun in order to avoid losing him.

Finally, nervousness must not turn to despair. Every student should remember that *someone has to pass, or the profession will die out.*

Forms of Question. Questions on Company Law fall into four main categories:

(*a*) The *direct* question asking for specific knowledge, phrased in a manner which makes it easily identifiable, e.g.:
By what machinery and in what circumstances can a company (*i*) increase its capital, (*ii*) convert shares into stock?

Here the examiner is being as explicit as possible. He wants to know if the student has learnt the material in XV, **19** and **20**.

Questions of this type *should always be attempted*, for it is almost impossible to misunderstand them.

(*b*) The *indirect* question asking for specific knowledge, usually by means of a citation from a judgment, report or text-book, e.g.:
Comment on and explain the following passage from the judgment of Lord Coleridge, C.J. in *Re Perkins* (24 Q.B.D. 613): "It seems to me extremely important not to throw any doubt on the principle that companies have nothing whatever to do with the relations between trustees and their *cestuis que trust* in respect of the shares of the company".

The student usually dislikes this type of question unless he has had legal training. He does not understand 24 Q.B.D. 613. He has not read *Re Perkins*. He does not know what happened in *Re Perkins*. What does Lord Coleridge, C.J. (Chief Justice? Charles James?) mean? Why does Lord Coleridge think it so important? And what is it that is so important? Why does he always have an examination on a day when he cannot think clearly?

A moment's reflection will restore confidence. First, unnecessary words must be ignored. "It seems to me extremely important not to throw any doubt on the principle that . . ." adds nothing to the question, so that it can be reduced to:

"Companies have nothing (whatever) to do with the relations between trustees and their *cestuis que trust* in respect of the shares of the company."

Now it should be clear that the question is on *trusts* of shares. Section 117 is the only section of the Act which concerns trusts. The answer therefore is to be found in XIII, **11–15**.

This type of question *should also always be attempted*, for it is easier than it looks.

(*c*) The *problem* question, often consisting of the facts of a decided case which the student may or may not recognise, e.g.:
X and Y hold all the issued shares of B Ltd. They also together hold 950 shares in C Ltd. The other shareholder in C Ltd. is Z, who holds the remaining 50 shares in its issued share capital. B Ltd. makes an offer for Z's shares in C Ltd. at a valuation made by the latter company's accountants. Z refuses the offer. What are the respective rights of X and Y on the one hand and Z on the other hand?

Here the student may at once recognise the facts as being similar to those in *Re Bugle Press* (1960). If so, he will find the question easier to answer than if he has never heard of this case. But he should not let his failure to recognise the case prevent him from answering the question. He can still get good marks for knowing the principles of law involved, and the statutory provisions contained in s. 209 (*see* XXXII, **6–9**).

If he has difficulty in understanding the legal situation described in the question, he should make a small diagram for himself on a piece of rough paper, e.g.:

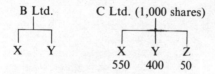

This sort of diagram indicates clearly that *the figures are important* and must be considered. But no diagram should ever be included in a script. The examiner is probably not a teacher and has therefore never drawn a company in his life, and he may well be baffled by pictures where he expects words.

Sometimes a problem question consists of entirely hypothetical facts, and if so, the student should first identify it in the way described earlier. He should then discuss the principles and statutory provisions applicable exactly as if the question were a direct one.

(*d*) The "gossip" question, e.g.:
Discuss the aphorism that a company, like a marriage, can be created more easily and cheaply than it can be dissolved.

This is by far the most dangerous type of question, for the student realises that with a little luck and a good command of English he can cover at least a page *without knowing anything at all*. But he should be careful: *the examiner realises this too*. No marks will be given for rhetoric. No marks will be given for an account, however entertaining, of the marriage ceremony or of the grounds for divorce. *This question is in a Company Law paper*. The examiner wants the candidate to compare the ease and cheapness of company *formation* with the ease and cheapness of *dissolution*. But there are four methods of dissolution: some are easier and cheaper than others. Presumably he requires a discussion of all four.

The difficulty of this question is now apparent. Some of the material required will be found in IV and XXV, but clearly a very wide discussion of formation and dissolution is needed and the student must have a comprehensive knowledge to deal well with such a topic. Unless a candidate writes excellent English, has a thorough knowledge of the subject, and a good academic background, he should *avoid this type of question if he possibly can*.

Index